Research and Debate in Primary Geography

Half the chapters in this book bring together recent papers which make important contributions to understanding and developing primary geography. The book considers primary teachers' and trainee teachers' knowledge of geography; how the primary curriculum uses geography; teachers' planning of geography teaching; the way in which aspects of geography are taught; what high quality geography might look like; and children's geographical understanding and voices.

Though geography curricula change quite often in countries around the world, the core matters noted above remain of constant and vital importance. The papers in this book either concern research with primary teachers and children, or consider key concerns in primary geography, providing important perspectives for thinking about future developments in geography teaching and curriculum initiatives in primary schools. This is a stimulating and enticing collection written by leading exponents of, and experts in, primary geography education.

The core of this book was originally published as a special issue of *Education 3–13*.

Simon Catling is Emeritus Professor of Primary Education at Oxford Brookes University. He taught in London primary schools before moving to Oxford Brookes University in the 1980s, serving as Dean and Assistant Dean in the 1990s and 2000s. He is a Past-President of the Geographical Association, author of *Mapstart* and *Teaching Primary Geography* (with Tessa Willy).

Research and Debate in Primary Geography

Edited by
Simon Catling

Routledge
Taylor & Francis Group

LONDON AND NEW YORK

First published 2015
by Routledge
2 Park Square, Milton Park, Abingdon, Oxon, OX14 4RN, UK

and by Routledge
711 Third Avenue, New York, NY 10017, USA

Routledge is an imprint of the Taylor & Francis Group, an informa business

Chapter 1 © 2015 Simon Catling
Chapters 2, 6, 7, 8, 10–13 © 2015 Association for the Study of Primary Education
Chapters 3, 4, 5, 9, 14 © 2015 Taylor and Francis

British Library Cataloguing in Publication Data
A catalogue record for this book is available from the British Library

ISBN 13: 978-1-138-89989-6

Typeset in Times New Roman
by RefineCatch Limited, Bungay, Suffolk

Publisher's Note
The publisher accepts responsibility for any inconsistencies that may have
arisen during the conversion of this book from journal articles to book chapters,
namely the possible inclusion of journal terminology.

Disclaimer
Every effort has been made to contact copyright holders for their permission to
reprint material in this book. The publishers would be grateful to hear from any
copyright holder who is not here acknowledged and will undertake to rectify
any errors or omissions in future editions of this book.

Contents

Citation Information   vii
Notes on Contributors   xi

1. Introduction: thinking about primary geography   1
   Simon Catling

2. Enquiring into primary teachers' geographical knowledge   21
   Simon Catling and Emma Morley

3. English primary trainee teachers' perceptions of geography   39
   Emma Morley

4. Contesting *powerful knowledge*: the primary geography curriculum as
   an articulation between academic and children's (ethno-) geographies   54
   Simon Catling and Fran Martin

5. Ethnogeography: towards liberatory geography education   73
   Fran Martin

6. More than just core knowledge? A framework for effective and
   high-quality primary geography   87
   Paula Owens

7. Geography and creativity: developing joyful and imaginative learners   103
   Stephen Scoffham

8. Subject-based and cross-curricular approaches within the revised
   primary curriculum in Northern Ireland: teachers' concerns and
   preferred approaches   117
   Richard Greenwood

9. Teachers' perspectives on curriculum making in Primary Geography
   in England   133
   Simon Catling

10. Children researching their urban environment: developing a methodology   160
    Elisabeth Barratt Hacking and Robert Barratt

11. *My Place*: Exploring children's place-related identities through reading
    and writing   173
    Emma Charlton, Gabrielle Cliff Hodges, Pam Pointon, Maria Nikolajeva,
    Erin Spring, Liz Taylor and Dominic Wyse

CONTENTS

12. Same old story: the problem of object-based thinking as a basis for
    teaching distant places   190
    Fran Martin

13. 'They are like us' – teaching about Europe through the eyes of children   205
    Daniela Schmeinck

14. Giving younger children voice in primary geography: empowering
    pedagogy – a personal perspective   217
    Simon Catling

    Index   241

Citation Information

The following chapters were originally published in *Education 3–13*, volume 41, issue 4 (August 2013). When citing this material, please use the original page numbering for each article, as follows:

Chapter 2
Enquiring into primary teachers' geographical knowledge
Simon Catling and Emma Morley
Education 3–13, volume 41, issue 4 (August 2013) pp. 425–442

Chapter 6
More than just core knowledge? A framework for effective and high-quality primary geography
Paula Owens
Education 3–13, volume 41, issue 4 (August 2013) pp. 382–397

Chapter 7
Geography and creativity: developing joyful and imaginative learners
Stephen Scoffham
Education 3–13, volume 41, issue 4 (August 2013) pp. 368–381

Chapter 8
Subject-based and cross-curricular approaches within the revised primary curriculum in Northern Ireland: teachers' concerns and preferred approaches
Richard Greenwood
Education 3–13, volume 41, issue 4 (August 2013) pp. 443–458

Chapter 12
Same old story: the problem of object-based thinking as a basis for teaching distant places
Fran Martin
Education 3–13, volume 41, issue 4 (August 2013) pp. 410–424

Chapter 13
'They are like us' – teaching about Europe through the eyes of children
Daniela Schmeinck
Education 3–13, volume 41, issue 4 (August 2013) pp. 398–409

The following chapter was originally published in *Education 3–13*, volume 42, issue 2 (April 2014):

Chapter 11

My Place*: Exploring children's place-related identities through reading and writing*
Emma Charlton, Gabrielle Cliff Hodges, Pam Pointon, Maria Nikolajeva, Erin Spring, Liz Taylor and Dominic Wyse
Education 3–13, volume 42, issue 2 (April 2014) pp. 154–170

The following chapter was originally published in *Education 3–13*, volume 37, issue 4 (November 2009):

Chapter 10

Children researching their urban environment: developing a methodology
Elisabeth Barratt Hacking and Robert Barratt
Education 3–13, volume 37, issue 4 (November 2009) pp. 371–384

The following chapter was originally published in *International Research in Geographical and Environmental Education*, volume 21, issue 2 (May 2012):

Chapter 3

English primary trainee teachers' perceptions of geography
Emma Morley
International Research in Geographical and Environmental Education, volume 21, issue 2 (May 2012) pp. 123–137

The following chapter was originally published in *International Research in Geographical and Environmental Education*, volume 23, issue 4 (November 2014):

Chapter 14

Giving younger children voice in primary geography: empowering pedagogy – a personal perspective
Simon Catling
International Research in Geographical and Environmental Education, volume 23, issue 4 (November 2014) pp. 350–372

The following chapter was originally published in *Curriculum Journal*, volume 22, issue 3 (September 2011):

Chapter 4

Contesting powerful knowledge*: the primary geography curriculum as an articulation between academic and children's (ethno-)geographies*
Simon Catling and Fran Martin
Curriculum Journal, volume 22, issue 3 (September 2011) pp. 317–336

CITATION INFORMATION

The following chapter was originally published in *Curriculum Journal*, volume 24, issue 3 (September 2013):

Chapter 9
Teachers' perspectives on curriculum making in Primary Geography in England
Simon Catling
Curriculum Journal, volume 24, issue 3 (September 2013) pp. 427–453

The following chapter was originally published in *Children's Geographies*, volume 6, issue 4 (November 2008):

Chapter 5
Ethnogeography: towards liberatory geography education
Fran Martin
Children's Geographies, volume 6, issue 4 (November 2008) pp. 437–450

Please direct any queries you may have about the citations to
clsuk.permissions@cengage.com

Notes on Contributors

Robert Barratt is Professor of Education and Head of Initial Teacher Education at Bath Spa University, UK. He is the founder of the Children Environment Research Centre at Bath Spa University, and a member of the Centre for Research in Education and the Environment, University of Bath.

Elisabeth Barratt Hacking is Director of Studies for the MA Education and MA International Education and Globalisation courses at Bath Spa University, UK. Her research interests relate to childhood and environment and children's participation, she has published widely in the fields of environmental education and education for sustainability.

Simon Catling is Emeritus Professor of Primary Education at Oxford Brookes University. He taught in London primary schools before moving to Oxford Brookes University, UK, in the 1980s, serving as Dean and Assistant Dean in the 1990s and 2000s. He is a Past-President of the Geographical Association, author of *Mapstart* and *Teaching Primary Geography* (with Tessa Willy).

Emma Charlton is a Faculty Member in the Department of Education at Deakin University, Melbourne, Australia. She was previously based at the University of Cambridge, UK.

Gabrielle Cliff Hodges is Senior Lecturer in Education at the University of Cambridge, UK. Her recent research has focused on students' development as readers and aims to discover more about the social and intellectual processes involved, with a particular interest in the students' own views on what motivates and supports their reading development.

Richard Greenwood is Senior Lecturer in Teacher Education (Primary) Geography at Stranmillis University College, Belfast, UK. He was previously a primary school teacher in Belfast. His current research includes the attitudes of Teacher Education students to the school subjects of History, Geography and Science, and teacher attitudes towards the implementation of the Northern Ireland curriculum.

Fran Martin is Senior Lecturer in Education at the University of Exeter, UK. She was previously an early years primary school teacher in Buckinghamshire. She is the lead academic of the Re-Place Research Group, and Senior Fellow of the Higher Education Academy. She is a Past-President of the Geographical Association and author of *Teaching Geography in Primary Schools: Learning to live in the world* (2006).

Emma Morley is Senior Lecturer in Education and co-ordinator for Professional Studies at the University of Winchester, UK. Her research interests include issues relating to the training of teachers generally, the training of students to teach geography, and primary teachers identities related to geography education.

Maria Nikolajeva is Professor of Education and Fellow of Homerton College at the University of Cambridge, UK. She is a member of several editorial boards of international professional journals and was one of the senior editors for the *Oxford Encyclopedia of Children's Literature*.

Paula Owens is the Curriculum Development Leader (Primary) for the Geographical Association, Sheffield, UK. Her professional interests include Education for Sustainable Development and outdoor learning. She recently co-authored (with Fran Martin) *Caring for our world: a practical guide to ESD for ages 4–8* (2008).

Pam Pointon is a Lecturer in Geography Education (Primary) at the University of Cambridge, UK. She previously taught Geography in London comprehensive schools for thirteen years. Her current research focuses on children's perceptions of, and relationship with, nature and the environment.

Daniela Schmeinck is Professor in the Institute of Primary Science and Social Sciences, University of Cologne, Germany. She has run a number of pan-European projects, including a study of primary pupils perspectives on teaching about Europe, which is reported in her co-edited book *Through the Eyes of Children* (2010).

Stephen Scoffham is a Visiting Reader in Sustainability and Education at Canterbury Christ Church University, Canterbury, UK. He has served as Honorary Publications Officer for the Geographical Association since 2005 and is an elected member of the GA governing council. His research interests include geography teaching, creativity, the environment and the global dimension. He is editor of the *Primary Geography Handbook* (2010) and *Teaching Geography Creatively* (2013).

Erin Spring is a post-doctoral Fellow in the Institute for Child and Youth Studies at the University of Lethbridge, Alberta, Canada. She was previously based at the University of Cambridge, UK.

Liz Taylor is a Senior Lecturer and Undergraduate Course Manager in the Faculty of Education, University of Cambridge, UK. She has a particular interest in cultural geography and the ways in which new ideas in the field can contribute to relevant and engaging geography in schools. *Representing Geography* (2004) gained the Gold Award for publications from the Geographical Association and was winner of the Scottish Association of Geography Teachers' book awards.

Dominic Wyse is Professor in the Department of Early Years and Primary Education at the Institute of Education, University of London, UK. The main focus of his research is curriculum and pedagogy, with a focus on the teaching of English, language, literacy, and creativity.

Introduction: thinking about primary geography[1]

Simon Catling

School of Education, Faculty of Humanities and Social Sciences, Oxford Brookes University

Introduction

Geography, when taught well, is an exciting, inviting and invigorating primary curriculum subject. Geography is, intricately and demonstrably, a dimension of our lives, takes us into the world, and challenges us. It connects our lives and places to others, and with the physical environment. It is the 'world subject' (Bonnett 2008). Geography gives, with other subjects, 'body' to the primary curriculum and extends and deepens younger children's learning. Its importance lies in developing their knowledge and understanding about the world as it is and their sense of its and their own futures. As a school subject its role is to engage, encourage and enable children's geographical thinking.

Geography is present in very many primary curricula around the world, most usually as a contributory component in curriculum areas such as social studies, as in the USA and Singapore. In other nations it has stronger links with science, for instance, to an extent in Germany and Finland. In some countries geography is a distinct subject, which is the case in Australia and Ireland, where there are also explicit national standards, expectations and curriculum programmes. In the United Kingdom geography is present in all four national primary curricula. It is a named subject, *geography*, in England's national curriculum. It lies in 'Knowledge and Understanding of the World' for 3–7 year olds and is a listed subject for 7–11 year olds in Wales. In Northern Ireland it is identified as a subject component of 'The World Around Us' area of learning. In Scotland it is integrated within social studies. It may be taught as a separate subject, strongly highlighted in a linked programme, or integrated within a cross-curricular or thematic course. Geography's appearance in various guises in the curriculum for younger children globally is certainly positive: the subject is recognised as providing distinctive insights about the world and is appreciated as important and of significance to younger children's learning nationally and internationally.

Research and Debate in Primary Geography brings together research findings and discussions about matters that are important for the present and future of primary geography. The chapters explore a number of topics to aid their better understanding. They indicate opportunities and developments for primary geography; even when critical, they provide a strong sense of optimism for the subject with younger children. This chapter contends that fostering children's geographical learning requires their engagement in geographical thinking. This is explored, as an example, through a review and consideration of the changes in 2014 to the English primary geography national curriculum and what is understood about high quality planning, teaching and learning in geography in primary schools (which is limited). It concludes by introducing the chapters of this book.

Geographical thinking

Pedagogy, encompassing the curriculum, teaching and learning in primary schools (Alexander 2000), aims to develop children's thinking through their explorations and uses of knowledge, understanding, skills, values, feelings, and perspectives. Thinking geographically requires knowledge about the world, but it is based in deep subject constructs not on surface information, and its development lies in engaging children's curiosity and enquiries (Martin 2006; Catling and Willy 2009; Scoffham 2010; Barlow 2013). Fundamental to understanding geography's perspectives and to applying geographical thinking is fostering children's developing and burgeoning appreciation of the underpinning concepts of geography, which for Jackson (2006, 199) are "place and space, scale and connection, proximity and distance, and relational thinking", the last of which refers to how we construct and contrast fair, just and balanced geographies of ourselves and others; these concepts involve knowledge and understandings about the environment, people's lives and cultures, human and physical processes, sustainability, diversity and difference, spatial distributions and patterns, and their effects. Intricately linked with these is how in geography we know about, find out, analyse, evaluate and communicate learning, including through fieldwork, investigations and enquiries, and evidence-based presentations, from local case studies to global overviews. Morgan (2013, 275) encapsulates this when he notes that

> To think geographically is to have a trained capacity to construct a mental map to see patterns, to recognise relationships, to see movement, to take that map and 'clothe it in meaning'. This is a form of visualisation, and one which is powerful because it is to make informed judgements, intelligent guesses and to situate itself in human culture.

Younger children cannot know, understand or value geography without doing and studying geography. They cannot deepen their understanding of the world or develop new ways to appreciate it and apply their learning unless they are engaged in geographical activities and reflection, the latter being vital. Children must be involved, not simply be observers of the world or accumulators of information about it. This is logical, since they are involved in geography as a daily practice. Morgan reflects this view for primary children when he states that it is important

> . . . to take seriously 'the popular wisdom of everyday life' that children have valid ideas and interpretations, and that academic geographers (and by extension teachers) do not have a 'uniquely critical insight' into the nature and affects of cultural roots. (Morgan 2013, 280)

In various ways younger children think geographically, whether or not we recognise this (Catling and Willy 2009). Through their learning in the 'everyday' world informally, serendipitously, as well as in school classrooms, they encounter and imbibe (to varying degrees) understandings about how the world works and their place in it, in their own contexts, locally, more extensively and globally. They do this through direct experiences in places but also through listening and conversations, as well as from media such as television and a range of internet sources, some interactive and some not. Not only do they construct and recall knowledge and understanding accurately but they will also develop misperceptions and partial and erroneous knowledge and perspectives, for instance, about natural and human geography processes and concerns. Primary children at various ages may well be able to discuss clearly aspects of their own locality, its features and activities there, and some of its benefits and limitations, but they may equally hold, for example, naive notions of river flow, food sources, commerce, population movements or mountain formation. The importance of focusing on geographical thinking in primary education is that teaching geography intends to help younger children use and enhance their developing local to global awareness and knowledge. It challenges their misconceptions, strengthens and deepens their understanding and their thinking about the world in an informed way, and begins to engage them with and apply geography's key concepts of place, scale, connections, spatial relationships and so forth. It will do this most effectively through a structured and progressive spiral curriculum which revisits key concepts with increasing demand and challenge, in new contexts and at increasing scales.

Geographical understanding is not a 'spectator' perspective; it lies at the heart of many of the decisions we make which affect our communities, places and environments and our own and others' lives. Geography is not outside us but part of us from our earliest years. Its focus is the here and now but its view is to the future. Geographical thinking is vital in and to our lives. It is about applying knowledge and using investigative and evaluative skills to understand the world and reflecting critically to create informed and improved futures (Hicks 2014). Thinking forward geographically is essential because we know that the effects of what we do have lasting impacts, for good or ill, on the places, environments and lives of current and future generations. Since we recognise this, we cannot act dispassionately, as if without or simply setting aside feelings and standpoints, ethics and preferences. Thinking geographically involves values and feelings alongside critically aware knowledge and understanding of the world and the skills to investigate it, however near to and distant from us, through direct experience and secondary, even third-hand, sources.

Geographical thinking is a turn of mind which curriculum, teaching and learning in primary schools seeks to stimulate and enhance. It is based in knowledge of the world at a range of scales, knowledge which evolves and shifts. Yet geography is more than a mechanism for identifying, classifying and analysing information and ideas; it is about acting and appreciating the impact of our actions on people and the planet. To be thoughtful and positive in doing this, primary children need to begin to understand geography's perspectives, to use its key ideas and ways of working, to build their knowledge of a selection of the myriad aspects of the Earth's physical and human world, and to develop values to act upon in the world. Through geographical understanding we position ourselves in relation to our places, environments and peoples locally and globally in their diverse circumstances and situations. Geography as a curriculum subject, taught in whichever context, seeks to promote knowledge of how our world is and works, as it also promotes how we must consider and treat our planet and all living on it, using learning to avoid simplistic assumptions and solutions (Morgan 2012). Geographical thinking is tough but vital.

Primary geography in a context: evolving content in England

Developing geographical thinking lies at the heart of the subject's curriculum requirements and teaching and learning approaches, even when it is not spelt out! Curriculum change in geography provides an example to reflect upon ways in which geographical thinking can be provided for primary children. England's 2014 geography curriculum is a particular example, which illustrates that there is more to a national curriculum content list than is apparent. Curriculum statements are open to interpretation and (re)construction by teachers. This encourages optimism about what primary schools can do. The more succinctly content is stated, the better the opportunities to interpret that content, to realise and extend learning of value with children, building on and from, as well as building up, their experiences, knowledge and understandings. A list need not constrain; it can be the basis for developing geographical thinking. Such opportunities need to be taken. Rueing revisions to a national curriculum at any time is not surprising, since it means further change to be implemented by hard-pressed teachers – and much change was put in place across all the primary curriculum subjects at the same time in England from September 2014 (DfE 2013). Treated as a catalyst, however, it provokes the challenge to explore the possibilities that such change presents.

Change in England's primary geography curriculum 2000–2014

The 2014 revised geography programmes of study (DfE 2013) for 5–7 year olds (key stage 1) and 7–11 year olds (key stage 2) appeared to be far reaching – and seemed a radical shift from what had been required up to that point – indeed, there was more to be positive about than the succinct content list intimated at first glance. It was only a list, not a curriculum. Yet, as with past amendments to primary geography requirements, there was continuity as well as change. There were evident opportunities to maintain good and pertinent practices and motivating work with primary children, while opening up studies and investigations in new and wider geographical pastures. Good practices in developing children's geographical thinking could continue while adapting to some new content. Since 1991 (DES 1991) the geography curriculum in England had undergone two completed and one aborted revisions (DfE 1995; DfEE 1999; QCDA 2010). During these it was reduced and reshaped rather than reconstituted. Revision 'four' in 2013 (DfE 2013) promoted several changes, restating subject content while maintaining various aspects from earlier versions. Looking 'thin' as a list of geography content – though not in what was needed to teach the geographical topics well – it was intended to seem lean; yet it was, if anything, fuller. In England's primary schools there were very real constraints on teaching time for geography in whichever curriculum context, since the pressure was for focused and high level outcomes in English and mathematics, almost regardless of anything else. A case could be made, on this basis, that the geography 'framework' allowed – even encouraged unintentionally – content choices to be made, curriculum balances to be shaped and the interests and needs of children in school to be addressed through curriculum decisions and approaches to teaching geography. In effect, making connections across the geographical content was required to create geographical coherence and to enable and enhance geographical thinking – challenging the sense of 'compartmentalisation' which the contents' lists displayed.

As an example of curriculum content change, it is useful and informative to note what had been retained, included and removed in this shift in primary geography from Curriculum 2000 (DfES/QCA 1999) to Curriculum 2014 (DfE 2013). In both curricula the primary geography programmes of study for key stage 1 and 2 had consistent structures, though they differed to an extent in content requirements. Both Curriculum 2000 and 2014 emphasised subject knowledge and geographical skills, though the key 'aspects' under which the geography content was grouped were retitled from the former to the latter to distinguish the 'resetting' of the geography requirements and to emphasise 'change' in the core components in school geography. These geographical aspects are given in Table 1 below.

Certainly, from 2000 to 2014 there had been modifications. Knowledge of place locations was present in both versions of geography, but it was highlighted overtly in 2014. Knowledge about the nature of places continued, and the various topics within human and physical geography were named, reorganised and extended in the 2014 version, which provided greater clarity given their centrality to the subject. Understanding geographical patterns and processes, a key heading in 2000, was more discretely included in the 2014 primary programmes. Though change in the environment was subsumed within human and physical geography, sustainability had apparently been removed as though it was not an aspect of geography to which to introduce younger children – an interesting move given sustainability's increasing prominence in global debates and actions for the planet and its

Table 1: The aspects of geography used as sub-headings in England's National Curriculum Geography programmes of study for 2000 and 2014.

	Aspects of Geography in England's Curriculum 2014	Aspects of Geography in England's Curriculum 2000
A common framework for Key Stages 1 & 2	• Geographical skills and fieldwork • Locational knowledge • Place knowledge • Human and physical geography	• Geographical enquiry and skills • Knowledge and understanding of places • Knowledge and understanding of patterns and processes • Knowledge and understanding of environmental change and sustainability

people, albeit not solely within geography (Robertson 2014). Table 2 provides the detail about the range of continuity and change, to enable a content comparison of the programmes for key stages 1 and 2 between the 2014 and 2000 requirements (DfE 2014; DfES/QCA 2000). In Table 2 the specific statements have been abbreviated and the content has been re-sequenced to enable comparison. It makes interesting reading to see what was revised, removed and added. Yet this can be viewed positively, for it provided for primary children and teachers a broader sense of geography. It formed a basis for developing their geographical thinking, if thoughtfully and creatively used.

A sense of purpose for primary geography

The overall purpose of teaching and learning primary geography remained to develop curiosity about the world and to foster a sense of wonder and fascination for younger children. These are intrinsic elements of thinking geographically, as motivating forces for lifelong interest. While they were not articulated, the key geographical concepts of place, space, scale, environment and interconnections underpinned the 2014 curriculum, and were the basis for making sense of it to build primary children's geographical thinking. The programmes of study encouraged understanding of the natural environment and the human diversity of the world, the processes and patterns at work across the planet, and interdependence and interrelationships from local to global scales. Interconnecting these is vital in thinking geographically; they were there to be used. Working outside the classroom was maintained as essential, a clear basis for active learning and thinking. Children would continue to undertake fieldwork, building their observational, investigative, recording and analytic skills: these essences of enquiry – with curiosity and inquisitiveness – remained central to geography's classroom-based and outdoor teaching and learning. Children continued to develop map skills, which are best integrated within their studies of places and environments, to be used outdoors as well as inside. Developing younger children's knowledge of the Earth and of where key places are, building their local and global mental maps, continued to be central to the geography curriculum. Children are fascinated doing this, just as they enjoy and gain much from studying their local area and other places, teasing out the commonalities and differences when comparing places, valuing diversity as the lifeblood of the Earth and its people, and recognising much that is shared across our lives and places. All of this ran through primary geography. Integrating these aspects goes to the heart of developing geographical thinking.

Table 2: A summary comparison of the 2000 and 2014 England's National Curriculum Geography framework for key stages 1 and 2.

	England's NC2014 Geography Programme	England's NC2000 Geography programme
Overall Purpose/ Importance statement and Aims statement	Geography is to inspire curiosity/ fascination and build knowledge/deep understanding about diversity of the world and its people and physical/ human processes/interactions, interdependence and spatial variations. Explain how features at different scales are shaped/interconnected/change. Contextual knowledge of locations, their characteristics and relationships. Use geographical skills, including fieldwork, to collect, analyse, communicate data. Use extended writing. Interpret sources of geographical information, eg maps, globes, photos and GIS.	Geography provokes/answers questions about natural/human worlds, using enquiry. Develops knowledge of places/ environments, maps, investigative/ problem-solving skills. Focus for understanding/resolving issues about the environment and sustainable development. Links natural and social sciences. Helps through studies of different cultures and societies recognise inter-nation reliance. Inspires thinking about one's own place in the world, about values, rights and responsibilities to others/the environment. Preparation for adult life/employment.
KS1/2 content focus	The *KS1/2 introductory statements* focus on: knowing about their locality, the UK, the world and named continents; global locational knowledge of significant physical/human features; physical/human processes; geographical vocabulary and skills/tools; use first-hand observation.	The *KS1/2 introductory statements* focus on: learning about the locality, the UK, the wider world and links between places; how people affect and are affected by the environment; skills of map work and out of classroom learning; use/nature of 'enquiry'.
KS1 programme of study (for 5–7 year olds)	*Geographical skills and fieldwork* Observational skills Fieldwork skills. Basic geographical vocabulary of named physical and human features. Use globes, world maps and atlases. Plan perspective and key. Identify features on aerial photographs. 4 compass directions and relative locational vocabulary to describe feature sites and routes on maps. *Location knowledge* Locational knowledge of continents/ oceans; UK countries/capitals/seas. *Place knowledge* School and its grounds and surrounding environment. Small area in UK and contrasting non-European country; key human/ physical features; geographical similarities and differences.	*Geographical enquiry and skills* Asking questions, observing, recording, expressing views, and communicating. Fieldwork. Geographical vocabulary. Maps and globes. Use secondary sources. *Knowledge and understanding of places* Locality/place/feature location. School's local area; contrasting local area in UK or overseas for comparison. Local area features/nature, development and change; links and comparisons. *Knowledge and understanding of patterns and processes* Relative locations and features in the environment. Changes in features.

Human and physical geography
Daily/seasonal weather patterns.
Locate hot/cold areas of world, related to Equator and North/South Poles.

Knowledge and understanding of environmental change and sustainable development
Environmental changes.
Sustaining environmental improvements.

KS2 programme of study (for 7–11 year olds)

Geographical skills and fieldwork
Use fieldwork to observe/measure/record physical/human features in local area, using range of methods.
Local area fieldwork methods, using sketch maps, plans, graphs digital technologies.

Maps, atlases, globes, digital/computer mapping for location and feature description.
Map symbols/key, 8 compass points, 4- & 6-figure grid references.
OS maps (and other maps) to build UK/world knowledge.

Geographical enquiry and skills
Asking questions, collecting/recording/analysing evidence; explaining varied view, communicating.
Fieldwork methods/techniques.
ICT in investigations.
Develop vocabulary.
Maps, atlases and globes.

Secondary sources.
Decision making.

Location knowledge
Locational knowledge of world's countries.
Locational knowledge of environmental regions, physical/human characteristics and major cities of Europe, and North and South America.
UK countries, cities, topographical features, land use and characteristics of regions, including how some aspects changed over time.
Position/significance of latitude/longitude, Equator, Tropics of Cancer/Capricorn, Arctic/Antarctic Circles, Northern/Southern Hemispheres, prime meridian, time zones.

Knowledge and understanding of places
Locations of significant British Isles, European and world places/features.

Locality/place location.

Place knowledge
Physical/human geography of a region of UK, of a European country, and within North or South American to understand geographical similarities/differences.

Study locality in UK and less economically developed country, for comparison.
Locality features/nature/activities; why/how of change up to now/for the future; geographical context and interdependence.
Place comparisons.

Knowledge and understanding of patterns and processes
Patterns made by physical and human features.
Physical and human processes; how these create changes to environments/places.

(Continued)

Table 2: Continued

	England's NC2014 Geography Programme	England's NC2000 Geography programme
	Human and physical geography Key aspects of physical geography, including: climate zones; biomes, vegetation belts; rivers, water cycle; mountains, volcanoes/earthquakes.	At a range of scales and in a variety of environments/places. Water (river or coastal) processes and affects on people.
	Key aspects of human geography, including: settlements; land use; economic activity and trade; natural resource distribution including energy, food, minerals and water supplies.	Ways settlements differ/change; their 'characters'. Land use issues.
		Knowledge and understanding of environmental change and sustainable development People damaging/improving environment; decisions affecting people's lives. How/why people manage environments sustainably; opportunities for personal involvement. An environmental issue arising from change.
Attainment Target	Children are expected to know/apply/ understand matters/skills/processes specified in the relevant Programme of Study.	5 Attainment Target levels for KS1/2 geography: Descriptive statements covering aspects for the key stages (KS1: L1–2/3; KS2: L2–4/5), against which children's achievements were judged for a 'best fit' decision by the teacher.

While there appeared greater emphasis on knowing where places are, this was not really the case; it had just been spelt out more directly; it was not to be overplayed. Locational knowledge had always been part of good geography, as one foundational element. Importantly, children in key stage 1 would continue to investigate their local area, and this would be followed up in key stage 2. Weather and seasons reappeared in the geography curriculum from key stage 1 (returning from the science curriculum), and children in key stage 2 would investigate global patterns of climates, biomes and vegetation, as new topics, extending their local scientific studies of plant and animal life and of their local weather in the school grounds. For 7 to 11 year olds the study of physical geography, which retained river and coastal studies, added learning about volcanoes and earthquakes, their processes, volatility and effects on environments and people's lives. A more rounded sense of the natural, physical environment of Earth was encouraged. Studies of settlements and land use continued in human geography and could be linked with understanding how places function and lives are lived – which might, for example, involve enquiries into shopping and work activities. These could be developed through investigating the uses of natural and human made and modified resources, involving studies of water, food, minerals and energy; their sources, distribution, uses, consumption and future needs would be vital elements of their geography. Such studies would extend from key stages 1 to 2 beyond the local area to the wider region in which the children and others lived, to aid investigation of another area of the UK, helping to build national knowledge, and to selected places and people's lives in another European country, to note the interconnections and to make continental comparisons. This reintroduction of a European dimension, through investigating a region of the continent, was to develop children's understanding of their home continent and to make links with one or more places and areas they may have visited or heard about. Not only were these aspects of geography available to foster broader and deeper geographical thinking, but they presented excellent and stimulating opportunities for cross-subject enquiries, such as with history, science and art, and in which literacy and numeracy could be used and developed.

Studying places and areas of the world has been a strong and positive element of primary geography. The focus from 1991 was to study the geography of local places and of urban or rural localities in countries in more economically diverse areas of the world and to make comparisons with the UK. This led very many primary schools to focus on countries such as Kenya, the Gambia and India. This focus was shifted deliberately in 2014 to require investigations of the physical and human geography of places and regions in North and South America. Few localities and features in South America had been the focus for primary geography investigations beforehand, though there were resources available. This change intentionally extended interests and choices beyond the Amazon River and forests, and city favelas and mountain villages, to the wider context of the continent. In South America river studies can look to the grand scale, and there exist excellent possibilities for investigating mountains and their environments, volcanoes and earthquakes, vegetation and climate zones – and the whys and wherefores of people's lives in these and a range of rural and urban places and environments. It opened many possibilities. Studies could be made of some of the continent's resources, their use and impact, from food production to tropical forest exploitation and mineral extraction. Issues could be examined. For instance, Brazil has been a magnet for study, given its scale, prominence, geographical diversity and the contrasts in its people's lives. It is a major world economy and host to global events. Within its borders it encapsulates a wide diversity of human and physical geography and places, much that is positive in development but also critical concerns. Other nations and areas of the continent offer equally rich possibilities, from Chile and Argentina to Columbia and Guyana. The continent can be revisited to focus on and integrate the various aspects of its geography in order to develop children's geographical thinking as they learn to understand geographical interconnections, scales, patterns and processes, and much more.

In North America, the self-promoting cities in the USA, from Los Angeles to New York, are known to many younger children. Regular news reports show the effects of tornado strikes in the mid-West and coastal hurricanes. Children are aware of – perhaps a few have been to – Disneyland in Florida, and they may know of the Rockies and have heard about actual and potential earthquakes. Many of the same possibilities for study exist for North America as for South America. The USA is a rich and distinctive nation, as is Canada, an equally vast country stretching into the northern polar region. People consider they know about these nations from news media and films, but perhaps they need to know and understand them rather better, not only in terms of items of information but more vitally in terms of how the parts relate to and create the whole. These are good reasons for investigating them with primary children. Both American continents are diverse. The shift of studies to North and South America from Africa and the Indian sub-continent offered good opportunities for deeper enquiries into aspects of these continents and their countries in order to recognise and appreciate them more fully. The countries of Central America and the Caribbean are integral to the Americas. There is richness to investigate in this region 'between' the continents, which some schools have done for many years. This change of focus provided for continuity alongside new avenues, scenes and lives to examine, to encourage and enable thinking geographically.

Studies in primary geography in England from 2014 offered a good range of possibilities. Yet, as Table 2 indicates, one aspect of geography was not discretely included. It seemed that something was missing – but perhaps that could not be, if geography was to be well grounded and studied fully and effectively. For example, it would be remiss when studying the topics of food and water not to consider their distribution and accessibility in different and contrasting communities in the world, and what the issues involved are where access is poor, such as links with poverty and famine – or plentiful and there is waste. Examining information about access to resources without investigating the effects, positively and critically, inhibits developing a full and coherent sense of geography – and, inevitably, constrains thinking geographically. School localities, other settlements and their land uses cannot be studied with geographical integrity unless a balanced understanding of what is happening and changing for people and the environment is considered: who and what is affected, to what extent and why, for better or worse, for instance, the nature and impact of floods in the UK and Bangladesh. Exploring sustainability and environmental change – enhancement, degradation and management – remain vital to developing younger children's understanding of the world as it is, as well as in relation to their own and other children's futures. Whether or not these ideas are mentioned in the geography requirements is, in fact, immaterial; geographical studies cannot bypass or ignore them without leaving out a key aspect of the subject, diminishing children's geographical learning and thinking.

It seems strongly to be the case that younger children are highly motivated by local care projects, value the natural environment and their own places, however urbanised, and are aware of wider world concerns about the environment, from oil spills to climate change (Alexander 2010; Freeman and Tranter 2011; Ofsted 2011; Davis and Elliott 2014). They encounter these through their direct experiences and through the media they use. This gives geography a key role in their education, that of helping them be better informed, challenging the misunderstandings and misconceptions they develop, and examining ways in which issues can be understood and tackled to provide positive directions for the future, indeed, for their future (Wooley 2010; Hicks 2014). This draws much in geography together and provides for thinking geographically. In doing this children encounter a variety of viewpoints and begin to recognise the effect of people's decision making, of how this can improve or damage the world around them and what individually and as a class might be appropriate perspectives, stances and actions for them to consider. Whether aspects of geography such as sustainability and environmental change were stated in the geography programmes was not the relevant issue; for geography to be taught viably and with integrity, environmental issues and impacts and the sustainability of the present and future of the Earth, its environments and places, and people's lives must be key aspects of place, and physical and human geography studies from the earliest years (Martin and Owens 2008).

Providing for progression in geographical learning

Enabling primary children to develop their thinking geographically raises the need to articulate how their thinking might progress between the ages of 5 to 11. A curriculum 'framework' which states the content to be covered within a particular age phase identifies what children might be taught, but it does not provide guidance about developing expectations in their learning. Stating that knowing, understanding and applying 'the content' by the end of primary education is the expectation provides no clarity for teaching or learning, and in England that was not the intention of Curriculum 2014 (DfE 2013). In contrast, what is required needs to go beyond the content list to encourage understanding of the key aspects and ideas of geography. It is children's growing awareness of these which supports their developing geographical thinking and their potential to apply this thinking. This is not the same as an account of what would be covered in each year or over two years; that is for a curriculum scheme or syllabus to state. Instead, the need is for an 'expectations' statement which focuses on the increasing rigour, sophistication and challenge in geographical understanding to which the teaching and learning of any particular content contributes. It should articulate progression in knowledge, understanding, skills and values in geography and enable teachers to make choices about which specific content they decide to teach when. The content to be taught is, after all, a matter for the school's overall planning and the organisation of this into topics or units of work and then into lessons. Setting out geographical expectations for different age groups must take a more fundamental focus, and go beyond a content which children might be introduced to at any particular age, to reflect what are regarded as important subject ideas. This is the basis for a spiral curriculum (Bruner 1960; Olson 2007), which is particularly apposite for developing children's geographical thinking.

The Geographical Association [GA] has provided an informative statement of expectations for progression in primary children's learning in geography. This is based on what it identifies as three aspects of geography: (1) "contextualising world knowledge"; (2) understanding the "conditions, processes and interactions" that explain features, distributions, patterns and change in places and environments; and (3) "competence in geographical enquiry" (GA 2014, 2). These aspects were constructed to give guidance about expectations across the ages of 5–7, 7–9 and 9–11 and are described by the GA as "benchmark expectations", to be used to aid teachers in planning progression in children's geographical learning throughout a school. They are based on five 'dimensions' of progress in geography stated by the GA (2014, 2):

- Demonstrating greater fluency with world knowledge by drawing on increasing breadth and depth of content and contexts;
- Extending from the familiar and concrete to the unfamiliar and abstract;
- Making greater sense of the world by organising and connecting information and ideas about people, places, processes and environments;
- Working with more complex information about the world, including the relevance of people's attitudes, values and beliefs;
- Increasing the range and accuracy of investigative skills, and advancing their ability to select and apply these with increasing independence to geographical enquiry.

Table 3 sets out the progressive expectations in primary geography of the three aspects, but they have been extended with further expectations. The Global Learning Programme [GLP] undertook a similar task to that by the GA to outline how progress in global learning in the context of geography is to be understood (GLP 2014). Inevitably there was much overlap between the two sets of statements but some elements vital to (primary) geography were stated explicitly in the GLP's expectations, while perhaps implicit in the GA's statement, in part reflecting the broader context expected in global learning, including about people's lives and needs, the effects of wealth and poverty and concerning sustainability and care for the environment. Those expectations which contribute to the fuller sense of geographical thinking expressed above have been included in Table 3.

Table 3: Benchmark expectations for progress in geographical learning and thinking for children in England between the ages of 5 and 11 years old (with acknowledgement to the Geographical Association and the Global Learning Programme).

Aspect of achievement: **Contextual World Knowledge** of locations, places and geographical features.

Dimension of progress: Demonstrating greater fluency with world knowledge by drawing on increasing breadth and depth of content and contexts.

Expectations by age 7, children:	By age 9, children:	By age 11, children:
Begin to find out about people and places in the local area, and to develop a sense of themselves as part of the wider world, becoming aware and gaining simple knowledge of other places, environments and cultures. Demonstrate simple locational knowledge about individual places and environments, especially in the local area, but also in the UK and wider world.	*Develop their awareness and knowledge of the wider world.* They have begun to develop a framework of world locational knowledge, including knowledge of places in the local area, UK and wider world, and some globally significant physical and human features.	Have a more detailed and extensive framework of knowledge of the world, including globally significant physical and human features and places in the news. *They learn about life in a locality or region of a developing country.*

Aspect of achievement: **Understanding**. Conditions, processes and interactions that explain geographical features, distribution patterns, and changes over time and space.

Dimensions of progress: Extending from the familiar and concrete to the unfamiliar and abstract; making greater sense of the world by organising and connecting information and ideas about people, places, processes and environments; working with more complex information about the world, including the relevance of people's attitudes, values and beliefs.

Expectations by age 7, children:	By age 9, children:	By age 11, children:
Show understanding by describing the places and features they study using simple geographical vocabulary, identifying some similarities and differences and simple patterns in the environment.	Demonstrate their knowledge and understanding of the wider world by investigating places beyond their immediate surroundings, including human and physical features and patterns, how places change and some links between people and environments. *They begin to explore how people and environments are connected and how they might be cared for.* They become more adept at comparing places, and understanding some reasons for similarities and differences.	Understand in some detail what a number of places are like, how and why they are similar and different, and how and why they are changing. *They can make comparisons with their own place.* They know about some spatial patterns in physical and human geography, the conditions which influence those patterns, and the processes which lead to change. They show some understanding of the links between places, people and environments.

They learn that people share the same basic needs. They begin to learn ways in which they are connected to other people, sometimes far away. They begin to understand the need to care for, and recognise changes to, familiar environments.	*They know that people share the same needs, and can give some examples of how people have improved their lives. They are aware of how they are linked with people in the wider world.*	*They know there are patterns of wealth and poverty in the world, some examples of how people have improved their lives in different places, and why people sometimes need support. They begin to develop their understanding of interdependence. They begin to think about how choices people make in their everyday lives affect people and places in other parts of the world. They begin to explore how people and environments interact and how environments might be cared for or improved in the future.*

Aspect of achievement: **Enquiry and skills**. Competence in geographical enquiry, and application of skills in observing, collecting, analysing and evaluating geographical information.

Dimension of progress: Increasing range and accuracy of pupils' investigative skills, advancing their ability to select and apply these with increasing independence to geographical enquiry.

Expectations by age 7, children:	By age 9, children:	By age 11, children:
Are able to investigate places and environments by asking and answering questions, making observations and using sources such as simple maps, atlases, globes, images and aerial photos.	Are able to investigate places and environments by asking and responding to geographical questions, making observations and using sources such as maps, atlases, globes, images and aerial photos. They can express their opinions and recognise that others may think differently.	Are able to carry out investigations using a range of geographical questions, skills and sources of information including a variety of maps, graphs and images. They can express and explain their opinions, and recognise why others may have different points of view.

Sources: Geographical Association (GA, 2014); *In italics: Global Learning Programme* (GLP, 2014). [The core of this table is the GA's complete framework of benchmark expectations, extended to develop global learning.] See: www.geography.org.uk/news/2014nationalcurriculum/assessment/.

High quality teaching in primary geography

Effective high quality geography teaching and learning in primary classrooms and schools is vital in the development and progression of children's geographical thinking, yet there are few studies of the practices of primary geography teaching and learning which provide guidance about this, though there is much advice. Useful studies by England's inspectors of schools have included investigations of geography education broadly and in samples of primary schools since 1991 (Ofsted 1999, 2008, 2011; see also Catling 2004) and earlier (DES 1989). These have looked particularly at geography teaching quality, children's achievements, the curriculum, and subject leadership and promotion. These inspection reports by the lead Her Majesty's Inspectors for geography have been a source of information about the range of quality in geography education. Their reporting of high quality geography education provides an optimistic message about what can be achieved through very effective teaching. This is important because a good geographical education underpins the development of children's geographical thinking. This section purposefully draws together what inspectors have identified about high quality primary geography.

The key to high quality geography throughout a primary school lies in the attitude of the school's leadership to geography as a primary curriculum subject. The headteacher's support for geography throughout the school needs to be unequivocal and evident (see also Catling et al. 2007). The teacher who leads geography – quite possible alongside one or more other subjects – must show enthusiasm for geography and give their colleagues confidence through demonstrable knowledge of and expertise in teaching geography. This role involves consistent monitoring and reviewing of the subject across the school, as well as providing encouragement, support and guidance for colleagues, with time available to do this. The geography leader may well have – though it is not essential – a background in geography but must undertake professional development to maintain and extend knowledge and understanding regularly, and quite possibly be a member of the Geographical Association (www.geography.org.uk), making use of its primary materials and events. The visibility of geographical learning in a primary school is important to stimulate children's interests, to help teachers' recognise its vitality and value, and to inform parents.

A high quality geography curriculum is based in a clearly structured and articulated school policy, regularly reviewed, which directs good practices in its teaching and learning. This involves balancing and interconnecting aspects of geography and promoting children's geographical thinking. Review processes involve colleagues and children, and take into account evaluations of learning using the school's geography curriculum priorities. This should lead to improvements and changes in the units or integrated contexts in which geography is taught. The curriculum is organised to maintain good progress in children's learning as they move through the school, to enable children's progression during a year from topic to topic and within topics. It is linked to national key stage requirements but not confined by them. High quality geography curricula draw on other key curriculum areas to develop primary children's understanding of the world and its complexities, such as global learning, 'global footprints' in sustainability and responsible citizenship. It makes links with other subjects appropriately and contributes to and enhances learning in literacy and numeracy and in outdoor learning. To support curriculum development and high quality teaching and learning in geography, teachers' knowledge, skills and practices and their own evaluations are used to develop in-service programmes in the school, as part of an annual action plan for development.

High quality geography teaching is multi-faceted, based, for instance, in effective geographical knowledge for the topics taught. Teachers engage children through their enthusiasm, notice and anticipate common misconceptions among their children, and give clear and helpful directions, descriptions and explanations. They plan their geography for the year and for each topic, but do not over plan or even stay inflexibly 'on plan' in each lesson or unit; the capacity to retain the initiative and adapt thoughtfully is essential, though this is contextualised by their focus on progress in children's learning. For example, they are likely to take account of their children's ideas and contributions and of new or unexpected opportunities, sometimes even outside the topic where this is evidently justified. Intentions are clear, expectations are high, and children understand what they are to do and how to go about their work, which is to say they can and should be involved in some of the decisions about their approaches to learning and in modifications to their topics. Good and better quality geography teaching employs a range of teaching approaches – and these may vary across a school, topics and lessons – including fieldwork, drama, experiments, role play, games, debates, enquiries and practical investigations, and paired/team cooperative working alongside independent studies. It is likely to be problem-based and structured through an enquiry approach (Catling 2004; Catling and Willy 2009). Depending on the topic and context, use is made of the school grounds regularly, alongside investigations in the locality and, at times, further afield. What is important is that geographical learning is meaningful and takes the children beyond what they appreciate or know at that time, while making motivational connections to and for them. It makes links with previous learning and might reflect topical matters and events of the day.

Good and better geography teaching is characterised by planning for the range of children in the class with needs and strengths supported and developed, the use of well-targeted and incisive geographical questioning, with high quality interactions between the teacher and the children. Geography teaching is purposeful, actively engaging children with the world (Catling 2004). Not only is there imaginative use of a variety of geographical resources, including via digital and other technologies, but children are actively involved in the selection, synthesis, organisation and recording of information from them. There are opportunities for reflection and discussion to foster deeper understanding – promoting geographical thinking – and for writing and visual presentations to clarify, sharpen and record children's geographical learning. This uses and develops an increasingly 'technical' geographical vocabulary in descriptions and explanations. Intrinsically an element in this, for the teacher, is the use of formative assessment during oral interactions, correcting misconceptions, extending information and understanding, giving clear guidance, marking work, and providing focused feedback on strengths and needs with joint consideration about the next steps for improvement. Periodically, summative activities are used to assess geographical knowledge, understanding and skills. There are clear records of children's geographical learning and achievements alongside indications of their engagement and motivation.

High quality teaching and learning is based in holding high standards to which the children are stimulated to aspire. The key effect is that children's developing geographical thinking is underpinned by effective knowledge, understanding and skills which they can apply. During their primary schooling children build good knowledge of places at local, national, European and global scales. They develop familiarity with their own locality and learn to make connections between their place and lives and those of others in other places, and they can make informed comparisons. They begin to appreciate the connections between different aspects of geography and to identify and give some explanation of natural and human patterns and processes at work in the world. They develop skills, such as in using maps and in making enquiries, and can apply these appropriately and selectively to find, record and explain data about places and in physical and human geography. This means that they are able to choose relevant resources to use. Children's development of good descriptive, reasoning, explanatory and reflective skills supports the consolidation of their geographical knowledge, understanding and skill-base, which is brought about through consistent good teaching in and across classes enabling good progress in their geographical learning. This provides the basis for children to be able to explain their understanding and to express and debate various perspectives about local and wider world matters and concerns they have studied. This indicates that younger children can achieve and exceed the expectations indicated for the end of primary education that are set out in Table 3.

This section has emphasised the characteristics of high quality primary geography. These align well with the practices of expert primary teachers (Eaude 2012). They have been signalled because developing primary children's geographical thinking requires, first, a well-grounded context for geography teaching, arising from the tone and aspirations set by the headteacher and the geography subject leader. Secondly, there needs to be in place, pertinent to that school's children and community and interlaced with geography curriculum guidance or national requirements – though these might be selected from and not used slavishly, and even extended – a well thought through rationale for geography's role in children's learning and a clear sense of how it enables progress in their learning through a progression-led curriculum. The third characteristic is high quality classroom teaching, which means that teachers need to be well versed in what they teach in any topic – that is, have sound knowledge of it – and make well chosen use of their pedagogic repertoire. Finally, teachers and children know and understand what they are learning about, what they understand better and are more knowledgeable about, and what they might need to address, as well as identify some future directions for their geographical learning. In this children become proficient at communicating what they learn and feel confident about, expressing and explaining their perspectives on matters geographical, in and beyond their direct experiences. The more that high quality teaching is taken up across primary schools, the stronger children's geographical knowledge, understanding and skills will be and the deeper their geographical thinking and enjoyment of the subject will become.

Themes and the organisation of the book

All but this first chapter in *Research and Debate in Primary Geography* have been published before in peer-reviewed research journals. They are drawn together from a number of sources, in particular from the journal *Education 3–13*, from which the stimulus and core of this book is drawn.[2] Eight of the chapters were originally published in *Education 3–13*, while others were published first in *International Research in Geographical and Environmental Education, The Curriculum Journal* and *Children's Geographies* (please see the Citation Information section for further information). They have been brought together to provide insight into a range of the research undertaken in primary geography and into some of the key debates within the subject in primary education. An important facet of (primary) geography is that the subject is both more extensive and longer-lived that any particular national curriculum set of requirements. The chapters consider matters that lie beyond the parochiality of any particular national curriculum in order to illustrate and raise questions and concerns pertinent to larger issues and needs in enabling the teaching and learning of good and high quality primary geography. The collection is not intended to cover all aspects of primary geography. Other sources can be consulted about such research (e.g. Robertson and Gerber 2000, 2001; Catling and Martin 2004; Schmeinck 2006; Wiegand 2006), though they are few.[3] This collection is designed to encourage consideration of and debate about the topics that are discussed, to encourage recognition of their importance and to provoke interest in developing research further.

The following chapters illustrate several themes pertinent to primary geography education. These themes are drawn from the discussion above. The first theme is teachers' and pre-service teachers' geographical knowledge and understanding. This is complemented by the theme of children's geographies – their awareness, experience, knowledge and understanding of the world. Interconnected with these is a third theme of geographical knowledge in the context of the school subject. Each of these interrelate, fourth, with personal (geographical) identities, for children and for teachers. Two further themes concern quality and opportunity in geography in the primary curriculum and responsibilities for and in primary geography teaching. Finally, running through the chapters is a theme about encouraging and developing geographical thinking. Often more than one theme – at times several – appears explicitly or implicitly as part of the research and debate within a chapter. This provides richness and, it is hoped, is stimulating and enticing. The chapter outlines which follow provide an introduction to the focus of each chapter and indicate the themes about which they provide some insight.

In Chapter 2 Simon Catling and Emma Morley enquire into what teachers understand by geographical knowledge. It is important to consider this at a time when teachers' and children's subject knowledge is being heavily promoted. This small-scale study raises some pertinent questions about what high quality primary teachers of geography understand about the subject. Making sense of geography and considering its value is important and not without its challenges. Emma Morley continues this theme in Chapter 3, investigating pre-service primary teachers' perceptions of geography and its educational purpose. This is a valuable study because it is concerned with the sense of geography and its role for primary children of those who will be teaching it. It provides insight into their state of understanding as they begin their teacher education course and may be indicative of the background of many future primary teachers. Simon Catling and Fran Martin take a different focus in Chapter 4, while continuing the debate about geographical knowledge. The 'knowledge turn' in the school curriculum has encouraged within geography education discussion about the notion of geographical knowledge as *powerful knowledge*. This underpins the argument that the teaching of subject knowledge in the school curriculum is, essentially, about taking children beyond their everyday experiences: indeed, Young and Lambert (2014), following Young (2008), argue that this is a school's essential educational purpose, though this is open to debate. Powerful knowledge seems to privilege subject learning over children's awareness and knowledge. Simon Catling and Fran Martin argue in the context of primary geography and younger children's geographies that this dichotomy is misconceived. They posit that the dialogue between academic knowledge and experiential, 'everyday' knowledge is fruitful for children's and teachers' geographical understanding and learning. In Chapter 5 Fran Martin pursues this argument more fully in the context of curriculum geography. She explores the concept of *ethnogeography* – teachers' and children's experiences and senses of geography – as a way to open up geographical education to create a more meaningful geography in the primary curriculum as well as in initial primary teacher education. She takes forward the case for the interplay between academic and 'everyday' geography.

Paula Owens picks up in Chapter 6 the discussion about the development of geography in the primary curriculum using a wider lens to explore how a high quality geography curriculum can be developed and have a positive impact for children, teachers and schools. She explains how the Geographical Association's *Primary Geography Quality Mark* is designed to help geography subject leaders and their schools enhance their geography curriculum and the quality of teaching and learning for their children. She points out that it is vital that children's perspectives are engaged with seriously to enable the development of their subject understanding and geographical thinking as engaged learners. She introduces also the role of teachers as curriculum makers and refers to creativity as essential in geographical learning. Stephen Scoffham, in Chapter 7, pursues the development of primary children's learning in making the case for creativity in geography in the primary curriculum. Using a range of approaches he shows how imagination and creativity are essential to good and better geography teaching (Scoffham 2013). Creativity includes how we help children become ever more thoughtful, imaginative and critically aware in looking to their futures. He argues that these are all essential to strong geographical learning, understanding and thinking. This requires that schools and teachers have high expectations of their children in their geographical enquiries and that they are stimulated by motivating and engaging studies.

In Chapter 8 Richard Greenwood returns to the focus on teachers' perspectives, which he investigated in Northern Ireland. He examines views about cross-curricular teaching, looking particularly at 'The World Around Us' Area of Learning in the Northern Ireland primary curriculum, in which geography sits alongside history and science, and where creative approaches to and subject understanding for teaching and learning are vital. He provides informative insights into the balance of teachers' views about subject and cross-curricular teaching and learning, and notes that whether teaching geography through subject-based or integrated curriculum approaches teachers need strong geographical knowledge and pedagogical skills to develop a high quality classroom curriculum. Simon Catling examines further the practices of 'curriculum making' among primary teachers in Chapter 9. Drawing on a geography-focused classroom-based teacher development project, he researched the dynamics of teachers' curriculum ownership and enactment. He explores matters of teacher control over their planning and pedagogy, their perceptions of children's capability and the role of subject knowledge, drawing out a number of features which appear pertinent to high quality curriculum making and teaching in primary geography.

Chapter 10 refocuses on children's geographies through their sense-making of their own locality. Elizabeth Barrett Hacking and Robert Barrett explore and reflect on their research approach and on older primary children's environmental experiences, investigating the role children can play as collaborative and participatory 'geographical' researchers. This chapter provides insight into children's capabilities and potential which has important lessons for primary (and secondary) education, as well as for geographical and environmental learning. The analysis considers how developing children as researchers enables their deeper engagement and involvement with their school and local community. This study is about the reality of children's geographical learning, both about learning geography and learning about how we understand our environments in more rigorous and pertinent ways. It connects children's everyday geographical understanding with geographical investigations. Chapter 11 also examines primary children's learning about their locality, but from a rather different perspective. Emma Charlton, Gabrielle Cliff Hodges, Pam Pointon, Maria Nikolajeva, Erin Spring, Liz Taylor and Dominic Wyse explored children's place-related identities over eighteen months through the use of a story. This interdisciplinary study connected geography with reading and writing, using *My Place* (Wheatley and Rawlins 2008) to encourage children to explore and share their sense of place and their connections with places. Though concerned with children's geographies, this study has valuable messages for primary teachers about the interplay of school subjects to stimulate children's thinking about their engagement with the world around them, their places in it and their place identities.

Fran Martin, in Chapter 12, draws us into the teaching of distant places, doing so through her research and reflections on teachers' knowledge and self-learning, and their senses of identity. She considers UK teachers' learning through study visits in two countries, India and Gambia, from within which locality studies of 'distant places' have often appeared in the geography curriculum: distant in that they are far away and in that they are beyond the children's and, usually, the teachers' personal experience. Her research focused on how teachers' direct experience of a culture, community and place outside their 'comfort zone' challenged their thinking about how they might conceive of, feel about and value others. She explored, too, how these teachers' reflection inform their teaching about distant places in the primary geography curriculum, particularly through heightening their awareness to 'difference' as a positive dynamic in life and learning, giving insight into their own lives as well as into those living elsewhere (see also Martin 2012). It raises pertinent questions for primary teachers about senses of self, identity and subject knowledge. Daniela Schmeinck reports in Chapter 13 on a cross-European project she co-ordinated which involved primary age children from several European countries. Its purpose was to enable children to help each other learn about other countries in Europe by communicating about common studies they had undertaken. They investigated aspects of the geography of their own nation, drawing on everyday life experiences and created information to share in text and visual formats with other children, who could then use this material to complement their own work and build a wider geographical sense of Europe. The aim was to promote greater international and intercultural awareness and appreciation among primary children. In doing so the purpose was also to contribute to sharing and shared European identities.

Finally, in Chapter 14 Simon Catling pursues a number of the themes that have appeared across these chapters through his focus on children's voice in primary geography. He interrelates considerations of geographical knowledge, identity and children's geographies with the variety of 'voices' which children might have in the curriculum and through teaching and learning. He aligns this with critical pedagogy and dialogic teaching and learning, arguing that such a perspective can help the curriculum, learning and teaching move beyond any national curriculum. He makes a case for children's strong engagement in primary geography and, implicitly, for reflecting on geographical thinking.

Conclusion

The chapters in *Research and Debate in Primary Geography* provide food for thought about curriculum, teaching and learning in geography. They raise questions about teachers' geographical knowledge and values, what teachers think they know about themselves as teachers of geography, and how they might want their geography curriculum to be for children and the challenges this raises. It considers, too, how children's voices might be heard and involved in their geographical studies, teachers and children's senses of identity, what good quality geography teaching and learning is, whatever its curriculum context, and ways primary teachers might approach the teaching and learning of geography. Each chapter encourages us to reflect further on what might influence the development of children's geographical thinking. These chapters are not uncritical; indeed, it is hoped that they provide not only food for thought but some provocation to press forward with research, development and improvement in primary geography. This provides a purposeful sense of opportunity and optimism for geography's future in primary education.

Notes

1 This chapter is a rewritten and extended version of the Editorial, 'Optimism for a revised primary geography curriculum', by the author, published in 2013 in *Education 3–13*, 41, 4, 361–167.
2 I must record my thanks to Mark Brundrett, editor of *Education 3–13*, who suggested and encouraged the development of this book. As this book shows, his interest and enthusiasm is a strong stimulus to action!
3 See also, for example, these journals: *International Research in Geographical and Environmental Education, Journal of Geography, Research in Geographic Education, Review of International Geographical Education Online, Primary Geography.*

References

Alexander, R. 2000. *Culture and pedagogy: International comparisons in primary education.* Oxford: Blackwells.
Alexander, R., ed. 2010. *Children, their world, their education: Final report and recommendations of the Cambridge primary review.* London: Routledge.
Barlow, A. 2013. "Geography and history in the local area." In *Teaching geography creatively*, edited by S. Scoffham, 100–111. London:Routledge.
Bonnett, A. 2008. *What is geography?* London: Sage.
Bruner, J. 1960. *The process of education.* Cambridge, MA: Harvard University Press.
Catling, S. 2004. "On close inspection." *Primary Geographer* 55:34–36.
Catling, S., R. Bowles, J. Halocha, F. Martin, and S. Rawlinson. 2007. "The State of geography in English primary schools." *Geography* 92 (2): 118–136.

Catling, S., and F. Martin, eds. 2004. *Researching primary geography*. London: Register of Research in Primary Geography.
Catling, S., and T. Willy. 2009. *Teaching primary geography*. Exeter: Learning Matters.
Davis, J., and S. Elliott, eds. 2014. *Research in early childhood education for sustainability*. London: Routledge.
DES (Department of Education and Science). 1989. *Aspects of primary education: The teaching and learning of history and geography*. London: Her Majesty's Stationary Office.
DES (Department of Education and Science). 1991. *Geography in the national curriculum (England)*. London: HMSO.
DfE (Department for Education). 1995. *Geography in the national curriculum: England*. London: HMSO.
DfE. (Department for Education). 2013. *The national curriculum in England: Framework document*. London: DfE. www.gov.gov.uk/government/uploads/system/uploads/attachment_date/file/210969/NC_framework_document_-_FINAL.pdf.
DfEE/QCA (Department for Education and Employment/Qualifications and Curriculum Agency). 1999. *The national curriculum for England: Geography*. London: DfEE/QCA.
Eaude, T. 2012. *How do expert primary classteachers really work?* Exeter: Critical Publishing.
Freeman, C., and P. Tranter. 2011. *Children and their urban environment: Changing worlds*. London: Earthscan.
GA (Geographical Association). 2014. An assessment and progression framework for geography. www.geography.org.uk/curriculum2014/assessment.
GLP (Global Learning Programme). 2014. Progression in global learning through geography. www.globaldimension.org.uk/glp/page/11043 [Download].
Hicks, D. 2014. *Educating for hope in troubled times*. London: IOE Press.
Jackson, P. 2006. Thinking geographically. *Geography* 91 (3): 199–204.
Martin, F. 2006. *Teaching geography in primary schools: Learning how to live in the world*. Cambridge: Chris Kington Publishing.
Martin, F. 2012. The geographies of difference. *Geography* 97 (3): 116–122.
Martin, F., and P. Owens. 2008. *Caring for our world: A practical guide to ESD for ages 4–8*. Sheffield: Geographical Association.
Morgan, J. 2012. *Teaching secondary geography as if the planet matters*. London: Routledge.
Morgan, J. 2013. "What do we mean by thinking *geographically?*" In *Debates in geography education*, edited by D. Lambert, and M. Jones, 273–281. London: Routledge.
Olson, D. 2007. *Jerome Bruner*. London: Bloomsbury.
Ofsted (Office for Standards in Education). 1999. *Primary education 1994–1998: A review of primary schools in England*. London: The Stationary Office.
Ofsted (Office for Standards in Education). 2008. *Geography in schools: Changing practice*. www.ofsted.gov.uk/resources/geography-schools-changing-practice.
Ofsted (Office for Standards in Education). 2011. *Geography: Learning to make a world of difference*. www.ofsted.gov.uk/resources/ geography-learning-make-world-of-difference.
QCDA (Qualifications and Curriculum Development Agency). 2010. *The national curriculum primary handbook*. Coventry: QCDA.
Robertson, M. 2014. *Sustainability: Principles and practice*. London: Routledge.
Robertson, M., and R. Gerber, eds. 2000. *The child's world: Triggers for learning*. Melbourne: ACER.
Robertson, M., and R. Gerber, eds. 2001. *Children's ways of knowing: Learning through experience*. Melbourne: ACER.
Schmeinck, D., ed. 2006. *Research on learning and teaching in primary geography*. Karsruhr: Pädagogische Hochschule Karlsruhr.
Scoffham, S., ed. 2010. *Primary geography handbook*. Sheffield: Geographical Association.
Scoffham, S,. ed. 2013. *Teaching geography creatively*. London: Routledge.
Wheatley, N., and D. Rawlins. 2008. *My place*. Newtown, NSW, Australia: Walker Books.
Wiegand, P. 2006. *Learning and teaching with maps*. London: Routledge.
Woolley, R. 2010. *Tackling controversial issues in the primary school*. London: Routledge.
Young, M. 2008. *Bringing knowledge back in*. London: Routledge.
Young, M., and D. Lambert, with C. Roberts, and M. Roberts. 2014. *Knowledge and the future school*. London: Bloomsbury.

Enquiring into primary teachers' geographical knowledge

Simon Catling[a,b] and Emma Morley[a,b]

[a]Faculty of Humanities and Social Sciences, School of Education, Oxford Brookes University, Harcourt Hill Campus, Oxford, UK; [b]Department of Initial Teacher Education, Faculty of Education, Health and Social Care, University of Winchester, Winchester, Hampshire, UK

Subject knowledge is an important component of primary teachers' repertoire, though it has not been studied widely beyond their understandings of aspects of science and mathematics. Evaluations of the quality of teachers' geographical knowledge for teaching primary geography indicate a disparity between high quality teachers and less strong teachers. Good or weaker geography subject knowledge influences primary teachers' capacity to plan well for and intervene effectively in children's learning. This small-scale interview-based enquiry explores several teachers' senses of geography subject knowledge. They are enthusiasts for geography and are identified as expert teachers of the subject in their classes and schools. Five themes emerge as very tentative findings from their reflections: the subject's breadth, knowledge about the world, a living subject, an accessible subject for children and need for geography to be visible in the curriculum. There are indications that these primary teachers have a sense of geographical knowledge as informational knowledge, conceptual knowledge and geographical thinking. However, there were limits to these teachers' clear articulations of their understandings. Questions emerge about the nature and value of subject knowledge in relation to pedagogical content knowledge for primary teachers.

Introduction

Subject knowledge has been central to the teaching of national curriculum subjects since 1988, as it always had been in schooling. Office for Standards in Education (Ofsted 2009) has highlighted the importance of subject knowledge in primary teaching across the range of subjects for primary teachers and children. Yet we enquire comparatively little into the nature of primary teachers' knowledge of the subjects they teach. There have been a range of studies over many years, focused both on early career and experienced primary teachers, examining most frequently aspects of their science and mathematics knowledge and understanding (Appleton 1995; Harlen and Holroyd 1997; Morris 2001) and on novice teachers' subject knowledge, largely in the same two subjects (Parker and Heywood 2000; Williams 2008; Witt, Goode, and Ibbett 2013). There has been limited investigation in subjects such as history and music (Harnett 2000; McCullough 2006), as there has been into primary teachers' and novice teachers' geographical knowledge (Catling 2004; Martin 2008; Morley 2012). Given the explicit re-emphasis of subject knowledge in children's school learning (Department for Education [DfE] 2010, 2013), it is timely to explore this topic further.

There is discussion in geography education about teachers' conceptions of geography, the nature of geographical knowledge and the forms of knowledge associated with the 'knowledge turn' in the national curriculum requirements (Brooks 2011; Firth 2011, 2013; Lambert 2011; Bustin 2012). Understanding primary teachers' knowledge of geography is of particular interest since the government requires that the English national curriculum should 'ensure that all children have the opportunity to acquire a core of essential knowledge in the key subject disciplines', in order to provide 'young people with the knowledge they need to move confidently and successfully through their education' (DfE 2011, 2–3). While much of this debate focuses around secondary school subjects (Lambert and Jones 2013), it is also important for primary education.

The development of primary teachers' subject knowledge is a key aspect of their pre-service education and training, since it is expected that many primary teachers will teach all the subjects listed for the Key Stages 1 and 2 curriculum. By 1993 the initial teacher training (ITT) criteria specifically required novice teachers to demonstrate their knowledge and understanding of the primary curriculum subjects they would teach so that it was clear that they were able to teach children effectively (DfE 1993). Through various revisions subject knowledge has remained a core component, although from 2002 to 2007 primary ITT courses could offer either geography or history if they so chose (Department for Education and Skills/Teacher Training Agency 2002); very few took this option, with those that did dropping geography. Further revisions to the criteria in 2012 restated the need for prospective primary teachers to 'have a secure knowledge of the relevant subject(s) and curriculum areas' they teach to enable them to 'impart knowledge and develop understanding' (DfE 2012, 5–6). Yet the contact time for the geography component, for instance in one-year postgraduate courses, varies markedly from institution to institution and is low, varying between 2 and 16 hours and averaging under 7 hours, having decreased by a quarter since 2006 (Catling 2006, 2013a). There is little comfort in recognising that this situation seems to be much the same for all of the foundation subjects. The subject timetables and inspection programmes of primary ITT courses are dominated by the core subjects of English and mathematics, with even science's time declining. The implication is that future teachers' knowledge of geography and other foundation subjects would seem not to be of significant importance, though they will teach a broad curriculum.

Primary teachers and geographical knowledge

It is expected that each primary teacher will develop their expertise in teaching and that many will become expert primary teachers employing a wide range of pedagogical capabilities, including subject knowledge (James and Pollard 2012), to enable children's development, progress and success (DfE 2010). The notion of the expert primary teacher has been of interest for many years (Taylor 1986; Eaude 2012). Taylor, exploring knowledge as one of the key facets of expert primary teaching, contended that there are two aspects to knowledge. One is 'knowledge about knowledge … the *what* of teaching' (Taylor 1986, 120), in effect subject knowledge and societal knowledge, while the other concerns understanding the practical dynamics of teaching, *how* to do it, including teachers' knowledge of their children, their range of teaching skills and techniques and their capacity to match the two to foster children's effective learning. Eaude (2012) concurs but notes that primary teachers will inevitably lack much specialist subject knowledge, though they may have greater expertise in some subjects than others. He foregrounds Shulman's case for pedagogical content knowledge (2004). This connects subject knowledge with understanding ways that are appropriate and effective in teaching subjects to enhance children's engagement with and learning of them. Eaude argues that what primary teachers really need, and do in fact make use of, is '*enough* understanding' of the range of subjects for the children they teach. As does Taylor, he sees subject knowledge as but one aspect of the teacher's repertoire, which includes setting the classroom climate, decisions on learning objectives, choices about teaching and learning activities, interpersonal relationships with children that support their learning, and providing feedback and guidance on their next learning steps. Teachers' real expertise, Taylor and Eaude contend, lies in their approaches to teaching their children; it is their pedagogical expertise.

The House of Commons Education Committee (2012) noted the importance of subject knowledge for teachers and the differing needs of primary and secondary teachers though it did not elaborate on this. Focusing on 'outstanding teachers', the Committee recorded that Ofsted considers such individuals to have 'exceptionally strong subject knowledge', enabling them to challenge and inspire learning in the children they teach (House of Commons Education Committee 2012, 16). This perception reinforces the view that in order to be an effective primary teacher subject knowledge is fundamental. It is supported by the findings of the Teaching and Learning Research Programme in the UK (James and Pollard 2012), which noted that 1 of the 10 principles of effective pedagogy is that it is vital to engage children with subjects and knowledge through their 'big ideas, key skills and processes, modes of discourse, ways of thinking and practicing, attitudes and relationships ...' (James and Pollard 2012, 4). This requires some depth of understanding in a subject if not necessarily being an expert in that subject.

An analysis of research in geographical education internationally notes that little is known about both secondary and primary teachers' geographical knowledge (Bednarz, Heffron, and Huynh 2013). While there has been limited investigation into 'expert' secondary geography teachers' geographical knowledge and its relationship to their teaching (Brooks 2011; Bustin 2012), such studies are lacking of 'expert' primary teachers. Indeed, it is not clear who are 'expert' primary teachers of geography. A rare study of a well-experienced 'expert' teacher of social studies in an elementary school in the USA indicates that other than high quality generic teaching skills, she 'routinely reinforces basic geographical concepts when opportunities arise, especially concepts associated with common confusions or misconceptions' (Brophy, Alleman, and Knighton 2009, 104). Clearly, this teacher uses her geographical knowledge to support and enhance children's geographical learning, but this is a capability she uses across all the subjects of her class' curriculum (Brophy, Alleman, and Knighton 2010). We do not learn what her knowledge and understanding of geography are, though we know she involves place and location studies, the use of globes and maps and covers aspects of geography such as food, transport and resources in her curriculum. She is not a geography specialist, and it seems more likely that she has effective, even very good, geographical pedagogical content knowledge which she has developed over many years in her practice.

Ofsted evaluates the quality of primary geography teaching, children's achievements, the curriculum and subject leadership. Its geography reports (Ofsted 2008, 2011) identify a mixture of high quality, ordinary and weak geography in primary schools. Discussing teaching which is good or outstanding, Ofsted states that 'good geographical knowledge' is one of the essential ingredients (Ofsted 2011, 12). Yet Ofsted says little about such knowledge (Ofsted 2009, 2013), other than that primary teachers need to have 'an understanding of what pupils should know about geography', a good sense of children's misconceptions (Ofsted 2008, 11) and include key aspects of the programmes of study in their curriculum. Ofsted's case is that a good knowledge of the subject supports teachers' high quality planning and teaching, just as it applies to success in the role of the geography subject leader. The good use of geographical vocabulary during teaching, encouraging children to use geographical terms contextually and accurately, is one way through which primary teachers use their subject knowledge well to enhance learning. Providing high quality subject-specific feedback on and about children's geographical work, particularly formatively, is another indicator of a teacher's good geographical understanding. These examples illustrate the effect of supporting children's achievements and of aiding progress in building their geographical knowledge and understanding (Ofsted 2013). In this context, Ofsted's critique of weaker geography teaching is informative of concerns about primary teachers' subject knowledge.

Martin notes that often primary teachers appear to have 'difficulty interpreting the nature of geography as expressed in the National Curriculum orders' (Martin 2013, 18). Ofsted (2008, 2011) identifies a key issue in the weaker teaching of geography as many primary teachers' low level of confidence in their understanding of the subject. This insecurity results in too many primary teachers not being able to

> interpret effectively the outline curriculum ideas that had been provided, and to ensure that high quality experiences for learning geography were interwoven into the topics they were teaching. As a result, many of the teaching units did not provide a clear and sequential structure which would enable pupils to develop and improve their geographical knowledge and understanding. (Ofsted 2011, 18)

A key point Ofsted (2008, 2011) reiterates is that while primary teachers generally have good generic teaching skills, for many their weak geographical knowledge compounds a poor situation when they are not clear about what constitutes good geographical learning for and by children. This results in opportunities being missed to extend children's understanding, such as by using further relevant examples within a particular geographical topic and by challenging children's misunderstandings. Indeed, some teachers may misinform children about, say, an environmental issue and not recognise when they themselves offer stereotypical perspectives about a distant place. Teachers' lack of awareness of specific geographical terminology inhibits children's chances to be more precise in their discussions, descriptions and explanations about geographical phenomena, patterns and processes and thus to deepen their understanding. Where knowledge is weak, questioning is likely to be less focused, and teachers find it difficult to respond to probing questions the children ask, just as they fail to provide real challenges for more able children in geography. Constraints in their geographical knowledge lead, in effect, to teachers developing only superficial studies with children. Some primary teachers' over-reliance on and too rigid use of commercial teaching units identifies insecurity in their geographical knowledge. In such circumstances, quite often not all aspects of a unit would be taught, with some ignored due to a lack of personal confidence, not simply the result of time constraints. In particular, the impact of this is seen in cross-curricular topics. A significant outcome of weak geographical knowledge and its effect on planning, Ofsted states, is fragmented geographical experience for children, undermining the development of their geographical understanding. A subject leader may well not recognise this situation if their own geographical knowledge has weaknesses, which frequently is the case, for very many geography subject leaders are not geographers nor necessarily interested in the subject. Being unable to tackle primary teachers' insecure subject knowledge is compounded further by the lack of opportunities for subject leaders and teachers to develop their geographical understanding through continuing professional development courses. Because it has low priority, many primary schools do not invest for their children's geographical education.

Few primary teachers see themselves as geographers, even when they might be the geography subject leader in a school (Ofsted 2011). In Martin's (2008) view, this lack of understanding by primary teachers of themselves as geographers places deep constraints on being able to work effectively as a teacher of geography. She argues that by the time prospective primary teachers begin their training, they have 'already built a body of knowledge about the world geographically but many do not recognise this' (Martin 2008, 36). She sees their personal geographical knowledge as built through their everyday experiences enabling them to operate perfectly well geographically, for instance in making travel, shopping and leisure decisions and in being aware of national and global matters which will affect them, such as movements in food prices linked to changing climate and trade patterns. She contends that all primary teachers have their own tacit 'ethno-geography' upon which they can draw as teachers if they are enabled to recognise and appreciate this. She recognises that ethno-geographies are not the same as academic geographies, but she argues that for many primary teachers developing their knowledge and understanding of geography as a school subject can be brought about through and from their ethno-geographies. Such understanding challenges and enables teachers to move beyond the constraints of their personal geographies to develop a broader understanding of the subject through awareness of its big ideas and conceptual frameworks. Yet, as has been noted (Catling 2013a), there is little time in initial teacher education courses for novice primary teachers to be given the opportunity to explore and understand their own geographical experiences and conceptualisations, just as there is often little or no opportunity to do so throughout their career. This seems likely to compound weak geographical knowledge.

Seeing yourself as a geographer is a challenge when you neither have understanding and sense of the subject nor appreciate that it is an aspect of your daily life. Yet being knowledgeable about geography is evidently vital for its effective teaching. Being a geographically aware and knowledgeable primary teacher has a positive impact on children's learning. It seems equally true that the converse is the case. From the level of subject leadership to day-to-day teaching, teachers' feeling secure in their geographical understanding seems vital to children achieving well and being able to make good progress in developing their own geographical knowledge during the year and across their primary career.

Enquiring into primary teachers' sense of geography

Unstated in all of this are assumptions about what geographical knowledge is; it remains implicit unless the subject is elaborated upon. However, neither is this straightforward nor is this the place to debate the contested nature of geographical knowledge (Bonnett 2008; Holt-Jensen 2009). Rather the interest is to investigate what primary teachers' sense of geographical knowledge might be. Indeed, it is helpful to explore this unencumbered by presumed notions of the subject, to understand what emerges rather than to provide perspectives to which teachers respond.

This enquiry explores their sense of geography with a small group of primary teachers. The participants work in primary schools which have been externally recognised either by Ofsted and/or by the Geographical Association (GA) through its Primary

Geography Quality Mark (GA 2013) as outstanding providers of geography for their children. The teachers involved have responsibility for coordinating and managing geography in their schools and are recognised as high quality teachers of geography in their classrooms and as effective subject leaders. The purpose of this study is to enquire into these teachers' relationship with geography and their sense of the subject. The investigation involved five career primary teachers who volunteered to participate. It is an opportunistic selective sample, a very small-scale study, in which those involved were recommended to be approached. It makes, therefore, no claims to be representative or for any generalisation from its findings, which must be considered highly tentative because of the small-scale and open-ended approach. It is a topic which needs much fuller and deeper research.

Data were collected through interviews with the participants, using questions that invited mainly open-ended responses. Before the interviews, each participant was visited in their school setting informally by one of the authors because, while recommendation was valued, it was vital to obtain each participant's agreement and to gain a sense of their valuing of geography. In each case they were very positive about participation and their involvement was endorsed by their head teachers. Each individual was enthusiastic about their role as geography coordinator. They were very willing and keen to promote geography as a curriculum subject to both colleagues and children. Ahead of the formal interview, each participant was sent a questionnaire to gather basic information such as qualifications, number of years teaching and the range of their teaching experiences, as well as details of any personal affiliations to organisations such as the GA or environmental bodies. All the participants were female. The length of time teaching varied from 10 to almost 40 years. One teacher was a non-core subject (including geography) curriculum leader, while two were very experienced teachers with deputy and assistant headship roles and were responsible for geography. The fourth teacher was a class teacher who was also her school's geography co-ordinator, and the fifth participant had recently left primary teaching to move to a role as a university primary teacher education tutor. Three had full or half geography degrees, while one had no educational qualification in geography. Two were active members of the GA, with a third in a member school; and another was involved with the National Trust. The study has not compared the individual cases; it has taken a cross-cutting approach to draw out tentative findings.

The interviews were semi-structured. The questions focused on exploring participants' understanding of the nature and purpose of geography and included questions about personal experience of being taught the subject, their level of confidence in teaching geography and about their understanding and valuing of the subject. Each interview was recorded and transcribed. Questions were explored using prompts appropriate to each participant's responses. Their interview transcript was checked by each participant. A constant comparison method was used in analysis of the transcripts (Glaser and Strauss 1967; Bryant and Charmaz 2007; Thomas 2009; Newby 2010). The approach was to identify topics and statements grounded in the data in relation to each of the questions and then between the question responses. Several themes emerged which appeared to have some significance in terms of the focus of the study. Inevitably such an interpretive method is constrained since it is to an extent subjective, even where two or more researchers are involved in comparing and agreeing judgements and outcomes.

This article presents and reflects on the participants' responses to two specific elements in this study. One concerned the teachers' sense of geography and what it means to them. The other asked how important subject knowledge is to them in their understanding of geography, and why this is the case. Their responses were informative though not always clearly expressed, which may have arisen from the process of interviewing as much as from the capacity of the participants to articulate their senses of geography. The analysis of the responses to these two topics produced five identifiable themes: geography's subject breadth; geography as knowledge about the world; geography as a living subject; the accessibility of geography for all; and the visibility of geography. These are now considered, illustrated by statements from the teachers involved.

Geography's subject breadth

The first theme to emerge drew largely on participants' responses to the question about what they thought the subject of geography to be. Participants viewed geography in very broad terms about people, places and environments, and saw it as particularly interested in people's lives and their interconnections. They appeared to see this *holistic* nature of the subject as one of its key assets.

> Well, I think it sort of encompasses everything, because it's all about people and places, so it's all about us as we are now, and places we go, places we've been, and for the children things for the future … I think it encompasses the environment … I think it's all about the here and now … I think it's about the world that we live in, and the people that are in the world, and the way that they interact. [T2]

Rawding (2013) argues that *holistic geographies* tend to be overlooked in geography teaching, since so often the focus in (secondary) geography teaching is very rarely on the sense of the planet as a whole than on particular aspects of its geography. It is informative that these primary teachers identify and value the encompassing nature of geography. The interviewees saw geography as a means to develop children's sense of wonder at the world as their home. They acknowledged that there are challenges in ensuring that children understand the nature of the subject, in particular its breadth, how it fits together and the application of geographical understanding, which Jackson (2006) has termed 'thinking geographically'.

> I think it's just about making them [children] aware of the wonder of what sustains them. Because they don't realise that everything that they do comes under the umbrella of geography. If you're in a traffic jam, you're suddenly thinking 'oh, which other route can I take?' They don't make that link, and I don't know where that stems from. [T4]

Their responses indicate that these teachers consider geography to be a broad subject, covering very many aspects of the world and lives lived in it. In this respect, the teachers' senses of geography might seem to go beyond the requirements set out in the national curriculum geography programmes on which they based their curriculum (Department for Education and Employment [DfEE] 1999), though none of them made the connection directly. Certainly, their views were intended very much as a positive endorsement of geography in primary education. Yet it can be argued that seeing geography as having this very breadth is a cause of some of the problems associated with defining its nature and interests, which raises the question: 'what is not geography?' (Bonnett 2008). It might seem too loose and unspecific an account of geography, not really providing a clear sense of the subject, yet it captures what Rawding (2013) argues is so often overlooked. These primary teachers want children to develop a sense of the world as a whole, not simply to have explored a selection of aspects of it, as well as to be fascinated and awed by and be curious about the world.

It was apparent from the participants' responses that they found it difficult to articulate any more specific or coherent statement about geography. Their sense of geography appeared to be quite general, though it offered a holistic view of the subject and was justified on the basis of children being informed about the world. It lacked sharp definition and the teachers involved did not attempt to describe or justify the range of aspects of the world which they implied might be elements in geographical studies with primary children, such as places or the environment.

Geography as knowledge about the world

Quite evidently the first theme indicates that geography includes knowledge about the world. This emerged more directly as a second theme in response to enquiring about the way these teachers viewed subject knowledge in their understanding of geography. However, they appeared unsure about the interpretation of the word 'knowledge' used in relation to geography. There was little doubt that they felt that knowledge was important, although there was a sense that they were almost embarrassed to admit this, implying that 'knowledge' meant facts. Indeed, while there was apparent reference to the essential 'foundations' of geography, it was not clarified.

> I think they're like layers in a way. You've got to have some foundations from which to build the other things. I don't think … any of them can be separated from one another. Alongside the traditional knowledge … I do believe in having skills. [T5]

The notion of traditional knowledge seemed to include factual information about the world, such as the names of countries, which it was acknowledged their children enjoyed. It was extended by reference to geographical skills, such as map reading.

> I think why teachers are quite happy to teach history rather than geography is that the history is not such a skill set. There are some certain skill requirements for geography, like the map reading and contours … and if people don't know that themselves, they find it difficult to teach it, whereas history just happens. [T4]
>
> Not that you want children to be reciting facts and figures, but they like that. You know, when we did the Olympics they got the flags out, and they desperately wanted to know which flags went with which countries. So although tenuous, it was important and they loved it. [T2]

The references to factual information and particular geographical skills would seem to be in line with the notion of 'core knowledge' used by the government to describe what it requires of a national curriculum (DfE 2010, 2011), in particular the specification of particular subject content, such as locating named countries and rivers and developing map skills in geography. But its use by these teachers seems not so much as to be about pre-specified content, as to refer to children's interest in and seeking of facts and using map skills. It is also inferred that teachers need to know such geographical information and skills to be able to teach geography effectively. Primary teachers need to be knowledgeable, but perhaps more in terms of what interests and motivates their children and how to develop this by using their understanding of children's subject needs than in being highly informed about the many aspects of geography. This implies the use of pedagogic content knowledge, of having 'enough knowledge' in Eaude's (2012) phrase.

Within this theme there is an evident sense of geographical knowledge including information about places and environments. It appears clear that knowledge may be used in another way to refer to the understanding and use of particular skills, while a third sense of geographical knowledge can be inferred from the reference to the 'layers' of the subject and the idea of taking different angles, perhaps meaning its conceptual base used in thinking about and providing structure to matters in the world around us. Yet there remains a constraint in that these expert primary teachers of geography find it challenging to express in clear geographical terms what they understand geography subject knowledge to be. This inhibits expression of and, perhaps, access to a depth of understanding about the subject, which might indicate that these teachers do not have a well-developed sense of what geography is about. It leaves inferences to be drawn about their knowledge of geography, rather than enables their sense of the subject to be readily identified and appreciated.

Geography as a living subject

> You know, you think of history being the past, but I think geography is always changing; it's quite vibrant, and just depending on what angle you take, you know you can go … different sorts of angles – human, or environmental. For the children as well, I think, there's always something in the news, every day … so it's constantly changing and quite exciting. [T2]

Geography is seen as connected with the everyday world, a subject that is living, dynamic and evolving. This perspective supports the notion of 'living geography', which is focused on developing geographical thinking, going somewhat beyond geography as a subject that can in its weaker teaching do little more than 'deliver a selection of the discipline's products in a packaged format' (Lambert 2009, 6) or as 'essential knowledge' (DfE 2011), whoever decides that. *Living geography* engages seriously with children's ethno-geographies; it explores aspects of geography at a range of scales setting the local in national and global contexts, going beyond the local; it encompasses physical and human geography processes and change, taking a critically thoughtful stance in inter-relating physical and human geography; and it understands the past in relation to the present and looks to the future (Lambert 2009). The dynamism of living geography applies as much with primary children as with secondary pupils. The participants saw this as a particularly positive feature of the subject.

> It's about being engaged in what's going on around you. [T1]

It was acknowledged that to be a living subject, geography requires active involvement. Such active engagement was viewed as giving the children both a key role in their learning and providing an opportunity for them to have an effect on the world, personally and locally, perhaps, as these teachers saw it, in a way not offered by any other subject in the primary curriculum. In this sense, it goes beyond activity-based teaching and learning to provide direct meaning for children through investigation, creativity, problem-solving and risk-taking (Monk and Silman 2011).

> It needs to be hands on … you need to be involved in it. You can't get a sense of the world or the place around you from a book – you've got to get out there. [T1]
>
> I think it's just vital that the children understand that everything they do has an impact, as a person, so it's not about countries, it's about people. And it's that connection between people and places locally and globally, and that we have a difference with everything we do. [T3]

This practical, involved approach to geography is most obviously seen in primary schools in the form of geographical fieldwork and enquiry in and beyond the classroom. These teachers endorsed this approach linking it with children's curiosity and greater worldly awareness. The GA's *Curriculum Consultation Report* (2011b) endorses this stance when it states that 'the best geography teaching is based on stimulating the curiosity of children and young people in order to ask questions and to generate a "need to know" about the wider world' (6). Geography is viewed by this sample of teachers as about engaging children with the world through active investigations, because they see geography as grounded in the everyday and the wider world as it is. Geography's knowledge is 'out there' to be sought, not simply to be brought in parcelled up. This indicates a sense of geography as investigative and of its knowledge as what is found out, what is discovered through enquiry, not just what is already known and simply passed on. This is about 'doing geography', not simply learning about it (Scoffham 2010).

The accessibility of geography to all

Connected with the idea of living geography is that the subject needs to be accessible. These teachers indicated that this should be thought of in at least four ways: in relation to geography's value in children's education, its contextualisation for them, that learning is matched to take children's geographical learning forward and that teachers should show their interest and enthusiasm for geography. Although the teachers said little specifically about geography's educational value, they were clear that it is important in children's education, echoing the view that 'geography is not a narrow academic subject for the few. It is fundamental for everyone' (GA 2009, 5). Children need to know their geography. In part this may have reflected their enthusiasm for geography, which underpinned their desire to promote it throughout their schools. It is about accessibility as giving children the opportunities to engage in geographical studies to enhance their own lives and learning. This is a statement about valuing geography, implying that learning about geography concerns developing children's knowledge of the world and its role in their everyday lives.

Underpinning this sense of accessibility, secondly, is the notion of geography's relevance. The teachers' responses concurred with Lambert (2011) who suggests that geographical subject knowledge needs to be contextualised for it to be meaningful to children. Participants were strongly in favour of new geographical knowledge being connected to children's personal everyday geographies (Martin 2008; Catling and Martin 2011). They saw this linking of new knowledge to existing knowledge as a key feature of good primary practice.

> You have to contextualise subject knowledge. If you just teach me about a pile of rocks it's not going to be interesting. I think … children have to know … why information is important, but I think that about all subjects. I mean if I was doing that in maths, I'd think the same. I need to know about area because I need to know how many bathroom tiles I need. [T5]

They indicated, third, that this includes making effective connections to previously taught geographical knowledge in order for the new content to make sense to children. Information and ideas are not isolated but only make sense in the larger whole, in geography as in any other subject and area of learning. This seemed to make sense for themselves as teachers, recognising how their geographical knowledge are inter-related. What came across was that the teachers recognised that their children's ethno-geographies were broadly based not simply linked to the locality but more worldly, with the implication that this was also the case for them. Geographical knowledge is seen to involve not only information and links but values about the environment as well.

> The geography I did in school wasn't connected to anything. It didn't appear to be connected to anything in my life or around it, and I know that has influenced what I've done, what I did as a teacher and what I do now. [T5]

> They are more knowledgeable than we were at our age. They know what's happening in the world. They know how they should be caring for it. I think when we were doing geography it was facts and figures, wasn't it? But I think now they're very knowledgeable. [T2]

Knowledge of the subject linked with knowledge about the children is a vital element of pedagogic content knowledge. It facilitates the relationship between geographical knowledge and enquiries and the children. These teachers saw relevance in terms of matching their studies to the children's current geographical understanding in order to develop it further.

> You need to understand the skills that children need to learn from that subject, and how they can transfer them in other subjects. And you need to think really carefully about what is age appropriate. I think sometimes, the temptation is to run before we walk, and then you've lost the children, and what was the point of that? So it's about age appropriateness, it's about being creative without losing sight of what it was you wanted to teach them. [T1]

The participants acknowledged the challenges of teaching geographical subject knowledge, particularly for those teachers with little background in the subject or specific subject training. Reinforcing the point made above, they felt that teachers need more than to be knowledgeable about a subject. Fourth, primary teachers need to show their interest in geography, even to be enthusiastic about it, to encourage children to develop similar attitudes, which reinforce their valuing of the subject. Access requires more than the opportunity to be taught geography; it requires of the teacher positive attitudes to motivate themselves and the children, and such enthusiasm came from being knowledgeable, not from ignorance or being only partially aware. Equally, interest in geography as a teacher implied the willingness to understand the subject more fully and deeply.

> If you don't ... have an interest in it yourself, I think it's even more difficult for you to actually access and teach enthusiastically. I think that's the barrier, you know. If you're not interested in it, it's difficult to get that enthusiasm. [T4]

The visibility of geography

The final theme concerns geography being explicit within the curriculum. Unless it is visible it can be lost; it becomes 'not known'. Ofsted (2011) noted that in some 10% of primary schools where foundation subjects such as geography are taught through creative, cross-curricular topics, geography is more or less absent. No reason is given for this situation, but it would seem to relate to two things. One is teachers' lack of confidence in teaching geography, which would almost certainly be compounded by their insecurity in their subject knowledge and by not valuing the subject. The other is the lack of leadership in geography in a school, linked with low status. The impact can be subject weakness and loss.

When asked about the nature and purpose of geography, this small sample of teachers made the point that, even in instances where their schools used an integrated topic-based approach, it is still vital for geography to be drawn on and out discretely. This means that teachers are clear and explicit for both themselves and the children about which aspects of their cross-curricular topics focus on geographical learning, rather than, say, historical learning, even if there is an extent of integration between the subjects.

> I think they [the children] need to know the term geography ... and what it encompasses ... ...
> Lumping them together ... I don't think you can! [T4]

> You've still got to keep your skills discrete. Because otherwise then I think you're going to lose
> things, and people are going to go 'well, what was geography?' and I think you've got to have
> that balance. You can do it in your holistic way, but I think you've also got to make explicit, ...
> this is a geography skill. [T1]

It is not simply a matter of including aspects of geography, which might be done in a low key manner; it is about foregrounding geographical foci, knowledge and enquiries. Barnes (2011) notes that the teaching of subject knowledge remains vital whether a subject is taught distinctively as a separate subject or within a cross-curricular or integrated studies topic. These teachers contend that being overt and explicit about geography is essential to enabling children to connect their topics and their learning with the subject. It helps their development of their knowledge of geography. For the teachers it foregrounds geography as a 'known' subject.

Reflections on expert primary teachers' knowledge of geography

These insights into this small group of teachers' sense of geography, its accessibility and its visibility in the primary curriculum give some indication of their knowledge of geography for its teaching. One justification for revisions to national curriculum subjects has been that the focus needed to shift to 'core knowledge', or its apparent synonym 'essential knowledge', in subjects like geography (DfE 2010, 2011) from an implied looseness in the subject descriptions in earlier curriculum requirements (DfEE 1999). It has been a matter of debate as to what this re-focusing means (GA 2011a; Lambert 2011). Firth (2013) suggests that the concept of 'core knowledge' is unhelpful, since it seems to be muddled and can be interpreted in too limited a way. Politicians may mean it in a broad or narrow sense, but they are unclear. This indicates a concern with using the term 'knowledge'. It may have a limited sense to some but a wider meaning for others.

To try to resolve this conundrum, the GA tackled the concern about knowledge head-on in its initial proposals towards a revitalised geography national curriculum (GA 2011a; Hopkin 2013). It identified three forms of knowledge appropriate to geographical content and learning, an approach which was strongly endorsed in the responses to the Association's consultation (GA 2011b).

Knowledge as information about the world, for which it used the phrase 'core knowledge', is to be thought of as the 'vocabulary' of geography. It refers to the facts which geography both draws on and refers to. It is seen as the public sense of geography, the view of the subject as dealing in facts about places and the physical and human environment, such as the knowledge of the names and locations of countries and capital cities, as well as of the world's rivers and mountain ranges, and such like. It is described as the traditional view of geography.

Knowledge as a subject's concepts is identified by the notion of 'content knowledge'. This focus is on the big ideas and generalisations that geography uses to understand and make sense of the world. It is called its 'grammar' and encompasses such key concepts as location, place, scale, space and environmental processes, as well as the meanings of such geographical terms as town, mountain and site. It encompasses values and differing perspectives on places and environments which give extended meaning to geographical concepts and their understanding.

Knowledge as thinking geographically is the subject's 'procedural knowledge'. This is characterised by appreciating place as a significant idea and by taking a relational or holistic approach in studies, such as exploring human and physical geography aspects in an enquiry and connecting local with global contexts (GA 2011a, 2–3). Thinking geographically applies geographical information and concepts in problem solving, creativity and decision-making.

Using this typology, all three elements of knowledge are identifiable to varying degrees in the teachers' reflections on their sense of geography. They recognise and appreciate that geography deals with facts; that it is about *knowledge as information* about the world. Less explicit but underlying what emerged is the notion of geography as *knowledge of a subject's concepts*. Here there seems to be emphasis on the more everyday concepts of geography, such as town and site, rather than on its big ideas, for instance, scale and location, though the concepts of place and environment are mentioned in the teachers' reflections. These underpin the third sense of knowledge, that of *knowledge as thinking geographically*. This appears where the teachers referred to the application of knowledge in problem solving and linking with everyday concerns and needs, though this is less explicit overall in their responses than in the first two. While a tentative finding, it might be concluded that these teachers have a sense of geographical knowledge which is useful in distinguishing the levels of knowledge and understanding with which children need to engage.

What comes through less evidently is how these expert primary teachers of geography might describe geography and what they feel its key elements are. They give considerable value to the subject of geography, and they believe that it contributes significantly towards a primary child's education, though they say almost nothing directly about what the benefit is. They connect it with everyday living and its role in daily decision-making and understanding of the world, near and far. It can be discerned that they recognise and value its breadth and relevance, and they see geography as a holistic subject inter-linking its various aspects to make sense of the world. It requires factual knowledge as much as conceptual understanding, but it involves the application of these in studies of places and environments, not simply the learning of them. They seem reasonably confident in their own geographical knowledge, although precisely what they understand by this is less clear, since their specific notions of geography are not well articulated. This supports a similar finding drawn in a separate study about primary teachers' perspectives on curriculum making, where those teachers recognised the value of their geographical knowledge in enhancing their own and their children's geographical learning, though, again, they did not elaborate on it in any detail (Catling 2013b). This is a matter to explore further. Yet, this sample of teachers sees geography as a dynamic, living subject, about the world today and in holistic terms (Rawding 2013). As importantly, they come across as enthusiastic, and they give the impression that they make every effort to find out what they need to know to be able to teach geography well, because they have a genuine interest in the subject. They appreciate the role of subject knowledge as an important ingredient in their teaching. They indicate also that their approach to their planning and teaching is one that resonates with the notion of curriculum making (Lambert and Morgan 2010; GA 2012; Catling 2013b), an approach which involves taking responsibility for the planning of their class' units of study. In this context, it can be inferred that they implicitly use a 'capabilities approach', which 'knowingly recognises the need to use the subject discipline as a resource to co-construct deeper conceptual understanding, so that young people can make sense of the world' (Lambert 2011, 258).

These teachers' sense of geography is positive, if not entirely clear, about geographical knowledge, which bodes well in their dealing with revisions to and developments in the subject (DfE 2013). However, they voiced concerns about the future of geography. In response to other questions in their interviews, they made the point that regular continuing professional development courses in geography, and making use of local authority and subject association expert help, are the key to reversing the picture portrayed by Ofsted (2008, 2011) of too many primary schools and classrooms where geography is not effectively taught and where teachers' lack of confidence in the subject inhibits children's learning. They appeared genuinely to want their colleagues and children to enjoy what they saw to be the benefits of studying and learning geography. In this context they also saw it as appropriate for geography to be linked with other subjects, as long as the distinctions remain clear and geography is evident in the planning and is named explicitly to the children when aspects of studies are geographical in nature. They spoke enthusiastically about using geography as the overarching 'umbrella' and central point for topics and about teaching their literacy and numeracy through geography. They indicate that they make connections in their teaching to and from geography consciously and subconsciously.

> I think I see geography in a completely different light, and realise that it just permeates absolutely everything we do in school, and I am just trying to communicate that, the awesomeness of it! …. Geography here is not just being packaged into a little box with the dreaded textbooks, it's all-encompassing … and they're [the children] gaining, so all their literacy's taught through it, all the writing, absolutely everything. [T3]

Brooks (2011) investigated the influence of subject knowledge in the practice of 'expert' secondary geography teachers. She concluded that it was relevant not only to know how teachers understand their own subject knowledge but also to examine how these individuals call upon their subject knowledge to develop their students' understanding. Martin's (2000, 2008) research with novice primary teachers' use of their geographical knowledge drew a similar conclusion. Evidence from this micro-survey suggests that these primary teachers both have and use subject knowledge, but there are indications, not fully explored, that this may rather be in the form of *enough* subject knowledge in the context of pedagogical content knowledge rather than deep geographical understanding. Perhaps this should not be considered unusual even among 'expert' primary teachers of geography, though this might be somewhat surprising given that three of the teachers are geography graduates. In fact, in the interviews there seemed to be no better articulation about geography by these three than by the two non-geography graduates.

Conclusion

This very small-scale enquiry generates a number of questions rather than provides clear answers. It was undertaken with too few primary teachers to be considered representative or draw more than tentative indications about their sense of geography. It sought to gain some insight through interviews with expert teachers of geography in primary schools into their geographical knowledge. What emerges is an interesting picture of such teachers who appreciate the role and value of geographical knowledge in their teaching, but it remains unclear what their deeper understanding of geography really is. Their responses tend towards the general rather than are specific or detailed. They provide a sense of the subject as broad and encompassing much, indicating at least three ways in which they appear to have understood geographical knowledge, but these teachers do not provide a focused description or definition of the subject or much sense of depth or breadth about what it covers. Perhaps, as Eaude (2012) infers, this goes beyond what they can reasonably articulate, indeed what they might reasonably be expected to know.

As primary teachers, responsible for teaching 10 or more subjects to their class, even as enthusiasts for geography, what really needs to be explored is the knowledge of the subject that is sufficient to teach it effectively, appropriate for the age group, that is, its pedagogic content knowledge. This could well be knowledge which goes beyond the stated curriculum content, but to what extent requires investigation and reflection in relation to notions of geography as a school subject, perhaps even as an academic discipline. There remains the question about the extent to which primary teachers are able to articulate this sufficient understanding of geography – and this connects with a question about the extent to which they might be able to do this for each of the subjects they teach. Is it that their expertise truly lies in their knowledge of teaching, incorporating enough understanding of geography, rather than in the depth of their subject knowledge? Taylor (1986) and Eaude (2012) counsel that it does. Their expertise as primary teachers may well hold them in good stead, able to seek and select, perhaps unconsciously using their everyday geographies, their informational and conceptual knowledge, and their geographical thinking relevant to a particular geographical topic or appropriate for a theme to which geography contributes, such that they ensure children have an authentic experience in their geographical learning. Yet we do not know that this is what happens in their teaching of geography even from Ofsted's evaluations. It is, perhaps, time for Ofsted's inspectors to express and explain their knowledge expectations more clearly and in greater detail than at present. Given that these teachers see it as their role to teach to the highest standards they can achieve, perhaps their expectations and personal standards are what drive their capability in teaching geography well with their classes. Domain or subject knowledge is one of the principles of effective pedagogy, but it is not sufficient; there is much else in pedagogy which enables and fosters children's engagement, learning and achievement (Alexander 2010; James and Pollard 2012). Further studies with primary teachers of geography might focus more evidently on pedagogical content knowledge which this study intimates might be a fruitful line of investigation.

There can be no doubt that this is and will remain a complex area which will continue to warrant attention, not least because some consider that concerns about teachers' subject knowledge has informed 'top-down reforms' (Poulson 2001, 40), an inference that might also be drawn, for instance, from Ofsted's geography reports (Ofsted 2008, 2011). Perhaps an unstated intention underlying the revision of the national curriculum (DfE 2010, 2011) is that it is not only the child who needs to know their subjects; teachers must be more knowledgeable about what they teach to be effective, and this drives the knowledge criterion in ITT courses. However, for the large majority of primary teachers this seems to be a catch-22 situation. Addressing weaknesses in geographical knowledge is an issue from the start of a primary teachers' initial training, because primary ITT course time for geography is very low, and it may well be more problematic in school-based courses, where there are likely to be few geography 'expert' teachers. Likewise, developing primary teachers' subject knowledge through continuing professional development in geography is a low priority. Tackling these needs and opportunities should be a key way to enhance primary teachers' and novice teachers' geographical knowledge.

References

Alexander, R., ed. 2010. *Children, Their World, Their Education*. London: Routledge.
Appleton, K. 1995. "Student Teachers' Confidence to Teach Science: Is more Science Knowledge Necessary to Improve Self-Confidence?" *International Journal of Science Education* 17 (3): 357–369.
Barnes, J. 2011. *Cross-Curricular Learning*. London: Sage.
Bednarz, S., S. Heffron, and N. Huynh, eds. 2013. *A Road Map for 21st Century Geography Education: Geography Education Research* (A Report from the Geography Education

Research Committee of the Road Map for the 21st Century Geography Education Project). Washington, DC: Association of American Geographers. http://natgeoed.or/roadmap

Bonnett, A. 2008. *What is Geography?* London: Sage.

Brooks, C. 2011. "Geographical Knowledge and Professional Development." In *Geography, Education and the Future*, edited by G. Butt, 165–180. London: Continuum.

Brophy, J., J. Alleman, and B. Knighton. 2009. *Inside the Social Studies Classroom*. New York: Routledge.

Brophy, J., J. Alleman, and B. Knighton. 2010. *A Learning Community in the Primary Classroom*. New York: Routledge.

Bryant, A., and Charmaz, K. eds. 2007. *The Sage Handbook of Grounded Theory*. London: Sage.

Bustin, S. 2012. "Geography Teachers' Conceptions of Knowledge." *Teaching Geography* 37 (2): 73–75.

Catling, S. 2004. "Primary Geography Initial Teacher Education." In *Geographical Education: Expanding Horizons in a Shrinking World*, edited by W. A. Kent, E. Rawling, and A. Robinson, *Scottish Association of Geography Teachers (SAGT) Journal* (special edn.) 33: 111–119.

Catling, S. 2006. *Plus or Minus One Point Five Percent: Geography Provision for Generalist Primary Trainee Teachers on PGCE Courses: A Report* (Unpublished). Oxford: Westminster Institute of Education Oxford Brookes University.

Catling, S. 2013a. "Challenges and Opportunities: Considering and Creating the Future for Geography in Primary ITE – 2013 and Beyond." Paper given at the Charney Manor primary geography conference: Researching and developing the primary geography curriculum, Charney Bassett, Oxfordshire, March 1–3.

Catling, S. 2013b. "Teachers' Perspectives on Curriculum Making in Primary Geography in England." *The Curriculum Journal* 24: 3.

Catling, S., and Martin, F. 2011. "Contesting Powerful Knowledge: The Primary Geography Curriculum as an Articulation Between Academic and Children's (ethno-) Geographies." *Curriculum Journal* 22 (3): 317–335.

Department for Education (DfE). 1993. *The Initial Training of Primary School Teachers: New Criteria for Courses*. London: DfE. Circular number 14/93.

Department for Education (DfE). 2010. *The Importance of Teaching: The Schools White Paper 2010*. London: TSO.

Department for Education (DfE). 2011. *Review of the National Curriculum: England*. Accessed January 22, 2011. http://www.education,gov.uk/schools/teachingandlearning/curriculum/nationn alcurriculum

Department for Education (DfE). 2012. *Teachers' Standards in England*. Accessed May 12, 2013. http://www.education.gov.uk/schools/teachingandlearning/reviewofstandards

Department for Education (DfE). 2013. *The National Curriculum in England: Framework document*. Accessed July 8, 2013. http://www.gov.uk/government/uploads/system/uploads/attachment_date/file/210969/NC_framework_document_-_FINAL.pdf

Department for Education and Employment (DfEE). 1999. *The National Curriculum for England: Geography*. London: HMSO.

Department for Education and Skills/Teacher Training Agency. 2002. *Qualifying to Teach: Professional Standards for Qualified Teacher Status and Requirements for Initial Teacher Training*. London: TTA.

Eaude, T. 2012. *How Do Expert Primary Class Teachers Really Work?* Plymouth: Critical Publishing Limited.

Firth, R. 2011. "Debates about Knowledge and the Curriculum: Some Implications for Geography Education." In *Geography, Education and the Future*, edited by G. Butt, 141–164. London: Continuum.

Firth, R. 2013. "What Constitutes Knowledge in Geography?." In *Debates in Geography Education*, edited by D. Lambert and M. Jones, 59–74. London: Routledge.

Geographical Association (GA). 2009. *A Different View: A Manifesto from the Geographical Association*. Sheffield: Geographical Association.

Geographical Association (GA). 2011a. *The Geography National Curriculum: GA Proposals and Rationale*. Accessed August 10, 2011. http://www.geography.org.uk/geographycurricul umconsultation

Geographical Association (GA). 2011b. *Geography Curriculum Consultation Full Report*. Sheffield: Geographical Association. Accessed January, 2012. http://www.geography.org.uk/geographycurriculumconsultation

Geographical Association (GA). 2012. *Curriculum Making*. Accessed May 12, 2013. http://www.geography.org.uk/cpdevents/curriculummaking/

Geographical Association (GA). 2013. *Primary Geography Quality Mark*. Accessed May 15, 2013. http://www.geography.org.uk/eyprimary/primaryqualitymark

Glaser, B., and A. Strauss. 1967. *The Discovery of Grounded Theory: Strategies for Qualitative research*. New York: Aldine de Gruyter.

Harlen, W., and C. Holroyd. 1997. "Primary Teachers' Understanding of Concepts in Science: Impact on Confidence and Teaching." *International Journal of Science Education* 19 (1): 93–105.

Harnett, P. 2000. "History in Primary Schools: Re-Shaping Our Pasts – The Influence of Primary Teachers' Knowledge and Understanding of History on Curriculum Planning and Implementation." *International Journal of Historical Learning, Teaching and Research* 1 (1): 5–17.

Holt-Jensen, A. 2009. *Geography: History and Concepts*. London: Sage.

Hopkin, J. 2013. "Framing the Geography National Curriculum." *Geography* 98 (2): 60–67.

House of Commons Education Committee. 2012. *Great Teachers: Attracting, Training and Retaining the Best*. London: TSO. Ninth Report of Session 2010-12.

Jackson, P. 2006. "Thinking Geographically." *Geography* 91 (3): 199–204.

James, M., and A. Pollard, eds. 2012. *Principles of Effective Pedagogy: International Responses to Evidence from the UK Teaching & Learning Research Programme*. London: Routledge.

Lambert, D. 2009. "What is Living Geography?" In *Living Geography*, edited by D. Mitchell, 1–7. London: Optimus.

Lambert, D. 2011. "Reviewing the Case for Geography, and the 'Knowledge Turn' in the English National Curriculum." *Curriculum Journal* 22 (2): 243–264.

Lambert, D., and M. Jones, eds. 2013. *Debates in Geography Education*. London: Routledge.

Lambert, D., and J. Morgan. 2010. *Teaching Geography 11–18: A Conceptual Approach*. Maidenhead: Open University Press.

Martin, F. 2000. "Postgraduate Primary Education Students' Images of Geography and how these Affect the Types of Teachers they Become." *International Research in Geographical and Environmental Education* 9 (3): 223–244.

Martin, F. 2008. "Knowledge Bases for Effective Teaching: Beginning Teachers Development as Teachers of Primary Geography." *International Research in Geographical and Environmental Education* 17 (1): 13–39.

Martin, F. 2013. "What is Geography's Place in the Primary School Curriculum?" In *Debates in Geography Education*, edited by D. Lambert and M. Jones, 17–27. London: Routledge.

McCullough, E. 2006. "I Don't Know Anything about Music: An Exploration of Primary Teachers' Knowledge about Music Education" Thesis submitted for a PhD, Northumbria University.

Monk, J., and C. Silman. 2011. *Active Learning in Primary Classrooms: A Case Study Approach*. Harlow: Longman.

Morley, E. 2012. "English Trainee Teachers' Perceptions of Geography." *International Research in Geographical and Environmental Education* 21 (2): 123–137.

Morris, H. 2001. "Issues Raised by Testing Trainee Primary Teachers' Mathematical Knowledge." *Mathematics Education Research Journal* 3 (1): 37–47.

Newby, P. 2010. *Research Methods for Education*. Harlow: Pearson.

Office for Standards in Education (Ofsted). 2008. *Geography in Schools: Changing Practice*. Accessed December 12, 2012. http://www.ofsted.gov.uk/resources/geography-schools-changing-practice

Office for Standards in Education (Ofsted). 2009. *Improving Primary Teachers' Subject Knowledge Across the Curriculum*. Accessed March 10, 2013. http://www.ofsted.gov.uk/resources/improving-primary-teachers-subject-knowledge-across-curriculum

Office for Standards in Education (Ofsted). 2011. *Geography: Learning to Make a World of Difference*. Accessed December 12, 2012. http://www.ofsted.gov.uk/resources/geography-learning-make-world-of-difference

Office for Standards in Education (Ofsted). 2013. *Geography Survey Visits*. Accessed April 18, 2013. http://www.ofsted.gov.uk/resources/generic-grade-descriptors-and-supplementary-subject-specific-guidance-for-inspectors-making-judgements (click on geography file).

Parker, J., and D. Heywood. 2000. "Exploring the Relationship Between Subject Knowledge and Pedagogic Content Knowledge in Primary Teachers' Learning about Forces?" *International Journal of Science Education* 22 (1): 89–111.

Poulson, L. 2001. "Paradigm Lost: Subject Knowledge, Primary Teachers and Education Policy." *British Journal of Educational Studies* 49 (1): 40–55.

Rawding, C. 2013. *Effective Innovation in the Secondary Geography Curriculum: A Practical Guide.* London: Routledge.

Scoffham, S., ed. 2010. *Primary Geography Handbook.* Sheffield: Geographical Association.

Shulman, L. 2004. *The Wisdom of Practice: Essays on Teaching, Learning and Learning to Teach.* San Francisco, CA: Jossey-Bass.

Taylor, P. 1986. *Expertise and the Primary School Teacher.* Windsor: NFER-NELSON.

Thomas, G. 2009. *How to do Your Research Project.* London: Sage.

Williams, P. 2008. *Independent Review of Mathematics Teaching in Early Years Settings and Primary Schools: Final Report.* Annesley: DCSF.

Witt, M., M. Goode, and C. Ibbett. 2013. "What Does It Take Two Make a Primary Maths Teacher? Two Trainee Teachers' Successful Mathematical Journeys." *Teacher Education Network Journal* 5 (1): 19–32.

English primary trainee teachers' perceptions of geography

Emma Morley

Department of Initial Teacher Education, University of Winchester, Winchester, United Kingdom

This paper summarises the findings of research conducted with one cohort of English undergraduate primary teacher trainees on point of entry to a 4-year course. The research examines the perceptions held of geography as a subject discipline and the purposes of teaching the subject. Two hundred and eleven trainees were asked to define geography and provide information about their pre-course qualifications as well as their perceptions of the current primary geography curriculum. A volunteer sample of 12 students then completed a nominal group exercise which explored trainees' understanding of the purposes of teaching geography and the skills that they considered they brought to the teaching of the subject. The findings indicate that trainees had an information-orientated perception of geography and did not appear to fully appreciate the breadth of the subject.

Introduction

Geography is a statutory subject in English primary schools and forms part of the National Curriculum (DfEE [Department for Education and Employment], 1999). Indications from the coalition government are that it will remain so, possibly as part of an "English Baccalaureate" (DfE [Department of Education], 2010, p. 41). Consequently, all graduates from teacher education courses are usually required to teach geography when they take up teaching positions within English primary schools.

Current teacher education course requirements set by the Training and Development Agency for Schools (TDA) do not specify either the course content or the percentage of time that should be spent preparing students to teach individual subjects. In addition, the current inspection schedule for such courses focuses on the overall effectiveness of each provider in securing high-quality outcomes for trainees and considers how well trainees meet the Qualified Teacher Status (QTS) standards (TDA, 2008). Although these standards require that successful students should "have a secure knowledge and understanding of their subjects/curriculum area and related pedagogy to enable them to teach effectively across the age and ability range for which they are trained" (TDA, 2008, p. 7) providers do not have to offer courses in any subjects other than English, Mathematics and Science.

The disappearance of subject-specialist courses from many institutions has resulted in increasing numbers of newly-qualified teachers teaching geography and taking on the role of subject coordinator when they have either limited or no subject background and often no access to in-service training (Bell, 2005; Catling, 2004; Catling & Willy, 2009). In addition, inspection reports have consistently reported on the poor state of geography in primary and secondary schools with the most recent report identifying "a polarised picture, with a sharp contrast between inadequate and outstanding practice" (Ofsted, 2011, p. 4). Inspectors have attributed this in part to "a lack of expertise and awareness of what constituted good geography" (Ofsted, 2011, p. 4). The Cambridge Primary Review (Alexander, 2010) also highlighted the marginalisation of the humanities in English primary schools and related this in part to the neglect of these subjects in teacher education courses.

This study examined the point from which *undergraduate* students on a 4-year teacher education course started their studies including how they defined geography and what they perceived to be the purpose of teaching geography to primary-aged (5–11) children and builds on previous work by Walford (1996), Martin (2000), Catling (2004) and Alkis (2009).

Students' perceptions of the nature and purpose of primary geography

Although Martin (2000) and Catling (2004) investigated postgraduate primary trainee teachers' perceptions of geography, research into student teachers' perceptions of the nature and purpose of geography has been limited with much of it based on the perceptions of trainees preparing to teach geography in secondary schools.

A small-scale study conducted with secondary postgraduate teacher trainees, by Barratt Hacking (1996), aimed to elicit individuals' geographical persuasions early on in the course and then consider the influence that this had on their professional learning. "Geographical persuasion" was viewed as being the participants' sense of geography drawn from their personal expertise, interests, experience and their ideology of the subject (Barratt Hacking, 1996, p. 77). A number of diverse interests and perspectives were identified amongst the sample and a number of individuals felt strongly about certain aspects of the discipline, in particular the "environmental" or "people-environment" perspective. It was noted that individuals viewed themselves as "geographers who bring a distinct ideology and distinct interests" (Barratt Hacking, 1996, p. 81) to the course. However, this conflicted with the findings that "geographical persuasion" appeared on the most part to be suspended when students undertook their planning and teaching in school. Barratt Hacking (1996) suggests that these findings reflect those of Calderhead (1988) in that newly qualified teachers appear to have some issues with self-confidence and draw heavily on observed practices rather than their own ideas.

Walford (1996) pursued this theme when conducting research with geography specialist secondary postgraduate initial trainees at the start of their courses over a 4-year period between 1990 and 1994. Each student was asked to produce a short definition of "geography" and each of the statements was then examined and categorised. Walford rejected previously used classifications which centred on word and phrase characteristics concluding that they did not allow the participants' "different stances [. . .] be detected and illuminated" (Walford, 1996, p. 73). A new fourfold classification which took elements from previous work was drawn up and applied to each of the statements (see Figure 1). Walford (1996) concluded his work by stating that "though the high tide of positivistic spatial analysis may have passed, a significant proportion of students couch their definitions of the subject in a way akin to hard science" (Walford, 1996, p. 76). He advocated that further research be conducted into the way in which the "philosophical and attitudinal positions of prospective geography teachers influence their own subsequent teaching and their later decisions in the field of curriculum policy" (Walford, 1996, p. 76). He also questioned whether or not non-geography graduates would hold similar views.

The focus for the work carried out by Martin (2000) was similar to that of Barratt Hacking (1996) in that it centred on trainee teachers' conceptions of geography and then examined the relationship between these and their style of teaching. By contrast, the sample

Geographical category	Geography as the study ....
Interactionists	...of the interdependence of and interaction between people and their environment and between peoples over the Earth's surface, i.e. linking human and physical environments in the study of geography.
Synthesisers	...that draws from a variety of disciplines, knowledge and understanding about people, places, cultures, the physical world and their interactions to develop a sense of global responsibility for managing human engagement with the Earth, i.e. synthesising the range of perspectives from within the discipline and beyond.
Spatialists	...of the spatial distribution, relation, processes and consequences of the interaction of physical and human phenomena over the surface of the Earth, i.e. geography as spatial analysis.
Placeists	...that locates, describes and theorises about places in terms of why places are where they are, why they are like they are and what that means, in order to foster a sense and appreciation of place, i.e. concerned with information and characteristics of places, regions and countries.

Figure 1.   Walford's classification of postgraduate secondary teacher trainees' definitions of geography. Source: Catling (2004, pp. 149–158), based on examples given in Walford (1996, pp. 73–76).

consisted of primary school trainees. Within the constructs identified by the trainees, "the traditional physical-human linkage identified by Walford" (Martin, 2000, p. 235) occurred most frequently. Findings indicated that many of the trainees held narrow views of geography as a discipline. Comparison of geography and non-geography graduates found that amongst the geography graduates, there was a small group whose constructs for geography as a discipline were no more elaborate than they were for the non-geographers. From a study of the trainees' image of geography and the subsequent plans that they produced for teaching geography, Martin (2000) concluded that "expertise in a subject does not mean expertise as a teacher of the subject" (Martin, 2000, p. 242). In addition, Martin (2000) identified that students appear to hold two images of the subject, that of geography as a subject discipline and that of geographical education. The findings from this research seem to indicate that ideas about geographical education were a stronger influence on students' teaching of primary geography than an individual's perceptions of geography per se.

Catling (2004) asked postgraduate primary trainees to provide definitions of geography. A classification derived from that used by Walford (1996) was then applied to the statements (see Figure 2). These students were also asked about the purpose of teaching geography to primary children, and the significant reason to emerge from this study was to emphasise environmental knowledge and understanding linked to previous findings highlighting the importance given to the physical–human aspects of the subject.

Bradbeer, Healey and Kneale (2004) explored geography undergraduates' from Australia, New Zealand, the United Kingdom and the United States conceptions of teaching, learning and geography by using phenomenography. No distinct patterns of national variation emerged between the group and the findings supported those of Marton, Dall'alba and Beaty (1993) in that they showed five different conceptions of geography held by participants. These conceptions ranged from the very general study of the world or the study of the distinct physical and human dimensions of the world to ideas of geography as people–environment interactions, spatial organisation or of areal differentiation.

A case study of two secondary school geography teachers undertaken by Walshe (2007) concluded that there was an "apparent relationship between a teacher's understanding of geography and their professional training, academic background and personal values"

Geographical perspective	Geography as the study ….
Globalists	… that develops an informed knowledge and understanding of the world, its human and physical features and environments and of the countries of the world.
Earthists	… of the Earth, its physical and human features and environments and of the forces and processes that shape them.
Interactionists	…of the interactions between and interdependence of people and their natural and social environments, of the processes that sustain these interrelationships and of their effects and influences as outcomes.
Placeists	…of people's lives and activities in places, communities and cultures to understand what they are like, why they are as they are, what this means for them and how they relate to others.
Environmentalists	…of environmental concerns and issues, locally and globally and about sustainability.

Figure 2.   Catling's classification of postgraduate primary teacher trainees' conceptions of geography. Source: based on examples given in Catling (2004, pp. 149–158).

(Walshe, 2007, p. 97). The implication from the findings was that these factors would impact on the experience that students have in the geography classroom, and the suggestion is made that further research into the subject understanding of geography teachers and even students working together with their teachers might "reveal a greater range of factors which affect the nature and structure of teachers' understanding of their subject" as well as encourage consideration of "the implications of this on practice" (Walshe, 2007, p. 118).

More recently research was conducted into Turkish secondary trainees' perceptions of geography by Alkis (2009) who examined their perceptions of geography as a discipline and the aim of geographical education. The findings were similar to those of Bradbeer et al. (2004) and Catling (2004) and again confirmed the traditional physical–human linkage. Many of the trainees appeared to have "a relatively simplistic conception of geography i.e. it is the study of the world around us" (Alkis, 2009, p. 130). A significant finding from this study was the dominance of the "environmentalist" view for trainees' reasons as to the purpose of teaching geography. The students focused on environmental concerns, issues and sustainability. Alkis (2009) concluded that the dominance of the environmentalist view may result from the introduction of the new geographical curriculum in Turkey (CDOP, 2005) which places a great emphasis on environmental education and includes learning about sustainable development. The research found similar results to those of Martin (2000) in that the students surveyed did not appear to perceive geography as a multidimensional subject.

Methodology

For the purposes of this study, an exploratory mixed methods design (Creswell & Plano Clark, 2006) was employed and data from 211 entrants to the BA (QTS) course during the period September to November 2009 were used. The sample used for this study consisted, for the most part, students who had recently left further education having completed either A-Levels or similar qualifications. A small number (1%) of students were mature (30+) and the year group consisted of mainly female students (90%) and 99.5% of students were Caucasian.

In the first phase, survey data was collected about trainees' geographical qualifications, their perception of what children might study in geography lessons and their preferences for each of 10 curriculum subjects studied in their previous phase of education. Additionally, students were asked to define the term "geography" by completing the sentence "geography is . . ." in less than 30 words.

Table 1. Primary trainee teachers' perceptions of themes covered in the primary geography curriculum.

Theme	Example of category content	% of students
Physical Geography	Rivers, coasts, erosion, the water cycle	56.8
Places	Where they are, flags, countries, capitals, continents	53.5
Maps	Grid references, compass points	30.8
Cultures	Differences between, other people's lives, food, jobs	28.9
Natural Disasters	Volcanoes, earthquakes	27.0
The Local Area	Where I live, our neighbourhood	23.2
Issues	Pollution, recycling, global warming, poverty, fair trade	22.7
Weather/Climate		22.7
Animals	Mini-beasts, nature, creatures, wildlife	15.1
The Environment		14.6
Human Geography	Population, tourism, rural, urban, cities, towns, national parks	14.2
Rainforests		9.5
Rocks and Soil		7.1
Ecosystems		2.4
Farming		1.4

The second phase of the research was conducted with a small volunteer sample of students taken from the original cohort. A nominal group exercise was undertaken in which students explored both individually and collectively the purposes of teaching primary geography and the skills that these individuals perceive that they bring to the subject.

Questionnaire design and administration

A semi-structured questionnaire was designed comprising three sections. The first asked participants about their geographical qualifications at point of entry to the course. This was followed by an open-ended question which asked respondents to "list up to 5 themes that you think primary aged children cover in their geography curriculum". Using content analysis, the themes listed were collated and similar themes were grouped together (see Table 1). The third part of the questionnaire asked trainees to rank in order of preference a number of subjects studied in a previous phase of education and which are currently part of the primary curriculum delivered in English schools. The scores for each subject were collated and a mean was established. Table 2 shows these mean scores in ascending order. The subject with the lowest mean was that most favoured by the students.

Table 2. Mean score for each of the subjects ranked by primary trainee teachers.

Subject	Raw total score	Mean score
Art	826	3.91
Design technology	889	4.21
History	1038	4.91
Physical education	1126	5.33
Geography	1172	5.55
Music	1191	5.64
Drama	1199	5.68
Information communication technology	1369	6.48
Religious studies	1368	6.48
Modern foreign languages	1439	6.81

Finally, participants were asked to write a definition of "geography" by completing the sentence "Geography is . . ." in no more than 30 words. As statements with similar content were identified, a code was decided upon and this was then applied to similar statements. Some statements had more than one code applied to them as it was felt that the content could be classified into more than one category. As previously noted, the starting point for the classifications used was the works of Walford (1996) and Catling (2004) but as it was found that neither of these sets of classifications could be adequately applied, a new set of classifications was drawn up. Table 3 shows the classifications that were used and the number and percentage of statements that were coded to each category.

Nominal group technique

For the second phase of the research, a nominal group technique (NGT) exercise was carried out with a self-selecting sample of 12 volunteers from the original cohort. This technique was originally developed by Van de Ven and Delbecq (1971) to "facilitate the generation of ideas while encouraging quality participation" (Asmus & James, 2005, p. 350). One of the main advantages of using the technique for the purposes of research is that according to its proponents, it reduces the influence of group dynamics of data collected thus affecting validity and reliability of the research process.

The choice of NGT was made after the consideration of the sample. The participants had only recently embarked on the course and, as a result, they had had little time to gain each other's confidence and it was felt that they may have been intimidated by either being asked their thoughts in either group or individual interviews. Additionally, it was hoped that the participants would speak freely without feeling that there was a "right answer" that they had to give. The procedure followed in this NGT exercise is outlined in detail in Figure 3.

In hindsight, it may have been beneficial to have repeated the exercise with a second group. Whilst the results achieved may limit the extent to which they represent the wider sample and because by asking participants to volunteer, they may by default have been particularly "keen" students, the exercise was still useful. If the results are viewed in the context of being from a particular situated case and alongside the data collected from the larger sample by questionnaire, they contribute to an overall "thick description" (Geetz, 1973) of the point from which one cohort of trainees start their BA (QTS) geography module.

Primary teacher trainees' images of geography

It emerged that statements could be identified in two of the same categories identified by Catling (2004) namely "interactionists" and "placeists". These categories were also identified by Walford (1996). The category "synthesisers" identified by Walford (1996) was also used to classify those students whose statements appeared to demonstrate an awareness of geography as a broad subject which included multiple elements. Examples of statements categorised under each of these headings were the following:

-Interactionists
"how we affect our planet"
-Placeists
"the study of area/country/maps and places"
-Synthesisers
"the study of the land and people in the world we live in. It aims to aid the understanding of different cultures and helps one understand why things are the way they are, including"

Table 3. Conceptions of geography held by BA (QTS) primary trainee teachers.

Geographical perspective	Geography as the study	Number of statements	% of statements
Global *"fact finder"*	... of knowledge and understanding of the world, its human and physical features and environments and of the countries of the world.	160	65
Global *"processor"*	... of the earth, its physical and human features and environments and of the forces and processes that shape them.	25	10
Interactionists	... of the interactions between and the interdependence of people and their natural and social environments, of the processes that sustain these interrelationships, and of their effects and influences as outcomes.	16	7
Facilitators	... that facilitates opportunities to engage with the environment, explore the outdoors and gather evidence / information.	12	5
Placeists	... of people's lives and activities in places, communities and cultures to understand what they are like, why they are as they are, what this means for them and how they relate to others.	10	4
Synthesisers	...that draws from a variety of disciplines, knowledge and understanding about people, places, cultures, the physical world and their interactions to develop a sense of global responsibility for managing human engagement with the Earth, i.e. synthesising the range of perspectives from within the discipline and beyond.	8	3

Note: 12 students (6%) gave a response that did not relate to the content of geography but rather to their feeling about the subject e.g. complicated and boring; 6 students (3%) gave no response.
Adapted from Walford (1996, pp. 73–76) and Catling (2004, pp. 149–158).

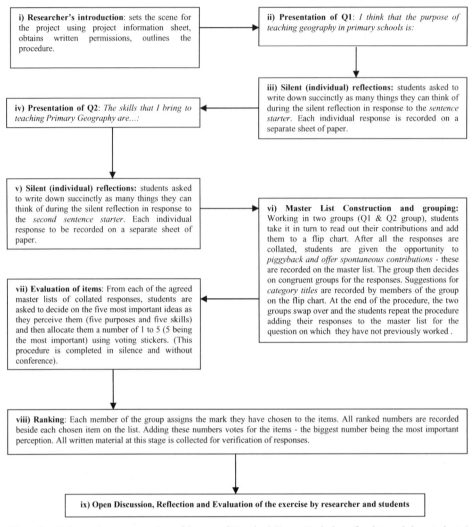

Figure 3.   Schematic representation of the use of Nominal Group Technique for determining students' perceptions of the purposes of teaching primary geography and identifying the skills that they bring to the subject at the start of a BA (QTS) degree. *Adapted* from Fuller, Gaskin and Scott (2003, p. 85.)

In the research conducted by Catling (2004) and replicated by Alkis (2009), two related but distinct categories emerged: the globalist and earthist perspectives. This piece of research identified two categories that relate to these perspectives but which were subtly different. The first of these was termed as "*global fact finder*" and was applied to students whose statements classified geography as the finding out of facts about the world, its human and physical features, its environments and countries. Significantly no indication of an alignment of process understanding to these facts was identified in these statements. Statements classified into this category included the following:

"the study of the world in all areas"
"knowledge about the world that we live in"
"a subject that teaches you about the world"

The second related category was called "*global processor*" and was allocated to those students who described geography as the study of the earth, its physical and human features and environments and the forces and processes that shape them. The significant word in this description is "processes" and statements were only categorised into this group when the word "processes" or "forces" was used. This category is similar to that termed *earthist* by Catling (2004). Statements classified into this category included the following:

"the study of how the physical world works"
"knowledge of how the world works (tech plates / volcanoes)"
"about how the land is formed and altered"

One category unique to this piece of research emerged. Some students did not make reference to any knowledge or understanding of geographical concepts or themes but merely defined geography in terms of providing an opportunity for pupils to engage with the environment, explore the outdoors and gather evidence/information. This group of statements were termed "*facilitators*". An example of such a statement is the following:

"a chance for children to explore the world through different activities and gain information based on their findings"

A small number of students (3%) either did not respond to this request for a definition of geography or provide a statement which contained no reference to geographical content (6%) but rather appeared to reflect their personal feeling about the subject, for example "complicated and boring". It would be interesting, in future studies, to follow up why certain students have these feelings.

One very dominant group of ideas about geography emerged: the global fact-finder perspective. The distinction between this group of statements and that of the global processor perspective is so subtle that it would appear that these two categories could justifiably be considered to represent one perspective – that of the student who appears to perceive geography purely as the study of the world in which we live. These findings are therefore similar to those of Walford (1996), Martin (2000), Catling (2004) and Alkis (2009) all of whom found that the majority of students see geography as concerned with the physical–human dimensions of the environment.

Slightly fewer students were classed as "interactionists" and "placeists" than in previous studies, but in general, the trends were similar to previous findings. In Catling's study (2004), 4.1% of the sample was classed as "environmentalists". These students identified geography as concerned with the impact of human influences and interventions in the environment. Whilst this percentage was small, there were at least some students who perceived a core focus in geography to be environmental issues and sustainability unlike this current study where no student was classified in this group. One or two students did make reference to sustainability but this was only as part of a wider definition and this did not appear to be what the participants saw as the core focus of geography. Whilst it is not impossible to rule out that some of the students may have used the word "environment" meaning concerned with environmental issues rather than using it as a term to describe their surroundings, this is not immediately obvious from the examination of the statements. This was a surprise given the increasing reference made to environmental issues in the media and the emphasis on "knowledge and understanding of environmental change and sustainable development" that is present in the current National Curriculum (DfEE, 1999) from Key Stage 1 through Key Stage 3. It could suggest that students do not identify geography as the subject in which such issues are taught and raise questions about the emphasis that may or may not be put on this aspect of the subject in English schools.

A large percentage (73%) of the statements analysed was short and contained only limited and simplistic vocabulary. This may be because the students were allowed only a very brief amount of time in which to complete the statements – a maximum of 10 minutes at the start of one of the taught geography sessions compared with Catling (2004) who allowed his participants a total of 15 minutes for this exercise; however, no students asked for more time to complete their definitions. Alkis (2009) identified 15% of the sample as "having a relatively simplistic conception of geography", figures which were similar to those of Bradbeer et al. (2004). It is possible that one-to-one interviews with participants may have revealed a broader understanding of the subject than the definitions suggest, and also that the definitions generated are no more than a reflection of the students' stage in the education process. Participants in this enquiry were undergraduates similar to the sample used by Alkis (2009), although only eight students were geography specialists, but it may also be an indication of a lack of understanding and/or engagement with the subject during a previous phase of education.

Caution should also be exercised when interpreting the results as they give no indication of how the individual characteristics of the trainees or their experiences impact on their perceptions. These are factors which both Brooks (2006, 2010) and Hopwood (2011) highlighted as needing consideration. Some of the participants will no doubt for example have been encouraged to travel and the experience that the sample had of "school geography" will also have varied greatly.

Primary trainee teachers' views of the purpose(s) of teaching primary geography

Unlike previous research (Alkis, 2009; Catling, 2004), the data gathered in order to answer the question "what are the new ITE recruits' views of the purpose(s) of primary geography?" were not collected using a survey. Participants were asked to complete the sentence starter "I think that the purpose of teaching primary geography is . . .". The responses were grouped by the participants into collections of those which they felt were similar and then each group was given a title before individuals allotted votes. This difference in data collection method makes direct comparison with the findings of Catling (2004) and Alkis (2009) more difficult; however, there are a number of similar and contrasting themes that do emerge.

This set of findings (see Table 3) also replicates those of Catling (2004) in that the "globalist" perspective described by the students in this enquiry as "the world in which we live" dominates as the main purpose for teaching primary geography. Physical geography is very strongly supported with 58% of the votes given by the students allotted to the groups "the world we live in", "physical geography" and "the environment". It is noticeable that the participants put far less emphasis on human features of the world compared with physical features – the group entitled "people and cultures" was allotted just 11% of the vote. It is difficult to ascertain the reasons for this without conducting individual interviews with respondents to clarify their intended meaning in using particular phrases and discussing the question posed, but these findings may suggest that those participants in this piece of research have been exposed to a very limited geography curriculum in a previous phase of education or that the physical geography studied had made more of an impact on individuals than other areas of the geography curriculum.

Discussion

The findings from this study appear to support those of previous researchers (Bradbeer et al., 2004; Catling, 2004; Martin, 2000; Walford, 1996) in that students' images of geography appear to be limited to an information-orientated perception of a subject which centres on the human–physical features of the world and the interrelationship between them. In this particular study, the acknowledgement of these interrelationships was less pronounced than in previous findings. The majority of students starting the course perceived geography as being predominantly about knowledge and understanding of the world in which they live and characteristics associated with physical geography dominated.

Although only just over half of the students (56.8%) surveyed had completed a pre-course qualification in geography, the responses provided by those without any qualifications were similar to those with qualifications. It may be that this is an indication that on entering an initial teacher training course, prior knowledge is of less importance than perhaps was previously thought. However, it should be noted that the students were not asked whether they were successful in passing their geography exams.

The information collected regarding primary teacher trainees' views on what they think primary children would study as part of their geography curriculum (see Table 1) appears to provide further evidence that on entering the course, trainees' perceptions of geography are narrow in comparison with the current requirements of the English National Curriculum (DfEE, 1999) which includes in addition to knowledge and understanding about particular places, geographical skills as well as knowledge of patterns and processes. These undergraduates did not appear to fully appreciate the breadth of the subject. Physical geography was the dominant theme that emerged, and a large number of students used technical language such as longshore drift and plate tectonics which would appear to derive from their secondary school. This may suggest that it is physical geography which has the most impact on students' geographical learning. Subsequent teaching sessions with the sample reinforced evidence of this narrow understanding, with most students showing surprise at what constituted the current primary geography curriculum particularly with regard to the skills that teachers are expected to teach. It is possible that this perception reflects the participants' own experiences of geography at secondary school.

It was also surprising how few students mentioned "environmental issues" as a key primary geography theme, but this may reinforce the fact that no student in this study viewed the main purpose of geography as being to teach about environmental issues and sustainability. However, when comparing the conceptions of geography held by primary trainee teachers and their understanding of the reasons for teaching geography, this is the most noticeable difference. A significant percentage of the nominal group asked to identify the purposes of teaching primary geography could be classed as environmentalists (see Table 4), in that they cited reasons such as "to lose ignorance of just accepting the world we are in, appreciate the world's natural beauty and improve others' awareness". Whilst it is encouraging that this study appears to suggest that some students perceive one of the central purposes of teaching geography is to promote awareness of environmental issues, the lack of reference to such issues by the larger sample suggests that this remains a cause for concern and needs to be prioritised by those involved in geographical education across all phases.

Places featured strongly on the students' lists of themes that they thought primary children covered in the geography curriculum which is slightly surprising as few students were classified as "placeists" when defining the subject. However, this may be because they did not see studying places as the primary component of geography and only focused on the main component in their short definition of the subject.

A certain amount of information was collected in order to gauge the participants' feelings about geography in relation to other subjects. When students were asked in a subsequent teaching session about the reasons that they had not chosen to take General Certificate in Secondary Education (GCSE) geography, there appeared to be three main

Table 4. Summary of nominal group responses to the sentence starter, *"the purpose of learning geography is . . .:"*.

Category Title (chosen by participants)	Number of Responses	Total Score
The World We Live In	23	51
Awareness	13	39
The Environment	6	33
Physical Geography	19	29
People and Cultures	14	22
The World's Resources	2	7
Maps	5	5
Subject Knowledge	2	5
Countries and Cities	5	4
Graphs	1	0
Living Things	1	0

reasons behind their decision. (a) A sizeable number of students were asked to choose between history and geography. It is often the case in England that students are encouraged to take a "double science" GCSE which would include for example physics and chemistry so it seems misguided that students who may have an interest in the social sciences are sometimes prevented from studying both history and geography. It is interesting to note that in the current cohort, twice as many students (16) are history specialists than are geography specialists (8), and both these figures are substantially less than the number of English specialists (25). (b) Another group of students did not choose to study geography because they felt that the teaching was inadequate, a factor which may support findings by Ofsted (2011) that geography in the first years of secondary school is often taught by non-specialists who have both limited knowledge of and interest in the subject. (c) A final group of students described the subject as "boring" and "dull" and consisting of textbook-based work and endless videos. Twice as many students surveyed preferred history to geography on entry to the course, and this may be as a result of some or all of these factors. It would be of value in future research to explore these themes in more detail through individual in-depth interviews with trainees to try and ascertain more precisely the reasons behind students' choice of specialist subject.

The most significant group of responses to the nominal group sentence starter "the skills that I bring to teaching primary geography are . . ." related not to specifically geographic skills but to generic skills such as enthusiasm, a questioning mind and patience (see Table 5). A number of students made reference to their own "personal geographies" by recording that they could bring personal experience, an appreciation of other cultures and knowledge of different places to the subject. This acknowledgement of one's own personal everyday geography concurs with what Martin (2005) terms "ethnogeography" which "reflects the view that all students are geographers because they all live in the world" (Martin, 2005, p. 367). It appeared that although participants in this enquiry had limited understanding of geography in terms of subject content, they appeared to be aware of generic pedagogic skills that they might be able to apply to geography when they were more familiar with the primary geography curriculum. It is possible then that this finding may support that of Martin who on discovering that students on school experience appeared to "suspend their image of geography in their thinking and planning in school" (Martin, 2000 p. 239) suggested that "perhaps it is students' image of teaching that is a more powerful influence" (Martin, 2000, p. 241).

Table 5. Summary of nominal group responses to the sentence starter, *"the skills that I bring to teaching Primary Geography are . . .:"*.

Category title (chosen by participants)	Number of Responses	Total Score
Teaching Characteristics	19	62
Different Cultures	4	29
General Knowledge	5	26
Outdoors	4	25
Resources and Data Collection	3	19
Personal Experience	5	16
Knowledge of Countries and Oceans	6	12
Maps	8	4
Knowledge of a Specialist Subject	7	1

Conclusion

There appear to be some significant questions which arise from these findings that need further consideration: firstly, what exactly is the "geographical diet" to which some of our secondary school pupils are being exposed and which results in the greater majority of students in this study starting their teacher training with a very limited understanding of the subject. Such information may be obtained from a larger, more in-depth study of initial teacher training students.

The second question concerns the preparation of students on initial teacher training courses to teach geography. Those graduates from initial teacher training who teach geography in English primary schools will quite possibly influence those who choose to study geography at a higher level and who subsequently move on to work as teachers in both primary and secondary schools and in other geography-related disciplines. Questions need to be asked about the preparation that these trainees receive particularly when it seems that early indications are that the new curriculum will promote a return to a focus on subject knowledge "the new National Curriculum will . . . have a greater focus on subject content, outlining the essential knowledge and understanding that pupils should be expected to have to enable them to take their place as educated members of society" (DfE, 2010, p. 42). The English Education White Paper (2010) goes on to suggest that "Teachers must be free to use their professionalism and expertise to support all children to progress". (DfE, 2010, p. 42). In order to "use their expertise", trainee teachers will need to firstly gain some expertise – this will continue to be a challenge in the current system where students only receive between 6 and 14 hours tuition on each of the foundation subjects (Catling, 2006). Secondly, we cannot assume that trainees and indeed teachers will be able to automatically "use" this expertise or "curriculum make" as Lambert and Morgan (2010) describe it.

The wider geographical community has been vociferous in its attempts to promote the value and importance of geography as a subject discipline in its own right, and in 2006, the "Action Plan for Geography" a DfE funded project was launched jointly by the Geographical Association (GA) and the Royal Geographical Society (RGS) with the aim of enhancing the teaching and learning of geography in school. As part of this wide-ranging specific subject initiative, a "primary champions" network was established with over 50 champions recruited to lead and enthuse primary teachers, 1500 of whom engaged with the network (www.geography.org.uk/eyprimary/champions). The advantage of such networks was acknowledged by Ofsted with the most recent report recommending that schools should "develop and make best use of networks in order to identify and share good practice, ideas and expertise in the teaching of geography" (Ofsted, 2011,

p. 7). The funding for this initiative ceased in March 2011, and although the subject associations continue to work hard to promote and support the teaching of geography, the findings from this study would seem to suggest that there are still a number of challenges to overcome to ensure that future teachers are able to deliver high-quality geography.

One of these challenges is undoubtedly the limited number of specialist geography teachers in primary schools. Alexander (2010) reignites the generalist versus specialist debate stating that "every primary school must have access to the range and depth of curriculum expertise which is needed in order to plan and teach, with consistent quality the full curriculum range" (Alexander, 2010, p. 432). He goes on to suggest that the arguments for specialists are rooted in the values which underpin our education system, "until there is acceptance that domain experience is so crucial to educational quality that it directly challenges the historical basis of primary teachers' professional identity as generalists . . . the highest possible standards of teaching . . . regardless of how much or little time each is allocated, will remain a pipe dream" (Alexander, 2010, p. 434).

The findings from this study replicate those of previous researchers (Catling, 2004; Martin, 2000) in suggesting that primary trainees need to widen their conception of geography to take into account all the areas that currently comprise the curriculum. However, the issues highlighted do not require a "short-term fix" but rather a range of sustained measures to ensure that future generations can benefit from and enjoy high-quality geographical education.

References

Alexander, R. (Ed.). (2010). *Children, their World, their Education Final report and recommendations of the Cambridge Primary Review*. London: Routledge.

Alkis, S. (2009). Turkish geography trainee teachers' perceptions of geography. *International Research in Geographical and Environmental Education, 18*(2), 120–133.

Asmus, C., & James, K. (2005). Nominal group technique, social loafing and group creativity project quality. *Creativity Research Journal, 17*(4), 349–354.

Barratt Hacking, E. (1996). Novice teachers and their geographical persuasions. *Journal of International Research in Geographical and Environmental Education, 5*(1), 77–86.

Bell, D. (2005). The value and importance of geography. *Primary Geographer, 56,* 4–5.

Bradbeer, J., Healey, M., & Kneale, P. (2004). Undergraduate geographers' understandings of geography, learning and teaching: A phenomenographic study. *Journal of Geography in Higher Education, 28*(1), 17–34.

Brooks, C. (2006). Geographical knowledge and teaching geography. *International Research in Geographical and Environmental Education, 15*(4), 353–369.

Brooks, C. (2010). Why geography teachers' subject expertise matters. *Geography, 95*(3), 143–148.

Calderhead, J. (Ed.). (1988). *Teachers' professional learning*. London: The Falmer Press.

Catling, S. (2004). An understanding of geography: The perspectives of English primary trainee teachers. *GeoJournal, 60,* 149–158.

Catling, S. (2006). *Plus or minus one point five percent: Geography provision for generalist primary trainee teachers on PGCE courses: A report*. (unpublished), Oxford: Westminster Institute of Education, Oxford Brookes University.

Catling, S., & Willy, T. (2009). *Teaching primary geography*. Exeter: Learning Matters.

CDOP. (2005). *Cografya dersi ogretim programi*. Ankara, Turkey: Gazi Kitabevi.

Creswell, J., & Plano Clark, V. (2006). *Designing and conducting mixed methods research*. London: Sage.

Delbecq, A.L., & Van De Ven, A.H. (1971). A group process model for problem identification and program planning. *Journal of Applied Behavioural Science, 17,* 466–492.

Department of Education (DfE). (2010). *The importance of teaching. The school's White Paper*. Retrieved from http://www.education.gov.uk/publications

Department for Education and Employment (DfEE). (1999). *The National Curriculum for England: Geography*. London: HMSO.

Fuller, I., Gaskin, S., & Scott, I. (2003). Student perceptions of geography and environmental sciences fieldwork in the light of restricted access to the field, caused by the foot and mouth disease in the UK in 2001. *Journal of Geography in Higher Education, 27*(1), 79–102.

Geertz, C. (1973). *The Interpretation of Cultures*. New York: Basic Books.

Hopwood, N. (2011). Young people's conceptions of geography and education. In G. Butt (Ed.), *Geography, education and the future* (pp. 30–41). London: Continuum.

Lambert, D., & Morgan, J. (2010). *Teaching geography 11–18: A conceptual approach*. Milton Keynes: Open University Press.

Martin, F. (2000). Postgraduate primary education students' images of geography and how these affect the types of teachers they become. *International Research in Geographical and Environmental Education, 9*(3), 223–244.

Martin, F. (2005). Ethnogeography: A future for primary geography and primary geography research. *International Research in Geographical and Environmental Education, 14*(4), 364–371.

Marton, F., Dall'alba, G., & Beaty, E. (1993). Conceptions of learning. *International Journal of Educational Research, 19*(3), 277–300.

Ofsted. (2011). *Geography learning to make a world of difference*. Retrieved from http://www.ofsted.gov.uk/publications/090224

Training and Development Agency for Schools (TDA). (2008). *Professional standards for qualified teacher status and requirements for initial teacher training* (Rev. 2008). London: Author.

Walford, R. (1996). What is geography? An analysis of definitions provided by prospective teachers of the subject. *Journal of International Research in Geographical and Environmental Education, 5*(1), 69–76.

Walshe, N. (2007). Understanding teachers' conceptualisations of geography. *International Research in Geographical and Environmental Education, 16*(2), 97–119.

Contesting *powerful knowledge*: the primary geography curriculum as an articulation between academic and children's (ethno-) geographies

Simon Catling[a] and Fran Martin[b]

[a]School of Education, Faculty of Humanities and Social Sciences, Oxford Brookes University, Oxford, UK; [b]School of Education, University of Exeter, Exeter, UK

The argument has been propounded that academic disciplines and school subjects provide a powerful, authoritative knowledge which is key to enabling children to better understand the world in which they live. Inherent in this perspective is that children's experience, knowledge and understanding are poorly formed and of limited everyday use and value. Yet it is appreciated that children's naïve knowledge can be a pedagogic starting point to initiate them into academic subjects. While appreciating the purpose and roles of academic subjects, this article challenges these assumptions, arguing that children's ethno-knowledges provide powerful learning bases of equivalent authority to subjects. Using the example of younger children's everyday or ethno-geography, the case is that children bring to school powerful (geographical) knowledge of their own. This can and should be recognised and valued in dialogue with authoritative (geographical) subject knowledge, not as subservient to it. It is argued that this perspective goes beyond that of the child/subject co-construction of knowledge to interrelate the developmental nature of children's everyday (geographical) learning with (geography) sense-of-subject evolution. This case is set in the context of geography but is applicable to other school subjects, where children's and subjects' powerful knowledges can mutually engage with and enhance each other.

Introduction

The purpose of this article is to explore the notion of *powerful knowledge* within the context of the primary curriculum. The ideas we develop stem from three sources: research into primary student teachers' conceptualisations of geography education and how to teach it (Martin 2008a, 2008b); the application of research into children's geographies to education (Catling 2003, 2005; Catling and Willy 2009); and Michael Young's recent argument for reasserting knowledge in the curriculum (Young 2008). In the context of the primary geography curriculum, teachers' lack of subject knowledge has been identified as problematic for some time (Bell 2005; Ofsted 2008, 2011). This has coincided with an apparent erosion of the importance of subject knowledge in schooling and with an inferred downgrading of the importance of curriculum in relation to experience:

> A school shouldn't start with curriculum content. It should start with designing a learning experience and then check it has met National Curriculum requirements. (Mick Waters, quoted in Wilby, *The Guardian* 2010)

The primacy of experience over knowledge – as if the former can be planned for without consideration of the latter – is causing some concern and is arguably behind Michael Young's call for a re-emphasis on subject knowledge, with a particular focus on what he calls *'powerful knowledge'* (Young 2008). This concern is reflected in the government's revisions to the National Curriculum which it is intended will retain a subject-based curriculum with, as expressed in the recent Schools White Paper (DfE 2010), 'core knowledge' being identified for each phase of education (DfE 2011). This is not a unique concern within England, as a cross-national evaluation of approaches to curriculum review reveals (Sargent et al. 2010), which notes concerns by governments to clarify the knowledge that should be taught to children, but that this should not be onerous. A key purpose for several countries is the need to make the curriculum more meaningful and relevant and to do this through connecting more appropriately with children's everyday lives. A concomitant interest lies in how to define knowledge and its relationship to subjects and, indeed, to children and their experience and learning.

The time, therefore, seems ripe for some reflection on the roles of knowledge and children's experience in a subject-based curriculum. We argue that while we agree with the need to 'bring knowledge back in' (Young 2008), we are less convinced by Young's notion of *powerful knowledge* as he presents it and we understand it. Although Young himself has said that his ideas are predominantly aimed at secondary education, we believe that it is relevant and vital to consider its application to primary education for two reasons. First, the curriculum review relates to *all* phases of statutory education in order to achieve the coherence and consistency that was arguably lacking following the revisions under the previous government (QCA 2007; Rose 2009). Second, as for current and previous versions of the National Curriculum (DES 1991; DfEE/QCA 1999), a top-down approach to curriculum design remains likely, with decisions being made for and at secondary level, then filtered 'down' to primary schools. The emphasis on the secondary phase is evident through the greater emphasis on secondary curriculum and assessment in the White Paper and curriculum review (DfE 2010, 2011) and in ministerial briefings and speeches on raising older secondary age pupils' achievements in comparison to other nations (Vasagar 2010).

We argue that *powerful knowledge* as conceived by Young is insufficient in the primary context because it valorises academic knowledge above the everyday or ethno-knowledges (Begg 2006) that pupils bring with them into school. It is our contention that primary pupils' (and primary teachers') everyday or ethno-geographies should also be seen as valid forms of powerful knowledge, and that their incorporation into the curriculum constitutes a kind of 'liberatory education' (Freire 1972). We offer a revised model, rebalancing Young's perspective, for how academic and ethno-geography can ground a geography curriculum that is based on a dialogic pedagogy (Alexander 2008). We are using geographical education here to illustrate an argument that we believe applies across the primary curriculum.

Ethno-geography in the primary phase

Ethno-geography as an idea emerged from the findings of a research study that showed how primary novice teachers' conceptualisations of geography predominantly relied on memories of the geography they were taught in school (Martin 2008a, 2008b). When thinking about geography in a primary education context, novice teachers did not appear to recognise the value of their everyday experiences as a potential source of geographical knowledge, nor did they express an awareness that their personal geographies connected in any way with school geography. This 'disconnection' with the subject is problematic for a number of reasons, particularly because those who do not perceive the relevance of the subject will be unlikely to teach it in a way that is relevant to pupils, and because their lack of awareness of their knowledge base affects their ability to recognise the academic potential of pupils' everyday geographies. This is supported by Ofsted's (2008, 2011) analysis that many primary teachers' geographical subject knowledge is weak.

We contend that, because of their disconnection with the subject, coupled with the very minimal time allocated to humanities subjects in Initial Teacher Training (ITT) (Catling 2006), primary teachers have a problem making a distinction between information, knowledge and understanding. Thus, when thinking about the subject for teaching, their attention is focused on knowledge as *information* rather than knowledge as *understanding* and the basis for informed action. Therefore, it seems imperative to develop a paradigm for primary geography that supports teachers (the very large majority of whom are non-specialists) in making a distinction between these different types of knowledge. We propose that this could be *ethno-geography*.

Ethno- (of the people and their culture) *geography*:

> reflects the view that all [teachers and pupils] are geographers because they all live in the world. They all negotiate and interact with a variety of landscapes (human and natural) on a daily basis. Through these daily interactions and decisions they will have built up a wide knowledge base about the world, near and far, through a range of direct and indirect experiences. What they don't perhaps recognise is that this knowledge is useful geographical knowledge and a point from which deeper conceptual understanding can be developed. (F. Martin 2005, 291)

An important point to note about the meaning of 'ethno' in *ethno-geography* is that it is about examining how people learn and use 'geography' – though they may not relate the term 'geography' or apply it directly to this experience and aspect of their lives – in distinct cultures and in everyday situations within cultures. Thus, in a parallel field of ethno-mathematics, Gilmer states:

> In this context, we may think of culture as acquired knowledge transmitted among groups. ... From this concept of culture, race is not a proxy for culture and 'ethno' in ethno-mathematics is not a proxy for ethnic. (Gilmer 2001, 80)

The cultures represented in the arguments made here are, therefore, those of the academic and everyday, each of which leads to different forms and structures of knowledge. The case presented is to reconnect these two cultures, and the structures of knowledge they produce, in the context of primary education and younger children's experience.

The view of knowledge inherent in ethno-geography is similar to Vygotsky's theory of knowledge as social activity-based, and which expresses a dialectic and interdependent relationship between everyday and scientific concepts (Young 2008). However, 'dialectic' implies that there is a tension between academic and everyday knowledges that needs to be resolved through discussion, the aim of which is to reveal or seek 'truth', the validity of which is traditionally based on generalised, abstract concepts, privileging them over their genesis in the everyday. Rather than a dialectic relationship, we propose a dialogic relationship. *Dialogic* is a discussion between two logics, each of which will be informed by the histories and cultures that produced them, in this case academic and ethno-geographies. Alexander (2008) states that the vocabulary we commonly share and use carries our personal interpretations, assumptions and values alongside their own evolution of meaning:

> In dialogic interactions, children are exposed to alternative perspectives *and* required to engage with another person's point of view in ways that challenge and deepen their own conceptual understandings. (Alexander 2008, 27)

The essence of dialogue is not privileging one perspective over another but the interaction between the two. The dialogue between academic and ethno-geographies deepens and enhances the understanding of both.

As equal partners in the dialogue, this is a distributed approach to knowledge construction. As such, ethno-geography is founded on Freirean liberatory education. Freire (1972) argued that the dominant discourse in education, and evident in the curriculum, is that of *the powerful* and it does nothing to reflect the lived experiences or culture of the learners. Freire developed a democratic pedagogy aimed at avoiding teaching that led to authority dependence. He developed a socially constructed, dialogic pedagogy in which learners and teachers learn from each other and together construct knowledge in ways that are meaningful to both:

> Teaching and learning become knowing and reknowing. The learners gradually know what they did not yet know and the educators reknow what they knew before. (Freire 1998, 90)

Powerful knowledge or knowledge of the powerful?

In his argument for 'bringing knowledge back in', Young (2008) begins by discussing Moore and Muller's (1999) critique of voice discourse theorists. Young shows how Moore and Muller, while providing a useful critique of the so-called 'experience as the foundation of all knowledge' (2008, 6), have brought sociology of education to a cul-de-sac because they dismiss the relevance of the everyday knowledge pupils bring with them to the classroom. Young, based on his reading of Vygotsky, reinterprets the problem of voice discourse, and proposes an alternative way forward in which acknowledgement of voice does not, de facto, result in a disavowal of 'scientific' or 'expert' knowledge. The arguments put forward by Young are complex and there is not space here to consider them in depth. We have chosen, therefore, to focus on that aspect of his argument which examines the relationship between academic/scientific knowledge and everyday/ethno-knowledge, as repre- sented in Figure 1.

Figure 1 represents our interpretation of Young's work and what he says about knowledge, objectivity and pedagogy. First, Young (2008) is

The authoritative	mediating between	The naïve
Academic →	The curriculum ←	Everyday
perspectives	as replacing	perspectives
	the naïve with the	
	authoritative	
[The discipline		*[The younger child*
of geography]		*with geographical*
		experience]
Powerful	Pedagogy	Ethno-knowledge
knowledge	draws on the *everyday*	(the *everyday*)
(the *academic subject*)	to reconstruct it as	
	the *academic subject*	
It has:		It is perceived as:
structure		untutored
coherence		tacit
rationale		implicit
concepts		unformed
and is systematic		unsystematic

Figure 1. The relationship between authoritative/powerful and everyday (geographical) knowledge (based on Young 2008, 2010).

careful to distinguish between knowledge of the powerful (high-status knowledge of the ruling classes) and *powerful knowledge*, which refers to the purpose of knowledge in the sense that it can move young people, intellectually, beyond their local and particular circumstances. Young differentiates between the forms of knowledge shown as academic and everyday, arguing that it is only academic knowledge that can claim objectivity because, although it has emerged from experience, it has been reformulated and developed into an abstract body that goes beyond the social circumstances of its generation. *Academic knowledge*, according to Young, has structure and coherence, is rational, and organises thought systematically through concepts. *Everyday knowledge*, on the other hand, is close to experience, personal, untutored, tacit, unformed and not systematic, and thus can have no claims to objectivity. Academic knowledge is therefore portrayed as authoritative and everyday knowledge as naïve.

Within the context of the school curriculum, Young argues that disciplinary or specialist knowledge is fundamentally more powerful because it is reliable and potentially testable knowledge that takes anyone *beyond their experience*. This accords with Young's view that the purpose of schooling is to give all students access to the knowledge that most of them will not have the opportunity to acquire at home or socially, and enables social mobility. In other words, Young's argument is one of social justice. However, unlike Moore and Muller (1999), he does not go on to dismiss completely voice discourse. Instead he proposes a middle way that recognises 'the inescapable role of experience in the production of new knowledge' (Young 2008, 2011) and that sees this as a valid starting point from which more academic, abstract knowledge can be developed. This is achieved through a Vygotskian social constructivist pedagogy that connects everyday, naïve knowledge to the more abstract scientific concepts that are inherent in subjects. In Young's view, consideration of knowledge and the curriculum cannot be done without consideration of pedagogy since how knowledge is acquired (everyday, tacit) relates directly to how it can then become organised (codified, abstract) within the curriculum:

> It follows that just as the sociology of knowledge is inseparable from the sociology of learning, so the study of the curriculum is inseparable from the study of learning and pedagogy. (Young 2008, 13)

Everyday knowledge is, therefore, of use *pedagogically* as a starting point and valuable to elicit in the classroom merely in order to rectify misconceptions and to restructure in the academic mould. Young is not using the argument that to focus on the local knowledge that students possess denies working-class children 'access to the knowledge required for social mobility' (Morgan and Williamson 2009, 47). He believes that 'such everyday knowledge should be the basis for teaching and learning' (Young 2008, 13) but appears to stop short of considering that this knowledge is powerful in its own right. To us, this constitutes a privileging of academic knowledge over everyday knowledge that is not helpful in the primary education context. Our understanding of ethno-geographies as powerful knowledge is based on Begg's (2006) and D'Ambrosio's (1985) call for the recognition of different dynamic forms of knowledge as a basis for the curriculum. Ethno-knowledges, as ethno-geographies and, indeed, an ethno-curriculum, are active, reflective upon experience, constructive and evolving, just as subjects and disciplines are seen to be. This provides the basis for a dialogic interplay between subjects and children's everyday knowledges.

An argument for the power of everyday knowledge

We intend to counteract the position put forward by Young, initially by drawing on the work of Freire, and then by applying ideas from post-colonial theory. We will draw on evidence from research in the field of children's geographies to support our ideas in the context of primary geography.

First, Young raises important points about the nature of knowledge and claims to 'truth' and objectivity. The assumption is that everyday knowledge cannot be objective because it is too close to experience, does not have a history behind it, and is unformed or lacks any rational structure. Freire counters this by observing that:

> In the first moment, that of the experience of and in daily living, my conscious self is exposing itself to facts, deeds without, nevertheless, asking itself about them, without looking for their 'reason for being' ... knowing that results from these involvements is that made from pure experience. In the second moment, in which our minds work epistemologically, the methodological rigour with which we come close to the object, having 'distanced ourselves' from it, that is, having objectified it, offers us another kind of knowing, a knowing whose exactitude gives to the investigator or the thinking subject a margin of security that does not exist in the first kind of knowing, that of common sense. (Freire 1998, 93)

We infer from this (and the use of the word 'moment') that it is in the very nature of being human to know at these two levels: the first level of 'being' and the second, almost instantaneous, level of reflection. Over time we will have a multitude of first and second moments and from this build knowledge that is structured and helps us to make sense of the world, albeit differently from the structure of the discipline. The culture of childhood thus produces knowledge based on social and environmental interactions, everyday geographies of the spaces and places negotiated either directly or indirectly. Because children's geographies are born of their culture(s) they are necessarily different from academic geographies, but this does not mean that they do not have structure or that they are not formalised in ways suited to their context (Matthews 1992; Freeman and Tranter 2011). We contest, therefore, Young's assertion that everyday geographies are not objective and cannot make claims to truth on the basis that he is using academic perceptions of knowledge as the basis for making this judgement, whereas we would argue that the only valid bases for judging the claims for truth and objectivity are children's own cultural and geographical contexts.

Second, the use of academic perceptions of knowledge as the standard by which to view the everyday, or ethno-knowledges, places the two in a binary discourse in which one holds the power and the other is 'oppressed':

> We have a strong tendency to affirm that what is different from us is inferior. We start from the belief that our way of being is not only good but better than that of others who are different from us. ... The dominant class, then, because it has the power to distinguish itself from the dominated class, first, rejects the differences between them but, second, does not pretend to be equal to those who are different; third, it does not intend that those who are different shall be equal. (Freire 1998, 71)

We would argue that those who privilege academic knowledge and perceive it as being 'superior' to the 'inferior' everyday knowledge are, in effect, 'Othering' and diminishing the everyday, and children along with it, in a way that is similar to western 'Othering' of the East or South (Said 1985). This seems an apposite comparison to make because, in colonial times, the 'Other' was often portrayed by the West as childlike, without rules or governing structures, and thus naïve and in need of the paternalistic hand of the West to develop. In this respect powerful knowledge is no different from the knowledge of the powerful that Young aims to distance himself from, a point supported by Begg in his observation that:

> formal education and subjects have not changed markedly over the last fifty years ... colonialism is alive and well ... and the ruling/upper classes are retaining power and privilege. (Begg 2006, 2)

Power relations in schools and classrooms have been the subject of much discussion, not least the power relations between teachers and pupils. But the power relations between the different knowledges represented by the academy and the everyday and how these might influence the curriculum have only been a small part of this debate. To be clear, this is not a discussion about who decides what gets taught in the classroom; it is a discussion about which knowledges derived from which sociocultural contexts have a right to be represented in the classroom. In our view, academic and everyday knowledges are powerful for different reasons and both need to be included in the curriculum. By arguing for the power of everyday knowledge we are not arguing against academic knowledge – we see both as being important aspects of any curriculum. This is distinct from the voice discourse argument, which seeks to *replace* the power of the academic voice with that of pupil voice. Liberatory education does not believe in replacing one discourse with another; it seeks to give voice to the suppressed and then to create a dialogue with the aim of co-constructing new knowledge. One way to illustrate the power of ethno-knowledges is through research into children's geographies.

Children's geographies

Children's geographies recognises that children's experience, views and understanding of the local and wider world are not the same as those of adults but are no less valid to recognise, investigate, appreciate and value (Horton et al. 2008; van Blerk and Kesby 2009), not only in the UK but globally (Aitken et al. 2008). Research into children's geographies shows that our younger people develop sophisticated understandings of their worlds, and that these understandings are structured and the basis for acting with agency in the world (Aitken 2001; Foley and Leverett 2011; Freeman and Tranter 2011).

This field of study investigates and provides a voice for children's perspectives on their use of space, places and the environment that identifies and clarifies their personal everyday or ethno-geographies. It draws out: how children feel they are perceived in the environment by adults; how experience in places engages them in practices of identity; the ways in which they utilise environments differently alongside adults, layering places with diverse meanings; as well as how they develop environmental and way-finding skills, understanding and knowledge. While past research has been interested to describe children's environmental and place experience, the focus of *children's geographies* has become increasingly engaged in understanding children's sense of their own geographies. Through such studies researchers have begun to appreciate that children not only develop their experience but construct their knowledge and understanding through that experience, including the affordances and constraints provided by places, their growing sense of values in relation to the environment and their encounters with the wider world through a variety of media.

Evidence suggests that while children constantly encounter a wide range of 'particulars' and items of 'information' as they learn, through trial and error, risk-taking and their application of skills and understandings to new contexts, they are constantly reflecting on, reconstructing and reapplying their growing 'geographical' knowledge and understanding (O'Brien 2003; Ba 2009). Through this broad-based everyday reconstituting of evolving schemas children develop a conceptual base about their local world and the wider world and environment, providing a basis for action, further reflection and reconceptualisation. This has been described from the days of early investigations into this area (e.g. Piaget 1929; Piaget and Inhelder 1956) and subsequently in terms of children's construction of their knowledge in, of and about the world, and is the basis for their everyday spatial, environmental and place competence, that is, their *ethno-geographies*.

Studies of children's experience of their locality reveal ways in which they construct their knowledge of the environment and their sense of place. The older primary age children in Ba's (2009) study of their exploration of their local area in New York, USA, identified how and what they learnt through experience from the *affordances* an area provides, such as which of the various commercial sites are child-friendly and will accommodate younger children 'hanging out' rather than as customers. Pike's (2008) studies in Dublin and Waterford, Ireland, noted that children's perspectives included ways in which they *appropriated* places, naming them for their own use, to be sites of activity. Similarly, Derr (2006) identified that the freedom to explore enables children not only to construct, for instance, 'dens' within their own locale but to recognise the specialness of sites that matter to them. Children's awareness of the potential and of its corollary, risk, in an environment is not simply a matter of the state of the physical aspects of the environment but is rooted strongly in the human dimension, the ways in which shopkeepers, park staff and other adults and youth respect and relate to children, providing child-friendly and social contexts for them, and the ways in which they *subvert* these.

Children's active engagement out in their locality was exhibited in Freeman's (2010; Freeman and Tranter 2011) study based in Dunedin, New Zealand. This linked with their *attachment* to their neighbourhood, which had a strong social relationships focus. Children who had ready and direct access to the neighbourhood and wider area, as in Ba's (2009) study, developed their sense of place through personal *exploration* and *social interaction*, giving rise to sensing their experienced places as both physical and social entities, a finding similar to that of Cele's studies in England and Sweden (2006). Pike (2008) argues that from this experience in their everyday places younger children develop effective *spatial and place knowledge* of their everyday environments along with understanding of the processes which shape their places. O'Brien (2003) noted London-based younger children's environmental concerns and interest in *place improvement*, their clear sense of neighbourhood quality. Their capacity to 'reconstruct' less pleasant parts of the environment, such as stairwells, into 'bases' did not deter them from clearly expressing their desire that those responsible for the quality and cleanliness of the local area, including its buildings, had a responsibility to undertake this effectively and consistently. Similar views were expressed by children who participated in research with Al-Khalaileh (2008) into their everyday environment in Amman, Jordan, where they argued that environmental improvements included not only collecting the litter and cleaning the streets but also improving the street environment through tree planting, reducing traffic congestion and noise, and tackling crime levels, another source of risk.

These world-wide examples illustrate that through their movement about and exploration of their environments children not only develop familiarity with places and learn their way around them, but they build an evident sense of the state of the environment, realise and make use of the opportunities that social responses afford, 'subvert' it for their own interests and ends, have a clear appreciation of the risks inherent in the 'real world' and develop views about how adults should undertake their responsibilities to places and the people who live there. Younger children are able to propose ways in which places can be improved and sustained, and they do not exempt themselves from such involvement to make a difference (Alexander and Hargreaves 2007). Children come across as informed, engaged and interested in both their own futures and those of others. They know about their places. This is knowledge and understanding which continues to evolve – as it does with adults – through daily engagement in their environments. It forms the heart of their ethno-geographies.

We contend not only that these are powerful aspects of children's lives, but that their personal geographies provide *powerful knowledge* which children use in their daily lives to make sense of their world as they encounter it, to reflect on it and to deepen their appreciation, under-standing and the uses they can make of it. Children do not enter schooling without a geographical background or without geographical skills, knowledge and understanding that are in and from their lived geographies. However, the notions that children use to understand and make use of their localities and their experiences in them, such as affordance, appropriation, subversion, exploration, social interaction, space and place knowledge, and environmental improvement, are largely not the terms that the academic discipline of geography uses to construct its discourse. The perspective that younger children develop *powerful geographical knowledge* accords with the argument within the sociology of childhood that we can and must take a more positive sense of childhood and of children's experience and learning through their lived lives (Holloway and Valentine 2000; Jenks 2005), that children bring valid and valuable experience, understanding and knowledge into the classroom which should be engaged with and not treated as lacking or impaired and needing simply to be replaced or amended (Slater and Morgan 2000).

A revised model of the knowledge–curriculum relationship

We noted earlier that Freire set out two initial levels or stages in developing everyday or ethno-knowledges. 'Moment one' introduced the idea of knowledge in the experience, and 'moment two' was explained as a reflection on that experience to know it a second time, epistemologically and as common sense. We suggest that there could further be third and fourth levels or stages – a dialogue with the academic (a meta-reflection) that causes a third sense of knowing, but that in this dialogue the teacher also has a 're-knowing' which develops/extends the sense of knowing the subject. The fourth stage is, then, the dialogue between the teacher knower and the subject community, in which the dialogue between the two in turn changes the subject/discipline – i.e. that teacher practitioners are part of the community that develops the subject as it relates to the school curriculum.

In this model both academic and everyday knowledges are powerful. We contest *Powerful Knowledge* (capital letters), which privileges the academic, and suggest a view of knowledge that is powerful (lower case) in which both academic and everyday knowledges are viewed as equally powerful, albeit for different reasons. These knowledges then come into dialogue with each other with the result that both are changed by the encounter in some way – new knowledge is created that has elements of both in it. We draw on Giroux's notion of *becoming* here – that as learners children (and, indeed, adults) are becoming (Freire 1998) and that teachers need to approach the job of teaching as learners, as always becoming. Indeed, this is the case with academic subjects, as discipline histories evidently testify (G. Martin 2005; Holt-Jensen 2009; Agnew and Livingstone 2011), that is, they have an identity of their own, but this identity is not fixed, since subjects are dynamic and constantly changing, thus *becoming*.

Giroux discusses the idea of a border pedagogy in which teachers and students occupy a space where meaning is suspended, and where there is space to negotiate meaning in the classroom, as explored in the 'Enquiring Minds' project (Morgan and Williamson 2009). In this project the curriculum:

> had to be constructed through the dialogue between students and teachers. It was a border pedagogy in the sense that it existed at the margins of the formal school curriculum. It was a different space, where ... students and teachers were involved in the co-construction of knowledge. (Morgan and Williamson 2009, 43)

What this co-construction of knowledge acknowledged is the authoritative voice of both the child and the teacher/subject – that both bring 'powerful knowledges' to the investigation and construction of knowledge and understanding. Using Hart's (2001) distinction between information, knowledge, understanding and wisdom, understanding is inclusive because 'the other is no longer separate but becomes part of our world and ourselves in a profoundly intimate way' (Hart 2001, 13). The essence of this argument is that children's everyday or ethno-knowledge and understanding is no longer 'Othered' but becomes the co-core, with the subject, at the heart of the curriculum and pedagogy. We have represented this in Figure 2, which reworks Young's model, outlined in Figure 1, to show the concomitant authorities which both children's everyday experience and understandings and subject interpretations and knowledge provide reciprocally for each other. Here the curriculum is an articulation of the interrelationship between the two '*powerful knowledges*' brought to bear by children and subjects and fostered by the pedagogical interactions between these two 'authorities'.

Considering two implications

There are various implications in the argument we have made. We will focus on aspects of just two. One is the applicability to other subjects in the primary curriculum. The other concerns the implications for teachers

Authority	held by both contexts	Authority
Powerful → knowledge	Curriculum as articulation	← Powerful knowledge
[*The discipline of geography*]		[*The younger child with geographical experience*]
Academic perspectives of geography	where the pedagogic, dialogic interrelationship lies	Everyday geographical perspectives (ethno-geography)
It is: rational conceptual systematic coherent structured		It is: rational conceptual systematic coherent structured

Figure 2. A revised model of the authority relationship of academic and everyday (geographical) knowledge.

and primary schools. We set these out briefly to indicate the need for fuller consideration by specialist and curriculum developers.

We have illustrated our argument with geographical education. There has been a similar, older interest in this debate in mathematics education, exploring the notion of ethno-mathematics. In the mathematical context arguments have been made challenging the false dichotomies between binaries encapsulated by the practical and the academic, action and reflection, subject and object, and concrete and abstract. Binaries are often used hierarchically to privilege one over the other, such as the objective over the subjective. In ethno-mathematics the argument is not that one aspect is more powerful than the other but that both have equal roles in the dialogue (D'Ambrosio 1985). A key element of the argument is that teachers must draw upon the context of their pupils to interrelate understandings of academic mathematics and ethno-mathematics. Studies have been undertaken that explore ways to connect the situatedness of children's everyday mathematics with academic mathematics (Gerdes 1997), which focus on the daily games, activities and commerce of children's and non-western people's lives. This also implies understanding children's social and cultural backgrounds to be able to draw effectively on their ethno-mathematics (D'Ambrosio 1994). Mathematics is thus a second subject in which the notions that we have discussed have been developed. While there appears to be negligible work on this topic in other subjects, we nevertheless consider this to be a fruitful avenue to explore.

Ofsted (2008, 2011) has identified concerns about the nature and depth of primary teachers' geography subject knowledge and understanding, which affects their confidence in teaching geography. Implicit in teachers' lack of subject knowledge are the limited residual school geography they recall and a minimal or lost awareness of their personal ethno-geography (Martin 2008a, 2008b). For very many primary teachers this has never been addressed in their minimal initial teacher education programme or through continuing professional development (CPD), which has become increasingly less available (Ofsted 2011). This has evident implications for younger children's learning. It identifies a need to address both the nature and length of geography units in initial teacher education programmes and the provision of CPD. One means of addressing this concern is to maintain the training of primary geography subject specialists. Such courses will need to engage novice teachers in developing their own connection with their personal or everyday geographies, alongside understanding children's ethno-geographies, and to develop their understanding of the academic structure and vocabulary of the discipline of geography. The Geographical Association in the UK has used the government-funded Action Plan for Geography (www.geographyteachingtoday.org.uk) to develop several such initial e-based CPD programmes (GA 2010). This implies that novice teachers should undergo the same dialogue that they then might undertake with their pupils, between their ethno-geographies and academic geography in their own programmes, as indicated in Figure 2.

Conclusion

Arising from the arguments presented above, we propose that equal value is given to everyday or ethno-geography and to academic geography. Everyday geographies are rational, conceptual and structured, but *differently* so from academic geography. While ethno-geographies are grounded personally and socially, providing the conceptual base for daily interactions, living and reflection, academic geographies provide an alternative aggregated reflection and conceptualisation, the basis for creating and using subjects. Our case is one of social justice, in which difference is encountered not as an 'Other' to be replaced by one dominant, powerful discourse, but to be brought into dialogue as a democratic partner in the mutual interplay of learning in the process of evolution within and between the everyday knowledges of children and the disciplinary knowledges of subjects. This relationship recognises that what is taken from classroom interactions is not a replacement of one set of experiences and understandings (in the 'subjective' child) by another set of experiences and understandings (from the 'authoritative' teacher/subject) but is the intersection and interaction of the two authorities, which both foster the child's personal learning of the everyday and of the academic, and feed into re-interpretations of the subject for the teacher and the discipline. Butt reinforces this point when he concludes in an analysis of the role of personal geographies in the geography classroom that:

> only when the geography classroom becomes reorganised as a space where children are entitled to know will they be addressed 'less as children and more as participants in a culture they share (Slater and Morgan 2000, 272)'. (Butt 2009, 21)

We have noted that the antecedents for this argument lie in the case for ethno-mathematics, and we consider that the argument here can be applied in other subject areas in relation to primary children's ethno-knowledges and their learning about subjects through the primary curriculum. Geography is a pertinent example of this argument because it is so much a part of children's lives from their earliest years, since without their engagement in knowing and understanding the physical and human everyday worlds, not only would they not undertake such apparently straightforward matters as way-finding but they would not construct their sense of their environments as lifeworlds in order to make use of the affordances they offer. Geography is a fundamental and essentially powerful aspect of being human from the earliest years.

In the coming years there will continue to be debates about the nature of knowledge and its role in the curriculum. This article is a contribution to that debate and one that calls for a fundamental rethink of the role of and relationships between knowledge and the curriculum in the primary context. We have argued that children are to be viewed as contributors to our shared knowledge and understanding of the world rather than as recipients and 'beneficiaries' of 'hand-me-down' curricula which emerge from bodies of ideas designed for secondary schooling and then diluted until suitable for primary consumption. Our argument proposes a reversal of thinking which might go far beyond the present debate to challenge and change classroom dynamics and perhaps contribute to fuller and deeper engagement of children with both their ethno-knowledges and academic subjects.

Acknowledgements

We wish to acknowledge the informative and helpful comments of the two reviewers in shaping this final version of this article. Nevertheless, the views expressed remain our own.

References

Agnew, J., and D. Livingstone, eds. 2011. *The Sage handbook of geographical knowledge*. London: Sage.

Aitken, S. 2001. *Geographies of young people*. London: Routledge.

Aitken, S., R. Lund, and A. Trine Kjørholt, eds. 2008. *Global childhoods*. London: Routledge.

Alexander, R. 2008. *Towards dialogic teaching: Rethinking classroom talk*. 4th ed. York: Dialogos.

Alexander, R., and L. Hargreaves. 2007. *The Primary Review interim reports: Community soundings*. Cambridge: University of Cambridge; Primary Review. http://www. primaryreview.org.uk (accessed November 22, 2007).

Al-Khalaileh, E. 2008. *Understanding children's environments: Where to go, where to play*. Saarbrucken: Verlag Dr Müller.

Ba, H. 2009. *Children's place exploration*. Saarbrucken: Verlag Dr Müller.

Begg, A. 2006. Ethno-mathematics, ethno-knowledge, and ethno-education. Paper presented at ICEm3, Third International Conference on Ethno-mathematics, February, in Auckland.

Bell, D. 2005. The value and importance of geography. *Primary Geographer* 56: 4–5.

Butt, G. 2009. Developing pupils' 'personal geographies' – Is the personalisation of geography education beneficial? *Research in Geographic Education* 11, no. 1: 5–23.

Catling, S. 2003. Curriculum contested: Primary geography and social justice. *Geography* 88, no. 3: 164–210.

Catling, S. 2005. Children's personal geographies and the English primary school curriculum. *Children's Geographies* 3, no. 3: 325–44.

Catling, S. 2006. *Learning to teach geography in ten-and-a-half hours*. Westminster Institute of Education. Oxford: Oxford Brookes University.

Catling, S., and T. Willy. 2009. *Teaching primary geography*. Exeter: Learning Matters.

Cele, S. 2006. *Communicating place*. Stockholm: Stockholm University.

D'Ambrosio, U. 1985. Ethnomathematics and its place in the history and pedagogy of mathematics. *For the Learning of Mathematics* 5, no. 1: 44–8.

D'Ambrosio, U. 1994. Cultural framing of mathematics teaching and learning. In *Didactics of mathematics as a scientific discipline*, ed. R. Biehler, R. Scholz, R. Straber, and B. Winkelmann, 443–55. Dordrecht: Kluwer.

Derr, T. 2006. 'Sometimes birds sound like fish': Perspectives on children's place experiences. In *Children and their environments*, ed. C. Spencer and M. Blades, 108–23. Cambridge: Cambridge University Press.

DES (Department for Education and Science). 1991. *Geography in the National Curriculum (England)*. London: DES.

DfE (Department for Education). 2010. *The importance of teaching: Schools White Paper 2010*. London: The Stationery Office. http://www.education.gov.uk (accessed November 24, 2010).

DfE (Department for Education). 2011. Review of the National Curriculum: England. http://www.education.gov.uk/schools/teachingandlearning/curriculum/nationalcurriculumreview (accessed January 20, 2011).

DfEE/QCA (Department for Education and Employment/Qualifications and Curriculum Authority). 1999. *The National Curriculum for England: Geography*. London: DfEE/QCA.

Foley, P., and S. Leverett, eds. 2011. *Children and young people's spaces: Developing practice*. Basingstoke: Palgrave Macmillan.

Freeman, C. 2010. Children's neighbourhoods, social centres to 'terra incognita'. *Children's Geographies* 8, no. 2: 157–76.

Freeman, C., and P. Tranter. 2011. *Children and their urban environment: Changing worlds*. London: Earthscan.

Freire, P. 1972. *Pedagogy of the oppressed*. Harmondsworth: Penguin Books.

Freire, P. 1998. *Teachers as cultural workers – letters to those who dare teach*. Trans. D. Macedo, D. Koike, and A. Oliveira. Boulder, CO: Westview Press.

GA (Geographical Association). 2010. My place, your place, our place. http://www.geography.org.uk/cpdevents/onlinecpd/myplaceyourplaceourplace.

Gerdes, P. 1997. Survey of current work on ethnomathematics. In *Ethnomathematics: Challenging Eurocentrism in mathematics education*, ed. A. Powell and M. Frankenstein, 411–28. Albany, NY: State University of New York.

Gilmer, G. 2001. Ethnomathematics: A promising approach for developing mathematical knowledge among African American women. In *Changing the faces of mathematics: Perspectives on gender*, ed. J. Jacobs, J. Rossi Becker, and G. Gilmer, 79–88. Reston, VA: National Council of Teachers of Mathematics.

Hart, T. 2001. Teaching for wisdom. *Encounter: Education for Meaning and Social Justice* 14, no. 2: 3–16.

Holloway, S., and G. Valentine, eds. 2000. *Children's geographies*. London: Routledge.

Holt-Jensen, A. 2009. *Geography: History and concepts*. London: Sage.

Horton, J., P. Kraftl, and F. Tucker. 2008. The challenges of 'Children's Geographies': A reaffirmation. *Children's Geographies* 6, no. 4: 335–48.

Jenks, C. 2005. *Childhood*. London: Routledge.

Martin, F. 2005. The relationship between beginning teachers' prior conceptions of geography, knowledge and pedagogy and their development as teachers of primary geography. Unpublished PhD thesis, University of Coventry.

Martin, F. 2008a. Knowledge bases for effective teaching: Beginning teachers' development as teachers of primary geography. *International Research in Geographical and Environmental Education* 17, no. 1: 13–19.

Martin, F. 2008b. Ethno-geography: Towards a liberatory geography education. *Children's Geographies* 6, no. 4: 437–50.

Martin, G. 2005. *All possible worlds: A history of geographical ideas*. Oxford: Oxford University Press.

Matthews, H. 1992. *Making sense of place*. Hemel Hempstead: Harvester/Wheatsheaf.

Moore, R., and J. Muller. 1999. The discourse of 'voice' and the problem of knowledge and identity in the sociology of education. *British Journal of Sociology of Education* 20, no. 2: 189–206.

Morgan, J., and B. Williamson. 2009. *Enquiring minds: Schools, knowledge and educational change*. Bristol: Futurelab. http://www.enquiringminds.org.uk (accessed December 7, 2010).

O'Brien, M. 2003. Regenerating children's neighbourhoods: What do children want? In *Children in the city*, ed. P. Christensen and M. O'Brien, 142–61. London: Routledge.

Ofsted (Office for Standards in Education). 2008. *Geography in schools: Changing practice*. London: Ofsted. http://www.ofsted.gov.uk (accessed February 24, 2008).

Ofsted (Office for Standards in Education). 2011. *Geography: Learning to make a world of difference*. London: Ofsted. http://www.ofsted.gov.uk (accessed February 15, 2011).

Piaget, J. 1929. *The child's conception of the world*. London: Routledge & Kegan Paul.

Piaget, J., and B. Inhelder. 1956. *The child's conception of space*. London: Routledge & Kegan Paul.

Pike, S. 2008. Children and their environments in Ireland. Unpublished EdD thesis, Queen's University, Belfast, UK.

QCA (Qualifications and Curriculum Authority). 2007. *Geography: Programme of study for Key Stage 3 and attainment target*. London: QCA. http://www.qcda.org.uk/curriculum (accessed January 27, 2009).

Rose, J. 2009. *Independent review of the primary curriculum: Final report*. Annesley: DCSF Publications.

Said, E. 1985. *Orientalism*. Harmondsworth: Penguin Books.

Sargent, C., A. Byrne, S. O'Donnell, and E. White. 2010. *Thematic probe: Curriculum review in the INCA countries: June 2010*. Slough: NFER.

Slater, F., and J. Morgan. 2000. 'I haven't fully discovered it yet': Children experiencing environments. In *The child's world – triggers for learning*, ed. M. Robertson and R. Gerber, 258–75. Camberwell: Australian Council for Educational Research.

van Blerk, L., and M. Kesby, eds. 2009. *Doing children's geographies*. London: Routledge.

Vasagar, J. 2010. Bad teachers out, social mobility in: Gove outlines goals. *The Guardian*, November 25, 16–17.

Wilby, P. 2010. Mick Waters, curriculum guru, takes stock. *The Guardian*, September 7.

Young, M. 2008. *Bringing knowledge back in: From social constructivism to social realism in the sociology of education*. London: Routledge.

Young, M. 2010. 'What is powerful knowledge?' Paper given at Communicating Public Geographies, session 5 of the ESRC Engaging Geography seminar series, October 13, at the Institute of Education, London. http://engaginggeography.wordpress.com/2-seminars/vi-communicating-public-geographies/.

Young, M. 2011. Discussion to Part 3. In *Geography, education and the future*, ed. G. Butt, 181–3. London: Continuum.

Ethnogeography: towards liberatory geography education

Fran Martin

School of Lifelong Learning, University of Exeter, St Luke's Campus, Exeter

In the context of education in England, an argument is put forward that Geography, as it is conceptualised in the National Curriculum, does not connect to either primary school pupils or their teachers. Reasons for this are explored and a proposal is made for a new paradigm for primary geography: ethnogeography. This proposal parallels work on ethnomathematics, which provides a political agenda to the study of maths and itself draws from Paulo Freire's politicization and consciousness raising through adult literacy. This pattern is applied to learning in geographical education. Drawing on the findings of a recent research project, a case is argued for ethnogeography and the implications for primary Initial Teacher Education courses, learners and the curriculum in primary schools and are considered.

Geography and the National Curriculum

In England, the National Curriculum for Primary schools (5–11 year olds) includes the subject of Geography, the content of which is organised under the headings of: geographical enquiry and skills; knowledge and understanding of place; knowledge and understanding of patterns and processes; knowledge and understanding of environmental change and sustainable development; and breadth of study (DfEE/QCA 1999). While the specifications under each heading differ according to the age group for which it is intended, these headings themselves are the same for primary and secondary schools, although this is due to change for secondary schools where a new curriculum (QCA 2007) is to be implemented from September 2008. For reasons of continuity it can seem appropriate for primary and secondary schools to have the same overall framework for the geography curriculum. However, at primary level a lack of teacher expertise in geography is severely affecting how this curriculum is interpreted and implemented. The evidence shows that, after an initial improvement in geography teaching following the introduction of the National Curriculum in 1989, over the last decade the status of geography has declined in primary schools and this is having a negative impact on the standards achieved (Bell 2004, Ofsted 2004, Catling *et al.* 2004).

Decline in overall quality in primary schools is 'associated with teachers' weak knowledge of geography, their lack of confidence to teach it and insufficient training to support them' (Ofsted 2008, p. 4) leading to an overall picture of a subject that is poorly taught (Bell 2004), not enjoyed by primary school pupils or teachers (Woodhouse 2006) and which does not relate to the real world concerns that geography has so much potential to help us understand (Geographical Association 2008). To counter this decline, in 2006 the DfES announced funding for an initial 2-year Action Plan for Geography (APG) to be delivered jointly by the Geographical Association (GA) and the Royal Geographical Society/Institute of British Geographers (RGS-IBG). The APG recognises the need to develop:

> ... well trained, up-to-date and enthusiastic teachers who understand and can use geography to help young people become confident in their learning, informed about the world around them, and responsible, productive, active citizens. (Geographical Association 2008)

In two publications (Catling and Martin 2004, IRGEE 2005) a number of researchers in geographical education have also made suggestions about how primary geography can be improved. Many of these have focused on using children's personal geographies as a basis for connecting pupils to a curriculum *for* children (Catling 2005). Catling also advocates connecting such a curriculum to the action orientated Citizenship curriculum as this, when

> ... integrated with a geography of reality, politicises the geographical enquiries that can be undertaken ... not in a partisan sense, but by moving such geographical investigations into active pupil engagement and into following through the findings of such studies by proposing community action. (Catling 2005, p. 336)

A connection between geography and active citizenship has been endorsed by the Action Plan for Geography (GA 2006) and the Office for Standards in Education (Ofsted 2008) and, although this is a contested area in geographical education (Ellis 2003, Standish 2003), it is something that is seen as vital to the aim of revitalising the subject and making it relevant to children's lives.

> A partnership between geography and citizenship ... will energise the former and give substance to the latter. Citizenship can be a breath of fresh air, making geography relevant, exciting, and most important of all, empowering pupils so that they know how they can make a difference. (Ofsted 2008, p. 24)

Empowering pupils is a laudable aim, and one that reflects the emphasis on listening to children's voices that is evident in, for example, the work of Robin Alexander (2006) and his approach to The Primary Review (2007) in England. However, in the English education system this aim usually falls short of giving children more control over the curriculum and their learning, yet this is precisely what Simon Catling proposes in his argument for improving the primary geography curriculum (Catling 2003, 2005).

Children's geographies and the Geography National Curriculum

Children's geographies straddle the areas of social sciences and environmental psychology with an emphasis on valuing children's voices and everydayness. Yet, as Catling observes, 'there is limited recognition of the role that children's geographies play in the English primary school geography curriculum' (2005, p. 325). Catling has long since called for children's voices and their personal geographies (described as 'worlds inside their heads', Bale 1987) to be integrated into the primary curriculum (Catling 2003). His argument for a child-centred geography curriculum is predicated on a deep understanding of children as active agents in constructing their own geographies, which he organises under the headings of children's personal geographies, the geographies that affect children's lives, and the geographies of children's participation. Drawing extensively on children's geographies literature, he argues that children are marginalised in their local neighbourhood and school environments (Catling 2005). He goes on to show how children are also marginalised in the primary school geography curriculum. This point is picked up by Martin (2006a) who argues that the current geography curriculum is dominated by a top-down approach which values the academic voice but does little to recognise the non-specialist voice common to most primary teachers. The influence of national policy has led to a curriculum that is an eclectic mix of a number of geographical paradigms such as scientific, humanist, and radical (Rawling 2001). However, the resulting framework for the geography curriculum described at the beginning of this paper is not easily recognisable to those (primary teachers or their pupils) whose geographies are implicit in their everyday lives.

Catling identifies a danger in such discontinuity between children's geographies as they experience them in their daily lives, and the geographies they experience in the curriculum:

> Their [children's] real world is kept at a safe distance from what must be learnt. It enables geographical topics to be taught comfortably, ... It stays with safe questions and safe answers, as well as avoiding controversy ... [it] presents a potentially sanitized, almost cosmetically dressed, 'reality' for consumption by parents, governors and politicians. (Catling 2005, p. 335)

The suggestion is that this discontinuity between children, their environmental experiences and the geography curriculum could be a key factor behind the decline in the status of, and standards in, geography over the last decade. The central thread of Catling's argument is that when the geographies about, of and for children are the subject of geography topics (and he gives vivid examples of how this might be achieved) pupils take part wholeheartedly because their own perspectives are shown to matter to them (Hart 1997, Matthews 2003). This goes beyond the view put forward by John Bale in the 1980s who was concerned to take account of children's personal geographies in order that these *'untutored or vernacular world views'* (Bale 1987, p. 30) could be challenged and made sense of in the light of academic geographical views and perspectives. Catling is not suggesting a simplistic focus on the child as the *object* of study, but a focus on children's interests, concerns and participation. He recognises that this 'requires an increased sense of flexibility from government, schools and teachers' and that primary school teachers adapt the curriculum 'anticipating what may be of interest to and motivating for their children' (p. 340).

Catling's ideas are welcomed by the geographical education community, but there is a major stumbling block to their successful implementation: primary teachers poor subject knowledge and their lack of awareness of their own personal geographies. In order for primary teachers to elicit and build on children's geographies in the ways suggested by Catling, it could be argued that primary teachers need to have a level of awareness of their own personal geographies: unless one understands the ways in which one's daily life has geographical dimensions is it possible to identify the geographical dimensions of others' lives? As the next sections of this paper shows, trainee primary teachers do not appear to have this level of awareness and this creates a barrier to their development as teachers of primary geography.

Beginning teachers' geographies

In England, although primary school teachers are required to teach geography as part of the National Curriculum, they have often had little geography education of their own. A small-scale research project (Martin 2005) found that of 79 student teachers studying a Post Graduate Primary Education (PGCE) Initial Teacher Training (ITT) course, only 13 had an 'A' level or equivalent in geography (the highest formal school qualification), of which 10 went on to do a degree that contained elements of geography. Of the remaining 66 students, 42 gained an 'O' level and the remainder chose not to study the subject beyond the age of 14 years. It is perhaps not surprising that 45 of the 79 students said they felt negative about their geography lessons when they were pupils, although 55 were approaching the geography component of their ITT course with a positive attitude.

The aim of the research was to investigate the relationship between student teachers' conceptions of geography, pedagogy and epistemology and their development as teachers of primary geography. Primary students' conceptions of geography were elicited before and after the geography component of the taught course using concept mapping techniques, and 12 of the 79 were interviewed using their concept maps as a stimulus for semi-structured interviews. Of the many findings that emerged from data analysis, one of the most significant concerned how geography was conceptualised when students were asked the question 'What is geography?'. Interviews revealed that they relied predominantly on memories of the geography they were taught at school. No student interviewed indicated that they thought everyday experiences could contribute valuable geographical knowledge nor that they had personal geographies that were nothing to do with the geography they were taught at school. Some students who did not take geography as a subject beyond the age of 14 years were of the opinion that they 'did not know any geography' at all. Thus, when thinking about geography for teaching, the majority cast their minds back to their own experiences as pupils at school, drawing on ideas about geography that are unnecessarily limiting and, because they do not perceive themselves as geographers, they struggle to teach creatively or with conviction.

For the students in this study the geography component of their PGCE course made efforts to link the National Curriculum for geography to their (and, by implication, pupils') life experiences as much as possible and for some this had an impact on their concept maps after the course. However, when on school placement, despite this apparent gain in confidence and awareness of what counted as geographical knowledge, they often reverted back to their prior conception. Two phenomena have been noted with regard to student teachers early school practice. Barratt Hacking (1996) observed that secondary PGCE students' image of geography in practice tended to reflect that of the school's geography department rather than their own – elicited at the beginning of their course. Calderhead and Shorrock (1997) report that at an early stage of their school practice, student teachers often revert to the novice ideas they held at the beginning of their course rather than putting into practice the ideas they have been gaining through the university input.

Clearly, in the case of novice teachers, these phenomena are to be expected. However, in the case of primary student teachers while there are continuing opportunities to develop their pedagogical conceptions, the opportunities to do the same for their geographical conceptions are extremely limited. As Catling (2006) has found, in Primary PGCE courses in England the amount of time devoted to primary geography varies from 4 to 16 hours, with a few courses not covering geography at all. Teachers who remain novice as teachers of geography can pass these limiting conceptions on to their pupils and perpetuate an image of geography that is out of date and does not reflect either the fact that geography is part of everyday life, or the 'new agendas' (Grimwade *et al.* 2000) of global citizenship and sustainable development. How this situation can be addressed is of great concern to the geographical education community in England. The argument put forward in this paper is that trainee teachers need to feel connected to their personal geographies and that this can be achieved by helping them to become aware of the geographies of their everyday lives. This would provide a foundation for their working in the ways suggested by Catling. To this end, a new paradigm for primary geography has been suggested (Martin 2005): that of ethnogeography – a geography of the people and their culture. How this idea developed will now be explored.

Liberating the learner and the development of ethnogeography

A recent academic field that has been applied to educational contexts is that of ethnomathematics, which combines the mathematics of everyday life with a growing awareness of political and power relationships in number use. It looks to ways in which mathematics education can be liberating, much as Paulo Freire (1972) did for adult literacy. Frankenstein and Powell (1994) and Powell and Frankenstein (1997), argued that academic mathematics has been developed eurocentrically and imposed upon the world to the detriment of local mathematical systems. Mathematics is not value-free and further is set out in ways which benefit the academically initiated. Boaler (1993), in distinguishing between different interpretations of ethnomathematics refers back to the originator, Ubi D'Ambrosio and states that:

> The great insight of enthnomathematics is in involving individual and group generation of mathematical problems. I believe that in offering the term ethnomathematics D'Ambrosio is referring to a *self-generated mathematics* [my italics] which may have derived from cultural groups and not a mathematics which is used by cultural groups ... this is important in consideration of ethnomathematics as central to a curriculum offered to bridge the gaps between school and the 'real world'. (Boaler 1993, p. 16)

In his distinction between academic mathematics (that studied in schools) and ethnomathematics (that which is practised within identifiable cultural groups) D'Ambrosio (1985) proposed that learned mathematics stifled the mathematics that was practised as part of everyday life and, for some pupils, acted as a barrier to further learning in the academic sphere: schooling effectively disempowered these pupils.[1] D'Ambrosio argued that a combination of academic and everyday mathematics which recognised the dialectic relationship between theory and practice would liberate children from the confines of either one. He was critical of an education that set up a false dichotomy between theory and practice and, as Freire before him in the context of adult literacy had done, sought to develop an approach to mathematics that is dialogic and in which teacher and learner work together

> not only in the task of unveiling ... reality, and thereby coming to know it critically, but in the task of re-creating that knowledge. (Freire 1972, p. 44)

Central to ethnomathematics and the liberatory paradigm on which it is grounded is an understanding that what counts as knowledge is embedded in power relationships, the dominant (i.e., academic) voice being the one that prevails. Gerdes (1998) has argued that academic mathematical knowledge is often presented as fixed and universal, whereas it is not the knowledge that is universal, but the mathematical *activity* that produces that knowledge.[2] Thus, mathematial activity is universal to all cultures, including the culture of the non-academic:

> A key assumption in this field ... is that, through interacting in a myriad of daily-life activities, people already think and, more specifically, they think mathematically. (Frankenstein and Powell 1994, p. 74).

There are obvious parallels between the circumstances that led to the development of ethnomathematics and those within which primary geography is operating today, as reported above. However, a major exception is that in the case of primary geography the teachers themselves are non-geographers and therefore part of the 'oppressed' group whose voices need liberating.

Ethnogeography is a term that has been used since late 1800s to refer to the geographies of indigenous peoples. In early anthropological studies, ethnogeography described the ways the tribes studied used knowledge handed down and developed generation by generation to use geographic and environmental features to their advantage, whether for hunting or medicine (Barrett 1908, Shimkin 1947). In the context of geographical education, ethnogeography is used in a new way to apply to the culture and ways of knowing the world that are particular to learners (whether pupils or students in training or primary teachers).

> Ethnogeography reflects the view that all learners are geographers because they all live in the world. They all negotiate and interact with a variety of landscapes (human and natural) on a daily basis. ... They will have built up a wide knowledge base about the world, near and far, through a range of direct and indirect experiences. What they don't perhaps recognize is that this knowledge is useful geographical knowledge and a point from which deeper conceptual understanding can be developed. (Martin 2006b, p. 180)

In some senses this is a geography of the everyday, but it goes beyond this to suggest that this knowledge is culturally specific and of value in itself rather than something that is 'naïve' (Golledge 2006) and in need of replacing by academic perspectives. When the everyday is in dialogue with the academic there is the possibility of the creation of new knowledge that can give learners a sense of social and environmental agency. In terms of pupils as learners, Catling has provided an agenda for how this might be achieved, as discussed above. In terms of teachers as learners it is a little more complex. How can beginning teachers' geographies be identified and built upon to develop the understanding required to enable them to develop a curriculum that is based on children's geographies?

Ethnogeography: implications for teacher education

In the field of ethnomathematics, Gerdes (1998) identifies four interrelated dimensions of 'developing an awareness of the social and cultural bases of mathematics and mathematics education' (p. 46) that he argues are a necessary part of mathematics teacher education (i.e., learning to teach). These four dimensions have been applied to geographical teacher education.

Becoming aware of geography as a universal activity

Geography, or being a geographer, is a universal activity in the sense that in all cultures geographical thinking takes place whether 'spontaneously or in an organized way'. For example, all people negotiate their way around, and interact with their environment and do so almost unconsciously from infancy. The nature of this mobility and interaction will be culturally and environmentally contextualised, but the act of finding ones way around the world and making sense of your interactions with it is common to all people. Teachers need to develop and have valued this type of awareness 'in order to never underestimate the capacities, know-how, and wisdom of their students and the students' communities' (Gerdes 1998, p. 47). In practical terms, this can be achieved by asking students to write down anything they have done that week, and then encouraging them to look at the event or activity through a geographical lens. Here the concept of Geographical Imagination, in the sense that Giddens (2001) discusses a Sociological Imagination, is useful. Developing a Geographical Imagination is akin to providing a geographical 'lens' on everyday experiences that enable these experiences to be seen anew – i.e., from a geographical perspective. It brings the everyday and the academic together in discourse with the aim of creating a curriculum that is relevant to learners and enables them to both make sense of, and act responsibly in, their world as geographers. As Margaret Roberts (2003) has observed, the curriculum does not exist outside the space of interaction between pupil and teacher.

Becoming aware of the multilinear development of geography

As indicated above, how that geographical thinking has developed is time, environment and culture dependent. The geographical thinking of Australian and American aboriginal peoples has developed in directions that are different to geographical thinking in the 'Western' world. Likewise the development of geographical thinking varies according to age, gender, race and ability. Teachers who are not aware of cultural differences in geographical thinking may well disadvantage some of their learners. However, where an awareness of cultural differences is applied through the use of alternative teaching tools, the geographical thinking of some children can be enhanced. An example of this can be seen in the use of 'journey sticks' as an approach to mapping. This approach has been adapted from a technique used by North American Indians and involves the use of physical artefacts attached to a stick in the field during a journey. The journey stick can then be used as the basis for a map in a way that allows for cognitive and affective mapping thus engaging the learners at deeper levels (Whittle 2006). In other words, it would be up to the skill of the teacher to recognise the features in different cultural and social contexts (children's geographies) that were common to all types of geographical thinking (i.e., the universal elements) and to make connections between the two for the learners. As Gerdes points out:

With this understanding an openness for [geographical] ideas in other cultures may develop. Along with an awareness that contrasting views ... may enrich the teacher's own conception of [geographical] ideas and help the
teacher to find didactic alternatives. (Gerdes 1998, p. 48)

This also implies developing an awareness firstly, that there is no one 'geography' but many
'geographies' and secondly, that these geographies are dynamic and, as knowledge is developed
through a continuous process of physical and human interaction, constantly changing.

Being aware of geography and geographical education as socio-cultural processes

Pedagogically, this awareness is founded on the understanding that knowledge is socially constructed and cannot be separated from the knowing subject who is constantly developing understanding (Vygotsky 1978). The implications of this for teacher education would be to develop an
explicit awareness of the socio-cultural and environmental influences on primary geography.
This would entail raising student teachers' awareness of their own images of geography
through, for example, concept mapping as described earlier in this paper, comparing these
with the geographies reflected in everyday activities, and then discussing the differences in
order to identify the influences on each. It would also entail raising awareness of the different
geographies (scientific, humanistic, radical) that have influenced the National Curriculum (as
described by Rawling 2001) and that it is therefore possible to select from a range of geographical lenses in order to illuminate a phenomenon. In the context of primary teachers this may be
especially important because, as demonstrated at the beginning of this paper, they may well hold
beliefs such as 'I don't know any geography' and 'I have no geographical ability'. Going through
a process of identifying their own personal geographies and the influences upon them will
broaden their awareness of the geographical knowledge they hold and their confidence and
ability to teach it as a result (Martin 2006a).

Developing among teachers an awareness of the geographical potential of their students

In turn, this awareness could be applied to their pupils as learners with an intended outcome
of teachers not underestimating, or making inappropriate assumptions about, the geographical
abilities or potential of the children in their class. Rather, there would be an awareness of
the need to listen to children's voices, eliciting their own geographies and using these as
valid topics for investigation. As identified above, what might be revealed through these elicita-
tions has been the subject of research in the field of children's geographies. As part of this
process of awareness Nick Hopwood (2006) has argued persuasively that pupils would also
need to work explicitly on their understanding of what the subject of geography is all about,
in the same way as their teachers have before them. The overall benefit of these approaches
would be that

This awareness empowers teachers [and learners], enhancing their self-confidence that they, themselves – and the
cultural groups to which they belong – are capable of doing, producing, and developing geography. (Gerdes 1998,
p. 49)

with obvious gains in levels of motivation and achievement.

Ethnogeography and the primary curriculum

In this final section I will begin by discussing ways in which the current curriculum for primary
geography offers scope for an ethogeographical approach. I will then address concerns that have
been expressed about an ethnocurriculum for geography and show how, based on the principles
of a spiral curriculum (Bruner 1960) it is possible to develop a curriculum that leads to the type

of politicised geography that Catling and Ofsted argue for. Furthermore, I will argue that an ethnogeographical curriculum has the potential to develop children as global citizens, able to take positive action for social and environmental justice.

Ethnogeography and the National Curriculum

As outlined at the beginning of this article, the programmes of study for geography in the National Curriculum for England (DfEE/QCA 1999) provide a framework that is relatively flexible (Figure 1). In some respects this is a useful framework that can help teachers to focus on key geographical concepts such as place, patterns and processes and it offers flexibility in the choice of content that will provide the context for development of these ways of thinking.

As it stands, it is therefore theoretically possible for an ethnogeographical curriculum to meet the requirements of the National Curriculum for geography. An example of how this might be done is provided in Figure 2.

In this example, children's own everyday knowledge of their locality is used as the starting point for identifying aspects of their locality that interest them. This information provides the basis for locations to visit during the fieldwork where children choose what to record and (to a certain extent) how to record it. In the location assessment it is the children's own ideas about what they like or do not that are important and, following the sequence of activities this might then provide a further focus for an issue such as 'How can our local area be improved?' that draws on their own direct experiences of how space is used and the extent to which it is suited to the ways in which they would like to be able to use it. These activities would enable pupils to meet the following specific objectives within the National Curriculum:

In relation to knowledge and understanding of places, at Key Stage 2 pupils should be taught:

a. to identify and describe what places are like;
b. the location of places and environments they study and other significant places and environments;
c. to describe where places are;
d. to explain why places are like they are; and
e. to identify how and why places change and how they may change in the future. (DfEE/QCA 1999, available online at www.nc.uk.net)

Such a focus could be enhanced if teachers, as part of their development of subject knowledge, became aware of research into children's geographies. To take just one example, Ross (2005) has shown how primary children feel their ownership of play spaces is inhibited by too much adult intervention and imposition of rules. Children have always enjoyed using unkempt spaces for their play and socializing, but the increasing sanitisation of these spaces and

1.	Geographical enquiry and skills
2.	Knowledge and understanding of place
3.	Knowledge and understanding of patterns and processes
4.	Knowledge and understanding of environmental change and sustainable development
5.	Breadth of study – which at KS1 (5–7 year olds) requires a focus on two localities, one of the school and the other a UK or overseas locality that contrasts with the school locality; at KS2 (7–11 year olds) requires a focus on two localities and three themes: a UK locality, a locality in an economically developing country; water (rivers or coasts), settlements (size, character, change in land use) and an environmental issue (with an example of managing the environment sustainably).

Figure 1. Geography National Curriculum for England: programmes of study headings for Key Stages 1 and 2.

Preparation: With the class make a list of the places they know well in their locality and what they do there. Think about which places are distinctive to their area. Encourage them to think about the character of a place, reminding them that places have a character just as they each have their own character. *What children perceive as contributing to a locality's character may well be different from what adults might think. This can provide a very informative basis on which to choose the locations to visit during the fieldwork, and the criteria by which to assess these locations.*

Fieldwork: The focus of the fieldwork should be determined by the children's interests. Each group will need a map, a disposable and/or digital camera, clipboards, paper and pencils. Each group decides which locations to visit (maximum 5). At each location they complete a location assessment, draw a sketch of something that interests them, agree as a group what they would like to photograph and why.

Follow up: Create a class annotated map using the data gathered. Develop children's awareness of the overall character of their locality, and that while it will have its character, how each person describes and represents it will differ according to their personal preferences. However, there may be, as a class, some things they can all agree on which will help them to give a class response to the question 'What sort of place do we live in?'

Figure 2. My place: enquiry-based fieldwork to develop a personal sense of place (from Martin 2006c, pp. 32–33).

marginalization of children in their own localities has led to an increasing appropriation of adult spaces by children for their own purposes (Valentine 2004). There is also evidence that the marginalisation of young people in physical spaces is leading to their creating virtual spaces in which to play and socialise (BBC 2007). These are local issues of concern to children that have global dimensions. They are issues of social and environmental justice and have the potential to form the basis of an extremely meaningful curriculum.

Nevertheless, there are aspects of the National Curriculum that are not so easily adapted to an ethnogeographic approach, such as the requirement to develop specified locational knowledge referred to as 'significant places and environments'. As Catling and Taylor (2006) have identified, the meaning of significance in geography is far from transparent and, almost by definition, the places and environments listed will not hold significance for every pupil in a class. A further feature of the current structure of the geography programmes of study is that the headings outlined in Figure 1 do not create a clear enough conceptual framework for the majority of primary teachers, who are non-specialists. The result is that the content selected becomes the main focus for learning, and the conceptual framework that could provide a geographical lens for making sense of that content gets lost. Until recently, the Key Stage 3 programme of study was governed by the same framework as KS1 and 2. However, from September 2008, KS3 will be required to implement a revised structure which is a big departure from the previous version and is organised under the headings: key concepts (of which there are seven), key processes, range and content, and curriculum opportunities. The government has commissioned a review of the primary curriculum, the initial findings of which are to be published in March 2009. It will be interesting to see whether the review advises a change of structure similar to that for the KS3 curriculum. Such a structure would have the benefit of a clearer conceptual framework, and greater flexibility in the selection of content, both of which would more easily support an ethnogeographical approach to primary geography. It would not be without its drawbacks not least, as has been evident with the KS3 revisions, the need for substantial In-service training for teachers.

Criticisms of ethnogeography

It has been argued that ethnogeography, with its focus on children's geographical experiences in their daily lives, might be both limiting in scope (P. Jackson 2006, personal communication by email) and dilute the essence of what geography is about (R. Golledge 2006, personal communication by email). I will address each of these criticisms in turn.

Firstly, the observation that ethnogeography might be limiting in scope supposes that a focus on the everyday is a focus on the mundane, and that the everyday implies limiting the scope to the local. I would argue that enabling children to see the geographical dimensions of their everyday experiences is not an exercise in studying the mundane; it is about creating the excitement that accompanies the discovery of something new, or of seeing something new in a familiar situation for the first time.

In addition, children in the twenty-first century are connecting to the wider world on a daily basis. Some of these connections are direct through, for example, the food they eat and the clothes they wear; others are indirect through television, film, the Internet. The geographical knowledge built from indirect experiences is just as valid a base to start from as the knowledge built from direct experiences. An example from Ian Cook shows how this has been achieved at undergraduate level:

> I run a final year undergraduate module . . . called Geographies of Material Culture. Here, students are encouraged to find out how their lives and those of countless 'usually unseen others', near and far, are interdependent and interrelated. They do this by exploring the biographies and geographies of the everyday, mundane stuff that helps them to do what they do, be who they are. (Cook *et al.* 2006, p. 38)

One of the students describes how, when investigating her ballet shoes, she discovered that the shoes were sold

> . . . in more than 70 countries worldwide. Thus, in purchasing this brand of shoe I contribute to Russia's increasingly dynamic market economy. Consequently this is why such things matter. We are not isolated entities, but a world-system, components. The chain of interconnectivity does not end in Russia. There's International Dance Supplies – the company that distributes Grishko in the UK. Dance and Leisure Wear, Drayton Road, Kings Heath, Birmingham. The sales assistant who fitted my shoes. Thousands of people, thousands of miles, like the layers of paper and glue within them, compressed and wedged into two small shoes (Cook *et al.* 2006, p. 39)

This type of activity, if conducted with student teachers, would enable them to develop an image of geography that is current, part of everyday life, and connects to the new agendas of Global Citizenship and Sustainable Development. It would also provide a model for 'anticipating what may be of interest to, and motivating for, children' as advocated by Catling (2005).

Secondly, while Golledge (2006) supports the idea of anchoring geographic teaching in Everyday Life, he also expresses the concern that the everyday, ethnogeography approach may fail to teach a geographic vocabulary (concepts, objects, processes). Two assumptions underlie this concern: that a focus on social theory somehow precludes a focus on spatial theory, and that the purpose of anchoring geographic teaching in everyday life is to formalise children's 'naïve' geographies by reference to an academic spatial framework. In some respects, the argument that a focus on the everyday might fail to provide children with a clear conceptual framework is a real danger and one of which I am mindful. For me geography has never made sense as a 'writing the earth' discipline and spatial techniques and understanding should be at the heart of any geographical paradigm, including ethnogeography. However, I am also wary of taking a predominantly cognitive approach to developing understanding. I personally would therefore also want to see the spatial dimension taught within a broader framework of concepts that help pupils develop as future global citizens who are able to contribute towards a just and sustainable future for the planet, as in the example from Cook above. An affective and moral stance on what, for example, Geographic Information Systems can be used for is essential. All these things can be taught at a level that young children understand thus providing a sound foundation on which to tackle the more complex understandings later on. This is what I am striving for.

The second assumption is that valid geographical knowledge cannot be generated from learners and that it is only useful to elicit this 'naïve' knowledge in order to correct the misconceptions that are revealed. This is not what ethnogeography is about. Liberatory education does not believe in replacing one discourse with another; it seeks to give voice to the suppressed and then to create a dialogue with academic voices with the aim of co-constructing new knowledge. As Frankenstein and Powell explain, learning is a social process,

> where gaining existing knowledge and producing new knowledge are 'two moments in the same cycle' (Freire 1982) ... Knowledge, therefore, is a negotiated product emerging from the interaction of human consciousness and reality; it is produced as we, individually and collectively, search and try to make sense of our world. (1994, p. 2)

An attempt to represent what an ongoing dialogue between children's geographies and academic geographies might look like in the context of a spiral curriculum (after Bruner 1960) is shown in Figure 3.

> We begin with the hypothesis that any subject can be taught effectively in some intellectually honest form to any child at any stage of development. (Bruner 1960, p. 33)

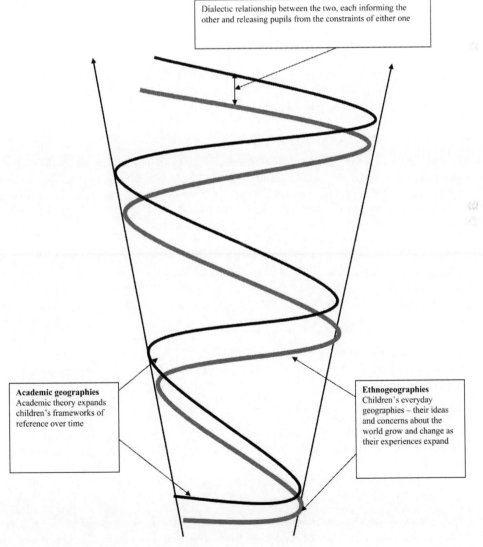

Figure 3. Ethnogeography and the spiral curriculam.

Here children's geographies, and their growing interests and concerns about the world, form the basis of a curriculum which would, through the skills of the teacher, be informed by and inform the academic frameworks of which Golledge speaks. The nature of this dialectic relationship would deepen and broaden as children's daily experiences expanded (shown by the direction of the arrows in Figure 3). The ethnogeographies would ensure that the curriculum was relevant to children's environments and culture, while the academic geographies would provide a conceptual framework that would enable children to make sense of their cultural and environmental experiences as geographers.

Ways forward?

This article has argued that Geography, as it is conceptualised in the English National Curriculum, does not connect to either primary school pupils or their teachers. Neither primary children's nor their primary teachers' (the latter of whom are usually non-geographers) personal and everyday geographies appear to represented in the formal school curriculum. Therefore a proposal has been made for a new paradigm for primary geography: Ethnogeography. This proposal parallels work on ethnomathematics, which provides a political agenda to the study of maths and itself draws from Paulo Freire's politicization and consciousness raising through adult literacy. Drawing on the findings of a recent research project, a case has been argued for ethnogeography and the implications for primary Initial Teacher Education courses, learners and the curriculum in primary schools and have been considered.

Thoughts about how to take the ideas forward are under consideration, but some of the implications for primary geography policy, practice and research are:

- The need to move away from a curriculum based on a content that is centrally prescribed to one that is based on a dialectic relationship between children's geographies and the key ideas/ concepts of academic geographies, mediated by primary teachers. What those key ideas might be could be developed from the key concepts outlined in the new Key Stage 3 curriculum for England (QCA 2007) and the key concepts as defined by the Geographical Association in the Action Plan for Geography (GA 2008).
- The need for an awareness of Children's Geographies research and methodologies by the teaching profession, with implications for Initial and In-service training.
- Government policy that allocates more time to geography in Initial Teacher Training courses (and by implication reduces over-emphasis on literacy and numeracy), and training that focuses on a combination of children's personal geographies and ethnogeography as described in this article.
- Continued funding for the Action Plan for Geography to continue work begun at with In-service teachers through the focus on, for example, Curriculum Making and Living Geography courses.

In terms of research, this implies a focus on:

- How to integrate children's geographies research into Initial and In-service Training courses.
- Investigating the impact of these courses on teachers' and children's learning in primary geography.
- Research, perhaps based on Action Research methodology, into the role of teachers and pupils as co-constructors of their geography curricula.

The last 2 years has seen the beginnings of a resurgence in the status of geography in England. The aim of the Action Plan for Geography has been 'to help young people become confident in their learning, informed about the world around them, and responsible, productive, active citizens' (GA 2008). It is the contention of this article that the above lists provide an agenda for action that could contribute to this aim.

Acknowledgements

The author would like to thank Dr Stephen Bigger for his comments on earlier drafts of the article, and the extremely helpful observations and recommendations of the two reviewers.

Notes

1. The General Teaching Council's Research of the Month, May 2006 (www.gtce.org.uk) contained a case study 'Development of pupils division strategies' which shows how young children (Year 5, 9–10 year olds) experienced less success when they tried to use a formal mathematical equation to solve division problems than when they used their own informal methods.
2. Gerdes (1998) provides examples of ethnomathematics in the context of working with adult learners in Mozambique. The mathematics that existed in their everyday lives through basket weaving, pottery making and house building were used as the basis for developing mathematical theorems. However, Boaler (1993) warns that 'culture' in ethnomathematics should not be narrowly interpreted. 'Race is not a proxy for culture and "ethno" in ethnomathematics is not a proxy for ethnic' (Gilmer 2001, p. 5). Gilmer goes on to give an example of mathematics in African American hairstyles, a brief overview of which can be found at www.math.buffalo.edu/mad/special/gilmer-gloria_HAIRSTYLES.html. What is liberating in these examples is the realization of the learners that they are mathematical and that the link between culture and mathematics can enhance their learning in relevant and meaningful ways.

References

Alexander, R., 2006. Alternative vision for primary children? *In*: *TES Platform*, October 13th, 2006.

Bale, J., 1987. *Geography in the primary school*. London: Routledge and Kegan Paul.

Barratt Hacking, E., 1996. Novice teachers and their geographical persuasions. *Journal of International Research in Geographical and Environmental Education*, 5 (1), 77–86.

Barrett, S.A., 1908. *The ethno-geography of the Pomo and neighboring Indians*, Vol. 6. CA: University of California Publications in American Archaeology and Ethnology.

BBC, 2007. The Today Programme: guest editors the geographers. Programme broadcast 01/01/07.

Bell, D., 2004. The value and importance of geography. *Primary Geographer*, 56, 4–5.

Boaler, J., 1993. The role of contexts in the mathematics classroom: do they make mathematics more real? *For the Learning of Mathematics*, 13 (2), 12–17.

Bruner, J., 1960. *The process of education*. Cambridge, MA: Harvard University Press.

Calderhead, J. and Shorrock, S., 1997. *Understanding teacher education*. London: Falmer Press.

Catling, S., 2003. Curriculum contested: primary geography and social justice. *Geography*, 88 (3), 164–210.

Catling, S., 2005. Children's personal geographies and the English primary school curriculum. *Children's Geographies*, 3 (3), 325–344.

Catling, S., 2006. Learning to teach primary geography in 10.5 hours. *IGU CGE Symposium*, Brisbane, Australia.

Catling, S. and Martin, F., 2004. *Researching primary geography*. London: Register of Research in Primary Geography.

Catling, S. and Taylor, L., 2006. Thinking about geographical significance. *Primary Geographer*, 61, 35–37.

Catling, S., Bowles, R., Halocha, J., Martin, F. and Rawlinson, S., 2004, unpublished. *Monitoring primary geography: 2003/04: a report for the QCA Geography Officers*. Oxford: Oxford Brookes University/QCA.

Cook, I., Montamedi, M. and Williams, A., 2006. Stuff geography. *Primary Geographer*, 61, 38–39.

DfEE/QCA, 1999. *The national curriculum for England*. London: DFEE.

D'Ambrosio, U., 1985. Ethnomathematics and its place in the history and pedagogy of mathematics. *For the Learning of Mathematics*, 5 (1), 44–48.

Ellis, B., 2003. Constructing a value map: a rejoinder. *Geography*, 88 (3), 234–235.

Frankenstein, M. and Powell, A., 1994. Toward liberatory mathematics: Paulo Freire's epistemology and ethnomathematics. *In*: P.L. McLaren and C. Lankshear, eds. *Politics of liberation: paths from Freire*. London and New York: Routledge, 74–99.

Freire, P., 1972. *Pedagogy of the oppressed*. Harmondsworth: Penguin.

Geographical Association, 2008. Action plan for geography. Available from: www.geography.org.uk/news/actionplanforgeography [Accessed 18.01.08].

Gerdes, P., 1998. On culture and mathematics teacher education. *Journal of Mathematics Teacher Education*, 1, 33–53.

Giddens, A., 2001. *Sociology*. 4th ed. Cambridge: Polity.

Gilmer, G., 2001. Ethnomathematics: a promising approach for developing mathematical knowledge among African American women. *In*: J. Jacobs, J. Becker and G. Gilmer, eds. *Changing the faces of mathematics: perspectives on gender*. US: National Council of Teachers of Mathematics.

Golledge, R., 2006. Geography and everyday life (again!). *Directions Magazine*, online journal available from: www. directionsmag.com [Accessed 24.10.06].

Grimwade, K., Jackson, E., Reid, A. and Smith, M., 2000. *Geography and the new agenda: citizenship, PSHE and sustainable development in the primary curriculum*. Sheffield: Geographical Association.

Hart, R., 1997. *Children's participation: the theory and practice of involving young citizens in community development and environmental care*. London and New York: Earthscan/Unicef.

Hopwood, N., 2006. Pupils' conceptions of geography: issues for debate, *Paper presented at the British Sub-Committee of the International Geographical Union, Commission on Geographical Education*, University of London, Annual Research Forum 21st October 2006, Institute of Education.

IRGEE, 2005. Forum: children's voices: younger children versus pedagogy. *International Research in Geographcial and Environmental Education*, 14 (4), 295–371.

Martin, F., 2005. *An analysis of PGCE primary students' conceptions of geography, education and knowledge and the relationship between these and their development as teachers of primary geography*. Ph.D Thesis, University of Coventry.

Martin, F, 2006a. Everyday geography. *Primary Geographer*, 61, 4–7.

Martin, F., 2006b. Knowledge bases for effective teaching: beginning teachers' development as teacher of primary geography. *In*: D. Schmeink, ed. *Research on learning and teaching in primary geography*. Karlsruhe: Pädagogische Hochschule Karlsruhe, 149–184.

Martin, F., 2006c. *Teaching geography in primary schools: learning to live in the world*. Cambridge: Chris Kington Publishing.

Matthews, H., 2003. Children and regeneration: setting an agenda for community participation and integration. *Children & Society*, 17 (4), 264–276.

Ofsted, 2004. *Ofsted Primary Geography Report 2003/04*. London: HMSO.

Ofsted, 2008. *Geography in Schools: Changing Practice*. London: HMSO.

Powell, A.B. and Frankenstein, M., 1997. *Ethnomathematics – challenging Eurocentrism in mathematics education*. Albany, NY: State University of New York Press.

QCA, 2007. *Geography programme of study for key stage 3 and attainment target*. London: Qualifications and Curriculum Authority.

Rawling, E., 2001. *Changing the subject. The impact of national policy on school geography 1980–2000*. Sheffield: Geographical Association.

Roberts, M., 2003. *Learning through enquiry*. Sheffield: Geographical Association.

Ross, N., 2005. Children's space. *International Geographical and Environmental Education*, 14 (4), 336–341.

Shimkin, D.B., 1947. *Wind River Shoshone ethnogeography*. CA: University of California Coyote Press facsimile reprint.

Standish, A., 2003. Constructing a value map. *Geography*, 88 (2), 149–151.

The Primary Review, 2007. Available from: www.primaryreview.org.uk/

Valentine, G., 2004. *Public space and the culture of childhood*. Hampshire: Ashgate.

Whittle, J., 2006. Journey sticks and affective mapping. *Primary Geographer*, 59, 11–13.

Woodhouse, S., 2006. 'But I didn't think that was geography!'. *Primary Geographer*, 60, 28–29.

More than just core knowledge? A framework for effective and high-quality primary geography

Paula Owens

Primary Curriculum Development and Quality Mark Leader, The Geographical Association, Sheffield, UK

The Primary Geography Quality Mark (PGQM) is a support mechanism for the development of successful school geography, which uses evaluative criteria to help subject leaders plan and lead the subject. Evidence from schools that have used the PGQM shows that whilst core knowledge is a necessary ingredient of geography, the knowledge and skill of teachers as 'curriculum-makers' is essential in blending other aspects of this dynamic subject together to ensure successful geographical experiences. Furthermore, schools find such a framework a powerful and enabling tool for curriculum development.

Introduction

The factors underpinning effective primary geography might be identified differently according to individual perspectives, cultural connotations, political imperatives or a mixture of all three. Catling and Willy (2009) identify well-taught geography as being exciting and enjoyable and drawing on a variety of teaching approaches and topical issues. They urge that teaching and content should pay attention to the needs and interests of children. Martin (2008) refers to the liberating notion of 'ethnogeographies' as an approach that helps to translate and extend the subject by legitimising everyday experiences as geographical knowledge, whilst Morgan (2011) recognises the tensions that exist between conceptions of place and notions of rigorous geography. Hicks (2006) urged that geography should have a temporal as well as a spatial element to give it a real futures perspective and validity. Scoffham (2013, 9), whilst emphasising the central importance of concepts and skills, reminds us that 'geography is an extensive area of study with many branches'. This mix of perspectives conveys an impression of rich, contested meanings to be made of and through geography, implying a range of knowledge and skills as well as emotional experiences.

England's coalition government places a high value on 'core knowledge' (DfE 2010). The proposed geography curriculum for primary and Key Stage-3 pupils is certainly very knowledge focused (DfE 2013). However, the Office for Standards in Education (Ofsted 2013a), which inspects geography education in schools alongside other subjects, has subject-specific grade descriptors for 'outstanding' geography which include references to knowledge, skills, attitudes and values. In the section on achievement, for example, it notes that pupils should: have a very good knowledge of where places are and what they are like; understand how to make connections between people and places at different scales and how human and physical environments are interrelated; be able to carry out increasingly complicated enquiry and have highly developed fieldwork and other skills. Ofsted's definition of outstanding geography also requires that pupils are able to work independently and collegially with a sense of passion and commitment towards the subject and real curiosity. Pupils need to be able to express opinions well rooted in very good knowledge and understanding about contemporary events and issues. The emphasis in the Ofsted (2013a) criteria on knowledge, skills and values and attitudes underpins an argument for high-quality geography being about more than a collection of static facts.

Geography in England

Geography in England has been undergoing a slight renaissance over the last few years, albeit in a rather fragmented and stilted fashion. A survey by Catling et al. (2007) investigated the state of geography in primary schools by interviewing subject leaders and drawing on subject reports from Ofsted. In this thorough and detailed report, these authors found that despite many negative findings about the (then) current state of the subject, it had improved in primary schools since the 1980s and that this was due in part to the introduction of the National Curriculum in 1991 which ensured that all schools were doing some geography.

A decade on from the introduction of the National Curriculum in England, evidence showed that although there was much more work needed to improve the subject in primary schools, some progress has been made in school standards in primary geography (Catling et al. 2007). By 2002 about a third of the primary geography teaching viewed in England was reported as good or better and pupils' attainment in a quarter of schools was deemed good or better when evaluated using the Ofsted criteria (Ofsted 2003). Recommendations for strengthening primary geography included ensuring schools engaged with more, and high quality, fieldwork, securing teachers' subject knowledge, and targeting support for subject leaders that would help them create strategies for the development of the subject (Catling et al. 2007).

A subject report from Ofsted in 2008 warned that there was still much to address in terms of pupil underachievement, poor management and declining provision in geography (Ofsted 2008). Teachers' lack of subject knowledge was again cited as a factor in this decline:

> In primary schools, this [unsatisfactory teaching and learning] is associated with teachers' weak knowledge of geography, their lack of confidence to teach it and insufficient training to support them. (Ofsted 2008, 2)

It is however worth noting that this report (Ofsted 2008) drew on visits and examples of practice gathered some two to three years earlier than the publication date and as such did not take account of any progress made through the 'Action Plan for Geography' (APG), a two-year project funded in England by the Department for Children, Schools and Families (GA 2011a). The APG commenced in September 2006 as a result of a perceived need to raise standards in geography. It was led jointly by the Geographical Association (GA) and Royal Geographical Society and in 2008, fuelled by evidence confirming its effectiveness, received funding for a further three years (GA 2011a).

The APG had a considerable and successful effect on the teaching and learning of geography at both primary and secondary levels and contributed in part to the ongoing, albeit slow, improvement of the subject in schools (GA 2011a). A survey of 91 primary schools by Ofsted between 2007 and 2010 found that achievement in half the visited schools was at least good and that the best geography was usually seen in schools which had participated in the APG programme (Ofsted 2011).

One of the attributed reasons for success of the APG was that is supported teachers in providing lively, current, relevant yet rigorous geography by developing both teachers' subject knowledge and their skill as curriculum-makers (GA 2011a). One way in which the APG achieved this was through a mix of face to face, online and mentored support over a period of time. This effective model of continual professional development (CPD) was used as the basis for the 'Young Geographers' project that enabled teachers to plan using everyday aspects of children's lives through fieldwork to develop geographical understanding (Catling 2008, 2011).

Therefore, by 2011, there was some evidence of improvement, by Ofsted standards, in the teaching and learning of primary geography in schools in England and some of this was linked to the work of the APG. However, Ofsted (2011) noted a polarisation between a growing number of good or better schools and those graded as unsatisfactory. It noted that in up to ten percent of primary schools geography was either negligible or non-existent (Ofsted 2011). While some schools were developing their geography standards, others were ignoring the subject or teaching so selectively as to provide a meaningless sense of the subject for their children. Ofsted remained clear about the need for improvement, not only by bringing geography back in but also by raising the quality of its teaching across the board, since little geography was outstanding. Some of the key recommendations identified by Ofsted for improving primary geography were that schools should:

- focus on developing pupils' core knowledge and a sense of place;
- ensure that geographical elements are clearly identifiable within topic-based work and that the curricular requirements are properly covered;
- maximise learning and motivation through more fieldwork opportunities;
- make the most of new technology;
- provide more opportunities for writing and focused reading;
- enable pupils to recognise their contribution to and responsibilities for people and places at different scales; and
- provide subject-specific support and professional development opportunities for teachers (Ofsted 2011).

The continued need for rigour is underlined by reference to ensuring that elements of geography are clearly identifiable within topic or creative curriculum work and, indeed, that the basic requirements of the curriculum are actually being covered. These areas for development identified by Ofsted were subsequently strengthened in the revisions of the Primary Geography Quality Mark (PGQM) framework. It is worth noting that both pupils' core knowledge and their sense of place required improvement, the latter phrase associated with sensory, dynamic interpretations requiring the application of geographical skills. Core knowledge and a sense of place might be thought of as a continuum where one extreme is represented by static knowledge and the other by a more esoteric understanding and interpretation of place as multi-faceted and open to interpretation.

Underlying reasons for the decline of geography

Although some of the blame for the decline of geography in England is attributed to teachers' poor subject knowledge (Ofsted 2008), the underlying mechanisms arguably go much deeper and relate to what Alexander (2009) identifies as a dual curriculum. The drive for improved standards in mathematics and English and the dominance of the Literacy and Numeracy Strategies have commandeered the curriculum since their introduction in 1998. This is a situation not peculiar to England. For example, in the USA, Leming, Ellington, and Schug (2006) found that social studies and associated subjects such as geography and history were considered less important in elementary and middle schools when compared to other school subjects such as mathematics and reading.

The pressure to perform well in certain politically favoured subjects has resulted in some schools eschewing a genuinely broad and balanced curriculum. Hence is it hardly surprising that many schools have not had geography on their list of priorities. Neither is it surprising that Initial Teacher Education has been shaped by a political imperative to ensure that emerging teachers are well versed in delivering Literacy and Numeracy strategies effectively rather than providing detailed guidance and expertise in teaching geography (DfE 2012).

The educational climate in recent years in England has not boded well for any foundation subjects, and geography seems to have been particularly affected. Evidence suggests that many teachers have low expectations of what primary-aged children can do in geography and this may well be connected with factors such as the low ranking of the subject within the school curriculum, the lack of time allocated for teaching and the limited subject knowledge of many teachers, especially about the localities in which they teach Catling (2011).

Therefore, a combination of factors has fuelled a spiral of decline in primary geography in terms of both provision and pupil attainment, mitigated to some extent by the intense support offered through the APG between 2006 and 2011 which has been in part responsible for a slight improvement in the subject's fortunes. The GA also produced the PGQM to help bolster the work of the APG and to articulate to teachers what they could do to strengthen the subject. The next section explains what this framework is and how it operates.

The primary geography quality mark framework

The PGQM is a framework of self-assessment designed to help subject leaders evaluate and develop strategies for improving the geography in their school. In its first, pilot year (2005–2006) nineteen primary schools trialled the process and were accredited by the GA with Bronze, Silver or Gold awards according to the best match between their application and the banded criteria. The 'Bronze' level recognises that lively and enjoyable geography is happening in the school; 'Silver' recognises excellence across the school and 'Gold' recognises excellence that is embedded and shared with the community beyond the school. Figure 1 shows the different levels of the Award and relates this to the influence and impact of the subject leader. Ofsted (2008, 2011) notes the importance of the role of the subject leader in enhancing the quality of geography teaching, learning and achievement in primary schools.

Feedback from schools

Feedback from schools about the benefits of this evaluative process are positive and varied, for instance: citing that the PGQM had aided the implementation of a 'creative curriculum'; improved the quality of boys' writing and helped to embed environmental and sustainability issues (North 2007).

Figure 1.   PGQM levels: your influence as a subject leader.

The self-evaluation audit toolkit, linked to the Ofsted Self-Evaluation Framework, has helped many geography subject leaders in the PGQM schools to lead the way when it comes to review-ing their subject within the curriculum. In one Gold Award primary school, the deputy head also used the self-evaluation tool as a model for the review for other subjects within the school. (North 2007, 46)

Since its conception, the PGQM has been on a journey of continual evolution, using feedback from users and other members of the geography community, as well as changes to the Ofsted framework, to tweak its criteria. In this sense it is a tool that is sen-sitive to temporal, education contexts yet robust in essential design. As it has begun to be adopted more widely beyond schools in England, it has also become more sensitive to spatial contexts. There are schools in Wales now with both the primary and secondary Quality Marks as well as some British Schools overseas.

At the time of writing, the PGQM framework is currently being reassessed in light of important contextual influences. One is the recently revised Ofsted (2013a) framework for schools in England which now has four categories for inspection: Achievement, Teach-ing, Behaviour and Leadership. The effect on the current framework is chiefly to reorganise the existing highly regarded criteria to be a better fit with the new categories and thus enable teachers and head teachers to find evidence more effectively that will support subject inspections as well as contributing to whole school inspections. There has been little need to change most of the key criteria, and they have so far survived scrutiny. It is envi-saged that the retention of the core messages of the framework will strengthen perceptions about high-quality geography as teachers interpret the demands of the new curriculum (DfE 2013).

Underpinning criteria

The PGQM framework is underpinned by key questions that probe achievement, teaching, leadership, curriculum and soon behaviour as well. For instance, one deceptively simple question in the current framework is: 'What is geography like in your school?' The full gui-dance and nuanced framework contains sub-questions requiring responses that evidence high attainment and pupil enjoyment and which convey the richness and challenge of the school's provision. Subject leaders are encouraged to give as full a picture as possible through a selection of images, children's voice, annotated pupil work, planning and other relevant documentation relating to policies, lesson observations and CPD provision. As the documentation states:

> This section asks you to look at what the learning environment looks like and what you are trying to provide for children through your geography curriculum and how your pupils feel about it. You will need to communicate the excitement and richness of the geography that your children experience. (GA 2013, 5)

The framework stresses an evaluative approach so that practitioners in schools ask themselves: 'What do we do? Why do we do it?' and, most importantly, 'How do we know it is effective for our learners? What impact is it having on learners?'

Figure 2 lists the core criteria that form the backbone of the framework and which give an overview of its content. In the full framework, there is a breakdown of what these criteria look like at the granular level of Bronze, Silver and Gold practices. Schools can use the framework either just to evaluate their geography provision and plan for improvement, or they may also wish to apply for the award, an evidence-gathering process which usually takes between 12 and 18 months. An award lasts three years and schools should then re-apply to maintain their accreditation, either at the current level or by applying for a higher level.

Approximately 50–60 primary and a similar number of secondary schools apply each year to gain accreditation. Many return for re-accreditation. Some schools for instance have worked their way from Bronze to Silver to Gold. Others have gone straight in to apply for Silver, or even for Gold, though the latter approach is a less likely one. Since many subject leaders use the framework to help develop their geography provision internally but choose not actually to go for the Award, its true impact is difficult to measure.

Evidencing criteria

The portfolio of evidence submitted by subject leaders for the PGQM has to 'tell the story' of geography in their school and evidence the criteria. More particularly the evidence has to explain, rather than describe, what is being done. It has to show why and how strategies are effective, how subject leaders know this and, most importantly, what impact it is having on learners.

A National Moderation Team of approximately 10 members evaluates the submissions each year, meeting to compare, discuss and moderate to ensure quality control. The team is a deliberate mix of classroom practitioners, school leaders and academics; all are experienced educators with some degree of expertise in primary geography as well as current or recent school experience. Each moderator has several applications to evaluate on their own or with a partner before coming together to review all applications made in that year.

The PGQM annual moderation process offers a chance to compare individuals' assessments, review those identified as borderline and make any necessary adjustments before the final feedback is returned to schools. A borderline application might be reviewed by as many as three moderators before a decision is reached. Most Gold applicant schools are visited by a moderator (an occasional Bronze or Silver applicant school may be visited too) and feedback from the visit is shared with the team. Applications can be upgraded or downgraded following moderation and this happens to a small number of schools in most years.

The process of moderation is valued as CPD by all of the team as it requires careful analysis of information, fine-tuned judgements and collaborative appraisal. One flaw in the system is that it is too costly to visit all schools, hence based on virtual evidence moderation has to be rigorous. As a result, schools are most likely to be judged solely on the

Key Question	Key Criteria*
1. Achievement How effective is geography in your school?	*Achievement is high and pupils make good progress when considered in relation to age, ability and prior experience.* • Children have good subject knowledge of where places are and what they are like. • Fieldwork, map -work, active enquiry learning and the use of ICT impacts on the way children learn geography. • Children's positive attitudes towards, and enjoyment of, geography support progress.
2. Teaching How effective is the teaching of geography in your school?	*Teachers have good subject knowledge and are up to date with current events and thinking.* • The teaching of core geographical knowledge underpins children's learning about the world. • Teachers use and apply their skill as curriculum - makers; geography challenges and engages children through effective enquiry and purposeful content. • Teachers have high expectations: assessment is valued as an essential tool in planning and monitoring pupils' progress. They model enthusiasm and regard for the subject.
3. Behaviour and Relationships How well does geography support positive behaviour and relationships?	*Geography teaching and learning promotes positive feelings, behaviours and relationships* • Geographical experiences promote a better understanding of safe and positive behaviours. • Through geography, children value their own and other's experiences in the world and have positive attitudes towards difference and diversity. • Children develop self -esteem through genuine opportunities for participation
4. Leadership How effective is subject leadership and management?	*Strong leadership ensures a shared vision, careful monitoring and high quality provision across the school.* • A vision for geography supports how it is taught, informs policy and guides the curriculum. • The subject leader has clear and effective development targets to ensure teaching and learning provision across the school impacts on pupils' achievement and enjoyment. • Geography supports other curricular areas /whole school ethos and enjoyment of learners.

Figure 2. The revised draft PGQM framework (overview of sections).

evidence they select to illustrate the quality of geography in their school. Schools are warned about this and online guidance supports subject leaders in putting together an effective portfolio for their school. CPD courses also support this process, arguably helping subject leaders to lead, evidence and reflect on what they do and why more successfully.

Why do schools bother with the PGQM framework as a tool for accreditation when they can use the Ofsted framework? It is true that they use the same headings and have some similarities in content yet the PGQM is more detailed and underpinned by supportive structures and resources that help subject leaders identify gaps in provision and plan for improvement.

Defining geography

Geography is a subject that has been described as having an ambition that is 'absurdly vast' (Bonnett 2008, 9) and hence, unsurprisingly perhaps, it sometimes struggles with identity issues. It is a subject that can be difficult to define and which is equally at ease with the humanities or the sciences. In addition, there is often a misconceived tension in curriculum subjects between knowledge and skills, which Alexander (2010) refers to as one of many misleading and false dichotomies in education.

The new geography curriculum in England (DfE 2013) focuses on knowledge that children ought to know by given stages in primary education. Although this document is identified as a skeletal curriculum to which local interpretation can be added, it cements an emphasis on the perceived value of 'core knowledge' which emerged with the Government White Paper on Education (DfE 2010). The anticipation of a greater knowledge focus in the new National Curriculum in England has caused some distracting discourse about the merits of a skills-led versus a knowledge-led geography curriculum.

Arguably the need is to develop knowledge and skills in tandem, alongside values and attitudes. This view is supported by the Ofsted criteria for outstanding geography, as noted above, and resonates completely with the thinking behind the PGQM criteria. However, while the PGQM framework requires evidence for all of these components it acknowledges that with a subject as broad as geography, schools need to develop a vision of what the subject is and what it can do for them and their learners. This vision is, in the best schools, shared with all stakeholders and the wider community and comes into being through a genuinely participative approach.

In schools where geography is done well, it has a clear and shared identity. Pupils and staff express their views as to what geography is about, which aspects they enjoy teaching and learning about and in which parts of the subject they feel they do well. Confident subject leaders encourage teachers and pupils to critique and contribute to curriculum content and design. Many of the high-achieving PGQM applications evidence pupils' questionnaires and 'pupil voice' about geography (Figure 3).

Core knowledge

The idea of core knowledge in a curriculum implies a central grounding of information or vital knowledge that is essential. Lambert (GA 2011b) states that it is helpful to think of three kinds of geographical knowledge and that each needs to be taught together; they are mutually interdependent.

- *Core knowledge*. This may be thought of as extensive world knowledge, in itself fairly superficial yet enabling. Examples of this might be: knowing the names of the continents and being able to locate them using an atlas, globe or map; naming the capital cities of certain countries or knowing the name of the longest river in England.
- *Content knowledge*. This is sometimes referred to as concepts or generalisations, and the key to developing understanding. It may also be thought of as more intensive world knowledge, taking in the realm of processes, different perspectives and values. An example might be the concepts of place and scale which requires a synthesis of different types of knowledge in explaining for instance where Uluru is, what it is like and why, and the meanings attributed to it by different cultural groups.
- *Procedural knowledge*. Thinking geographically is a distinctive procedure; high-quality geographical enquiry which might include decision-making or problem-

Year	Children's definitions of geography
2	"Geography is all about the world" "Geography is fun and exciting and you learn about other countries" "It's fun to learn new things and some countries are very different"
3	"It's fun because I have to think" "It's fun because you are active and it has fun things to learn"
4	"It's learning about the world, the different countries and climates" "It's about the Earth and how it's changing" "I find it interesting because I could learn how to make the world a better place" "It's fun to learn about the Earth and the atmosphere because you never know what you're going to find out next" "It's good to know what's happening around the world at different times"
5	"Geography is about places, map reading, countries, cultures, local areas etc." "Geography is about the environment" "Geography is about the world we live in" "Geography is about the world and countries and cultures" "Geography is about looking at where things are and looking at characteristics"
6	"Geography is about the environment and getting out and about" "Geography is learning about the world, how it works and looking after it" "You get to learn about the earth, different countries and cultures, also what the world might be like in the future and how it will affect us" "Geography is the study of people and places" "Geography is people and their relationship with countries" "Geography is the study of places around the world and it is also the natural things such as rivers" "It's interesting because it might be us that's making global warming and we want to know what's going on around the world so we can help"

Figure 3. Children's definitions of geography.

solving scenarios such as where to site an owl box in the school grounds, taking into account factors such as neighbours, microclimate, habitat and access. It includes a certain way of thinking about the world that may be relational and/or holistic and it recognises the significance of place and unique context.

Martin and Owens (2011) argue that developing core knowledge in a context devoid of understanding is worthless. In an example from Ofsted (2011) pupils had been learning about aspects of Kenyan life but were unable to locate Kenya on a map or name any of its border countries. This prevented these pupils from making connections between description and location and being able to offer explanations about how and why location influenced climate, for example. A description of what a 'place' is like might be detailed and rich but unless there is a spatial context and a sense of scale, is it truly geography? Such tensions between notions of place and geography and how they relate can be further explored through Morgan (2011).

The PGQM framework requires schools to evidence how they are underpinning learning with core knowledge but does not stipulate what this core knowledge should be. It is for schools and subject leaders to interpret their statutory curriculum accordingly and make selections where appropriate. As one subject leader reported, choosing what to focus on as essential was challenging:

This has been one of my biggest challenges over the last 3 years as the core Geography provision can only ever cover a very limited number of localities, themes and issues. (Halterworth Primary School, Silver PGQM 2009, 7)

Some schools have been ensuring that children develop a greater body of knowledge by playing games and through enquiry-based research.

> Great emphasis is placed on geographical knowledge and every lesson begins with a fun starter to develop core geographic knowledge or skills. A range of different activities and games are used during the starters such as: 'maps from memory', European cities/countries loop cards, odd one out, picture reveals, Who wants to be a millionaire?, listening to sound clips from around the world and plotting on a map geographical features, Pictionary, snap, Taboo and the yearly Geography/History Week Quiz (Elmwood Junior School PGQM 2011, 6).

> Pupils' understanding of physical geography and knowledge about the world is also developed within topics. For example, pupils learn about river features and processes, coastal features and process, along with the appropriate vocabulary to describe these in the context of specific localities. Pupils develop this knowledge and understanding through research, watching videos, discussions, fieldwork, role-play, art and writing. (Elmwood Junior School, Silver PGQM 2011, 6)

Many school submissions evidence an emphasis on locational knowledge and on developing a sound geographical vocabulary.

> All children make full use of atlases, large maps, plans and ICT programs at varying levels, to develop their knowledge of the world around them. They enjoy locating places and geographical features on maps and particularly like to use 'multimap' and 'Google Earth' to find places they know or have visited. The children love the challenge of quizzes involving geographical research and are encouraged to use appropriate subject-specific vocabulary at all times. (Ingleby Mill Primary, Bronze PGQM 2011, 7)

> In the Junior School the children's exercise books have vocabulary lists, appropriate for each year, stuck in the front to reinforce the learning of geographical terminology. When marking, attention is given to correct use and spellings of geographical words. (Ryde Junior School, Gold PGQM 2012, 9)

These examples demonstrate different approaches to ensuring that core knowledge is taught in primary geography but, as previously argued, this is not enough. Hence, the PGQM framework invites schools to consider and evidence how they develop teaching and learning of core knowledge in purposeful contexts that also require content and procedural knowledge. The selection of content is one challenge for teachers, while blending knowledge skills and contexts is another.

Conceptual knowledge

Young (2008) has urged a return to a deeper consideration of the role of knowledge within the school tradition and how it translates into structures of curriculum policy and organisation.

> My assumption is that the acquisition of knowledge is the key purpose that distinguishes education ... from all other activities. It is for this reason that debates about knowledge are crucial; by this I do not mean specific knowledge contents, although they are important, but the concepts of knowledge that underpin curricula. (Young 2008, 81)

Whilst commending much of Young's thinking, Firth (2011, 151) warns that it raises very important questions, such as 'in what way is geographical knowledge powerful knowledge?' and 'How should such knowledge be organised within the curriculum?'

Space and place are two core concepts of core geography (Martin 2011) which blend locational and contextual thinking together, providing 'entry level' geographical experiences as well as more complex thinking. If just these two ideas are used together to frame questions for geographical teaching such as: why is this a good place to live? It is likely that the resultant learning experiences will contain some rigorous geographical thinking. Places can be described, compared and explained with regard to their locational setting. To some extent a regard for the central, overarching concepts of geography and the questions that underpin them can be a touchstone for ensuring rigour in geography planning no matter which particular national curriculum is being followed. Whilst acknowledging that 'attempts to define a 'core' for the discipline of geography is fraught with difficulties' Matthews and Herbert (2004, 377) agree that space and place are integral parts of core geography, the latter evoking and inspiring geographers through a range of personal meanings and attachments that can be made.

Other key geographical concepts include scale, human and physical processes, environmental interaction, sustainable development, cultural understanding and diversity. Blending in aspects of other key ideas to refocus the geographical lens aids more sophisticated thinking and analysis about the world, adding new layers of enquiry. To return to the example given earlier about understanding Uluru using concepts of space and place, one could add scale and ask how the significance of that place changes as one 'zooms' in further or 'zooms' out to a country or continent scale. Adding in the concept of sustainability might then elicit questions about the tourism trade, the revenue it brings in and the social tensions and environmental impacts that occur as a result. Bringing such ideas together to make sense of separate aspects of knowledge about the world is what geographers do.

Thinking geographically

Core geographical knowledge is not an end in itself, and 'geographical capability' requires much more (Catling and Willy 2009). It is an essential starting point and provides a kind of specialised 'vocabulary' that gives learners the ability to engage in beginning dialogues about the world, such as knowing place names. But the 'grammar' of the subject is also vital (GA 2009). If core knowledge is geography's vocabulary then the conceptual framework of geography is its grammar (GA 2012), and it is this that helps to put the vocabulary together in ways that make sense, that make relevant and useful connections. For instance, knowing that places such as Uluru can be defined not just in terms of static knowledge such as name and location but also in terms of user perspectives, the meaning that they bring to a place and how this impacts on what is place is like and might be in the future, requires, indeed is, 'thinking geographically' (GA 2012).

Personal and emotional aspects of geography

Martin (2004) likened views of geography to a continuum. At one end is knowledge and factual information whilst at the other are subjective, emotional and personal responses that are laden with value. This can be equated in a sense to the big ideas of 'space' and 'place', the former being defined in more functional terms and the latter in more multi-dimensional and contested terms. Standish (2008) has warned that we need to consider carefully how we negotiate exploring values in geography education as children need to learn facts rather than be indoctrinated by views and agendas. Whilst agreeing that educators ought to avoid indoctrination, it is the role of educators surely to allow learners full access to relevant information. Geography is messy in the sense that it deals with issues that often have opposing views. Arguably, it is impossible to ignore attitudes and values when studying geography as they influence how people think and act. In turn, how people think and act shapes the physical and human environments.

One of geography's basic tenets is that there is a reciprocal and ongoing dynamic between people, places and environments. Places are never value free but are contested by people or groups with conflicting views about how spaces should be used and who by. Understanding how different values underpin people's views and actions helps geographers to think more impartially about causes and consequences. This is a part of what Lambert and Owens (2013) call 'empathic geographies' and is a creative act. Engagement with this facet of geography helps to develop children's imaginations as they put themselves in others' 'shoes'.

> Year 5 considered happiness, of themselves and other children from around the world. Then they were introduced, via a story about a greedy king, to the Happy Planet Index. (Ryde Junior School, Gold PGQM 2012, 8)

Developing empathy as a skill enables children to build a sense of place and is as vital as core knowledge. We ought to remember that teaching is not value free and that children develop attitudes and values as a result of or despite the teaching and learning experiences that they engage with. Thus, we have a moral obligation to evaluate and openly discuss the choices people make and why.

Geographical skills

Subjects also require the application of skills, which may comprise generic as well as associated and specialised skills. For example, communication and collaboration are skills that you would expect to use across the entire curriculum, while graphicacy denotes a set of skills, such as interpreting maps, photographs and charts, associated with, but not unique to, geography. Within graphicacy, making and using maps is considered to be a specialised, geographical skill, as is fieldwork. Skills are tools of the trade that help unlock knowledge and which by definition need to be practised to be improved and refined.

> Field work, and first hand exploration continues to be central to the way children at Two Rivers learn and investigate geography. (Two Rivers Special School, Gold PGQM application 2012, 6)

In good geographical practice, children use enquiry and fieldwork skills as well as information technology and mapping skills to gather, analyse and evaluate information that is set within a purposeful context. They blend different types of knowledge and develop positive attitudes and values in a learning environment that values creativity as well as critical thinking, and teachers ensure that this happens through careful teaching.

Teachers as curriculum-makers

The mix of knowledge, skills, attitudes and values as well as the precise selection of content are dependent upon choices made by teachers and subject leaders. Curriculum-making happens when teachers draw on rigorous aspects of geography and their own knowledge of the subject, their knowledge of their pupils and their needs, and select content for learning that is purposeful and relevant and lively. Effective teachers blend different kinds of knowledge, skills, attitudes and values and ensure progression in breadth of learning as well as depth (Catling, forthcoming). Curriculum-making is more than just facilitating learning; it is about developing pupils' knowledge beyond their everyday experience (Lambert 2011). The act of curriculum-making requires teachers to have good subject knowledge.

Teachers also need permission to take risks, adapt and innovate. A good subject leader will collaborate, support and inspire teacher agency. PGQM submissions evidence in varying degrees how subject leaders are encouraging curriculum flexibility, deviation and innovation. These extracts are typical of what subject leaders are saying at Silver or Gold levels of the Award:

> Many new schemes of work have been written in school, often addressing some extremely complex and challenging issues (e.g. climate change through the Antarctica unit in Year 5), and this work is now beginning to embed into our broader Geography curriculum. ... I believe this has had a huge impact on the children's understanding of the relevance and purpose of the subject more broadly. (Halterworth Primary School, Gold PGQM application 2011, 12)

There is evidence of flexibility, where staff allow the curriculum to evolve and be relevant for their pupils.

> The Geography curriculum is evolving to embrace more local and global issues, to be more topical and relevant to children's lives and to offer the pupils the opportunities for direct contact with the outside world. (Orchard House School Silver, PGQM application 2011, 8)

As well as flexibility and adaptability, confident teachers are not afraid to rewrite completely their curriculum for their pupils if necessary.

> The curriculum expertise that is held within our school was highlighted by OFSTED in our outstanding report in 2009.
> The huge expertise that staff bring to bear on promoting learning ensures every pupil makes significant progress no matter how complex their learning difficulties may be.
> The challenges our sensory pupils face in accessing the geography curriculum or knowledge and understanding element in the early years has resulted in a team of staff in school writing a specific sensory curriculum to meet their needs and their way of learning, at the end of the academic year 2011. This was implemented in September 2011 and is currently under review. However early indications are that this new sensory curriculum is making an impact on their learning. (Two Rivers Special School, Gold PGQM application 2012, 5)

Curriculum-making is at the heart of successful geography because it involves teachers drawing on their subject knowledge to select content that is relevant for their children and setting, and which has relevance in the real world as well. In actively solving the questions, 'What should I teach, why and how?', curriculum-making can also evidence one of the hallmarks of creativity in curricular design.

Creativity

There are other insights into what capable teachers can do when given support to practice curriculum-making. As part of a project previously referred to as 'Young Geographers, a Living Geography project for Primary Schools' (Catling 2008, 2011, forthcoming), groups of primary teachers received mentoring support to develop new learning sequences that incorporated local fieldwork in contexts relevant to learners. This learning was creative in ways identified by the Roberts Report (2006), namely it was imaginative, original (to the learner), purposeful and valued. Whilst the planning for this project was cross-curricular, it was led by geography that had rigour at its heart. Retaining subject rigour is essential as otherwise the real value of learning can be lost or diluted. One way in which participants were helped to plan both creatively and with subject rigour was by thinking how they could include key geographical concepts such as place, space and scale.

Creativity is also about problem-solving, lateral thinking and hypothesising; and applies across the curriculum. Geography synergises the curriculum and as such can be a powerful lens through which to focus on high-quality learning. Ofsted (2013a, 2013b) identified some successful instances of the creative curriculum at work that were led by high-quality geography.

> Geography is given a high profile across the school and forms a large part of the creative curriculum. As you [the head teacher] stated, 'It's the glue that holds the curriculum together'. (Ofsted 2013b, 3)

> This example [of geography teaching and learning] shows … what can be achieved with creativity linked to good subject expertise. (Ofsted 2013c, 2)

Geography has a very real role to play within a truly creative curriculum not just because it is creative in its own right but because it offers topic work meaningful and relevant contexts for enquiry. The twin companion of creativity is critical thinking and within creative teaching and learning they work together when pupils have opportunities to apply their learning to original and valued contexts. Real, current world issues offer plenty of scope for this kind of activity.

Doing geography is a creative act (Lambert and Owens 2013), gives children a real voice (Catling 2009) and also provides an agenda of hope (Hicks 2006) that is often needed when thinking about possible and preferred futures through concepts such as sustainability. Although sustainability is a whole school issue, geography has teaching and learning content and strategies consistent with those needed for sustainable debate and learning (Owens 2011, 2012). Whilst Martin (2011) warns that sustainability is a complex concept with no easy answers, it has both a strong spatial component that helps to explain production and distribution of resources and has a central concern with human–environment interactions. Geography must, by its very nature, engage with sustainability to help explain and predict global changes and connections. In return, engagement with this concept offers the subject serious creative credibility.

Maintaining momentum

It is pertinent to conclude by reflecting on how, in the best examples of geography practice, teachers not only ensure that core knowledge is used effectively but use their own professional judgements and autonomy through curriculum-making to apply knowledge in creative contexts. The evidence from PGQM submissions is encouraging and often inspiring. It provides additional evidence to that of Ofsted geography subject inspections about how the subject is thriving in many schools thanks to reflective and committed practitioners and visionary subject leaders who can give that 'permission' to innovate. In the words of a Gold PGQM school subject leader:

> Geography continues to play a major part in the life of the school. It is very much in children's minds and thinking; I think we encapsulate the aims of 'Living Geography'. We aim to produce enjoyable and stimulating lessons and activities to engage our children. We take every opportunity, both in and out of lessons, to ensure current geographical issues are considered and that whole world knowledge is enhanced. We have built up our use of local examples and never use a text book example if we can use a local case study or visit. (Ryde Junior School, Gold PGQM application 2012, 14)

Frameworks such as that used for the evaluation of the PGQM are tools that help provide diagnostic and reflective mechanisms for professional conversations about the health of the subject. Such frameworks can be powerful and encourage conditions for what Durrant and Holden (2006) call new participative and shared decision-making models that facilitate the growth of learning communities.

Acknowledgements

Thank you to the schools, teachers and pupils who have provided annotated evidence as part of the PGQM application process.

References

Alexander, R. 2009. *Towards a New Primary Curriculum a Report from the Cambridge Primary Review, Part 2: The Future.* Cambridge: University of Cambridge. Accessed February 18, 2013. http://www.primaryreview.org.uk/search.php?q=Towards%20a%20new%20primary%20curriculum%3A%20a%20report%20for%20the%20Cambridge%20Primary%20Review%20Part%202

Alexander, R. ed. 2010. *Children, Their World, Their Education Final Report and Recommendations of the Cambridge Primary Review.* London: Routledge.

Bonnett, A. 2008. *What is Geography?* London: Sage.

Catling, S. 2008. *Young Geographers: A Living Geography Project for Primary Schools, an Evaluation Report.* Sheffield: Geographical Association.

Catling, S. 2009. "Creativity in Primary Geography." In *Creativity in Primary Education*, edited by A. Wilson, 189–198. Exeter: Learning Matters.

Catling, S. 2011. "Children's Geographies in the Primary School." In *Geography, Education and the Future*, edited by G. Butt, 15–28. London: Continuum.

Catling, S. Forthcoming. "English Teachers' Perspectives on Curriculum Making in Primary Geography." *The Curriculum Journal* 24 (3).

Catling, S., and T. Willy. 2009. *Achieving QTS: Teaching Primary Geography.* Exeter: Learning Matters.

Catling, S., R. Bowles, J. Halocha, F. Martin, and S. Rawlinson. 2007. "The State of Geography in English Primary Schools." *Geography* 92 (2): 118–136. (The original paper of which this article is a development can be found at. Accessed January 20, 2013. http://www.brookes.ac.uk/schools/education/rescon/THE%20STATE%20OF%20PRIMARY%20GEOGRAPHY%20IN%20ENGLAND.pdf)

Department for Education (DfE). 2010. *The Importance of Teaching: The Schools White Paper.* London: HMSO.

DfE. 2012. *Teachers' Standards.* London: HMSO.

DfE. 2013. *The National Curriculum in England: Framework Document for Consultation*, July 2013. London: DfE.

Durrant, J., and G. Holden. 2006. *Teachers Leading Change, Doing Research for School Improvement.* London: Sage.

Firth, R. 2011. "Debates about Knowledge and the Curriculum: Some Implications for Geography Education." In *Geography Education and the Future*, edited by G. Butt, 141–164. London: Continuum.

Geographical Association (GA). 2009. *A Different View: A Manifesto from the Geographical Association.* Sheffield: Geographical Association.

GA. 2011a. "The Action Plan for Geography: Final Report." Accessed November 12, 2012. http://www.geography.org.uk/download/GA_APGFinalReport.pdf

GA. 2011b. "Curriculum Proposals and Rationale." Accessed November 10, 2012. http://www.geography.org.uk/download/GA_GIGCCCurriculumProposals.pdf

GA. 2012. "Thinking Geographically." Accessed November 13, 2012. http://www.geography.org.uk/download/GA_GINCConsultation12ThinkingGeographically.pdf

GA. 2013. "The Primary Geography Quality Mark Framework." Accessed May 24, 2013. www.geography.org.uk/pgqm

Hicks, D. 2006. *Lessons for the Future: The Missing Dimension in Education*. Victoria, BC: Trafford Publishing.

Lambert, D. 2011. "Reviewing the Case for Geography and the "Knowledge Turn' in the English National Curriculum." *The Curriculum Journal* 22 (3): 243–264.

Lambert, D., and Owens, P. 2013. "Geography." In *Creativity in the Primary Curriculum*, edited by R. Jones and D. Wise, 98–115. London: Routledge.

Leming, J. S., L. Ellington, and M. Schug. 2006. "The State of Social Studies: A National Random Survey of Elementary and Middle School Social Studies Teachers." *Social Education* 70 (5): 322–327.

Matthews, J. A., and D. T. Herbert. 2004. "Unity in Geography: Prospects for the Discipline." In *Unifying Geography, Common Heritage, Shared Future*, edited by J. A. Matthew and D. T. Herbert, 369–393. London: Routledge.

Martin, F. 2004. "Creativity Through Geography." In *Unlocking Creativity*, edited by R. Fisher and M. Williams, 117–132. London: David Fulton.

Martin, F. 2008. "Ethnogeography: Towards Liberatory Geography Education." *Children's Geographies* 6 (4): 437–450.

Martin, F. 2011. "Global Ethics, Sustainability and Partnerships." In *Geography, Education and the Future*, edited by G. Butt, 206–224. London: Continuum.

Martin, F., and P. Owens. 2011. "Well What Do You Know? The Forthcoming Primary Review." *Primary Geography* 75: 28–29.

Morgan, A. 2011. "Place-Based Education versus Geography Education?." In *Geography, Education and the Future*, edited by G. Butt, 85–108. London: Continuum.

North, W. 2007. "Going for Gold: the Primary Geography Quality Mark." *Primary Geography*, no. 62: 46.

Ofsted. 2003. "Geography in Primary Schools: Ofsted Subject Reports Series." Accessed May 23, 2013. http://www.ofsted.gov.uk/resources/annual-report-200203-ofsted-subject-reports-primary

Ofsted. 2008. *Geography in Schools: Changing Practice*. London: HMSO.

Ofsted. 2011. *Geography: Learning to Make a World of Difference*. London: HMSO.

Ofsted. 2013a. "Geography Survey Visits." Accessed May 15, 2013. www.ofsted.gov.uk/resources/generic-grade-descriptors-and-supplementary-subject-specific-guidance-for-inspectors-making-judgements (click on geography file).

Ofsted. 2013b. "Ofsted 2012–13 Subject Survey Inspection Programme: Geography Hursthead Junior School, Cheadle." Accessed February 14, 2013. http://www.ofsted.gov.uk/inspection-reports/find-inspection-report/provider/ELS/106053. Inspection date 12 May 2012.

Ofsted. 2013c. "A Creative Curriculum to Support Outstanding Teaching and Learning in Geography: Corsham Primary School." Accessed January 18, 2013. www.ofsted.gov.uk/resources/good-practice-resource-creative-curriculum-support-outstanding-teaching-and-learning-geography-corsh

Owens, P. 2011. "Why Sustainability Has a Future." *Primary Geography*, no. 74: 7–9.

Owens, P. 2012. "Geography and Sustainability." In *Teaching Geography Creatively*, edited by S. Scoffham, 154–167. London: Routledge.

Roberts, P. 2006. *Nurturing Creativity in Young People A Report to Government to Inform Future Policy*. London: DCMS.

Scoffham, S. 2013. "Geography and Creativity: Making Connections." In *Teaching Geography Creatively*, edited by S. Scoffham, 1–13. London: Routledge.

Standish, A. 2008. "Keep 'Global Issues' Out of the Classroom." Accessed November 13, 2012. http://www.spiked-online.com/index.php?/site/article/6039/

Young, M. 2008. *Bringing Knowledge Back In*. London: Routledge.

Geography and creativity: developing joyful and imaginative learners

Stephen Scoffham

Faculty of Education, Canterbury Christ Church University, Canterbury, Kent, UK

Creativity is a complex and contested notion but is now widely recognised as a feature of learning across the curriculum. This article explores how primary geography teaching can be enriched by creative practice. It goes beyond simply suggesting imaginative ways to devise geography lessons, to outline a pedagogy which places children at the heart of learning. In doing so, it shifts attention away from the transmission of knowledge towards the process of learning. The failure of government reports to make the connection between geography and creativity, and the need for greater recognition of how creativity promotes learning through enjoyment, health and emotional well-being are highlighted.

Introduction

The formulation of a new primary curriculum presents great opportunities for teachers in England. The parameters for the discussions which have taken place over the last few years were set out in the Schools White Paper, *The Importance of Teaching* (DfE 2010), which the coalition government published soon after it took office in 2010. Here, it is clearly stated not only that the National Curriculum should set out the essential knowledge and understanding that all children should acquire but that teachers should decide how to teach this most effectively (DfE 2010, para 4.1). The discussion about core geographical knowledge and how it can be structured raises complex questions about curriculum design, geographical concepts and educational values (Scoffham 2011). The stakes are high and establishing what should constitute core knowledge in a balanced and forward-looking geography curriculum has occupied much of the energies of the Geographical Association and other interested groups.

The current focus on core knowledge has diverted attention away from pedagogy, yet in many ways divorcing curriculum content from curriculum delivery creates a false divide. Alexander (2010) reminds us that even if a curriculum looks inspiring on paper it will make little headway unless teachers can find ways of engaging children in learning. In other words, *how* children learn is as important as *what* they learn (Alexander 2010, 257). Immordino-Yang and Damasio (2007) make an even bolder claim. Drawing on a range of neurological evidence they conclude that emotional engagement is a critical force in learning and that emotions provide a subtle and pervasive influence on all human thought and action. Without some form of emotional engagement it seems that students are unlikely to learn anything at all.

This paper builds on these perspectives to set out a case for re-uniting curriculum content and pedagogy. It explores how harnessing creative responses can motivate children, enhance their well-being and promote lasting learning. It is argued that we need to go beyond devising novel and unusual approaches to lesson planning. Instead, we need a vision of primary geography teaching which respects the integrity and individuality of children as playful and imaginative learners and places them at the heart of schooling and education. This vision of creative pedagogy and practice has the potential to redefine the boundaries of the formal curriculum and encourage flexibility and innovation at a time when the curriculum, because of its focus on knowledge, runs the danger of becoming rigid or inert.

Perspectives on creativity

Creativity is a contested notion with multiple interpretations. Once regarded as being restricted to certain gifted individuals, it is now seen as a feature of learning across the curriculum. Theorists and commentators have highlighted a number of different elements. Koestler (1964) emphasises the links between creativity, surprise and humour and coined the term 'bi-sociation' to describe the creative spark which is generated when different modes of thought combine. De Bono (1999) argues that binary approaches are limited and instead proposed strategies such as the 'thinking hats' approach which allow people to pool their ideas. Craft (2001) directs attention to imagination and originality through the notion of 'possibility thinking'. Another distinction which has proved useful is between the kind of thinking which changes how we see the world ('big C' creativity) and everyday problem solving ('small c' creativity). This makes the point that we are all creative in humble and unassuming ways, even if we fail to recognise it.

One of the other features of creativity is that it involves being open to suggestions and making links between ideas. Lucas and Claxton (2011) offer a metaphor that helps to explain the value of reflective states of mind. They suggest that playful and dreamy states help us to generate new ideas because they correspond to a relatively flat mental landscape. In this mode, our thoughts tend to bleed into each another giving rise to unusual or unexpected associations. By contrast, more mountainous modes of thinking keep our ideas flowing down deep valleys and establish channels which have the advantage of allowing us to make quick judgements and decisions. Flat mental landscapes may be particularly conducive to creativity but switching between modes is also important as it enables us to get the best of both worlds.

Any attempt to characterise creativity raises questions about agency. Moran and John-Steiner (2003), for example, extend Vygotsky's theories of social constructivism to argue that creative thought is an on-going process which draws on our imagination and personal sense of meaning to generate public outcomes which can themselves be internalised in a further cycle of creativity. This approach recognises the role of social and cultural factors. It also suggests that creativity, rather than being exclusively vested in individuals, may also be seen as distributed amongst groups who generate new thinking by bouncing ideas between each other. Studies by Feldman (1999) and Rogoff (2003) add weight to this argument.

Viewing creativity as a process rather than a product means that it is also culturally relative. In recent times, Western European thinking has tended to emphasise and reward innovation and individual achievement. Eastern perspectives, on the other hand, have focussed more strongly on notions of fulfilment, inner truth and a sense of oneness with the world. Craft (2011) highlights these differences when she reminds us that creativity, rather than being universal, needs to be understood within its temporal and cultural context. A further, and perhaps even more important, observation is that creativity is in itself morally neutral. It can be harnessed just as easily in the service of sinister and distasteful causes as it can be used to promote joy and happiness. Ultimately, educational activity requires us to be clear about what we value. A focus on creativity challenges us to do this.

If defining creativity is problematic, an alternative is to explore the qualities which characterise it. Foremost amongst these are (a) play and curiosity (b) imagination (c) new thinking and (d) problem solving. However, here too there are difficulties. For example, should creativity be viewed as disinterested and experimental? The National Advisory Committee on Creativity and Cultural Education (NACCCE 1999) argue that creative thinking requires a definite focus – it needs to be both directed towards an objective and lead to outcomes that are of value. In this interpretation, fantasy, day dreaming and speculation can only be viewed as creative if they yield useful results. Play and speculation are similarly marginalised. The fact that the NACCCE definition has been widely adopted by Ofsted and other government organisations for more than a decade highlights some of the tensions surrounding the notion of creativity in education today.

Creativity and personal growth

There is a significant link between the opportunities which children have to engage in creative activities and their long-term health and well-being. Evidence from educationalists, psychologists, psychotherapists and neuroscientists corroborates this claim. There is an extensive literature, for example, about the benefits of free play and the contribution that it makes to children's social, emotional and cognitive development (Chawla 1992; Louv 2008; Moss 2012). Creative activity also builds children's sense of self-esteem. Harding and Chaudhuri (2008, 7) make the bold claim that creative moments are the foundation stones or 'bedrock of experiences that make us who we are'. Such thinking chimes with study of gifted individuals which led Csikszentmihalyi (1997) to claim that creativity is a central source of meaning in our lives.

The link between creativity and personal growth is worth exploring further. Csikszentmihalyi (1997) argues that we find creative activities fulfilling because they fascinate us and challenge us to make full use our skills and abilities. Focussing on subjective aspects of creativity, he coined the term 'flow' to characterise those states of mind when we are so engrossed in what we are doing that we lose our sense of time, forget our worries and focus so intensely that even our fear of failure drops away. Flow experiences are especially linked to physical and creative activities. In school settings flow is most often encountered in playground games, sports and practical work. Other common examples include those moments when pupils manage to ignore external distractions despite the odds or are genuinely too busy with what they are doing to be aware of time passing. At their most intense, flow experiences can generate an ecstatic sense of meaning and oneness with the world.

Fredrickson's 'broaden and build' theory elaborates on this argument a stage further by focusing on personal development. Drawing on empirical evidence over a period of two decades, Fredrickson (2005) argues that we build enduring personal resources when we are in a positive mindset, that is, when we are happy, curious and creative. She postulates two mechanisms. First, positive states underlie expansive and outward-looking mindsets in which we broaden our thought-action repertoire. Second, the resources (physical, intellectual and social) that we acquire as a result of broadening processes enable us to build our resilience for the future. Furthermore, Fredrickson, along with Seligman (2003), argues that positive experiences have the potential to undo the damaging effects of negative ones. This holds out the tantalising prospect that long-term daily exposure to creative activity has the potential to maximise personal fulfilment and initiate a spiral of upward growth and development based on positive emotions.

Fredrickson's theory is not without its critics. Held (2004) points out that what counts as a positive or negative experience is a matter of judgement and that the distinction between positive and negative is both polarising and simplistic. It is also important to recognise that challenging and destructive experiences can be particularly powerful stimuli for creative endeavour. The life stories of exceptional artists such as Beethoven, Dostoyevsky and Van Gogh, all of whom found inspiration in adversity, illustrate this point. Yet, it would be misleading to conclude that a pedagogy which seeks to promote happiness and well-being runs the risk of removing challenge and creativity from education. On the contrary, it has the potential to maximise the opportunities for children to flourish. As Scoffham and Barnes (2011) point out, only a few resilient individuals draw strength from suffering. The vast majority are much more vulnerable.

Creativity in school settings

Government reports published over the last decade confirm that creativity contributes to young people's cognitive and emotional development. One particularly influential summary, the Government Response to the Roberts' Report, unequivocally declares that 'creativity and standards go hand in hand' (DCMS/DfES 2006, 4). Additionally, the Ofsted report into Creative Partnerships – a programme which worked with a million young people between 2002 and 2011 – reaches the same conclusion (Ofsted 2006). Meanwhile, a report by the House of Commons Education and Skills Committee, which appeared at about the same time, makes it clear that 'creativity has a value in its own right' (House of Commons Education and Skills Committee 2007, para 21).

The idea that creativity has a value in its own right chimes with the views of many teachers who saw the publication of two key reports, *Excellence and Enjoyment* (DfES 2003) and *Every Child Matters* (DfES 2004), as an opportunity to adopt what has come to be known as the 'creative curriculum'. This term has been applied in strikingly different ways across the country but generally represents a more flexible and integrated cross-curricular approach to teaching and learning (Barnes 2011). Despite these trends what happens in schools has remained heavily constrained by the inspection regime. Dobson (2009) is not alone in noting the irony of promoting creativity within a performance driven-system that is focussed on accountable standards and outcomes. He argues that the climate in which teaching occurs is a key influence on creativity and laments the fact that teachers' voices are rarely heard in educational debates. He notes, for example, that the teachers in his small scale study 'consistently' felt that a creative focus was more in line with the way children actually learn as opposed to a fragmented, unit based, structure which is the dominant mode (Dobson 2009, 102). This research adds further weight to the conclusion reached by Jeffrey (2008) that creative teaching involves making learning relevant to learners and enables them to take ownership of their learning.

Creativity, though it may be seen by teachers as a 'good thing', raises problems at a classroom level. Not only is the concept itself fluid and ill-defined, there are also questions about the extent to which creativity links to particular character traits – concerns which are compounded by the fact that some of these traits, such as dreaminess, playfulness and divergent thinking, fit rather uneasily into the current education system. Sternberg (2003) links creativity to what he calls 'legislative' styles of thought and argues that originality almost always involves adopting a contrary position. He proposes a 'creative investment theory' in which people buy low and sell high in the world of ideas. If independence of judgement is one side of the creativity coin, the other side is the ability to persuade others of the validity of your thinking.

From a teacher's point of view creativity is also difficult to manage. To begin with it takes time to nurture and develops erratically rather than in allocated timetable slots. Furthermore, it is hard to quantify and assess, being neither neatly progressive nor uniquely attributable to individuals. A further consideration is the extent to which judgements about creativity are variable and subjective. At a time when outcomes and targets overshadow educational practice, creativity sits rather uneasily alongside dominant agendas. In the absence of hard evidence, creativity is all too often seen as woolly or insubstantial; as a way of engaging less able children, while the high fliers get on with the 'real' business of learning substantial and quantifiable knowledge.

Finally, it is worth noting that creativity is still widely associated with artistic achievement. The idea that creativity and creative thinking are central to every subject, while it may be superficially acknowledged, is not deeply rooted. For example, *All Our Futures* (NACCCE 1999) has over 300 references to the arts. By contrast science is mentioned approximately 150 times, mathematics 60 times, humanities and history around 40 times each and geography 23 times. Whatever the argument in the text, the message that comes across is that creativity is less relevant and important in subjects which are not directly to do with the arts.

An analysis of Ofsted geography reports reveals further ambiguities. For example, the 2011 report, *Geography: Learning to Make a World of Difference* (Ofsted 2011), contains a number of case studies of highly creative teaching. We learn how in one reception class children hunted for flight tickets for a pretend flight to Mexico, mimed going on the journey and searched for messages left by an imaginary character called Carlos (Ofsted 2011, para 15). In another class, year six pupils found out about conflict in the Middle East. Two children acted in the role of newsreaders, while others took on the role of 'expert witnesses', conducted interviews or researched information (Ofsted 2011, para 83). Despite these inspiring examples of creative practice, the report contains no direct discussion about creativity and how it can enhance teaching. Indeed, the term itself is only used once where it occurs in a phrase that links it to spontaneity. Similarly, 'play' is mentioned on just three occasions and 'imagination' twice. By contrast, 'knowledge' receives 43 mentions, 'assessment' 33 and 'challenge' 20. Current curriculum and policy priorities dominate the report and issues to do with pedagogy are relegated to the side-lines. Just as the NACCCE (1999) report fails to make meaningful links across subjects, the Ofsted geography report fails to make links between geography and creativity, as Figure 1 illustrates.

Geography and creatively

Geography and creativity are fundamentally aligned. Trying to make sense of the world and understanding the forces that act upon it – key geographical endeavours – require us to think creatively. The information available to geographers at any particular time will inevitably be fragmented and partial. It may even be contradictory. Synthesising and transforming this information into a coherent body of knowledge challenges us to ask questions, envisage alternatives, assess possibilities, make judgements, construct narratives and devise theories. It also requires us to position ourselves socially, culturally, historically and philosophically. Other subjects face similar challenges. However, when Catling

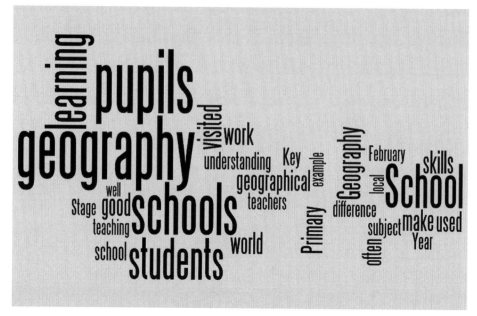

Figure 1. A word cloud of the 30 most common words in the Ofsted geography report (2011) – a strong focus on management and performance: creativity is notably absent.

(2009, 189) declares that 'geography is an active subject at the heart of which lies creativity', he makes an important point. Geography and creativity are not usually associated in the popular imagination and this is a misconception that needs to be challenged.

One of the most striking features of geography is that it synthesises different ways of thinking. Physical geographers study the processes operating in the world around us using techniques which draw heavily on the sciences. By contrast, human geographers explore the way that people respond to their surroundings using approaches which are more akin to the arts and humanities. These different perspectives are brought together in a creative interface through studies of concepts such as interdependence, environmental interaction and cultural understanding. Koestler's notion of bi-sociation (1964) and the observation by Csikszentmihalyi (1997) that creativity flourishes at the frontiers of a subject are particularly relevant here.

The way that geographers present information also requires creative approaches. Few other subjects make such extensive use of graphical techniques such as graphs, charts, diagrams and pictures. One technique in particular is central to geography. Maps of many different types and forms are the geographers' stock in trade; and they are not the dry, descriptive documents which they are sometimes thought to be. Every cartographer has to decide what to include, what to leave out and how best to portray the information they have selected. On one level this means that maps can be regarded as highly imaginative representations of reality. At another level, the complexities of digital mapping and the analysis of spatial information, which is now available using geographical information systems, represent cutting edge scientific thought. Again, the Janus-like quality of the subject is immediately apparent.

At the heart of all geographical studies stands the concept of place. Place is a complex and contested notion. On a physical level, places include landscapes, habitats and settlements in all their diversity. The difference between places, the way that they are linked, how they are changing and what makes them unique are rich areas of study. However, these studies go beyond exploring the physical setting to include human dimensions. It is the dynamic interplay between people and places – how people affect places and how places affect people – which help to make geography such a fluid and stimulating subject. It also lends itself to creative thinking. Massey (2005) has explored how places can be viewed in terms of nodes and connections which come together at particular moments in time. Digital technology, because it allows us to occupy multiple spaces at the same time, is making the notion of place even more diffuse.

There is also a sense in which geographical studies of all kinds look towards the future. The analysis of trends and the theories which emerge from them inform our thinking about what is happening in the world. Children also speculate about what may happen with respect to the care of their locality and the planet. A central part of this process is the construction of narratives. What we think is important and the significance that we give to phenomena are matters of judgement. Switching from small to large scale views and drawing on different types of information to reach conclusions based on meaningful evidence is a highly creative endeavour. It is no co-incidence that the notion of the 'geographical imagination' has begun to feature in the literature of the subject. The way that we interpret the world around us is necessarily tentative, incomplete and culturally situated. At a classroom level teaching geography involves envisaging different possibilities. As Catling (2011) argues, the ways in which children engage with, think and feel about the world – their geographical imaginations – are central to geography and creativity.

Geography also favours pedagogies which draw on and develop creative thinking. Asking and answering questions are key techniques, along with active learning and practical investigations. The enquiry process which moves through a sequence of discovering, dreaming, deciding and doing (Pickering 2013) is central to good practice. So too is fieldwork. The engagement which results from interacting with the environment can be a powerful catalyst for learning, raising problems and provoking creative thinking. There is increasingly powerful evidence from both neuroscience and psychology that the foundations of place attachment are laid in childhood, that fieldwork exploits fundamental biological drives and that outdoor work provides a context for exploring ideas which can stimulate unusual and imaginative responses (Barnes and Scoffham 2013).

Before concluding this section there is a further angle to consider. How do children themselves view geography and what do they want to learn from it? The questions which upper primary school children spontaneously ask about geography have been investigated by Scoffham (2013). His study of 134 pupils from schools in five different areas of England, found that around half the children's questions focussed on factual information. The other half were to do with processes, puzzles and existential speculation about how the world came to be. Significantly, a proportion of the questions were underpinned by a sense of awe and wonder – one of the avowed aims in the original version of the geography National Curriculum (DfE/WO 1990). The links between geography and other subjects were also apparent as many of the questions related to more than one discipline, especially science. The evidence from this, admittedly limited, research study suggests that some children have a natural tendency to approach geography from a creative stance and are fascinated by the larger, often imponderable questions, about the world.

Creative approaches to teaching geography

It is not the remit of this article to give detailed advice on creative ways of teaching the geography curriculum but this section gives a general overview of some of the possibilities.

One key distinction which needs to be made from the outset concerns the difference between creative teaching and teaching for creativity. Creative teaching focuses on the teacher and their personal enthusiasm and curiosity. Teaching for creativity is about devising situations where children's creativity can flourish. The two are not necessarily the same. A flamboyant and showy teacher may be creative in themselves but fail to provide enough space for children to develop their own ideas. By contrast, a teacher who adopts a more subdued or questioning approach to learning sometimes fosters a secure but stimulating environment where imagination and creativity can flourish. Whatever the personality of the teacher, there is wide consensus that creative teaching is not an easy option. It involves being flexible, taking risks and is predicated on sound subject knowledge. It also involves, as Cremin, Barnes, and Scoffham (2009) argue, a creative mindset. The most creative teachers appear, rather tautologically, to be aware of and value creativity in themselves and seek to promote it in others.

Starter activities

Children learn in lots of different ways. A puzzle, problem or game, if well targeted, has the potential to engage children creatively and support imaginative learning. Whyte (2013) outlines a wide range of word games, riddles, map exercises and small scale investigations which can be used as starter activities in either competitive or collaborative settings. He recommends the use of jokes, stories, music and artefacts to prompt questions and stimulate curiosity. As well as being fun, such an approach has the potential to cater for different learning styles. Furthermore, as Whyte (2013, 16) points out, 'the way a lesson begins will often affect the way the children respond throughout the rest of the topic'. A creative beginning encourages a creative response.

Stories

Picture books, stories and poems have the potential to introduce children to geographical topics in imaginative and stimulating ways. The interplay between text and illustrations makes a powerful combination which can transport pupils to places beyond their immediate knowledge and experience. Tanner and Whittle (2013) argue that stimuli of this kind help to build children's 'geographical imagination'. In addition, picture books are particularly effective at making complex problems such as global warming, over population and biodiversity accessible, even to the youngest children. Many teachers will find ways of incorporating such texts into larger and more extended pieces of work. As well as appealing to children's natural desire for narrative, picture books are also often adroit at using a sense of empathy to present weighty problems in a light-hearted and positive manner. This is important because creative engagement is predicated on a spirit of optimism and hope. Without it, Craft's notion of 'possibility thinking' (2001) is seriously undermined.

Trails

Another creative and engaging approach to geography teaching involves the use of trails in and around the school. Trails can take many forms but always involve a route punctuated by activities. In educational contexts trails can be targeted on quite specific objectives, ranging from mathematical shapes and patterns to environmental issues as demonstrated by Whittle (2013). However, trails can also be experiential and exploratory or even specifically designed to be creative in their own right. Children enjoy the freedom to roam which trails afford and often relish the chance to take responsibility for their learning either as individuals or in collaboration with others. Getting out of the classroom and gaining first-hand experience of places provides a platform for creative responses and introduces some of the complexities of the real world into learning situations.

Place making

Place making activities such as den building give pupils the opportunity to engage with their surroundings, develop interpersonal skills and deepen their sense of place. Such activities have particular appeal to children in middle childhood and have the potential to harnesses deep-seated psychological drives. Setting up a camp, creating a shelter or making home for animals (real or imaginary) can be both enjoyable and engaging. Witt (2013) advocates immersion activities in which children are encouraged to explore fantasies and construct stories. In one example, pupils were encouraged to build a house to attract elves. Not only did the children eagerly suspend their disbelief but by the end of the activity Witt reports their experience of the local area had been infused with a sense of 'wonder, beauty and enchantment' (Witt 2013, 55). Another approach is to encourage children to engage with the natural world through making sculptures, dressing trees or making pictures from found objects. Creative play in which children change their surroundings through adaptation, construction and transformation makes use of 'slow pedagogies' which, as Payne and Wattchow (2009) explain, allow children to pause and dwell in spaces developing their sense of belonging through stillness, silence and reflection. Such approaches have been explored to great advantage by Forest Schools (Knight 2011). They also have the potential to provide children who have been raised in restricted, often urban, environments with rich and meaningful experiences to compensate for what Louv (2008) terms 'nature deficit disorder'.

Planning issues

Change is a constant feature of the built and natural environment and in any locality there are likely to be plans for new buildings and developments. There may also be proposals to safe-guard or enhance local habitats. Investigating these issues and considering questions about the future can lead to some exemplary work. Ofsted reports (Ofsted 2008, 2011) consistently extol the value of studies which focus on local issues which are of personal relevance to pupils. The pedagogies involved – investigation, role play, simulations, drama and debates – often stimulate some particularly original and perceptive pupil responses. Such studies have the added advantage of being both relevant and authentic, with all the complexity and contradictions that this involves. Catling and Pickering (2010) argue that it is the messiness of the real world which provides the basis for meaningful engagement, connects us with people and places and leads us to value our surroundings. It also encourages critical and creative thinking in the search for solutions.

Outdoor learning

Multi-sensory, first-hand experience of real environments distinguishes outdoor settings from other learning contexts. Activities which promote physical and emotional engagement and which have a clear geographical focus sometimes lead to exemplary learning, not least because of the immediacy of the experience and the impact of almost instantaneous feedback (Waite 2011). There are also particularly rich opportunities to nurture imaginative and creative responses. With the youngest children sensory and environmental walks provide excellent opportunities for using and developing vocabulary. The opportunities for enacting stories are also particularly rich. Witt recounts how one reception class, inspired by *Winnie the Pooh* (Milne 1995), used the school ground to go on their own 'expotition to discover the North Pole' (Witt 2013, 49). Older pupils might evaluate and compare the qualities of different local environments using words, diagrams and pictures. Discussing the hidden bias in photographs and place images, while comparing them in their actual setting, opens up further creative possibilities.

Finding out about the UK

Finding out and learning about places around the UK, mainland Europe and other parts of the world is a central geographical concern. There are many contentious questions surrounding the notion of national identity (Scoffham and Whyte 2011). Exploring these issues and recognising the need for multiple perspectives is a highly creative endeavour. Finding out about links and connections between the UK and other countries is another way of challenging and deepening thinking. Although we live in a modern globalised economy the disparities within and between countries is every bit as deep, if not deeper, than in the past. Trying to make sense of such paradoxes and speculating about future trends requires both deep knowledge and imaginative thinking. There are plenty of opportunities for making this work enjoyable. One approach which draws on a wide range of skills is to get pupils to devise a board game based on a theme or topic. Apart from the initial challenge of devising the game, the feedback which children gain from playing their games with each other will serve to enhance their learning.

Finding out about the wider world

How do children learn about the wider world beyond the UK? Even before they come to school children will have gained an idea about other countries and places (Wiegand 2006). To begin with, the alphabet charts that adorn the bedrooms of many toddlers include pictures of tigers and kangaroos. In addition, the pictures that they see on television will have brought people and places into their living-room, often projecting images of poverty and distress. They may have lived abroad or have close relations overseas. There are many creative ways of developing children's understanding of the world. On a prosaic level, exploring and interrogating the world map can provide a valuable entry point. The outline of the world which adults carry in their heads is invariably orientated towards the north. Reversing the orientation so that south is at the top can prove quite disturbing as shown in Figure 2. It also provokes all manner of questions. Which way up is correct? Who decides that the UK should be at the centre of the map? Is the Equator actually in the middle of the map? Are the outlines of the continents drawn accurately and in proportion to each other? Could we draw the map better? What would 'better' mean? Developing the creative learning opportunities which stem from such questions can lead in many different directions.

Environment and sustainability

Our relations with the natural world and the challenge of finding sustainable ways of living are arguably the meta-narrative of the twenty-first century (Bonnett 2004). One approach is to focus on current events. Many teachers set up a 'news corner' in their classroom or draw on news stories in their geography lessons. These bring an immediacy and relevance to learning. However, as Hicks (2002) argues, it is important to take a positive stance and not to be overwhelmed by doom and gloom scenarios. Engaging pupils in investigating

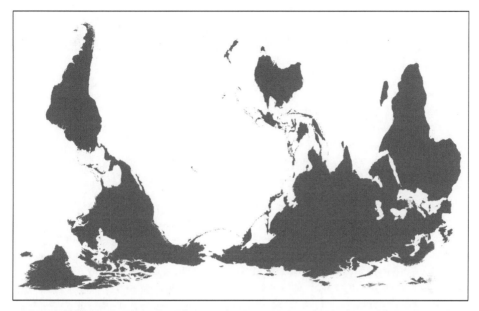

Figure 2.   A Pacific-centred world map orientated towards the south – it can provoke questions and challenge our preconceptions.

the facts and speculating about possible solutions harnesses creative thinking and increases their sense of agency. Alexander (2010) reports how in one class finding out about global warming helped to mitigate children's fears and gave them hope for the future. It is one of the features of environmental issues that they operate at a range of scales. Global warming, for example, affects people on the other side of the world just as it affects us locally. Making links and connections and switching from one scale to another are just as central to geography as they are to creative thought.

All the examples outlined above involve (a) collaborative and active learning, (b) enquiry, and (c) reflection and analysis. They place the learner (in this case, children) at the centre of the learning process. The way in which creative learning assists in the development of meaningful learning identities has been investigated by Jeffrey (2008). The key features which he identifies – relevance, control, ownership and innovation – are all represented in these examples. But there is a further quality which needs to be considered – namely a sense of playful engagement and fun. Trying to teach children without engaging them emotionally is likely to be a futile endeavour. It is when pupils enjoy what they are doing that they are most likely to develop a lasting love of knowledge.

Conclusion

Creativity is fundamental to what it means to be human and is one of the qualities that distinguish us from machines. When each of us does something which is at the cutting edge of our abilities, when we each become aware we are doing something creative, it contributes to our sense of identity. Every child needs to feel that they are expert at something. Geography offers us many opportunities to be experts. By contributing to children's sense of place attachment, creative activities build their sense of identity in other ways too. We define ourselves to some extent at least through the relationship we have with places, particularly those that we experience in our youth.

Creative approaches to geography teaching could simply be seen as interpreting a pre-scribed curriculum in an imaginative way. However, a pedagogy which sees creativity as the dynamo at the heart of joyful and ethical learning has much more to offer than this. In particular it:

- respects the autonomy and agency of the child, thereby enhancing their well-being;
- acknowledges that children learn in different ways at different speeds and with different motivations;
- recognises the complexity and messiness of ideation and
- attributes value to emotional and existential knowing alongside more visible cognitive achievements.

Further research is needed into the relationship between creativity and the development of children's geographical understanding. Robust empirical studies would, for example, buttress the extensive case study evidence and professional wisdom that already exist. There is also a need for a better theoretical and applied understanding of the mechanisms that link creativity, enjoyment, health and well-being. In the years ahead it seems likely that neuroscience research will yield results which will develop our thinking in this and other related domains. Despite these deficits, there is already sufficient evidence to affirm the benefits of creative geography teaching. Children value those subjects, as Alexander (2010, 213) reminds us, which spark their curiosity and encourage them to explore. Geography is in a prime position to harness this energy. Exploring different ways to promote creative geographical learning brings fun and enjoyment to geography teaching for both pupils and teachers alike.

References

Alexander, R. 2010. *Children, Their World, Their Education*. London: Routledge.
Barnes, J. 2011. *Cross-Curricular Learning*. London: Sage.
Barnes, J., and S. Scoffham. 2013. "Geography, Creativity and the Future." In *Teaching Geography Creatively*, edited by S. Scoffham, 180–193. London: Routledge.
Bonnett, M. 2004. *Retrieving Nature: Education for a Post-Humanist Age*. Oxford: Blackwell.
Catling, S. 2009. "Creativity in Primary Geography." In *Creativity in Primary Education*, edited by A. Wilson, 189–198. Exeter: Learning Matters.
Catling, S. 2011. "Children's Geographies in the Primary School." In *Geography, Education and the Future*, edited by G. Butt, 15–29. London: Continuum.
Catling, S., and S. Pickering. 2010. "Mess, Mess, Glorious Mess." *Primary Geographer* 73: 16–17.
Chawla, L. 1992. "Childhood Place Attachment." In *Place Attachment*, edited by I. Altman and S. Low, 63–86. London: Plenum.
Craft, A. 2001. "Little c Creativity." In *Creativity in Education*, edited by A. Craft, B. Jeffrey, and M. Leibling, 45–61. London: Continuum.
Craft, A. 2011. *Creativity and Futures Education: Learning in a Digital Age*. Trentham: Stoke on Trent.
Cremin, T., J. Barnes, and S. Scoffham. 2009. *Creative Teaching for Tomorrow: Fostering a Creative State of Mind*. Deal: Future Creative.
Csikszentmihalyi, M. 1997. *Creativity: Flow and the Psychology of Invention*. New York: HarperPerennial.
DCMS/DfES. 2006. *Government Response to Paul Roberts' Report on Nuturing Creativity in Young People*. London: DCMS.
De Bono. 1999. *Six Thinking Hats*. London: Penguin.
DfE (Department for Education). 2010. *The Importance of Teaching: Schools White Paper*. London: DfE.
DfES (Department for Education and Skills). 2003. *Excellence and Enjoyment: A Strategy for Primary Schools*. London: DfES.

DfES (Department for Education and Skills). 2004. *Every Child Matters*. London: DfES.

DfE/WO (Department for Education/Welsh Office). 1990. *Geography for Ages 5-16*. London: HMSO.

Dobson, K. 2009. "Teacher Creativity Within the Current Education System: A Case Study of the Perceptions of Primary Teachers." *Education 3–13* 37 (2): 95–14.

Feldman, D. H. 1999. "The Development of Creativity." In *Handbook of Creativity*, edited by R. Sternberg, 169–186. Cambridge: Cambridge University Press.

Fredrickson, B. 2005. "The Broaden and Build Theory of Positive Emotions." In *The Science of Well-Being*, edited by A. Huppert, N. Baylis, and B. Keverne, 217–238. Oxford: Oxford University Press.

Harding, J., and S. Chaudhuri. 2008. *Creative Wellbeing*. Abingdon: Creative Partnerships.

Held, B. 2004. "The Negative Side of Positive Psychology." *Journal of Humanistic Psychology* 74 (1): 9–46.

Hicks, D. 2002. *Lessons for the Future: The Missing Dimension in Education*. Oxford: Trafford.

House of Commons Education and Skills Committee. 2007. *Creative Partnerships and the Curriculum*. London: Stationery Office.

Immordino-Yang, M., and A. Damasio. 2007. "We Feel Therefore We Learn: The Relevance of Affective and Social Neuroscience to Education." *Brain, Mind and Education* 1 (1): 3–10.

Jeffrey, B. 2008. "Creative Learning Identities." Education *3–13* 36 (3): 253–263.

Knight, S. 2011. *Risk and Adventure in Early Years Outdoor Play: Learning from Forest Schools*. London: Sage.

Koestler, A. 1964. *The Act of Creation*. London: Hutchinson.

Louv, R. 2008. *Last Child in the Woods*. New York: Algonquin.

Lucas, B., and G. Claxton. 2011. *New Kinds of Smart*. Maidenhead: Open University.

Massey, D. 2005. *For Space*. London: Sage.

Milne, A. A. 1995. *Winnie the Pooh: The Complete Collection of Stories and Poems*. Godalming: The Book People.

Moran, S., and V. John-Steiner. 2003. "Creativity in the Making." In *Creativity and Development*, edited by R. K. Sawyer, V. John-Steiner, S. Moran, R. J. Sternberg, D. H. Feldman, J. Nakamura, and M. Csikszentmihalyi, 61–90. Oxford: Oxford University Press.

Moss, S. 2012. *Natural Childhood*. Swindon: National Trust.

NACCCE (National Advisory Committee for Creative and Cultural Education). 1999. *All Our Futures: Creativity, Culture and Education*. London: DfEE.

Ofsted. 2006. *Creative Partnerships: Initiative and Impact*. London: Ofsted. www.ofsted.gov.uk/resources/creative-partnerships-initiative-and-impact

Ofsted. 2008. *Geography in Schools: Changing Practice*. London: Ofsted.

Ofsted. 2011. *Geography: Learning to Make a World of Difference*. London: Ofsted.

Payne, M., and B. Wattchow. 2009. "Phenomenlogical Deconstruction, Slow Pedagogy and the Corporeal Turn in Wild Environmental/Outdoor Education." *Canadian Journal of Environmental Education* 14: 15–22.

Pickering, S. 2013. "Keeping Geography Messy." In *Teaching Geography Creatively*, edited by S. Scoffham, 168–179. London: Routledge.

Rogoff, B. 2003. *The Cultural Nature of Human Development*. Oxford: Oxford University Press.

Scoffham, S. 2011. "Core Knowledge in the Revised Curriculum." *Geography* 96 (3): 124–130.

Scoffham, S. 2013. "A Question of Research." *Primary Geography* no. 80: 16–17.

Scoffham, S., and J. Barnes. 2011. "Happiness Matters: Towards a Pedogogy of Happiness and Well-Being." *The Curriculum Journal* 22 (4): 535–548.

Scoffham, S., and T. Whyte. 2011. *The UK: Investigating Who We Are*. Sheffield: Geographical Association.

Seligman, M. 2003. *Authentic Happiness*. New York: Basic Books.

Sternberg, R. 2003. *Wisdom, Intelligence and Creativity Synthesized*. Cambridge: Cambridge University Press.

Tanner, J., and J. Whittle. 2013. *Everyday Guide to Primary Geography: Story*. Sheffield: Geographical Association.

Waite, S. 2011. "Making a Difference: Learning on a Grand Scale." In *Children Learning Outside the Classroom*, edited by S. Waite, 201–212. London: Sage.

Whittle, J. 2013. "Geography and Mathematics: A Creative Approach." In *Teaching Geography Creatively*, edited by S. Scoffham, 112–127. London: Routledge.

Whyte, T. 2013. "Fun and Games in Geography." In *Teaching Geography Creatively*, edited by S. Scoffham, 14–30. London: Routledge.

Wiegand, P. 2006. *Learning and Teaching with Maps*. London: Routledge.

Witt, S. 2013. "Playful Approaches to Outdoor Learning." In *Teaching Geography Creatively*, edited by S. Scoffham, 47–58. London: Routledge.

Subject-based and cross-curricular approaches within the revised primary curriculum in Northern Ireland: teachers' concerns and preferred approaches

Richard Greenwood

Stranmillis University College, Belfast, Northern Ireland, UK

A revision of the Northern Ireland Primary Curriculum took place in 2007. It promotes strongly a cross-curricular or thematic approach to planning and teaching and has an 'Area of Learning' structure which includes geography alongside history and science and technology in an area called 'The World Around Us'. Responses from teacher questionnaires and interviews with teachers and 'stakeholders' reveal wide-ranging opinions, mostly positive, about the effectiveness of this approach in improving pupil learning. A significant number of teachers have adopted a pragmatic, balanced and reflective approach to their planning, something which requires a high skill level in 'curriculum-making' which, in turn, can be enhanced by effective in-service training.

Introduction

The Northern Ireland Curriculum (NIC) was revised in 2007. Like the proposals in the Cambridge Primary Review (Alexander 2009) and the Rose Report (Rose 2009), it is not structured in single subjects but in 'Areas of Learning'. These include 'Language and Literacy', 'Mathematics and Numeracy', 'The Arts' (art and design, drama and music) and 'The World Around Us' (WAU), an area which includes history, science and technology and geography. Cross-curricular or integrated approaches to planning and teaching, termed 'Connected Learning' within the NIC, are encouraged, along with the use of active learning methods, Assessment for Learning (AfL) techniques and a focus on 'Thinking Skills and Personal Capabilities'.

In one of its introductory sections, the curriculum document produced by the Northern Ireland Council for Curriculum, Examination and Assessment (CCEA) states that 'Children learn best when learning is connected' (CCEA 2007, 10). It encourages relevant connections and integration between all of the Areas of Learning using cross-curricular approaches:

> Although the curriculum has been set out under six Areas of Learning, further integration is encouraged to help children better understand the links between the different aspects of learning. (CCEA 2007, 16)

Previous versions of the NIC, which became statutory in 1990 and 1996, had noted the importance of cross-curricular teaching, but it was not encouraged as overtly as in the 2007 curriculum. In it the formation of the Areas of Learning structure, the provision of exemplar materials – the 'Ideas for Connected Learning' (ICLs) and 'Thematic Units' (TUs) – and the emphasis on thinking skills and 'connected learning' have all combined to give cross-curricularity (CC) a much higher profile than before.

This paper discusses the pros and cons of cross-curricular and subject-focused approaches in primary school teaching with a focus on primary geography. It describes research into the opportunities and the concerns identified by the teachers and other educators by looking at the tensions which exist between the desire to highlight and celebrate subject distinctiveness while teaching within a 'connected learning' context. It is based on interview and questionnaire data provided by teachers and individual educational 'stakeholders'.

Literature review

There is no shortage of published material on the pros and cons of subject-focused and integrated approaches. In the last six years, three textbooks using the word 'cross-curricular' in their titles have been published in the UK: Rowley and Cooper (2009), Barnes (2011) and Kerry (2011). These books, along with the publication of a number of journal papers and articles, signal a significant renewal of interest in the area.

Terminology

The debate about whether a cross-curricular or a subject-based approach is more effective in terms of pupil learning is beset by the problem of terminology and definitions. A plethora of terms is found in the literature for cross-curricular teaching – for example, 'topics', 'projects', 'integrated teaching' and 'thematic teaching'. In the primary school, it is common for 'integration' to mean, in practice, a non-differentiated exploration of a theme or 'topic' using generalised and common-sense enquiry procedures. One of the best-known definitions of cross-curricular or topic work was given by Alexander, Rose, and Woodhead (1992, 21):

> … a mode of curriculum organisation, frequently enquiry-based, combining aspects of various subjects under a common theme.

Within this paper, the terms 'cross-curricular' and 'integrated' are used synonymously. They are defined as: approaches to planning and teaching which attempt to bring together within the same unit of work or topic, aspects from different subject areas which are taught concurrently and which contribute in a meaningful and appropriate way to the unit's whole. Each unit or topic must have core content, usually based on one, or possibly two, central subjects, and learning in one area must be supported by learning in the others (Martin 2002). The topic as a whole must be strengthened by the links, and the links should not focus just on content but also on skills and concepts. The intent of curriculum integration is to construct meaningful bridges to show connections in development and learning (Wortham 1996). Barlow and Brook (2010) brought together a number of these threads by arguing that an essential aspect of any cross-curricular approach is the idea that one theme may offer wide opportunities for quality learning in several subject areas (saving time and avoiding repetition), while at the same time this can create broader and more cohesive learning experiences, with greater consideration of how pupils learn.

In a booklet which preceded the NIC, addressing some of its implementation issues, CCEA (2006) used the phrase 'connected learning' in the context of the proposed revision of the curriculum and defined it as including:

> ... connecting new learning to learners' prior experience; making explicit meaningful relationships between knowledge and skills in different contexts; and encouraging the transfer of knowledge and skills across different contexts. (CCEA 2006, 2)

In this definition, the idea of pupils connecting new learning to learning which they already have, irrespective of whether these connections cross subject boundaries, is suggested. In addition, the idea of knowledge and skills being used *in* and *across* 'different contexts' is taken to encompass cross-curricular teaching and a flexible approach to structuring the curriculum in general.

Writing specifically about geography teaching in the primary school, Catling (2010, 84) argued that 'No aspect of geography can really be taught in isolation'. In the same book, Krause and Millward (2010, 335) stated that 'Geography lends itself to cross-curricular work and provides a context for exploring many other subject areas'.

CC in Northern Ireland education

The Northern Ireland educational system has had a different history from the educational system in the rest of the UK. It has been characterised as being more conservative and less 'liberal' in its structures and management, allowing teachers less freedom to experiment with curriculum change (Caul 1993). In other words, the 'pendulum of educational fashion' had never swung as widely in Northern Ireland education as it has in England. However, because Northern Ireland has had long periods of direct rule government controlling the educational system, it has tended to be the case that when Westminster made changes in educational policy, Northern Ireland education followed suit – usually a little later and in a less radical way. Northern Ireland has followed fairly closely the pattern of curriculum prescription in England and Wales: before the early 1990s, there was very little 'top-down' control of what was taught in primary schools. In Northern Ireland, a common curriculum was introduced in 1990, one year after the National Curriculum in England and Wales, and was set out in a similar, subject-based structure. The revision in 1996 (DENI 1996) reduced content and overlap in the curriculum in a process mirroring the Dearing review in England and Wales (Dearing 1994), but it was not in any way a radical re-appraisal. The statutory requirements of this revision remained in place for 11 years. Encouragement to teachers to use cross-curricular approaches was set out in both the 1991 and 1996 curriculum materials. In the 1996 revision (DENI 1996), the introduction to the Programme of Study for Geography at Key Stage 1 suggested that the content set out might be used flexibly in the planning of appropriate topics which might be cross-curricular or geography-led.

A revised NIC was introduced in March 2007 (CCEA 2007). In terms of CC, it can be seen as the most radical curriculum in the UK or Ireland. In this revision, geography, history and science and technology were placed into an Area of Learning called 'The World Around Us'. CCEA set out what it saw as the key features of the new curriculum; these included flexibility, active learning, integrated assessment, skills development and matching the learning to the learner. In addition, it described 'Connected Learning' and encouraged relevant connections and integration between all of the areas of learning in a cross-curricular approach: 'Although the curriculum has been set out under six Areas of Learning, further integration is encouraged to help children better understand the links between the different aspects of learning' (CCEA 2007, 16). In order to encourage the creation of strong and appropriate links across the curriculum, CCEA introduced a series of exemplar topics called 'ICLs' and 'TUs'. Many of these have a geography focus, for example, a topic for 6–8-year olds on their school and its surroundings, called 'School's Cool', a topic aimed at 8–9-year olds on water and its uses, called 'Liquid Gold' and an environmental topic called 'Eco Warriors' for 9–11-year olds. All are available as PDFs on the NIC website (http://www.nicurriculum.org.uk/).

Arguments in favour of CC

Arguments concerning the use of either subject-focused or cross-curricular approaches to learning have been hotly debated for many decades, with commentators either ardently supporting or opposing implementation of the various approaches in schools. Integrated approaches have been described as being a better reflection of the realities of pupils' experiences outside school (see, e.g. Tann 1988; Palmer and Pettitt 1993; Laurie 2011). Alleman and Brophy (1993, 287) put their point bluntly: 'Curriculum integration is one of those ideas that is obviously good'.

Educationalists who have written either in favour of or in opposition to cross-curricular approaches to planning and teaching have done so using a number of arguments. These have included psychological arguments concerning the nature of the mind of the learner and the conditions in which learning will occur, following work by famous educationalists such as Dewey and Vygotsky. Pragmatic arguments have also been made which allude to the idea that workers in the future will need to have the ability and flexibility to draw from many fields and solve problems that have interrelated factors. Further details on some of the arguments for cross-curricular teaching and learning have been set out in list form by both Morrison and Ridley (1988) and Cohen, Manion, and Morrison (2011).

A number of authors have proposed philosophical or epistemological arguments concerning the nature of knowledge itself (Bernstein 1971; Blenkin and Kelly 1981; Walkerdine 1983; Ward 1996; Kerry 2011). One of the strands within these kinds of arguments is that it is even more important for teachers who plan using integrated approaches to understand the 'deep structure' of each subject than it is for those teaching separate subjects (Bernstein 1975). Knight (1993, 3) concurred, stating that: 'A major problem with integration is simply that it demands sharp subject-matter understanding'. Thus, there is a body of evidence to suggest that a teacher's subject knowledge and understanding are directly related to the quality of the children's learning in a cross-curricular structure (Ryan and Jones 1998) and that an integrated approach to the primary curriculum demands of teachers high levels of skill and a wide 'pedagogical repertoire' (Burgess 2004; Wood 2011, 39). However, many teachers will argue that they have not had adequate training to allow them successfully to teach using a cross-curricular approach. In relation to geography, the 2008 Office for Standards in Education (Ofsted) subject report found that that many primary teachers were not confident in teaching geography and had little or no opportunity to improve their knowledge of how to teach it (Ofsted 2008). Three years later, the geography Ofsted report expressed concern over primary teachers' weak knowledge of geography, their lack of confidence in teaching it and insufficient subject-specific training (Ofsted 2011).

One of the main arguments in favour of an integrated curriculum is that pupils are more motivated to learn when the curriculum is organised in this way. Darling (1994) stated that the motivation gained by young children in following their own interests, albeit under teacher guidance, was fundamental to successful learning. The idea that pupil motivation is tied up with pupils' views of the relevance to their everyday lives of the work with which they are engaged has been suggested by some researchers. Hayes (2010) wrote about how cross-curricular approaches emphasise a fusion of ideas and concepts within and across subject areas and broader life experiences in an attempt to make education more relevant and meaningful for children. Such approaches are often seen as a way to support the transfer of learning and skills from one situation to another, teaching pupils to think and reason, and provide a more relevant curriculum to engage their interest (see also Thomson, McGregor, and Sanders 2009).

Arguments against CC

It is argued by those supporting disciplinary or subject-focused approaches to the curriculum that the retention of sharply defined subject boundaries provides for a more rigorous explanation of and a sense of order about our complex world (see, e.g. Gardner 2004). At a practical level, cross-curricular work is seen by some as not being the most efficient way for children to learn; for example, Entwistle (1970, 10) suggested that integrated studies seemed a 'poor instrument' for acquiring knowledge and skills in a manageable, disciplined form. The argument is that it may be difficult for pupils to make sense of experiences and knowledge without the benefit of the conceptual structures which disciplines provide (Morrison 1986; Kerry and Eggleston 1988; McNamara 1994). In the 'Three Wise Men' report, Alexander, Rose, and Woodhead (1992, 21) argued that to deny children access to subjects was to '... deny them access to some of the most powerful tools for making sense of the world which human beings have ever devised'. Rather than focusing on the ideological arguments in favour of or against subject teaching, they advocated recognising the empirical limitations of topic work and the benefits of subject teaching.

For many teachers, the main arguments about the practical difficulties associated with the implementation of an integrated curriculum have centred around five main issues: the fact that subjects can lose their distinctiveness; that topic work can often result in low order work being set; that the links made between subjects in planning may be weak and contrived; that there is frequently a lack of progression and that assessment is a major difficulty (see, e.g. Knight 1993; Coe 2010; Johnston 2011).

A compromise position

A compromise position between the extremes of strict subject planning and overly elaborate topic-based approaches has been suggested by a number of authors to be a desirable way forward. This position includes the idea that topics should not be too broad, but be more limited in scope (Palmer and Pettitt 1993; Barnes 2011) and that topics should have links which are natural, meaningful and purposeful and have conceptual coherence, rather than being tenuous and spurious (Martin 2002; Alexander et al. 2008; Rowley and Cooper 2009). In addition, various authors have advocated that teachers should vary their planning approaches between whole class topic work, individual topics and modular units of work with a single curriculum focus, taking into consideration the context of the school and the children's specific needs. A central question for teachers in their planning should not be: 'How can these concepts be integrated?' but rather 'How can these concepts best be taught?' (Lonning and DeFranco 1997).

Part of a practical, compromise way to work involves teachers deciding on the level of CC that they might use for any topic or unit of work which they are planning. Following the introduction of the subject-based National Curriculum in England and Wales in the late

1980s, a number of UK-based authors set out their preferred structures for thinking about the levels of CC that might be used by teachers in schools (Tyler 1992; Foley and Janikoun 1996; Bell 1996; Ward 1996). The compromise approach advocates that the most effective curriculum is one which is flexibly managed and combines teaching through separate subjects and through topics, exploiting the advantages of both approaches.

Research methods

The research for this study sought information on the extent to which Northern Ireland primary school teachers have developed cross-curricular topics, as well as investigating teachers' and other educators' opinions about the introduction of the revised NIC, with a particular interest in the role and context of geography. These topics required research approaches which were both qualitative and quantitative. A mixed-methods approach was used, involving initially the use of individual and small group interviews followed by the administration of a questionnaire to a large number of teachers.

Interviews

Six individual interviews were carried out with officers from each of the five Area Boards in Northern Ireland, as well as with an officer responsible for the 'WAU' Area of Learning at CCEA and a member of the Northern Ireland Schools Inspectorate. In addition, nine small group interviews were carried out with teachers in their schools, sampled so that they spanned three of the five Area Boards as well as a variety of urban to rural locations and a range of school sizes. In each school, teachers spanning the full range of primary classes took part.

The interview procedure followed best practice principles discussed by Punch (2009) and Cohen, Manion, and Morrison (2011). They lasted, on average, 45 min. They were semi-structured in format and the respondents were supplied with the questions two weeks before the interviews took place. The questions used in the individual interviews and the group interviews covered much of the same ground. They addressed respondents' opinions and perspectives about the pros and cons of 'connected learning' and the WAU grouping of geography, history and science within the new curriculum. The teachers were asked to give examples of topics which they felt had been effective with regard to pupil learning, and if they felt cross-curricular approaches promoted differentiation and motivation. Transcripts of the interviews were analysed using content analysis where the codes created were derived from the data responsively rather than being determined preordinately. The semi-structured nature of the question schedules produced a degree of predetermination, but the analysis of the interviews has followed an emergent pattern, allowing categories to develop from the text.

Questionnaires

A questionnaire was posted to all teachers of Primary 5 and 6 pupils (ages 8–10) in all 878 Northern Ireland Primary schools. The reason for this focus on upper primary teachers arose from responses made in the school group interviews, in which many Foundation Stage and Key Stage 1 teachers indicated that, for them, the introduction of the revised NIC with its emphasis on Connected Learning had not required them to make great changes in their planning and teaching. On the contrary, upper primary teachers said that they had had to make major changes in the ways in which they planned and taught. Primary 5 and 6 teachers

Level of cross-curricularity	Nature of cross-curricularity level	Description of level
1	No cross-curricularity	Geography content/ideas/skills taught entirely discretely.
2	Weak cross-curricularity	A small amount of integration, with a main focus on one subject, but content/ideas/skills used from one or two other subjects.
3	Medium level of cross-curricularity	A limited cross-curricular topic, still with a focus on a main subject, but content/ideas/skills used from three or four other subjects.
4	Quite a high level of cross-curricularity	A broadly-based topic/project with content/ideas/skills used from around five to seven subjects.
5	Strong cross-curricularity	A high level of integration producing a very broadly-based topic/project with content/ideas/skills from a wide range of subjects (eight to ten) as part of the topic

Figure 1.   Levels of CC from subject-focused to strongly cross-curricular.

had been, at the time when the questionnaires were administered, formally implementing the curriculum in their classroom for either two or three years.

The questionnaire was broad in scope, covering a number of aspects of the implementation of the new curriculum and teachers' opinions of it. The teachers were asked to give some information about their school and about themselves, but their anonymity was maintained. In addition, the teachers were asked to list all the WAU topics they were teaching during the academic year in question, and beside each one to indicate the level of CC they felt they had applied in the teaching of the topic, using a scale from Level 1 to Level 5, following descriptors and examples provided in Figure 1. The questionnaires were analysed using counts and descriptive statistics as well as parametric and non-parametric tests.

In total, 225 useable questionnaires were returned. The teachers who completed them came from all five of Northern Ireland's Area Boards and from small 2-teacher schools to 28-teacher schools. The teachers were predominantly female (79%) and their teaching experience ranged from 1 year to 37 years (mean = 14 years). It is estimated that returns were obtained from 168 different schools – 19.2% of the total number of primary schools in Northern Ireland.

Findings

The research upon which this paper is based was wide-ranging, encompassing teachers' and other stakeholders' views of a variety of aspects of the revised 2007 NIC. The main focus of this paper is to report on the views of the interviewees and the respondents to the questionnaire survey concerning the teaching of 'subjects' (with an emphasis on geography) within a curriculum which strongly encourages cross-curricular approaches. Initially, before discussing these issues, the results of a previous, pre-revision survey of geography teaching and CC in Northern Ireland primary schools are compared to the equivalent results from the current, post-revision survey.

Geography and CC: pre- and post-curriculum revision surveys

In 2005, before the revised curriculum was implemented, a questionnaire survey of primary school teachers in Northern Ireland was carried out to gain information on the geography-based topics which were then being taught and the levels of CC used for each topic (Green-wood 2007). Comparisons can be made to the present questionnaire data by looking only at the information concerning P5 and P6 teachers and only at topics that are clearly geography-led topics (2005: $n = 99$ teachers; 2010: $n = 225$ teachers). The most important aspect of comparison – that of levels of CC – is discussed below.

The number of topics taught at each of the five levels of CC in both surveys is illustrated in Figure 2. These figures reveal that there has been a significant change in the levels of CC reported by the two sets of respondents in the pre- and post-revised curriculum surveys, in that there has been a marked shift to the right side of the graph in 2010 compared with 2005. In the 2010 survey, a much greater proportion of the topics were taught at the higher CC Levels 4 and 5 while a much smaller percentage of topics were taught at the lower CC Levels 1 and 2. In 2005, the mean CC figure for all geography-based topics taught in P5 and P6 was 2.93 (SD = 0.94); in 2010 that figure had risen to 3.64 (SD = 0.93). Using a 't'-test, the difference between the two means (utilising the transformation $\sqrt{(x + 0.5)}$ as advised by Sokal and Rohlf 1995) was found to be highly significant ($t_{695} = 9.701$, $P = 6 \times 10^{-21}$).

It is clear that teachers have responded in an obvious way to the recommendations concerning connected learning set out in the revised NIC. However, as will be seen below, while the majority of teachers indicate that they are favourably disposed to CC in general and the creation of the WAU Area of Learning in particular, there is a significant minority of teachers whose responses indicate either an ambivalence or antipathy towards these changes.

Opinions about cross-curricular teaching

In both the individual and group interviews, the interviewees were asked about their understandings of the pros and cons of teaching using a cross-curricular or a subject-focused

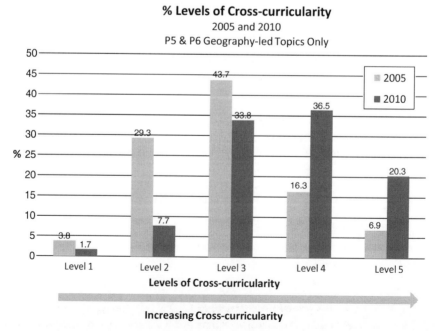

Figure 2.   Comparison of the CC levels of P5 and 6 geography-led topics in 2005 and 2010.

approach. In general, the response of the teachers interviewed was that the 'connected learn-ing' approach within the NIC produced more creativity and was more holistic, meaningful and relevant for the pupils or that the pupils were helped to be more independent and con-fident. Three of the individuals interviewed alluded to the benefits of 'joined-up experience' and the idea that subjects are artificial constructs for young children. The point was made that it was vital that pupils made the connections, not just teachers, and a significant number of teachers said that they saw evidence that this had occurred.

> A cross-curricular approach helps children make connections and see relevance. It backs up and underlines learning in other areas and underlines work they have already done. (P5/6 teacher)

Similarly, individuals from the Area Boards and CCEA also spoke about the potential for cross-curricular approaches to improve pupil understanding and confidence. One Board officer discussed pupil 'learning entitlement' and said that:

> Topics have the potential to act as the immediate vehicle to join up children's learning experi-ences in a way that subjects can't. (Board Officer)

A significant number of the questionnaire responses concerning teachers' opinions of 'con-nected learning' were also very positive: 77 of the 225 teachers responding to a question about 'connected learning' in the NI Curriculum said that, for them, it works well, using descriptors such as 'a great idea', 'useful', 'appropriate', 'valuable' and 'adds depth and meaning':

> I have found great benefits from connecting the children's learning. It makes it all click into place for them! (P5 teacher)

The questionnaire respondents were asked if they thought the grouping of science, history and geography into one Area of Learning was a good idea. Of the 221 who responded to this question, 63.4% said 'Yes', 31.2% said 'No' and 5.4% were 'Undecided'. Some of the most frequently made comments at this point were that the combination of history, geography and science was a natural, meaningful and relevant one. A number of the respondents said that they, as teachers, always tried to link these subjects, and that topics provide more depth and detail, more variety and a better learning experience than single subject teaching. The respondents were asked to list any advantages or disadvantages in the group-ing of geography, history and science in one Area of Learning. A significant number of tea-chers recorded some advantages but no disadvantages, using words like 'connected', 'cohesive' and 'holistic' to describe the potential curriculum benefits. However, 36 of the teachers recorded for 'Advantages' that there were 'None'.

Skills development and motivation improvements

Some of the most important positive arguments made in both interviews and questionnaires centred on the benefits which teachers felt had accrued in terms of skills development and increased pupil motivation. In seven of the interviews, teachers spoke about how they felt that a 'connected learning' approach lowered the risk of an over-emphasis on content while at the same time it facilitated the development of skills, stressing the importance of trans-ferable skills. Teachers in almost all of the group interviews described how they felt that pupils were more interested, involved and excited if teaching was carried out in a cross-curricular way, a number of them using the word *ownership*. Increased pupil enthusiasm and enjoyment were noted by a number of the questionnaire respondents.

Another (unforeseen) factor which emerged from both interviews and questionnaires was an increase in teacher enjoyment, seen by some as a vital pre-requisite for pupil enjoyment. For example, one teacher who was interviewed spoke about her teaching within the NIC by saying:

> I think my children are enjoying it more because I am enjoying it more. (P4 teacher)

A total of 88 of the questionnaire respondents wrote unprompted about how the introduction of the revised curriculum had proved to be a very positive experience for them personally, increasing their interest, enthusiasm and enjoyment in teaching, partly due to what they saw as an increase in teacher autonomy and *empowerment*.

Critical concerns

A significant number of respondents to the questionnaire as well as the individual and group interviewees reported a number of disadvantages and problems with 'connected learning' and the WAU Area of Learning. The most frequently voiced responses of this kind contained the idea that topics may be more contrived than subject-based planning. The danger of contrivance and artificiality and the temptation to include too much content in topic planning were noted by all five of the Area Board officers, who called for teachers to use a mixture of planning approaches, including subject-based teaching. One suggested that:

> There will be times when you have to teach something discretely; you make connections where appropriate. (Board Officer)

Worryingly, a number of questionnaire respondents wrote that they had felt pressure to create strongly integrated topics which resulted in them contriving curricular links, some implying that the guidance they had received in training courses had led them in this direction in their planning. Some wrote about the dangers of 'difficult', 'confused' or 'artificial' links in planning topics.

A second major issue raised was the possibility of the loss of specific content and skills associated with the three WAU subjects. A fear expressed was that cross-curricular planning could over-emphasise content as opposed to skills. Nine teachers in their questionnaire responses stated clearly that they preferred the structure of separate subjects to cross-curricular planning. One was particularly vehement in her opposition to connected learning; in answering whether or not it is a good idea that the subjects have been linked in the WAU Area of Learning, she wrote:

> Absolutely not! Definitely not at KS2. Children are not learning as much as previously – the curriculum in these subjects has been diluted. (P5/6 teacher)

The teachers who expressed concerns about a connected learning approach most frequently cited the possible loss of science skills and content (as opposed to geography or history). A total of 80 comments about loss of science were made in questionnaire responses. It was felt that this focus on science stems from the fact that in the previous iteration of the curriculum science had status as a 'core' subject alongside literacy and numeracy, and many primary schools had science coordinators. In many teachers' eyes, science had suffered a serious demotion.

This finding is reinforced by the results of a small-scale survey of primary school teachers by Johnson (2013). The majority of the teachers in her survey (90% of 29 teachers) said that they were spending less time teaching science than previously, with 50% saying that that this reduction was substantial. A number of teachers considered that topic work lent itself more easily to history and geography rather than science. Johnson concluded that teachers did not always recognise opportunities to link science to topic work in a meaningful way and that training and support were needed if they were successfully to make these conceptual links. She expressed concern that science was being watered down and had the potential to become 'lost' in the WAU.

Eleven teachers complained more generally that subjects were losing their identity or that their pupils were unaware of what 'subject' they were doing:

> I find my class think they are missing out on subjects; they ask – 'when are we doing history/geography/science?' (P5/6/7 teacher)

Some of the teachers interviewed asserted that subject-based teaching could at times be more in-depth while cross-curricular work could, paradoxically, be 'bitty'. In one school where interviews took place, the KS2 teachers agreed that teaching using a subject focus avoids the dilution and superficiality that can occur when using a cross-curricular approach, noting also that it was easier for them to monitor coverage and progression when focusing on subjects.

Overall attitudes to change

The responses of each teacher to six of the questions in the questionnaire concerning opinions about CC in the NIC were analysed to determine his or her overall 'Attitude to Change' (ATC); each respondent was designated as being essentially positive, negative or ambivalent. The result was that 70.6% of the 225 respondents were classified as being broadly positive in their attitude to the changes listed above; 24% gave answers which suggested a degree of ambivalence to the changes; and 5.3% were classified as being broadly negative. The only other recent canvassing of teacher opinion about the revised NI Curriculum has been a report entitled *Teachers' Voice 2010* compiled by the General Teaching Council for Northern Ireland (GTCNI 2011). This survey covered both primary and post-primary teachers. The response to one question relating to the NI Curriculum produced a similar response to the ATC figures reported above: in the GTCNI survey 71% of the respondents felt that the new curriculum had impacted on the effectiveness of their teaching in a positive way; negative impact was reported by 12% of the respondents and 13% responded 'Not at all'.

Discussion

The section above has discussed the opinions of teachers and stakeholders on CC and WAU reported in the interviews and questionnaires. A wide range of views was expressed, some vehemently negative, but the majority of teachers were positive or very positive towards 'connected learning' and the placing of geography, history and science within the one

Area of Learning. Around 86% of the questionnaire respondents were able to list at least one advantage of this way of arranging the curriculum.

Balanced approaches to CC and WAU

One aspect of how teachers have put cross-curricular planning into practice within the revised NIC is revealed in the interview and questionnaire responses: a significant number of teachers can be said to have taken a balanced and pragmatic approach to CC in their planning and teaching, stressing that there is no one 'right' organisational method, and that in fact a variety of approaches was beneficial for pupils. For example, one P6 teacher said:

> I don't think you can say that one approach works and the other doesn't. I think you have to assess what the children are learning and at the end of the day judge which is the best way forward for them. (P6 teacher)

Some stated that not everything integrates easily or equally, that some topics do not lend themselves naturally to a strongly integrated approach and that at times it was more efficient and effective to teach aspects of the curriculum as separate subjects:

> It is important not to forget about the science, history and geography areas that do not lend themselves to connected learning. (P4/5 teacher)

It seems also that the majority of teachers appear to be using cross-curricular approaches in a reasonably 'restrained' way – that most WAU topics listed were being taught at a medium to 'quite high' level of CC, and a relatively small percentage of topics were being taught at the highest level of CC – Level 5 – where it is more possible that topics can become unfocused and 'woolly'. The teachers who, in their questionnaire responses, were most strongly opposed to CC as a concept may have had in mind, perhaps based on previous unhelpful experiences, very wide-ranging, unfocused topics which proved ineffective in terms of pupil learning in their classrooms. Respondents at both ends of the CC 'Levels' spectrum might benefit from being shown a 'middle way'. For example, teachers who expressed serious concern about the loss of subject content might be 'won over' to cross-curricular planning if they saw topics set out where the subject content was clearly at the core of a weakly integrated or subject-focused topic (as argued for by, e.g. Alexander, Rose, and Woodhead 1992; Palmer and Pettitt 1993; Barnes 2011). Similarly, respondents who felt under pressure to 'connect everything' would benefit from seeing clear exemplars of topics where CC is 'weak' – that the links with other subjects or Areas of Learning are few, but the links which are made are purposeful and provide strength to the topic as a whole.

Effective learning – a combination of elements

During some of the interviews and in a number of the questionnaire responses, teachers made it clear that they believed that, in order to maximise the effectiveness of pupil learning, connected learning needed to be used in conjunction with pupil involvement in planning and an element of pupil choice in topics. Where possible the topic being studied should be linked to the pupils' own experience and involve a high degree of activity-based learning. It was agreed by the majority of the individuals interviewed that if the only change within the revised curriculum was a change to cross-curricular work, then no great increase in effective learning would be achieved; rather, all of the aspects listed above needed to be developed at the same time. If this occurred, improvements in pupil learning should be seen. It was also noted, however, that while these changes might prove very effective for pupils, they are not easy changes for teachers to make and require teacher time and effort, and ideally a substantial and effective training programme. One of the skills which teachers and schools working within the revised NIC have to develop more so than previously is the skill of 'curriculum-making'. The term 'curriculum-making' (Halocha 2010; Owens 2010) is described in The Geographical Association's 'Manifesto' (GA 2009) and was encouraged through its *Action Plan for Geography* (GA 2011). It is defined as

> ... the creative act of interpreting a curriculum specification and turning it into a coherent scheme of work. [It]lies at the heart of good teaching and heightens the enjoyment of teaching. (quoted in Owens 2010, 8)

This skill is especially important in the area of WAU since the provision in the revised NIC of a wide degree of teacher choice has produced the possibility for teachers of devising a great variety of cross-curricular topic permutations, which is something with which many of today's teachers are unfamiliar; they would benefit greatly from specific in-service training in this area.

Linked with curriculum-making, and of specific relevance to geography-based topics, cross-curricular local studies work was seen by many of the respondents as an aspect which, when done well, can result in excellent work being produced. A number of teachers referred specifically to feeling that they now had greater opportunity to engage in the planning and teaching of topics which have local, topical, current, relevant elements or involved 'spontaneous' teaching. The Board officer member of the Inspectorate who was interviewed stressed that a great deal of effort is required before high quality local studies work can happen because it is personalised to the area and needs a great deal of research, planning and skill on the part of teachers.

Conclusion

The present research is timely because it has taken place during a period when, arguably, what is taught and how it is taught in primary schools in Northern Ireland has changed more radically and at a greater pace than at any time previously. Evidence of the uptake of 'new' initiatives such as activity-based learning, thinking skills and AfL approaches as well as 'connected learning' is visible in many primary school classrooms. For some teachers, the change to the revised curriculum has been nothing short of a revolution in that they have seen the potential benefits of the new approaches and embraced them positively and wholeheartedly, altering radically the ways in which they plan and teach in their classrooms. Some teachers had adopted these approaches even before they were statutorily required to do so. Others have been more resistant and some have been openly negative to the changes. This spectrum of views emerged most strongly in the questionnaire survey in this research and which allowed the respondents to convey their views anonymously.

On the basis of the results of this study, the authors of the revised NIC should be heartened that such a major curricular change has been implemented effectively and relatively seamlessly by Northern Ireland's primary school teachers. A comparison of the 2005 geography-based survey and the 2010 questionnaire survey within this research shows that teachers in P5 and P6 classrooms are now planning and teaching topics at higher levels of CC than they were before the implementation of the new curriculum. However, in doing this, a significant number of teachers have adopted a pragmatic, balanced, thoughtful and reflective approach to their planning.

An integrated approach to the primary curriculum requires teachers to have high levels of skill in terms of curriculum subject knowledge and teaching methods (Shulman 1987; Burgess 2004) as well as 'curriculum-making'. Similarly, Wood (2011, 39) suggested that teachers utilising cross-curricular approaches need a deep and sophisticated understanding of learning and a wide 'pedagogical repertoire'. Teaching cross-curricular topics is not easy. Effective teaching of topics within 'WAU' may mean that teachers will include open-ended and flexible approaches in their delivery, and use a range of resources and a mixture of whole class, group work and independent work. All of these aspects require of teachers a degree of confidence as well as knowledge and skill – aspects which can be developed by the provision of substantial, effective in-service training. This is what is needed.

References

Alexander, R. 2009. *Children, Their World, Their Education. Final Report and Recommendations of the Cambridge Primary Review*. London: Routledge.

Alexander, R., J. Rose, and C. Woodhead. 1992. *Curriculum Organisation and Classroom Practice in Primary Schools: A Discussion Paper*. London: DES.

Alexander, J., P. Walsh, R. Jarman, and B. McClune. 2008. "From Rhetoric to Reality; Advancing Literacy by Cross-Curricular Means." *The Curriculum Journal* 19 (1): 23–35.

Alleman, J. and J. Brophy. 1993. "Is Curriculum Integration a Boon or Threat to Social Studies?" *Social Education* 57 (6): 287–291.

Barlow, C. and A. Brook. 2010. "Geography and Art: Local Area Work." *Primary Geographer* 72 (Summer): 16–17.

Barnes, J. 2011. *Cross-Curricular Learning 3–14*. 2nd ed. London: Paul Chapman.

Bell, P. 1996. *The Primary School National Curriculum Topic Book*. Preston: Topical Resources.

Bernstein, B. 1971. "On the Classification and Framing of Educational Knowledge." In *Knowledge and Control: New Directions for the Sociology of Education*, edited by M. Young, 47–49. London: Macmillan.

Bernstein, B. 1975. *Class, Codes and Control Vol 3*. London: Routledge and Kegan Paul.

Blenkin, G. M., and A. V. Kelly. 1981. *The Primary Curriculum*. London: Harper and Row.

Burgess, H. 2004. "The Primary Strategy: A Chance for a 'Whole' Curriculum." *Education 3–13* 32 (2): 10–17.

Catling, S. 2010. "Understanding and Developing Primary Geography." In *Primary Geography Handbook*, edited by S. Scoffham, 74–91. Sheffield: Geographical Association.

Caul, L. ed. 1993. *A Common Curriculum: The Case of Northern Ireland*. Belfast: LRU Stranmillis College.

Council for the Curriculum, Examinations and Assessment (CCEA). 2006. *The Revised NI Curriculum: Planning for Implementation*. Belfast: CCEA. Accessed January 24, 2011. www.nicurriculum.org.uk/docs/background/DVD_Booklet.pdf

Council for the Curriculum, Examinations and Assessment (CCEA). 2007. *The Northern Ireland Curriculum: Primary*. Belfast: CCEA.

Coe, J. 2010. "Areas of Learning." *Education 3–13* 38 (4): 395–402.

Cohen, L., L. Manion, and K. Morrison. 2011. *Research Methods in Education*. 7th ed. London: Routledge.

Darling, J. 1994. *Child-Centred Education and Its Critics*. London: Paul Chapman.

Dearing, R. 1994. *The National Curriculum and Its Assessment: Final Report*. London: School Curriculum and Assessment Authority.

Department of Education, Northern Ireland (DENI). 1996. *The Northern Ireland Curriculum: Programmes of Study and Attainment Targets*. Belfast: HMSO.

Entwistle, H. 1970. *Child-Centred Education*. London: Methuen. Accessed December 20, 2010. www.etini.gov.uk/index/surveys-evaluations/

Foley, M. and J. Janikoun. 1996. *The Really Practical Guide to Primary Geography*. 2nd ed. Cheltenham: Stanley Thornes.

Geographical Association (GA). 2009. *A Different View: A Manifesto for Geography*. Sheffield: Geographical Association.

Geographical Association (GA). 2011. *The Action Plan for Geography 2006–2011: The Final Report and Evaluation*. www.geography.org.uk/download/GA_APGFinalReport.pdf.

Gardner, H. 2004. *Changing Minds: The Art and Science of Changing our own and Other People's Minds*. Boston, MA: Harvard Business School.

General Teaching Council for Northern Ireland (GTCNI). 2011. *Teachers' Voice 2010*. Belfast: GTCNI. Accessed February 2, 2012. www.gtcni.org.uk/publications/uploads/document/Teachers%20Voice%20Survey%20Report%20Bookmarked.pdf

Greenwood, R. 2007. "Geography Teaching in Northern Ireland Primary Schools: A Survey of Content and Cross-Curricularity." *International Research in Geographical and Environmental Education* 16 (4): 380–398.

Halocha, J. 2010. "A Geographical Opportunity? Taking a Fresh Look at the Primary Curriculum." *Primary Geographer* 72 (Summer): 5–7.

Hayes, D. 2010. "The Seductive Charms of a Cross-Curricular Approach." *Education 3–13* 38 (4): 381–87.

Johnson, A. 2013. "Is Science Lost in 'The World Around Us'?." *Primary Science* 126 (January/February): 8–10.

Johnston, J. 2011. "The Cross-Curricular Approach in Key Stage 1." In *Cross-curricular Teaching in the Primary School: Planning and Teaching Imaginative Lessons*, edited by T. Kerry, 71–95. London: Routledge.

Kerry, T. 2011. *Ed. Cross-curricular Teaching in the Primary School: Planning and Teaching Imaginative Lessons*. London: Routledge.

Kerry, T., and J. Eggleston. 1988. *Topic Work in the Primary School*. London: Routledge.

Knight, P. 1993. *Primary Geography, Primary History*. London: David Fulton.

Krause, J. and J. Millward. 2010. "The Geography Subject Leader." In *Primary Geography Handbook*, edited by S. Scoffham, 334–347. Sheffield: Geographical Association.

Laurie, J. 2011. "Curriculum Planning and Preparation for Cross-Curricular Teaching." In *Cross-curricular Teaching in the Primary School: Planning and Teaching Imaginative Lessons*, edited by T. Kerry, 125–141. London: Routledge.

Lonning, R. and T. DeFranco. 1997. "Integration of Science and Mathematics: A Theoretical Model." *School Science and Mathematics* 97 (4): 212–215.

McNamara, D. 1994. *Classroom Pedagogy and Primary Practice*. London: Routledge.

Martin, F. 2002. "Primary Historians and Geographers Learning from Each Other: Making Supportive Cross-Curricular Links to Enhance Learning and Teaching." *Primary History* 30 (January): 18–21.

Morrison, K. 1986. "Primary Schools Subject Specialists as Agents of School-Based Curriculum Change." *School Organisation* 6 (2): 175–83.

Morrison, K. and K. Ridley. 1988. *Curriculum Planning and the Primary School*. London: Chapman.

Office for Standards in Education (Ofsted). 2008. *Geography in Schools: Changing Practice*. London: Office for Standards in Education.

Office for Standards in Education (Ofsted). 2011. *Geography – Learning to Make a World of Difference*. London: Office for Standards in Education.

Owens, P. 2010. "Re-Making the Curriculum." *Primary Geographer* 72 (Summer): 8–9.

Palmer, J. and D. Pettitt. 1993. *Topic Work in the Early Years – Organising the Curriculum for 4- to 8-Year Olds*. London: Routledge.

Punch, K. 2009. *Introduction to Research Methods in Education*. London: Sage.

Rose, J. 2009. *The Independent Review of the Primary Curriculum*. Final Report. Accessed March 5, 2011. www.education.gov.uk/publications/standard/publicationdetail/page1/DCSF-00499-2009

Rowley, C., and H. Cooper, eds. 2009. *Cross Curricular Approaches Towards Teaching and Learning*. London: Sage.

Ryan, A., and J. Jones. 1998. "Teaching the Foundation Subjects – Geography and History." In *Teaching in Primary Schools*, edited by A. Cashdan, and L. Overall, 155–168. London: Cassell.

Shulman, L. 1987. "Knowledge and Teaching: Foundations of a New Reform." *Harvard Educational Review* 57 (1): 1–21.

Sokal, R., and F. Rohlf. 1995. *Biometry*. 3rd ed. New York: Freeman.

Tann, S. ed. 1988. *Developing Topic Work in Primary Schools*. London: Falmer Press.

Thomson, P., J. McGregor, and E. Sanders. 2009. "Changing Schools: More than a Lick of Paint and a Well-Orchestrated Performance?" *Improving Schools* 12 (1): 43–57.

Tyler, K. 1992. "Differentiation and Integration of the Primary Curriculum." *Journal of Curriculum Studies* 24 (6): 563–67.

Walkerdine, V. 1983. "It's Only Natural: Rethinking Child-Centred Pedagogy." In *Is There Anyone Here From Education?* edited by A. M. Wolpe and J. Donald, 79–87. London: Pluto Press.

Ward, S. 1996. "Thematic Approaches to the Core National Curiculum." In *The Primary Core National Curriculum – Policy Into Practice*, edited by D. Coulby, and S. Ward, 71–95. London: Cassell.

Wood, E. 2011. "Cross-curricular Teaching to Support Child-Initiated Learning in EYFS and Key Stage 1." In *Cross-Curricular Teaching in the Primary School: Planning and Teaching Imaginative Lessons,* edited by T. Kerry, 39–51. London: Routledge.

Wortham, S. 1996. *The Integrated Classroom: The Assessment-Curriculum Link in the Early Childhood Classroom*. Englewood Cliffs, NJ: Prentice Hall.

Teachers' perspectives on curriculum making in Primary Geography in England

Simon Catling

School of Education, Faculty of Humanities and Social Sciences, Oxford Brookes University, Oxford, UK

The phrase 'curriculum making' has recently been used to describe medium-term planning and teachers' enactment of such planning in the classroom. This narrows the term's initial use from that in the first half of the twentieth century when it was employed inclusively from national programmes to lesson planning. While considering related studies about curriculum making, this paper focuses on the interpretation described and used by the Geographical Association (GA) to encourage more open approaches to medium-term curriculum planning in England by teachers. It reports the outcomes of a small-scale study of primary teachers' perspectives on their experiences of curriculum making during one GA project, 'The Young Geographers Project'. It identifies a number of 'curriculum dynamics', including teachers' feelings of liberation, children's agency in curriculum making, the importance of subject knowledge, engaging with children's everyday experiences and interests, and purposefulness for curriculum topics while retaining flexibility and openness. Reflecting on these findings, 10 features pertinent to curriculum making are noted.

Introduction

Since the late 1990s primary schooling in England has been affected by a wide range of government initiatives, which throughout the 2000s emphasised the development of children's literacy and numeracy capabilities while seemingly constraining the wider curriculum. This inhibited all the foundation subjects (Alexander, 2010). Meanwhile evidence accrued of improvements in children's learning, though there had been some narrowing in approaches to classroom teaching in many schools (Alexander, Doddington, Gray, Hargreaves, & Kershner, 2010). Teachers felt increasingly constrained in their curriculum and teaching practices (Tymms & Merrell, 2010). Nonetheless some considered that opportunities provided by curriculum guidance at the turn of the 2000s, for example in primary geography (QCA/DfEE, 1998/2000), helped them focus their curriculum to meet the English national curriculum subject requirements more effectively (DfES/QCA, 1999). Others viewed these changes to be more inhibiting (Catling, Bowles, Halocha, Martin, & Rawlinson, 2007). The government's response was to encourage refreshment in teachers' approaches to the primary curriculum, teaching and learning (DfES, 2003). A broader-based curriculum and greater flexibility for teachers were encouraged to enable them to use their professional skills to develop challenging and motivating pedagogy, though the reality of this occurring was questioned (Alexander, 2008a). Primary schools were invited to be more creative and adventurous, while using cross-curricular and subject approaches. This was reinforced in the 2008–9 review of England's primary curriculum (Rose, 2009), which drew on pertinent examples to illustrate how teachers could exercise increased autonomy in their classroom curriculum decision-making while working with national curriculum requirements and guidance. In particular, there was encouragement to focus on active learning strategies in the primary classroom (Monk & Silman, 2011).

Linked with these developments, England's then Training and Development Agency for Schools (TDA) offered funding to promote teachers' development of curriculum opportunities as a mechanism to reinvigorate and develop their teaching. This funding was focused on subject leaders who might consequently foster curriculum development and innovation in their schools (TDA, 2007). The Geographical Association (GA) successfully bid for funding from this stream (GA, 2007) and initiated a curriculum enhancement project, *Young Geographers – A Living Geography Project for Primary Schools*. At the heart of this project was what the GA termed *curriculum making*. The project provided opportunities for teachers to develop a class curriculum topic, with a strong geographical focus, which they could initiate and structure outside their normal scheme of work, but which would enhance it by opening new or additional lines of enquiry with their children. The project was undertaken in the context of the GA's *living geography* model which encouraged teachers to draw on and engage children's environmental experiences (GA, 2007; Mitchell, 2009). This article examines the teachers' emergent perspectives from their engagement in *The Young Geographers Project*, focusing on their reflections about *curriculum making*.

The term *curriculum making*: antecedents and meanings

The phrase *curriculum making* has been used for a century and more. Bobbitt's (1918) seminal text on curriculum argued that 'curriculum making' was poorly developed in the early twentieth century as a rigorous and well-structured approach to curriculum design and content decisions. By adopting a 'scientific method' to curriculum making Bobbitt proposed that the school curriculum must focus on what was to be taught in schools for children's learning and understanding to go beyond their everyday life experiences and knowledge (Bobbitt, 1918, p. 44). He identified extensive lists of human characteristics and abilities from which a curriculum should be created and organised to extend and deepen academic and vocational knowledge (Bobbitt, 1918, 1922). Such content information would be structured and sequenced to enable the curriculum to be planned across year groups as the basis for lessons. Amongst others, Draper (1936) identified an intermediate stage in planning between school and year programmes and lessons, which he termed 'units of work'. These, he argued, would be fully prescribed and arranged by the teacher who was the key curriculum maker, organising and structuring each unit. Draper also included a more 'progressive', child-centred approach to planning units of work, where children would contribute ideas co-operatively with the teacher to their planning and would be engaged through what today are described as 'active learning' approaches (Monk & Silman, 2011), influenced, it would seem, by the arguments of Dewey (1902).

In subsequent decades, the term 'curriculum making' was less frequently applied, while the literature and debate about the nature and use of curriculum in schools extended considerably. Curriculum making was described using other terms in England and elsewhere, for example curriculum design, curriculum organisation, curriculum planning and curriculum construction. It was allied with other phrases, such as curriculum processes and curriculum delivery, to explain curriculum construction and implementation from national to school to classroom levels. These terms encompassed the same aspects as initially set out for 'curriculum making', namely curriculum aims and intentions, curriculum and learning objectives or targets, curriculum content and subjects, schemes of work, units of work and lesson plans, as well as assessment foci and methods. Other terms such as syllabus, programme and course became commonplace to refer to the nature of curriculum prescriptions, plans and structures influencing or enacted by schools (Brady & Kennedy, 1999; Posner & Rudnitsky, 1986). But, at all levels, this was contentious. Goodson (1988) and Kelly (2009), for example, recognised the curriculum as an arena of conflict – where curriculum content and sequence, and implicit and essential approaches to organisation and teaching, could be contested at levels from government to the classroom. At the level of units of work, taught for periods of half to a whole term, there remains debate about the extent to which teachers should follow pre-determined outlines and pre-structured units or have the flexibility and freedom to decide, organise and develop units which they see as most appropriate for their children

(Alexander, 2010; Cox, 2011; Male, 2012). The social and political basis for curriculum intentions and, consequently, for the nature of classroom curriculum decisions is not neutral (Mufti & Peace, 2012). In recent years English primary education has focused on the impact of the national curriculum and the emphasis placed on the core subjects of English and mathematics. However, primary curriculum discussion has re-engaged with curriculum focus and organisation and debates about product or process approaches to design and practice, as consecutive governments have emphasised strongly curriculum 'delivery' by teachers (Alexander, 2000, 2010; Kelly, 2009; Wyse et al., 2012). Ways to enact the primary curriculum at times appear contradictory – even in the same school and classrooms – as teachers use a more structured and formal format when teaching the core subjects, while they try to apply a 'creative curriculum' approach to the rest of the subjects (Alexander, 2010) through their medium-term units of work.

Over the years curriculum construction, design, organisation and planning have explored how the values and perspectives of teachers influence their own approaches (Hawthorne, 1992) and to what extent even in more controlled contexts curricula 'emerge' as teachers determine how to shape them in practice (Grundy, 1988, Wyse et al., 2012). There is much now that 'curriculum making' encompasses, but a narrower interpretation is the focus in this study. At the turn of the twenty-first century the term *curriculum making* re-emerged, for instance in the context of post-compulsory education curriculum construction in the late 1990s (Bloomer, 1997) and in reflections on policy, professionalism and design issues affecting the primary curriculum and its future (Hulme & Livingston, 2012). Recently Edwards, Miller, and Priestley (2009a) have considered curriculum making at the classroom level of a unit of study. This and another study (Clayton, 2007) serve as preludes to introducing the use and meaning of *curriculum making* by the GA as a context for its recent projects.

The University of Stirling's *Curriculum Making in School and College* research project was initiated to investigate curriculum making practice in an upper secondary school and a further education college in Scotland. The focus was 'cultures of curriculum making' (Edwards et al., 2009a, 2009b), particularly in relation to teacher and student perspectives and the enactment of the curriculum in classroom settings. In reviewing the related literature, five factors affecting curriculum making were identified:

- *contextual factors*, e.g. national policy, funding arrangements;
- *organisational factors*, e.g. nature and size of institution and subject departments, styles of management, levels and types of resources, locus of decision-making, internal and external assessments;

- *curriculum factors*, e.g. the ways in which curriculum is prescribed, nature of the curriculum, i.e. academic or vocational;
- *micro-political factors*, e.g. collegial, hierarchical or individualistic, expectations of students and parents; and
- *individual factors*, e.g. professional formation and dispositions of teachers, student backgrounds and prior experiences. (Edwards et al., 2009a, p. 30)

Edwards (2009, p. 1) describes these factors as 'external to curriculum making practices and explanatory of them', in the sense that they describe the contexts of and influences on curriculum making in the classroom. Findings from the project noted particularly the influence of *organisational factors*, for instance the impact of timetabling and the effect of physical teaching space; *micro-political factors*, such as students' motivations, expectations and preferences in shaping their engagement in the curriculum; and *individual factors*, including the role of teachers' subject knowledge experience, their preferred approaches to teaching and interacting with students, and the variety of teachers' and students' performativity (Edwards et al., 2009b). Inherent in these factors are opportunities and limitations for teachers' sense of their own agency in their curriculum making which may be influenced by a sense of 'fidelity' or challenge to national or school requirements and educational cultures (Priestley, Edwards, Miller, & Priestley, 2010).

An American study of beginning teachers investigated their approach to curriculum making through their initiation of curriculum projects in schools (Clayton, 2007). The students reflected on their perspectives of themselves as teachers, using as their context their practice of planning and implementing curriculum at classroom level. These novice teachers explored their relationship to the curriculum, their subject knowledge and their sense of curriculum ownership. This involved confronting and reappraising their preconceived views of teachers as curriculum managers and transmitters of knowledge. They began to recognise what their pupils bring into school and to raise the expectations of those pupils while involving them in developing the curriculum project. This context is explored in the *Young People's Geography Project* in England, undertaken with experienced secondary school teachers (Biddulph, 2011, 2012, 2013). Clayton's study, though limited, postulates that a praxis approach to developing knowledge of oneself as a teacher and to providing opportunities for self-reappraisal can be fostered through curriculum making. Curriculum making can be seen here not only as being about curriculum decisions, organisation, resourcing and practice but also about self-exploration and awareness aligned with evaluation of personal perspectives and practices, as a basis for enhancing teaching and learning.

The GA's interpretation of 'curriculum making'

Working parallel to these research studies, the GA's development work with secondary and primary teachers focused on what it termed *curriculum making* (GA, 2012). Developed through the *Action Plan for Geography*, a government funded project from 2006 to 2011 (GA/RGS, 2006, 2011), curriculum making was described as:

> The creative act of interpreting a curriculum specification or scheme of work and turning it into a coherent, challenging and engaging and enjoyable scheme of work. (GA, 2012)

At the heart of curriculum making, the GA describes three core components: the subject, teacher choices about what is to be taught, and students' personal experience, interests and motivations. These are fundamentally inter-related, which Figure 1 illustrates. A key focus is allied to Bobbitt's (1918) aspiration for the curriculum and teaching to take children beyond what they already know, understand and appreciate, in this case through developing subject understanding using curriculum planning and the teaching repertoire.

There are several aspects of this perspective on curriculum making presented in the GA's and others' literature. First, geography (or any subject or area of learning) is a *subject resource* which helps pupils to appreciate and deepen their understanding about the world more effectively and

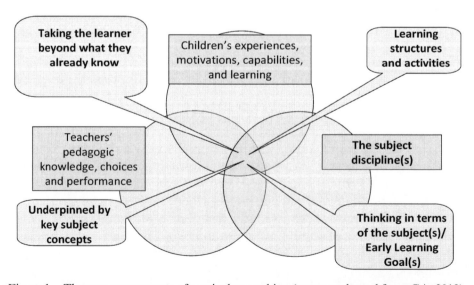

Figure 1.   The core components of curriculum making (source: adapted from GA, 2012).

fully. Secondly, curriculum making is about *'enacting geography'* through its teaching, the point of which is to give it 'purpose'. Purpose includes the intention to develop geographical understanding, as well as to be purposeful for children, which involves studies making sense to them, providing insight and being pertinent to their lives. A key teaching and learning approach to employ through curriculum making is 'enquiry', which requires teachers to 'perform a delicate balancing act', drawing upon the students' experiences, the subject resource and their own knowledge and craft skills. Third *children's experiences, attitudes and understandings* should be brought to the subject and their learning, such as their geographical experiences in their personal, daily lives. The GA states that through 'curriculum making' these three aspects are held in balance (GA, 2009a, 2012). Its key ingredients are the approaches and techniques teachers use, their expertise and practical skills, students' needs, interests and ways of learning, and geography as a dynamic, evolving subject and its role and value.

Within this vision of curriculum making teachers are to use their passion and enthusiasm for geography to create motivating and engaging, even surprising, studies, based in the school's or department's geography schemes of work. At the heart of the GA's case is that curriculum making is a professional activity, the purview of 'confident, autonomous teachers'. It is argued that:

> Designing the curriculum is not just a technical matter, specifying objectives and a course of study to meet them. It is a moral concern, and should reflect what we think we should be teaching. (GA, 2009a, p. 27)

Curriculum making, then, gives the teacher permission to decide how they are going to work in relation to the subject, to the children and in terms of their range of approaches and techniques in teaching – and that these decisions are to be more than pragmatic: to be true to the teacher's subject appreciation, teaching practices and values in relation to children as learners. It is vital, it is argued, in the context of curriculum making that teachers 'have a productive, ongoing relationship with the subject...' which '...gives them the confidence to innovate, to respond to the unexpected and at the same time maintain high standards of disciplinary enquiry' (GA, 2009a, p. 28). Not only should teachers understand their children and their learning and have a strong repertoire of stimulating approaches and techniques for teaching, but they must appreciate that geography, as any subject, is not static but evolving and that its approaches to understanding the world develop and change. Teachers, whether primary or secondary, need to appreciate the value of geography and the ways it enables children to view their lives and experiences. This requires that they have a clear sense of its subject content on which to draw to teach engagingly. Biddulph (2011, p. 50) sees a clear role for school pupils, where they 'share in democratic ways, both their own and their owned knowledges as well as disciplinary knowledge', drawn out through creative teaching processes. She sees curriculum making as a 'conversation' between pupils and teachers and sets it in the context of participatory engagement in curriculum and learning for children and teachers (Hopwood, 2007, 2012).

Curriculum making draws on 'living geography' (Mitchell, 2009), which emphasises the teaching of geography to bring it 'alive' for pupils. The key principles of living geography are:

- embracing children's and young people's geographies, by taking and treating their views seriously;
- being past, current and futures oriented;
- exploring often 'locally', but always set in the wider (global) context, fostering understanding of interlocking scales;
- investigating the processes which change environments and places;
- encouraging critical understanding of key geographical ideas, such as sustainable development, to help pupils appreciate the inter-connected nature of 'the physical and human worlds'. (Lambert, 2009, p. 7)

Living Geography concerns looking at and for 'local solutions' in curriculum making, appropriate to the school's context. It has been a 'banner' under which the GA has run a number of primary and secondary geography projects, including the *Young Geographers Project, Young Geographers Go Local/Go Global/Go Green* (GA, 2010) and *Making Geography Happen* (GA, 2011).

Lambert and Morgan (2010) argue that teachers are, inevitably, the curriculum makers. They distinguish curriculum making from curriculum planning and curriculum development. They see the latter occurring at levels 'above' curriculum making, which is given a context by national and regional curriculum policies and prescriptions as well as by school-level schemes of work for age phases, such as key stage 1 (5–7-year-olds) and key stage 2 (7–11-year-olds). Equally, they resist the notion that curriculum making occurs at the level of lesson planning, which they view as too specific. Curriculum making, as the GA also notes, lies at the level of turning school curriculum specifications into units of work, which are coherent and the basis for lesson sequences and which enable children to develop progressively their understanding and use of geographical ideas. It is this making of the classroom curriculum that draws together the three core components of: the subject(s) to develop pupils' understanding, the teacher's repertoire to create stimulating learning, and pupils' experiences, interests and learning. Brooks (2009) appreciates that this can seem a daunting challenge, but sees, in the context of a less prescribed set of national geography requirements, a positive opportunity for teachers to regain agency and thus develop effective, professional curriculum making.

The *Young Geographers Project*: investigating teachers' perspectives

The GA's *Young Geographers Project* was initiated to encourage primary school geography subject leaders to take initiatives in their professional practice as curriculum makers, as a prelude to curriculum development in their schools. Two cohorts of 10 primary teachers, with varied subject backgrounds in geography but who were strongly committed to the development of high quality geography in their classrooms and schools, participated, supported by two primary curriculum leaders in the GA. The project involved five aspects of practice:

- engaging practically in curriculum making through creating a class-based geography unit of work;
- using the motivation of 'living geography';
- engaging in learning outside the classroom, through fieldwork activities;
- focusing on education for sustainable development (one of the four aspects of the key stage 1 and 2 geography programmes of study);
- involving use of the local environment.

It encouraged the use of 'local solutions', to enable the projects to be appropriate for each school's context, including its children and its locality. The projects were run over one school term.

The geography subject leaders in the two cohorts – one in the north and one in the south of England – met on two occasions to discuss their project ideas and present their work to each other. Following the first meeting they were encouraged to maintain contact across their cohort, as a basis for sharing their ideas for topics, curriculum making approaches and the challenges facing them, and to support and aid each other. This recognised that geography subject leaders, perhaps the only geography enthusiast in their school, were often isolated. In a climate of declining local authority support the teachers found using email communication to exchange ideas and share frustrations enhancing and invigorating.

The focus of the study reported here was to investigate and evaluate the perspectives of the teachers about their experience of curriculum making (Catling, 2011a). The study was constrained by time, funding and the geographical distribution of the participants. Working with the two curriculum leaders, questionnaires and interviews were used to gather the teachers' responses to open-ended questions. An interpretivist approach was taken in this small-scale study (Dey, 1993; Thomas, 2009) which examined participants' views about what they intended to gain from their involvement, their confidence in teaching geography, their experience of fieldwork, the gains they anticipated for the children and the benefits and obstacles they anticipated or found through curriculum making. Participants completed a pre-project questionnaire as they began their curriculum making and a post-project questionnaire on completion of their class topic. A follow-up telephone interview was undertaken with half the teachers in each cohort three months after completing the project (Thomas, 2009; Robson, 2011). A number of the project outcomes were written up by teachers and posted on the GA's website (GA, 2009b). This study focuses and draws on the post-project questionnaires, interviews and written evaluations of 16 of the participants, since four were not able to undertake or engage fully with their projects.

The teachers involved were geography subject leaders in their school (and most had more than one subject to lead). They required the support of their head teacher to participate since the Project encouraged them to work outside their prescribed geography or humanities curriculum for the term. This was, essentially, an opportunistic sample of primary teachers who had an interest in teaching geography well (Newby, 2010; Cohen, Manion, & Morrison, 2011). They came from urban and rural schools of varied sizes and catchments. Only some had studied geography in their first degree or teaching qualification, and they varied in their length of time, teaching experience and responsibility held in their respective schools. The limitations of this small and self-selecting sample are recognised, as are the constraints of questionnaires and interviews. The study did not intend to investigate the classroom practice of these teachers but focused on their reflections on their experience of curriculum making. Inevitably, it was based on self-reporting and responses were taken on trust. It drew also on written material provided by some teachers about their projects and on a number of the presented outcomes placed on the GA's website (GA, 2009b). The views of the two curriculum leaders were sought to gather their reflections on the teachers' engagement with curriculum making.

The variety of data gathered was reviewed and analysed using a constant comparative method (Thomas, 2009; Newby, 2010; Cohen et al., 2011). This enabled a number of themes to emerge, based in the responses to the questionnaires and interviews. It was found that there were evident links with the GA's account of curriculum making. This is not surprising in view of the context in which the teachers involved undertook their projects. What it indicated, though, were additional insights and a number of features in the teachers' experience of curriculum making that can provide guidance for primary (and secondary) teachers. This article reports and discusses the emergent themes from the study.

Curriculum making: the teachers' perspectives

Two key characteristics for being a successful curriculum maker are enthusiasm and commitment (GA, 2009a). The teachers involved in the *Young Geographers Project* brought these qualities, yet at the same time were, mostly, somewhat nervous of the opportunity provided to them – since their teaching practice was not infrequently inhibited by the constraints instilled by the directives of the national strategies which still affected primary teaching (Alexander, 2010). Thus, the teachers viewed the opportunity offered by the project as both novel and risky while giving them some freedom to try different approaches to their curriculum and teaching. Several were beginning to experiment with a 'creative curriculum' which a number of head teachers encouraged. All the heads were supportive of their teachers' involvement in the project. This does not indicate that there were no constraints, but they were few given the supportive contexts within which the teachers worked. The key limitation the participants reported was the time factor, since the wider curriculum was not to be set aside and no additional time was available. They were required still to work to core subject requirements within their respective schools. Geography competed in their classes with other curriculum demands. At times they found themselves switching during the day between curriculum making and curriculum delivery, though, like the children, they seemed to cope with this. In one case a teacher was not allowed to take children off the school premises, though she could use the school grounds for field and 'local' work; she adapted her original intentions appropriately. There were, inevitably, some resource constraints, but teachers used the web and other means to circumvent these.

Given the committed nature of the participants in the *Young Geographers Project*, it is not surprising that the findings have a largely positive feel to them, though there are some surprises. Seven characteristics emerged from the project grouped under two categories. These categories are termed here *curriculum dynamics*. These are the 'ingredients' which provided opportunities for teachers to be proactive and to have agency as curriculum makers. What seems central to these characteristics is that they are, at heart, reflective of teachers' *attitudes* to themselves, the children and the potential of curriculum making. Without positive attitudes supporting them these characteristics would not function. This is consistent with the concept of curriculum making which, while reflective of curriculum requirements, requires teachers to be flexible and evolutionary in approach, providing direction and having goals while being discretionary, considering options and being decision-makers as a class project develops. The two categories of *curriculum dynamics* are termed 'contextual dynamics' and 'subject dynamics'.

Contextual dynamics

Contextual dynamics refer to the circumstances affecting teachers' attitudes to involvement and engagement in curriculum making. Three emerged from this study. One concerns the teachers' confidence to take a more open and less structured approach to planning the whole of a geography topic. A second identifies the need, nonetheless, to be clear about the purpose of the class topic. The third is about the extent to which teachers feel confident about their pupils' roles in curriculum making.

First, for the teachers in this project, at the heart of curriculum making lies a sense of giving yourself *permission to take curriculum responsibility*:

> [I was] able to carry out a project of my own choosing with the opportunity to do unbridled geography! [F/Yr2][1]

Allied with this was the concomitant agreement of the head teacher to take the curriculum beyond the normal set of requirements, such as extending or refocusing the listed topic in the school's geography scheme of work. This requires both the teacher and the head teacher to be confident in each other and to be willing to see opportunities and to take agency in adopting a more open and less pre-determined approach to enacting flexible approaches to medium-term planning. These 'personal attitudes' create circumstances in which teachers, buoyed by the confidence of others, as these participants reported they were, feel able to grasp opportunities and explore possible solutions to the challenges of a more thoughtful direction in their curriculum planning:

> The project allowed me to pilot creative ways of using fieldwork with my class. Our film making project allowed the children in my class to evaluate their own environments and familiar locations. [M/Yr2]

It enabled them to focus on achieving aspirations such as drawing children into a dialectical engagement with their studies as contributors and investors in the class curriculum, not simply as recipients of it. By sharing their ideas the teachers also grew in confidence as they felt their colleagues in other schools, working along the same lines, give them permission through mutual encouragement.

A second contextual dynamic to emerge was that teachers require *clarity of purpose and focus* as curriculum makers, having a clear and organised plan within which they could operate flexibly. The teachers felt the need to remain 'in charge' of their topic and that goals to aim at were essential, though they recognised that these could evolve with the topic and the children's learning. They reflected that a creative and open-minded approach to the curriculum still needs an evident sense of direction though change may occur and the children have an increased say:

The project [was] modified to the needs of the learners and we had a fully planned programme that altered and was dependent on progress. Great! [M/Yr5]

What this requires is an attitude of 'openness' to considering the avenues for development of the topic, by both the teacher and the children. It was not always easy to do, since the children were often highly motivated:

Perhaps one of the hardest aspects of the topic to manage was maintaining a focus due to over-enthusiasm, rather than lack of enthusiasm or lack of direction. [F/Yr2]

The topics, as this study required, needed a focus with a particular geographical interest. Teachers focused on such topics as hazards in the children's familiar environment, packaging and recycling, the school environment, habitats, and journeys and streams, which required developing understanding of particular geographical concepts and skills. In practice, since the teacher ensured the children were informed about and discussed the possibilities for the topic, children engaged in contributing to and developing the lines and nature of its enquiries. Most teachers saw this as a 'risky' approach since they were unclear where it might lead. However, they realised it involved a willingness to diverge and to engage consistently with the children in critical evaluation of the enquiries, avenues pursued, what had been informative and what inhibited effective planning.

This signals the third contextual dynamic, which was that teachers saw the *children as active curriculum agents*. For curriculum making to develop well, regardless of the age of the children, teachers found that they needed to recognise what children bring to the curriculum and to have confidence in their capabilities and potential to contribute, which they ensured played a significant role:

[The children] feel valued – they were able to have their say about things in their environment. [F/Yr5]

I read a text – The Journey – that would form the starting point for our next experiences and activities within our theme: Journeys and Jobs. Using the discussion that followed about the children's interests in journeys, streams and rivers I was able to plan for the next few weeks. Their involvement at this planning stage was crucial to its success and their learning and enjoyment. I also felt confident that the planned activities would work because of their enthusiasm and commitment to the project. [F/FS]

[I am] more confident now on gauging their views and allowing them to formulate and guide the curriculum. In the summer term I am not the curriculum maker, they will be. [M/Yr5]

The class topics involved were chiefly locally focused. What the teachers found was that children's enthusiasm and local knowledge and understanding could be harnessed in curriculum making. Children could make rational and reasonable choices about lines of investigation, about sequences and organisation of studies, themes and tasks. They could take responsibility to shape directions within the topic. For many teachers this was an understanding of pupils' roles which they developed through the topic. It was not that they had not elicited children's awareness and knowledge in the past but that they had not brought the children into the development of previous topics as partners. By being more open to pupils' involvement from the start, teachers realised that what the children could offer was able to be brought more into the mainstream as the topic evolved. Children's agency emerged and increased alongside teachers' developing confidence in them and themselves.

Subject dynamics

Subject dynamics describe those characteristics which relate to the three core components in curriculum making described by the GA: the subject, the children's experience and understandings, and the teachers' subject teaching repertoire (Lambert & Morgan, 2010; GA, 2012; Biddulph, 2013). Four subject dynamics were identified. The first is teachers' personal appreciation of their subject knowledge. Second was their recognition of the children's geographical awareness and knowledge, particularly locally. The third concerned children's developing realisation of their geographical understanding and of the subject. Fourth was teachers' reinforcement and development of their teaching repertoire.

The participants in this study largely felt *confident in their subject knowledge and understanding*, the first subject dynamic, though it enabled them to extend their appreciation and use of that knowledge:

> I was already reasonably confident as I have a geographical background and am very interested in geography and teaching of geography. This project has enabled me to think about the concepts of geography in a different way. [F/Yr3]

> [I] Really [have] been able to embrace with the children what 'living geography' is about in a purposeful and meaningful context. The children have been able to learn through the outdoor environment and really bring the outdoors in. [F/Yr4]

Amongst the geographical foci for the *Young Geographers Project* was sustainable development. Several of the schools where the teachers worked were involved in eco-school activities and promoted a responsible concern for the environment, while in others this was not such an evident element. A few schools were also working towards the GA's *Primary*

Quality Mark accreditation (GA, 2006), seeking to have their school awarded a gold, silver or bronze mark as a reference point for developing and achieving a high standard of geography teaching in their school. This involves clarity of understanding about geography. There were variations in how the teachers perceived and understood sustainable development. While most related it to recognising people's use of and impact on environments and to be about developing responsible attitudes to environmental activity locally and globally, several viewed it more narrowly as related to locally evident concerns such as litter and traffic issues. It was evident that there were variations in appreciating what a level of subject knowledge and understanding meant. Overall, teachers considered their subject knowledge had an positive impact on how they saw the potential of their topic and recognised that to provide the fullest and deepest learning opportunities they needed to be knowledgeable and well-informed themselves. A few teachers realised they needed to enhance their understanding of sustainable development, and that subject knowledge was a key aspect of curriculum making which affected the quality of their teaching.

The Project involved aspects of local study, an element of its 'living geography' dimension. This connected with the children's familiar environment, providing the opportunity for teachers to draw on the children's everyday geographies (Catling, 2005, 2011b; Martin, 2008; Catling & Martin, 2011):

> [It] has shown me how children are part of geography in their daily lives, and that they are aware of many issues relating to sustainability and their immediate environment at their own level. [F/FS]

While the teachers drew occasionally on children's awareness and knowledge in their previous geography topics, largely through elicitation activities, they were required in this project to engage the children more fully, such as in considering and agreeing what might be studied and investigated and where this could be done locally. What teachers expressed was surprise that the children had much more to offer than they had previously recognised. By providing opportunities for children to contribute local information and their own ideas and views, it became clear that children had a more complex, deeper knowledge and understanding of their locality than teachers credited them with:

> Do younger children value their environment? Absolutely, but not only this, they can also see the link between actions and consequences – they dislike muddy carpets and appreciate plant life and grassy areas and can accept that sliding down a bank to reach the classroom may no longer be acceptable. [F/Yr1-2]

The teachers realised that children also could offer ideas about how to approach their investigations, as well as in making proposals related to local and wider environmental care, improvements and management:

> [The children] have a greater understanding of the local environment around them and their role in the world and their responsibility to look after the school, local environment and the wider world. They have developed positive attitudes and enjoyment towards this very important area of the curriculum. [F/Yr4]

As the projects evolved *teachers recognised that children had geographical knowledge*, the second subject dynamic, helping them realise what children can bring to curriculum making. That the teachers knew the area of the school less well than their children helped them to appreciate that there was other expertise available in the class.

Connected to this, teachers perceived that children realised that they had more to offer than either they or their teachers had previously provided opportunities for. Through their involvement in developing the geography topic, children became more motivated and began to appreciate what they could contribute:

> The children were very keen to communicate new learning to others – often voluntarily. They were enthusiastic about what they were learning and many went home and did further research which they enjoyed sharing with us back in school. [F/Yr2]

More than this, the children began to realise the value of their geographical learning, not least because it was not 'apart' from them but intrinsically connected to their experience and knowledge of the area of study, their fieldwork and their perspectives on sustainability, as well as to their values about 'their place' and the wider world. The project enabled children's geographical learning to be evident to them and to want to take this further:

> [They saw] development of their own personal geographies. They began to perceive the familiar locations of their environment in different ways. They became more critical and evaluative. [M/Yr2]

> The children are very enthusiastic about their local environment and are keen to develop the project further to a national scale – looking at London. [F/Yr3]

Thus, as the third subject dynamic, teachers saw their *children valuing geography more positively*, in part because they enjoyed the active learning approach but also because they knew they had real knowledge and understanding to share and could learn from each other:

[The children developed] empowerment and excitement about wind energy. They now see themselves as geographers. [F/R]

A requirement of the *Young Geographers Project* was that teachers engage in local fieldwork. The teachers valued this requirement not least because it required working and learning outside the classroom. In fact, all but one of the teachers was able to work off site while many used the opportunity also to work in the grounds:

Being outside is essential to teaching – geography in particular; if you're outside you're automatically 'hands on'. [F/FS]

This reinforced their learning about their children's local geographies and developed their own local knowledge. It meant also that they needed to consider with the children the aspects of the locality which linked with sustainable development that they could investigate at first hand, such as local hazards, feeling about the local seafront, stream study and ways they could 'make a difference'. Teachers also found their sense that field-work was motivating strongly reinforced:

They have enjoyed it so much especially putting their hands in the compost. They have started to recycle at home too. [F/Yr4]

This engaged the teachers in considering *the variety of ways they might teach and the children work* to undertake their studies and investigations which would be engaging, insightful and motivating for learning. This was the fourth subject dynamic. There was increased discussion and debate, the use of enquiry in teaching and learning, a stronger focus on teamwork and sharing ideas and findings, and in employing drama and role play, for instance.

Discussion: learning about curriculum making

For some time the phrase 'curriculum making' has meant curriculum design and planning from the national to the school and to the class level. For the GA the term is focused on the creation of medium-term planning, derived from a scheme of work, which becomes the basis for lesson planning. This study has focused on the reflections of a self-selected sample of primary teachers who were involved in the *Young Geographers Project* and engaged with the sense of curriculum making described by the GA (GA, 2012). It is this interpretation of curriculum making that is now considered.

A key enabling factor to emerge is that the teachers felt *liberated* by the opportunity to make their own curriculum with their children in a subject they valued. They perceived that they had regained control of their subject, geography, and of decision-making about their teaching. This was a refreshing, almost novel, feeling for them, as they had often found themselves constrained by national and school prescriptions in their teaching across the curriculum. This *liberation* re-energised their commitment and enthusiasm, not least because they felt supported to take control and responsibility. While for some time their role might have been described as being 'agents of change' in children's learning on behalf of the government through its edicts about curriculum content, structure and outcomes and about teaching approaches (Cox, 2011; Kelly, 2009), they began to see themselves as having *agency as teachers*, retaking command of their professional expertise, authority and aspirations (Priestley, Biesta, & Robinson, 2012). This was, to an extent, daunting, but it enabled them to recognise their capability and potential. Curriculum making was *emancipatory* (Grundy, 1988; Kincheloe, 2008) and they felt themselves to be learning again.

Edwards (2009) described five factors impacting on curriculum making. Each is reflected in the findings of this study. *Contextual factors*, such as the English national programmes of study for key stage 1 and 2 geography (DfES/QCA, 1999), formed a backdrop to the *Young Geographers Project*, since the study encouraged three elements of these programmes: study based in the local area of the school, the use of fieldwork and a focus on sustainable development. These were not inhibiting but rather enabled a clear focus linked with the subject of geography while providing guidance on aspects of the subject to engage with. This connected the 'knowledge-base' of geography with the children. *Organisational factors* included the issue of time as a key resource for teaching and developing children's learning and understanding, as well as the permission given by the head teacher to be involved in the project and to work outside the prescribed curriculum requirements and expectations, albeit for only a limited part of the working week. This linked closely with *curriculum factors*, in terms of the interpretation of the national curriculum requirements teachers could make. The liberation teachers felt enabled this to be a positive opportunity rather than a constraint, since planning for and with the children would be outside the required plans of the school's geography scheme of work. This overlapped with *micro-political factors*, not only through the sense of permission to work more 'riskily' but because it refocused teachers' reflections and self-evaluation on their attitudes to such matters as their ownership of the curriculum and the fuller engagement of the children as partners in curriculum making. The strongest influence was *individual factors*, which described the opportunity teachers took to reassert their sense of themselves as professionals, to draw on their subject knowledge, and to develop their confidence in drawing the children into the class project. Their enthusiasm and commitment to geographical learning and to exercise agency provided a powerful frame for their curriculum making. This supports Clayton's (2007) suggestion that self-appraisal and questioning one's own values in the process of curriculum making are essential elements. These may be as important as, or more important than, decision-making about topics and lines of study and about who is to be involved and how in this process. Here curriculum making can be described as praxis (Grundy, 1988). For Clayton, the need through self-reflection to re-evaluate and reconsider personal values and practices is the basis for changing and enhancing how teachers work best, particularly in terms of inclusivity and equity, as curriculum makers in their own classrooms.

Draper (1936) presented one approach to curriculum making as medium-term planning which he described as 'progressive', in that it expressed an active learning focus to engage and involve children directly. It has been taken further in this project. Draper's notion is deepened by Alexander (2008b) in his work on dialogic teaching, which is informative for this study. The principles underlying Alexander's case for dialogic teaching include the need not simply to listen to children but to *hear* what they say. This means giving children time and support to convey what they want to, and to consider thoughtfully what children propose, rather than dismissing their ideas. It involves mutuality in collective approaches to enquiry, questioning and probing, and means considering together the lines of enquiry to follow, while evaluating at intervals and reappraising directions of study, including agreement to digress where there is useful interest or potential in doing so. This supports the teachers' perspectives about enhancing children's engagement in active curriculum making as agents in their own learning. As in a secondary school geography study, the primary teachers recognised children's need to be listened to and heard clearly and fully, so that a dialogue emerged as a result of teachers' openness to children's contributions and partnership (Biddulph, 2011, 2013; Hopwood, 2007, 2012). Likewise, the need for teachers' teaching repertoires to be broad-based, building on and taking forward enquiries, involves a dialogic approach for this to be meaningful, moving beyond being active to *activating* children's contributions.

This would appear to be enabled, as Biddulph (2011, 2012) found with secondary geography teachers, when teachers are knowledgeable about their subject, to the extent that they can recognise children's understandings (and misunderstandings) in the subject and appreciate the relationship of children's subject learning to their everyday experiences. While most of the primary teachers felt confident in their geography subject knowledge, what surprised them were the greater extent of children's knowledge of their local environment and their awareness and views about sustainable development which were more informed than expected – in the past children's views were less fully engaged with in class. Geography topics, it would seem, are frequently for children to undertake and learn about, rather than opportunities for children learning through sharing their geographical understanding and delving more deeply into it while connecting it with their own experiences. That the teachers, in the main, lacked this appreciation of children's developing personal geographies through their life experiences (Butt, 2009; Catling, 2005, 2011b; Freeman & Tranter, 2011; Scourfield, Dicks, Drakeford, & Davies, 2006; Spencer & Blades, 2006) indicates that they need, alongside their personal geographical understanding, to recognise, value and draw in children's geographical experience and learning beyond school. This last point challenges Bobbitt's (1918) sense that school learning should essentially *only* focus children's learning beyond the everyday. Rather, it supports the GA's approach to curriculum making which argues that curriculum experience must make effective connections with children's everyday lives so that they see value in their classroom learning (Biddulph, 2011; GA, 2012).

The approach used in curriculum making and the perspectives expressed by the teachers illustrate aspects of Ofsted's findings about innovation in English schools (Ofsted, 2008a) and in relation to high quality practices in geography teaching in primary schools (Ofsted, 2008b, 2011). Findings about the impact of innovative practices include increased motivation amongst children, raised achievement and more open approaches by teachers to curriculum making. It has been reported that greater curriculum flexibility is vital to support improvements through innovation, an opportunity which teachers often considered was not available to them but from which they may well have benefited. Ofsted notes that innovation supports personal development, and that it helps children see themselves as more involved and as improving their learning. Indirectly, this supports the view of the primary teachers that children in their classes felt they were learning from their geographical studies and valued the subject more. In their recent evaluations of the state of geography in primary schools, Ofsted (2008b, 2011) have identified the importance of teachers' subject knowledge and reinforced the view that this is vital for increasing the effectiveness of geography teaching – a point also noted by teachers in this study. Equally these reports illustrate the importance of a repertoire of teaching approaches and techniques, in particular drawing out the value and relevance of fieldwork experience and engagement for children, offsite as well as in the school's grounds. Findings reinforce the importance of a 'local solutions' approach where schools are innovative and involve the children in the development of geographical studies. They offer informative examples of investigations in the local area and of ways to develop children's understanding of sustainable development which illustrate curriculum making findings summarised here. Where a number of key features of innovative teaching and co-operative planning with children are brought together effectively, curriculum making is an exciting process and informs and enables deeper learning by children in geography.

Reflecting on this discussion, there are features of engagement and practice in curriculum making which emerge for teachers generally to take into account in their curriculum making. These are drawn from the approach advocated by the GA and from the *curriculum dynamics* which were identified in the teachers' perspectives on their practice. The first four reflect particular aspects of teachers' attitudes as essential underpinnings for curriculum making. The second six emphasise decision-making and organisational aspects as essential to effective curriculum making practices. While not suggested to be original, these features support several aspects of the UK Teaching, Learning and Research Programme's espoused 10 principles (James & Pollard, 2012), characteristics of active learning (Monk & Silman, 2011) and a range of elements of effective pedagogic practice (Hattie, 2009, 2012; Leach & Moon, 2008). The 10 features are expressed directly to reflect the potentially important role they contribute to effective curriculum making.

Attitudes underpinning curriculum making

- *Be confident in yourself as a curriculum maker.* This involves appreciating the value of working from the focus and plan of a topic to look for the opportunities it presents; seeking proposals and ideas from all in the class to discuss and lead to decisions, to appreciate that being open-minded involves a capacity to take risks, and to remain flexible to exploit thoughtfully unrecognised possibilities that arise; and being active as a curriculum maker.
- *Be confident in yourself as a teacher.* This involves using the skills of listening, hearing, observing and seeing as well as of leading and responding, in order to be able to direct and intervene to encourage and promote understanding of subject ideas and to support children's ways of learning.
- *Be confident in and inclusive of the children.* This involves valuing what children bring to the classroom and the topics they study; harnessing their enthusiasm and interests; engaging them in discussion and decision-making; involving them in planning and organising themes, foci for study and activities for investigation, analysis, evaluation and communication; and working with them as active curriculum agents.
- *Be active in your development of your subject understanding.* This involves developing and deepening your knowledge of the subject areas and topics you teach; responding to children's enquiries by investigating with them to broaden your knowledge, understanding and skills; and being an appreciative learner of knowledge, to encourage its reflection by the children.

Decision-making and organisational aspects of curriculum making

- *Be clear about the purposes of the topics you study*. This involves having a clear sense of direction, based on evident intentions shared and discussed with the children; keeping these uppermost and evaluating them together periodically; being open to additional lines of enquiry and/or a change in direction if the study rationally warrants these.
- *Limit your planning*. This involves planning for the medium term partially, not fully; identifying and setting lines of intent and goals; being open-minded to ideas, opportunities and possibilities; being flexible, ready to adapt the focus of study and open new avenues where this is potentially beneficial to do.
- *Recognise and draw upon children's subject potential and engagement*. This involves using elicitation, sharing, planning and organisational activities to draw in children's subject, for instance geographical, understanding to the topic of study; working with the children to consider, explain and justify what their knowledge can contribute and to provide insights into both what they know and their misconceptions, how these shape their sense of the subject and what uses their contributions can provide; raising with them new lines of subject enquiry, as well as the gaps in their knowledge, and encouraging them to investigate; and involving the children in reflecting on and evaluating their understandings of subjects and areas of learning.
- *Look always to use and extend your repertoire of teaching skills*. This involves choosing wisely to select effective teaching strategies and approaches; taking opportunities to trial approaches new to yourself and the children, being open with them that you want their feedback (as well as that of colleagues you share your ideas with), as well as undertaking self-evaluation; encouraging the children to offer ideas about and undertake teaching tasks and activities as part of the class topic; encouraging and supporting their ideas but engaging them in critical examination of their proposals; working with the children, to provide guidance and direction for their learning; ensuring they justify and explain what they plan to do, reflect on it periodically and evaluate it afterwards; and seeking to make future use of, adapt or reject teaching techniques that you try out.
- *Provide active and experiential learning*. This involves teaching inside and outside the classroom, engaging the children practically with the topic; focusing to ensure that the topics studied have meaning for and impact on the children; and engaging the children in planning and risk assessment.
- *Be open to discussion and debate*. This involves making your curriculum a 'conversation', as an active dialogue; being responsive and

proactive to challenges; being creative; being willing to take risks and to diverge; and reflecting critically on potential lines of development, with the children.

Conclusion

Curriculum making is the translation of and transition from school curriculum directions, requirements and schemes into classroom lessons. It is a loose rather than tight approach providing for evolving lesson planning and activities. It is exploratory and discretionary while having direction, works within a timescale rather than to a timetable, is based on proactive thinking and decision-making, and is rational, justifiable and defendable. Curriculum making is proactive and enactive, is purposeful, engaging and rigorous, and is flexible and open to justified divergence. It requires thorough reflection on and evaluation of its process and its practice, with the children, to enable progress in their learning and in teachers' teaching. Curriculum making returns agency to primary teachers as professional decision-makers in their own classrooms, while engaging children's agency in their learning.

Unsurprisingly, perhaps, this study has supported the centrality of the principal elements of curriculum making: the vitality of teachers' subject knowledge, the value and importance of children's subject-related experience and developing understanding, and the role which teachers' pedagogic knowledge and choices play. Its limitation is that it expresses this support only from a small-scale investigation of teachers' perspectives on their experience. Yet this is an aspect of recent study in curriculum making which has been under-pursued. Future studies need to engage more with the practices of curriculum making, both teachers' and children's, to explore further, even challenge, findings that have been noted here and elsewhere. Nonetheless, while undertaken with confident teachers, the *Young Geographers Project* has provided insights which stress the potential of an open and inclusive approach to medium-term planning in the classroom. It has identified a number of aspects which might be investigated further through curriculum making as praxis. In an evolving curriculum context in primary schools (Oates, James, Pollard, & Wiliam, 2011) these aspects might be useful to take into account in developing practice within what may at the same time be both a directed and a more open primary curriculum environment.

Acknowledgements

The co-operation and support of the GA, who obtained the funding which supported the primary curriculum project on which this study is based.

Note

1. This notation refers, by gender and age group taught, to the teachers who made the quoted statements. All primary age groups were represented in the study from Foundation Stage/ Reception to Year 6 by more than one teacher. The quotations are drawn from across two-thirds of the participants.

References

Alexander, R. (2000). *Culture & pedagogy: International comparisons in primary education.* Oxford: Blackwell.

Alexander, R. (2008a). *Essays on pedagogy.* London: Routledge.

Alexander, R. (2008b). *Towards dialogic teaching: Rethinking classroom talk.* York: Dialogos.

Alexander, R. (Ed.). (2010). *Children, their world, their education: Final report and recommendations of the Cambridge Primary Review.* London: Routledge.

Alexander, R., Doddington, C., Gray, J., Hargreaves, L., & Kershner, R. (Eds.). (2010). *The Cambridge Primary Review research surveys.* London: Routledge.

Biddulph, M. (2011). Young People's Geographies: Implications for secondary geography. In G. Butt (Ed.), *Geography, education and the future* (pp. 44–62). London: Continuum.

Biddulph, M. (2012). Young People's Geographies and the school curriculum. *Geography, 97*(3), 155–162.

Biddulph, M. (2013). Where is the curriculum created? In D. Lambert & M. Jones (Eds.), *Debates in geography education* (pp. 129–142). London: Routledge.

Bloomer, M. (1997). *Curriculum making in post-16 education.* London: Routledge.

Bobbitt, J. (1918). *The curriculum.* New York: Houghton Mifflin.

Bobbitt, J. (1922). *Curriculum-making in Los Angeles.* Chicago, IL: University of Chicago Press.

Brady, L., & Kennedy, K. (1999). *Curriculum construction.* Sydney: Prentice Hall.

Brooks, C. (2009). Teaching living geography – making a geography curriculum. In D. Mitchell (Ed.), *Living geography: Exciting future for teachers and children* (pp. 203–210). Cambridge: Chris Kington Publishing.

Butt, G. (2009). Developing pupils' personal geographies – Is the personalisation of geography education beneficial? *Research in Geographical Education, 11*(1), 5–23.

Catling, S. (2005). Children's personal geographies and the English primary school curriculum. *Children's Geographies, 6*(3), 325–344.

Catling, S. (2011a). The Young Geographers Project: Lessons for curriculum making in and beyond the U.K. In A. Demirci, L. Chalmers, Y. Ari, & J. Lidstone (Eds.), *Building bridges between cultures through geographical education: Proceedings of the*

IGU-CGE Istanbul Symposium July 8–10 2010 (pp. 243–254). IGU Commission on Geographical Education/Fatih University. Retrieved August 8, 2011, from www. igu-cge.org or http://igucge2010.fatih.edu.tr

Catling, S. (2011b). Children's geographies in the primary school. In G. Butt (Ed.), *Geography, education and the future* (pp. 15–29). London: Continuum.

Catling, S., Bowles, R., Halocha, J., Martin, F., & Rawlinson, S. (2007). The state of geography in English primary schools. *Geography, 92*(2), 118–136.

Catling, S., & Martin, F. (2011). Contesting powerful knowledge: The primary curriculum as an articulation between academic and children's (ethno-) geographies. *The Curriculum Journal, 22*(3), 317–335.

Clayton, C. (2007). Curriculum making as novice professional development: Practical risk taking as learning in high-stakes times. *Journal of teacher education, 58*(3), 216–230.

Cohen, L., Manion, L., & Morrison, K. (2011). *Research methods in education* (7th ed.). London: Routledge.

Cox, S. (2011). *New perspectives in primary education.* Maidenhead: Open University Press.

Dewey, J. (1902). *The child and the curriculum.* Chicago, IL: University of Chicago Press.

Dey, I. (1993). *Qualitative data analysis.* London: Routledge.

DfES (Department for Education and Skills). (2003). *Excellence and enjoyment: A strategy for primary schools.* Annesley: DfES Publishing.

DfES/QCA. (1999). *National curriculum: Handbook for primary teachers in England.* London: QCA.

Draper, E. (1936). *Principles and techniques of curriculum making.* New York: D. Appleton-Century Co.

Edwards, R. (2009). *Curriculum-making in vocational education: Translating tokens.* Retrieved July 24, 2012, from www.ioe.stir.ac.uk/events/documents/Paper_020_RichardEdwards.pdf

Edwards, R., Miller, K., & Priestley, M. (2009a). Curriculum-making in school and college: The case of hospitality. *The Curriculum Journal, 20*(1), 27–42.

Edwards, R., Miller, K., & Priestley, M. (2009b). *Cultures of curriculum naking in schools and colleges: Research briefing number 1.* Stirling: The Stirling Institute of Education, University of Stirling. Retrieved April 8, 2012, from http://www.ioe.stir.ac.uk/research/projects/CurriculumMaking.php

Freeman, C., & Tranter, P. (2011). *Children and their urban environment.* London: Earthscan.

GA (Geographical Association). (2006). *Primary geography quality mark.* Retrieved from www.geography.org.uk/eyprimary/primaryqualitymark

GA. (2007). *Subject CPD award: Pilot funding for CPD activity to support the development of subject leaders in primary schools.* Sheffield: Geographical Association.

GA. (2009a). *A different view: A manifesto from the Geographical Association.* Sheffield: Geographical Association. Retrieved February 7, 2011, from www.geography.org.uk/projects/adifferentview

GA. (2009b). *Young Geographers – A living geography project for primary schools.* Retrieved March 26, 2011, from www.geography.org.uk/projects/younggeographers

GA. (2010). *Young geographers go local/young geographers go global/young geographers go green.* Retrieved March 26, 2011, from www.geography.org.uk/cpdevents/onlinecpd/younggeographersgolocal; www.geography.org.uk/cpdevents/onlinecpd/younggeographersgoglobal; www.geography.org.uk/cpdevents/onlinecpd/younggeographersgogreen

GA. (2011). *Making geography happen.* Retrieved March 26, 2011, from www.geography.org.uk/projects/makinggeographyhappen

GA. (2012). *Curriculum making.* Retrieved February 28, 2012, from www.geography.org. uk/cpdevents/curriculummaking

GA/RGS. (2006). *Geography in action 2006–2008: The action plan for geography* [information leaflet]. Sheffield: Geographical Association/London: Royal Geographical Society. Retrieved July 24, 2012, from www.geography.org.uk/projects/ actionplanforgeography

GA/RGS. (2011). *The action plan for geography 2006–11.* Retrieved September 23, 2012, from www.geography.org.uk/projects/actionplanforgeography

Goodson, I. (1988). *The making of curriculum.* London: Falmer Press.

Grundy, S. (1988). *Curriculum: Product or praxis.* London: Falmer Press.

Hattie, J. (2009). *Visible learning.* London: Routledge.

Hattie, J. (2012). *Visible learning for teachers.* London: Routledge.

Hawthorn, R. (Ed.). (1992). *Curriculum in the making.* New York: Teachers College Press.

Hopwood, N. (2007). *Young people's geographies: Evaluator's report.* Retrieved April 4, 2010, from www.youngpeoplesgeographies.co.uk/download/ypg_evaluation.pdf

Hopwood, N. (2012). *Geography in secondary schools: Researching pupils' classroom experiences.* London: Continuum.

Hulme, M., & Livingston, K. (2012). Curriculum for the future. In D. Wyse, V. M. Baumfield, D. Egan, C. Gallagher, L. Hayward, M. Hulme, R. Leitch, K. Livingston, I. Menter, & B. Lingard (Eds.), *Creating the curriculum* (pp. 129–144). London: Routledge.

James, M., & Pollard, A. (Eds.). (2012). *Principles for effective pedagogy.* London: Routledge.

Kelly, A. (2009). *The curriculum: Theory and practice* (6th ed.). London: Sage.

Kincheloe, J. (2008). *Critical pedagogy* (2nd ed.). New York: Peter Lang.

Lambert, D. (2009). What is living geography? In D. Mitchell (Ed.), *Living geography: Exciting futures for teachers and children* (pp. 1–7). Cambridge: Chris Kington Publishing.

Lambert, D., & Morgan, J. (2010). *Teaching geography* (pp. 11–18). Maidenhead: Open University Press.

Leach, J., & Moon, B. (2008). *The power of pedagogy.* London: Sage.

Male, B. (2012). *The primary curriculum design handbook.* London: Continuum.

Martin, F. (2008). Ethnogeography: Towards liberatory geography education. *Children's geographies, 6*(4), 437–450

Mitchell, D. (Ed.). (2009). *Living geography.* London: Chris Kington Publishing.

Monk, J., & Silman, C. (2011). *Active learning in primary classrooms.* Harlow: Longman.

Mufti, E., & Peace, M. (2012). *Teaching and learning and the curriculum.* London: Continuum.

Newby, P. (2010). *Research methods for education.* Harlow: Pearson Education.

Oates, T., James, M., Pollard, A., & Wiliam, D. (2011) *The framework for the national curriculum: A report by the expert panel for the national curriculum review.* London: DfE.

Ofsted. (2008a). *Curriculum innovation in schools.* Retrieved December 7, 2008, from www.ofsted.gov.uk/publications

Ofsted. (2008b). *Geography in schools: Changing practice.* Retrieved February 12, 2008, from www.ofsted.gov.uk/publications

Ofsted. (2011). *Geography: Learning to make a world of difference.* Retrieved January 29, 2011, from www.ofsted.gov.uk/publications

Posner, G., & Rudnitsky, A. (1986). *Course design: A guide to curriculum development for teachers.* New York: Longman.

Priestley, M., Biesta, G., & Robinson, S. (2012) *Teachers as agents of change: An exploration of the concept of teacher agency.* Working paper No. 1, Teacher Agency and Curriculum change project. Retrieved July 25, 2012, from www.ioe.stir.ac.uk/events/tacc.php

Priestley, M., Edwards, R., Miller, K., & Priestley, A. (2010). *Teacher agency in curriculum making: Agents of change and spaces for manoeuvre.* Stirling Online Research Repository. Retrieved June 5, 2013, from https://dspace.stir.ac.uk/bitstream/1893/3119/1/The%20role%20of%20teacher%20agency%20in%20curriculum%20making_final.pdf

QCA/DfEE (Qualifications and Curriculum Authority/Department for Education and Employment). (1998/2000). *A scheme of work for key stages 1 and 2: Geography.* London: QCA.

Robson, C. (2011). *Real world research* (3rd ed.). Chichester: Wiley.

Rose, J. (2009). *Independent review of the primary curriculum: Final report.* Annesley: DCSF Publications.

Scourfield, J., Dicks, B., Drakeford, M., & Davies, A. (2006). *Children, place and identity.* London: Routledge.

Spencer, C., & Blades, M. (Eds.). (2006). *Children and their environments.* Cambridge: Cambridge University Press.

TDA (2007). *Invitation to tender for pilot funding for continuing professional development (CPD) activity to support the development of subject leaders in primary schools and the development of subject networks of secondary school teachers.* London: TDA.

Thomas, G. (2009). *How to do your research project.* London: Sage.

Tymms, P., & Merrell, C. (2010). Standards and quality in English primary schools over time. In R. Alexander, C. Doddington, J. Gray, L. Hargreaves, & R. Kershner (Eds.), *Cambridge primary review research surveys* (pp. 435–460). London: Routledge.

Wyse, D., Baumfield, V. M., Egan, D., Gallagher, C., Hayward, L., Hulme, M., . . . Lingard, B. (2012). *Creating the curriculum.* London: Routledge.

Children researching their urban environment: developing a methodology

Elisabeth Barratt Hacking[a] and Robert Barratt[b]

[a]Department of Education, University of Bath, UK; [b]School of Education, Bath Spa University, UK

Listening to children: environmental perspectives and the school curriculum (L2C) was a UK research council project based in schools in a socially and economically deprived urban area in England. It focused on 10/12 year old children's experience of their local community and environment, and how they made sense of this in relation both to their lives and the school curriculum. Issues faced by the research team in developing and implementing the project methods are explored including the challenge to promote children's equal involvement with adults in all aspects of the research. A case is made for promoting participatory and collaborative research with children in school settings. It is suggested that through the L2C project, the children developed an approach that was sensitive to children's personal experience and that developed their capacity as researchers and their understanding of the value of research.

Introduction

Research that makes the most of children's abilities, and treats them with respect, can provide children with opportunities that bring significant improvements in their own wellbeing. These include greater opportunities to acquire knowledge, to develop new skills, to build new friendships and wider support networks, to be heard and to have their concerns taken seriously. (Save The Children 2004, 10)

This contribution discusses some of the methodological challenges faced when undertaking participatory research with children aged 10–12 years. It draws on the experience of research in schools in England (Staffordshire and South Gloucestershire) which focused on children's local urban environment experience. A pilot research project was conducted in a school in Staffordshire (Barratt and Barratt Hacking 2008). This was the genesis of '*Listening to children (L2C): environmental perspectives and the school curriculum*', a project undertaken by University of Bath researchers with children and teachers from a secondary school and one of its feeder primary schools in South Gloucestershire (see e.g. Barratt Hacking et al. 2007; Barratt Hacking, Scott, and Barratt 2007). In both projects the schools involved recognised the potential of listening to children's local experiences and involving children in local environment research in order to take account of children's concerns and so contribute to their wellbeing.

The L2C project is used to exemplify methodological challenges in research with children. A range of issues are explored that the Research Team faced in developing and implementing the methodology and methods for the project. Primarily, the project aimed to develop context-specific research approaches designed by children that would gain access to 10–12 year old children's personal experience of the urban environment. In this contribution the background to the L2C research project is provided. The rationale for local environment research with children and the methodological challenges of participatory research are explained. The methodological approach is illustrated using examples of children's research from the L2C Project. Finally, reflections on the experience of researching with children are used to provide insights for researching with 10–12 year old children.

Background to the Listening to Children Project

Listening to children: environmental perspectives and the school curriculum (L2C) was a UK research council project (RES-221-25-0036, ESRC Environment and Human Behaviour Programme) based in schools in a socially and economically deprived urban area in South Gloucestershire. The project set out to investigate how children's local environmental perspectives might become a part of their school curriculum experience. The research was undertaken by a Research Team comprising of sixteen 11/12 year old children and four of their 16/17 year old mentors, two teachers, a parent and four university researchers. It focused on 10/12 year old children's experience of their local community and environment, and how they make sense of this in relation both to their lives and the school curriculum. This area exemplifies the sorts of social, economic, environmental and educational challenges that urban communities are facing nationally, and in the developed world more generally, and there is concern about the impact of such environments on children's wellbeing (Sustainable Development Commission 2008). The school recognised the need to involve local people in school development, and the L2C project provided an opportunity to involve parents, children and local voluntary bodies in curriculum change.

The L2C project aimed to explore:

(1) 10–12 year old children's experience in the local environment and community.
(2) How the curriculum can become more relevant to children, their families and the local community, and ways of involving children in both curriculum development and action in the local community.
(3) How local environmental and educational policy can change to take account of children's perspectives.

These aims reflect national and international agendas to improve education and the environment at the local scale, for example, in the sustainable schools guidance for schools in England (Sustainable Schools n.d.) and in local sustainability initiatives proposed at the Earth Summit (Earth Summit 2002). L2C provided key opportunities to consider how the community and its schools, parents, children and teachers can meet the challenge of growing up in an urban setting. It also explored ways of making closer connections between children's everyday experience and the school curriculum whilst enhancing children's opportunity to make a positive contribution in the school and local context (DfES 2003). There is evidence to suggest that children still have limited opportunities to contribute to school and local development (see, for example, Ofsted 2007; Roe 2007).

The two phases of the study were:

Phase 1 which involved establishing and planning the project then gathering and analysing evidence about the nature of 10–12 year old pupils' local environment experience (May 2004–December 2004); and

Phase 2 which used the evidence gathered and analysed in Phase 1 to develop, implement and evaluate a curriculum project (January 2004–May 2005).

Here the first phase of the project is mainly drawn upon, in particular, the nature of 10–12 year-old pupils' local environment experience (Research aim 1) in order to illustrate a number of methodological challenges in undertaking participatory research with children.

Why do local environment research with children?

The research discussed adopted an ecological perspective; in this the child is viewed within their family, social, environmental and cultural context. It is widely acknowledged that child development is not just biological but is also a product of experience (Kagan 1994; UNICEF 2004). The authors' interest in environmental education and environmental learning in schools is underpinned by a belief that children's everyday experience of their local community and environment is a significant influence on their learning and development (Barratt and Barratt Hacking 2008; see also Baacke 1985; Bronfenbrenner 1979; van Matre 1979). Evidence from the pilot Staffordshire project suggested a dissonance between the child's local experience and the school curriculum and that the children welcomed the opportunity to share their community experience in school and consider its relevance to the school curriculum (Barratt and Barratt Hacking 2008).

The rationale for undertaking local environment research with children is also based on the premise that communities need to engage those in the present who will determine future needs and wants. The UN Convention on the Rights of the Child set a global agenda for children's participation in democratic societies (United Nations 1989). In England, the Children's Bill and the new Children's Commissioner require that local authorities recognise the contribution made by children to society (DfES 2003). There is a policy commitment that children will 'actively be involved in shaping all decisions that affect their lives' (Children's Commissioner n.d.). Engaging children in local research can provide children with the skills and opportunities to make a contribution to society through local decision making:

> Children's participation (in research) makes children more active citizens as it … challenges the status quo in terms of what children can realistically contribute and accomplish'. (Save the Children 2004, 14)

Local research can therefore support children in:

- making stronger links between their everyday experience and learning in school (and so enhancing the relevance of the school curriculum for children and communities);

- developing a deeper knowledge and understanding of the everyday local environment and its links with other environments;
- using children's research findings to formulate and pursue their aspirations for the local environment, for themselves, others and for wildlife; and
- developing capacity as researchers and as local citizens, for example, by applying research skills and findings to their current and future role as consumers, residents, employees, stakeholders and voters.

Developing genuine participation and participatory research in a school setting

Participatory research has been defined as an approach that:

gives a 'voice' to those being researched, by questioning the acquisition and usefulness of knowledge, the power relationship between the researchers and the researched, and the stance of the 'objective' researcher. (Clark 2004)

This form of research developed out of concerns to i) understand the experience of community members and ii) work towards community improvement through providing opportunities for members to be partners in research. Examples include work with less advantaged communities and children (Hart 1997) and recipients of health services (Laws et al. 1999). The development of participation and participatory research has been less evident in school settings where 'providers and policy-makers have been slower to realise the potential of consulting "consumers"' (Flutter and Rudduck 2004, xi). However 'there is clear evidence that the political and social climate has begun to warm to the principle of involving children and young people but we must wait to see whether schools will provide the right conditions for pupil voice to grow' (Flutter and Rudduck 2004, 139).

Participation and participatory research is interpreted differently by different researchers and in different contexts. De Koning and Martin (1996, p. 3) suggest a range of interpretations including where the researcher and research community design the research together in contrast to where researchers design the study and then collect data with the help of the community. The approach adopted for the L2C project represents the former interpretation, also described as 'researching collaboratively with children' (Barratt and Barratt Hacking 2008; Garbarino, Stott, and Faculty of the Erikson Institute 1989). Children and young people are one of the most heavily researched groups in society. However, despite attempts to get beyond mere observation to extended dialogue with young people and reporting findings in their own words, the process still tends to be controlled by professional adults, that is, teachers and researchers (Clark et al. 2001; Kellet 2005a):

There is a lot of research done by adults 'on', 'about', and even 'for' children, but very little research in which children play an active and meaningful role. (Researching children n.d.)

In contrast the intention was that children would take an equal responsibility in developing all stages of the research from agreeing research questions through to developing methods, analysis, evaluation and dissemination. However, the opportunity for children to be genuine participants in a school-based research project can be limited by issues of compliance. The L2C project began to tackle such issues by adopting a participatory and collaborative approach to the research. This approach reflects a trend in educational and social science research from research *on* children to research *with* children and, more recently, towards the 'new paradigm' of research *by* children which involves 'children as active researchers' (Kellet 2005a, 2005b; see also Alderson 2000, 2001; Christensen and Allison 2000; Kirby 2004b).

Responding to research design issues in collaborative research with children

Four issues in collaborative research with children are discussed in the following sections:

1. *Establishing genuine consent to participate*

> Consent in research ... involves taking time to decide, being able to ask questions about the research, and then being able to say yes or no. Consent should be also seen as ongoing, rather than as a one-off event. (Morrow 2008, 54)

Within ethical debates surrounding research and children there is recognition of the difficulty of obtaintaining reliable consent in school settings. This relates to the notion that children will consent to adult expectations in relation to work and behaviour (Miller and Bell 2002; David 2007). In this respect 'assumed consent' (Heath et al. 2004), where the gatekeepers (teachers, senior managers) consent to participation on children's behalf, means that children do not necessarily exercise choice about their involvement. For example, children may believe that a research project is just part of normal class or school work and therefore that they are expected to participate in it (David, Edwards, and Aldred 2001; Morrow 1999). For these reasons there was a concern in the L2C project to ensure that children genuinely consented to participate and understood their right to withdraw as the project developed.

Prior to the involvement of children the school- and university-based researchers explored ways of approaching the issues around informed consent. The idea to open up the project to volunteers (through a year group assembly led by the teacher researchers followed by a question and answer session) attempted to ensure that:

(i) the project was presented in an appropriate way for 11/12 year olds;
(ii) children understood what they were volunteering for, the risks involved and expectations of them; and
(iii) there was equality of opportunity.

Out of about 200 children in the assembly, 50 stayed behind to ask questions and decide whether to volunteer. Through a negotiated process, eight girls and eight boys (representing all the tutor groups, a range of scholastic ability, parental background, in-school behaviour, and motivation to study) joined a parent, two teachers and university researchers in the Research Team.

In the first Research Team meeting ethical issues were explored including confidentiality and mutual expectations of the project. Children's right to withdraw from the project was discussed and clarified at the outset, repeated in writing to parents/ carers and revisited at different stages of the research. Children were offered debriefing if they decided to withdraw; one child chose to withdraw part way through the project and requested debriefing. These and similar matters were revisited throughout the life of the project. The emergent nature of L2C's research design meant that the project started out with research aims and questions but not with a fully determined research design. The approach that developed came out of a process of discussion and negotiation with children and hence consent to participate became an ongoing process as the project evolved.

2. *Developing appropriate and valid research methods and considering safety issues in the subsequent data gathering*

The L2C project adopted an *emergent* research design in that participants shaped the direction of the project through a process of discussion and negotiation. The Research Team met weekly in one hour off timetable sessions and began to focus on developing research methods. The challenge was to find ways of empowering children to use skills that are usually conducted in an adult domain associated with developing and implementing social science research methods. The approach adopted attempted to develop the children's skills and confidence as researchers whilst building on their natural research skills, for example, enquiring minds and ability to ask questions together with their interest and expertise in using technology. It also recognised children's ability to design:

> appropriate and innovative research tools which help to engage young respondents in research. (Kirby 2004b, 276)

In an early Research Team meeting the children:

(i) explored their understandings of the term 'local environment and community';
(ii) planned how they might find out about how other children behave in the local environment; and
(iii) considered how they might research children's likes, dislikes and feelings about the locality.

In addition, there was a focus on developing research skills for data gathering such as designing questionnaires, interview techniques and using information and communication technology (ICT) equipment including dictaphones and digital cameras. This was an essential first step in building children's capacity to engage in research and thus participate fully in the project.

The children's ideas were used as the basis for all decision making, for example, some children suggested making video and photographic diaries of their local experience using mobile telephones. The children also suggested asking groups of children who lived near each other to compile a large 'neighbourhood' map reflecting their local experience. There were also opportunities for the children to seek advice from the adult researchers who largely acted as facilitators. Through a negotiated process, the child members of the Research Team decided that they would gather data, not only from their year group peers in school, but also from younger, primary aged children who would join the school the following year. The research instruments included:

- Children's photographic and video diaries of their local environment experience (using mobile phone technology and digital cameras).
- Children's personal maps (with a children's questionnaire) which the children termed the 'little map' for all the year group at secondary school (90 children) and 20 children from the primary school.

- Children's group map drawn on a very large sheet of paper by a group of children who live in the same neighbourhood which the children termed the 'big map' (primary school children).
- Group interview 1 discussing the group neighbourhood map (primary school children).
- Group interview 2: discussing children's individual personal maps and annotating a digital version of the local street map (primary school children).
- Parents'/carers' (and grandparents) group interview.
- Curriculum audit (for teachers).

The research instruments were developed by the children in consultation with the adult researchers across the following weeks. Some issues arose with the photographic and video diaries; the children wanted to make weekend diaries of how they used their independent time in the locality with digital cameras. However, through discussion the team decided that this was inadvisable as it would be impossible to safeguard children from becoming targets whilst using expensive equipment in the community. Equally, the team was concerned about the ethical issues related to capturing images of children. In a compromise the children kept diaries using their personal mobile telephones and avoided capturing images of children not working in the L2C project.

In terms of the questionnaires, maps and group interviews 10–11 year olds from a nearby feeder primary school were invited to the school for a day during which the Research Team children conducted a circus of research activities with support from the adult researchers. As the subjects were younger this provided an opportunity to develop confidence in interviewing. The group interview sessions demonstrated how effectively the children were able to illicit younger children's thinking about their environmental experience by using child-friendly language, appropriately phrased questions and putting them at ease (Kirby 2004a). The children built on this experience by sharing responsibility for joining tutor group sessions in their own school to set up and conduct the questionnaires for their whole year group.

The adult researchers had anticipated that the children would find it difficult to engage in the development of research methods. However, this did not materialise:

> What we actually delivered over time was generated by the pupils ... down to individual (questionnaire) questions ... the balance of child and adult decision making was probably 70:30 towards children ... we facilitated children's decision making. (teacher researcher)

3. Engaging children in the complexities of data analysis

In the next stage of the project the Research Team faced the task of analysing a range of data sets that had been gathered from ninety 11–12 year olds in their school and around twenty 10–11 year olds from a feeder primary school. The Research Team held a two day Data Analysis Conference to begin this task; the children worked for most of the time in small groups supported by four year 12 mentors (16/17 year olds) who had volunteered to join the L2C project.[1] These older students were able to bring a range of expertise to the data analysis including their greater experience in the local community and their own research and ICT skills.

The data analysis was also facilitated by one of the university researchers who introduced a qualitative framework for the analysis of each data set as follows:

- You will need to read, look at maps, listen to the audio tape or look at the video in order to familiarise yourself with the data. Do this on an individual or group basis, whatever seems best.
- Re-look at the data, start to think about what is important about what children are saying.
- Make notes of what strikes you as important – each point should be added to a sticky 'post it' note.
- Talk to your partner add your notes to his/her notes.
- Make one set of notes for the whole group using the lap top.
- Organise your notes into different groups of ideas.

After initial support from the university and teacher researchers the groups worked mostly independently of adults and, as a consequence, this enabled the children to avoid adult interpretations:

> Participation of children in research can often produce better quality data, as it helps ... clarify the analysis and the interpretation of data. New insights are provided by children. (Save the Children 2004, 13)

Part way through the two days each small group interviewed a sample of children from whom they had gathered the data to corroborate the findings. This corroboration process gave the children confidence that their findings were sound and valid.

The data analysis conference concluded with presentations of findings from each group to an audience made up of the Research Team including the university- and school-based researchers involved in the project, the Head teacher and the two Deputy Head teachers. This gave the team the opportunity to synthesise their findings and review interim findings about children's local environment and community experience (Figure 1). This also built children's confidence; for the first time their work was disseminated and an important and influential audience was listening to them. The children's reflections on the analysis phase demonstrated a heightened awareness about children's experience of the local environment and that they were starting to consider the relationship between their local community and school experience:

> I've learnt that not everyone thinks we're being taught enough that's relevant outside school and for us later on so it's great to give our views. (Shane, year 8)

The adult members of the Research Team were surprised by the way in which the children approached this new and complex task. Kirby suggests that analysis has to be taken on by adults or shared between adults and children as it is 'one of the hardest stages of participatory research' and perceived by children as, 'difficult' and 'boring' (2004b, 278). In contrast Bragg suggests that although 'young co-researchers tend not to get involved in data analysis ... where they have been in control of the process, their involvement has been shown to be successful' (2007, 19). This latter point is reflected in the L2C project; the children responded positively to the challenge of analysing their data and, with the support of their mentors, worked mostly independently of adults.

1. **Children have an intricate knowledge of their local community and consider the quality of their local environment to be of great importance.**
   - *We have similar concerns and interests about the community and environment ... 'personal' (e.g. health, family and friends), 'safety / danger' (e.g. people, roads, vandalism), 'play' and 'shopping'.*
   - *Most of us move around without adults now... on foot, bike, bus and skateboard; we know lots of routes through the area and we know how to be safe.*
   - *We have detailed knowledge that is different to that of adults and we use our knowledge differently to them.*
   - *The environment is important to us. We want more wildlife, we want a cleaner and safer environment; we want to care for the environment.*
   - *The local community does not provide things for us to do and places for us to be.*
   - *We are concerned about how well the community provides for minority groups.*

2. **Children have difficulty taking action to achieve what they want for their local environment because they do not know how to go about it.**

3. **Children's knowledge of their local community and ideas to improve their environment are not included in the school curriculum. However, children feel strongly that their schools should support them in achieving their goals.**

Figure 1. Children's research findings about 10–12 year old children's experience in the local environment and community.

4. *Developing an ethical approach to the dissemination of children's research findings*

In terms of a research project where children and adults collaborate it would be easy for the adults to take responsibility for dissemination not least because of their greater experience with conventional forms of dissemination such as written reports and papers. Planning how and where dissemination should take place was an ongoing task for the Research Team which agreed on the importance of children's role in this and the impact they could have on both adult and child audiences:

> Involving young people themselves in the dissemination has been shown to have a strong impact on adult audiences. (Bragg 2007, 19)

Consideration was afforded to different forms of dissemination for the range of audiences, not least the children who had been researched (Kirby 2004b, 278).

The dissemination methods employed by the children included:

- Power Point presentations to the school Senior Management Team;
- sending an email to the local Member of Parliament (MP) and later meeting with him;
- giving interviews reported in local newspapers;
- contributing photographs and reports to a regular school newsletter and wall displays;
- planning and implementing a Children's Conference to which 11–12 year old children, teachers and local community officials and academics were invited;
- making and burying 'time capsules' in the school grounds for children and people of the future;
- making a DVD film;[2] including a future scenario acted and filmed in the local park;

- making an oral presentation to a Local Authority conference; and
- leading an open forum discussion with two academic visitors to the University of Bath who separately visited the school.

Three important conditions for children's successful participation in dissemination have therefore emerged through the L2C project experience. These are that:

(i) children's authentic views and words are represented;
(ii) forms of dissemination are concomitant with children's own interests and skills; and
(iii) children play a key role in deciding how and when ideas emerging from the project should be disseminated.

Reflections

In reflecting on the challenges of undertaking participatory research in school settings the over riding and ongoing concern has been to promote children's equal involvement with adults. Given that children had existing relationships with the school-based adults in this project it was difficult for children to move away from their existing compliant role. However, evidence from end of project interviews with children and adults involved in the research suggests that through their involvement the children felt more empowered and skilled to engage in research and contribute to school and local decision making. In addition, the teacher-researchers appreciated children's potential in this respect. The children also had a sense of frustration that, without the project, their potential would not have been realised. The teacher-researchers were keen to embed the project in school life but appreciated the difficulties of extending the principles of participation to the wider community of teachers, adults and children in the school:

> Within the project children are viewed differently, however, outside of the project there's status quo. The project has come so far but there's still much to do to make it a proper reform to transfer across the school. (teacher researcher end of project interview)

A number of other challenges were faced during the L2C research. The emergent nature of the research led to issues around obtaining informed consent to participate as it was not possible to predict to what children were consenting. Furthermore, in developing the research there were tensions between the school agenda and the research agenda, for example, the need for Research Team children to miss lessons to do the research, or to use lesson time to conduct data collection with the year group. Equally, concerns about children's health and safety in undertaking local environment research prevented children using some of the data gathering methods that they had planned.

Nevertheless, there seem to be three positive outcomes from the research experience in terms of children's role in the research. Firstly, the children played a significant role in developing and implementing research methods. They were able to develop 'child friendly' methods that were sensitive to children's environmental experience and that enabled children to express themselves in different ways appropriate to their age and ability. Secondly, the children grew in confidence and capacity as researchers and in decision making. As the research progressed, the children played an increasing role in driving and implementing the research process and the adults' main role became one of support and facilitation; the introduction of older students as 'mentors' seemed to promote children's confidence and independence as researchers and reduce their reliance on adults. Thirdly, through this project the children came to see the value of research; they had a strong desire to share this and their findings with others and had plans to continue their local environment research and take action from this. At the end of the project the children talked in groups about their experience of the project, how it might impact on the school in the future and what else they would like to do:

> I'd like it (L2C) to keep going ... but we should try to get even more involved with our community ... and use the research to try to get a new way of doing it like kids maybe building something inside the school like composting and show it to the adults ... so we can bring change into the community. (Gemma, year 7)

The examples and issues discussed have illustrated the capacity of children as researchers; we believe that the ability of children to do research is vastly underestimated by many adults. From her international literature review of research by children Alderson (2001) concludes how often:

> adult researchers note their surprise at child researchers' competence ... (and) frequently emphasise the value of listening to children, a point that is made more effectively when children can express themselves through doing the relevant research. (151).

We have shown some of the possibilities for researching collaboratively with children in school settings and enabling children's participation in school decision making. These have demonstrated that children might be better placed than adults to undertake research into children's experiences. For such an endeavour to be successful children need the opportunity to be genuine research partners, and not research subjects, and to focus on issues that matter to children.

Notes

1. During Research Team meetings it became evident how much the year 7 children valued their year 12 mentors and so mentors were approached to become involved in L2C; four volunteered. The school has a system of mentoring whereby each tutor group is allocated two year 12 mentors who are given some training; this was initially set up to support children with bullying issues and their role is primarily pastoral.
2. The children made the DVD themselves and this was the children's original idea. The children sought the help of a range of people to make this including representatives from the local Children's Fund, the school IT technician and an older student with experience of acting on television and in the theatre.
3. The final report of the L2C project and some of the other publications arising from this project can be found at http://www.esrcsocietytoday.ac.uk/ESRCInfoCentre/ViewAward Page.aspx?AwardId=2576.

References

Alderson, P. 2000. Children as researchers: The effects of participation rights on research methodology. In *Research with children*, ed. P. Christensen and A. James, 241–57. London: Falmer Press.
Alderson, P. 2001. Research by children. *International Journal of Social Research Methodology* 4, no. 2: 139–53.
Baacke, D. 1985. *Die 13–bis 18–jährigen: Einführung in probleme des jugendalters* [13 to 16 year olds: Introduction to problems of adolescence]. Weinheim: Beltz.

Barratt, R., and E. Barratt Hacking. 2000. Changing my locality: Conceptions of the future. *Teaching Geography* 25, no. 1: 17–21.

Barratt, R., and E. Barratt Hacking. 2008. A clash of worlds: Children talking about their community experience in relation to the school curriculum. In *Participation and learning: Perspectives on education and the environment, health and sustainability*, ed. A. Reid, B.B. Jensen, J. Nikel, and V. Simovska, 285–98. Dordrecht: Springer.

Barratt Hacking, E., W.A.H. Scott, and R. Barratt. 2007. Children's research into their local environment: Stevenson's gap and possibilities for the curriculum. *Environmental Education Research* 13, no. 2: 225–44.

Barratt Hacking, E., W.A.H. Scott, R. Barratt, W. Talbot, D. Nicholls, and K. Davies. 2007. Education for sustainability: Schools and their communities. In *Environmental and geographical education for sustainability: Cultural contexts*, ed. J. Chi-Lee and M. Williams, 123–37. New York: Nova Science Publishers, Inc.

Bragg, S. 2007. *Consulting young people: A review of the literature*. London: Creative Partnerships. http://www.creative-partnerships.com/content/gdocs/cyp.pdf (accessed May 22, 2008).

Bronfenbrenner, U. 1979. *The ecology of human development*. Cambridge, MA: Harvard University Press.

Children's Commissioner for England. n.d. http://www.childrens-commissioner.co.uk/html/aboutus2.html.

Christensen, P., and J. Allison, eds. 2000. *Research with children: Perspectives and practices*. London: Falmer Press.

Clark, J. 2004. Participatory research with children and young people: Philosophy, possibilities and perils. *Action Research Expeditions* 4: 1–18. http://arexpeditions.montana.edu/articleviewer.php?AID=83&PAGE=2 (accessed June 22, 2008).

Clark, J., A. Dyson, N. Meagher, E. Robson, and M. Wootten. 2001. *Young people as researchers: Possibilities, problems and politics*. York: Youth Work Press.

David, M. 2007. Changing the educational climate: Children, citizenship and learning contexts? *Environmental Education Research* 13, no. 4: 425–36.

David, M., R. Edwards, and P. Aldred. 2001. Children and school-based research: 'Informed consent' or 'educated consent'? *British Educational Research Journal* 27, no. 3: 347–65.

De Koning K., and M. Marion. 1996. Participatory research in health: Setting the context. In *Participatory research in health: Issues and experiences*, ed. K. De Koning and M. Martin. London: Zed Books Ltd.

DfES. 2003. *Every child matters*. London: DfES. http://www. everychildmatters.gov.uk/_files/EBE7EEAC90382663E0D5BBF24C99A7AC.pdf (accessed June 22, 2008).

Earth Summit. 2002. http://www.earthsummit2002.org/.

Flutter, J., and J. Rudduck. 2004. *Consulting pupils: What's in it for schools?* London: Routledge Falmer.

Garbarino, J., F. Stott, and Faculty of the Erikson Institute. 1989. *What children can tell us*. San Francisco: Jossey-Bass.

Hart, R.A. 1997. *Children's Participation: The theory and practice of involving young citizens in community development and environmental* care. London: Earthscan.

Heath, S., V. Charles, G. Crow, and R. Wiles. 2004. Informed consent, gatekeepers and go-betweens. Paper presented at the International Association Sixth International Conference on Social Science Methodology, August, in Amsterdam. http://www.sociology.soton.ac.uk/Proj/Informed_Consent/ISA.rtf (accessed April 5, 2008).

Kagan, J. 1994. *The nature of the child*. New York: Basic Books.

Kellett, M. 2005a. *How to develop children as researchers: A step by step guide to the research process*. London: Sage.

Kellett, M. 2005b. Children as active researchers: A new research paradigm for the 21st century? Published online by ESRC National Centre for Research Methods, NCRM/003. http://www.ncrm.ac.uk/publications.

Kirby, P. 2004a. *A Guide to actively involving young people in research: For researchers, research commissioners, and managers*. Hampshire: Involve. http://www.invo.org.uk/pdfs/Involving_Young_People_in_Research_151104_FINAL.pdf (accessed March 24, 2008).

Kirby, P. 2004b. Involving young people in research. In *The New handbook of children's rights, comparative policy and practices*, ed. B. Franklin, 268–84. London: Routledge.

Laws, S., D. Armit, W. Metzendorf, and P. Percival. 1999. *Time to listen: Young people's experiences of mental health services*. Manchester: Save the Children.

Miller, T., and L. Bell. 2002. Consenting to what? Issues of access, gate-keeping and 'informed' consent. In *Ethics in qualitative research*, ed. M. Mauthner, M. Birch, J. Jessop, and T. Miller. London: Sage.

Morrow, V. 1999. 'It's cool ... 'cos you can't give us detentions and things, can you?': Reflections on research with children. In *Time to listen to children*, ed. P. Milner and B. Carolin, London: Routledge.

Morrow, V. 2008. Ethical dilemmas in research with children and young people about their social environments. *Children's Geographies* 6, no. 1: 49–61.

Ofsted. 2007. TellUs2. Questionnaire summary sheet: National, Ofsted. http://www.ofsted.gov.uk/assets/Internet_Content/CSID/files/National_Summary.pdf (accessed February 3, 2007).

Researching children. n.d. http://www.researchingchildren.org/main-goals/index.php?Itemid=101.

Roe, M. 2007. Feeling 'secrety': Children's views on involvement in landscape decisions. *Environmental Education Research* 14, no. 2: 467–85.

Save the Children. 2004. *So you want to involve children in research?* Sweden: Save the Children.

Sustainable Development Commission. 2007. *Every child's future matters*. London: Sustainable Development Commission. http://www.sd-commission.org.uk/publications/downloads/ECFM_report.pdf (accessed March 25, 2008).

Sustainable schools. n.d. http://www.teachernet.gov.uk/sustainableschools/.

United Nations (UN). 1989. *Convention on the rights of the child*. Office of the UN High Commissioner for Human Rights. http://www.unhchr.ch/html/menu3/b/k2crc.htm (accessed February 15, 2008).

United Nations Children's Fund (UNICEF). 2004. *The state of the worlds' children*. New York: UNICEF.

Van Matre, S. 1979. *Sunship earth: An acclimatization program for outdoor learning*. Martinsville, IN: American Camping Association.

My Place: Exploring children's place-related identities through reading and writing

Emma Charlton, Gabrielle Cliff Hodges, Pam Pointon, Maria Nikolajeva,
Erin Spring, Liz Taylor and Dominic Wyse

Faculty of Education, University of Cambridge, Cambridge, UK

This paper considers how children perceive and represent their placed-related identities through reading and writing. It reports on the findings of an 18-month interdisciplinary project, based at Cambridge University Faculty of Education, which aimed to consider children's place-related identities through their engagement with, and creation of, texts. This paper will discuss the project, its interdisciplinary theoretical framework, and the empirical research we conducted with two classes in primary schools in Eastern England. A key text used in our research was *My Place* by Nadia Wheatley and Donna Rawlins. Drawing on our interdisciplinary theoretical framework, particularly Doreen Massey's notion of place as a bundle of trajectories, and Louise Rosenblatt's notion of the transaction between the reader and the text, this paper will examine pages from *My Place*, children talking about how this text connects with them, children talking about their sense of place, and maps and writing the children produced based on their place.

Introduction

The recent spatial turn in education, within and beyond the discipline of geography (Soja 2009), has led to increasing interest in research into the ways people interpret and create the world through reading and writing (Leander and Sheehy 2004; Bavidge 2006; Leander and Rowe 2006; Mackey 2010; Comber et al. 2006; Kostogriz and Tsolidis 2008). In this paper, we consider the ways children perceive and represent place-related identities through reading and writing. We draw upon two theoretical concepts in considering both the text that we used, and the texts that were produced by children within our research. These theoretical concepts – place as bundle of trajectories (Massey 2005) and the transaction between the reader and the text (Rosenblatt 1938/1995), both of which are discussed more fully below – encourage connections to be made between place, identity and text, and point to the importance of such connectedness in children's educational experiences. We will offer a brief outline of our interdisciplinary theoretical framework, including how it relates to *My Place* (Wheatley and Rawlins 2008), the text we used as a stimulus for some of the classroom-based work in the research. We will then show how two of the theoretical concepts from the framework were applied to some of the texts the children created to consider their place-related identities and the ways they are constructed.

My Place

My Place, written by Nadia Wheatley and illustrated by Donna Rawlins, was first published in 1987, with a twentieth anniversary edition being brought out in 2008. Set in Australia, *My Place* takes one house and its surrounding area and tells the story of this place from the perspective of a child who lives there, moving in reverse chronological sequence decade by decade from 1988 back to 1788. Each double-page spread represents a different decade, and is narrated by a different inhabitant. Some families remain in the house for several generations, others for much shorter periods. Through the written text, maps of each narrator's 'place' and illustrations, the text reveals information about family members, their cultural heritage (Greek, Irish, German, American and Chinese heritage, as well as Indigenous Australian), and something about their reasons for coming to this place and/or moving from it to somewhere else.

Each double-page spread also indicates something about the customs and traditions the residents have brought with them from elsewhere and which they enact in this 'new' place. Celebrations are a continual reference point throughout the book, and in some instances these festivities change over time to become new celebrations. For example, in 1878,[1] Mr Wong's family are represented celebrating with fireworks in their garden, and then in 1908, the entire town is celebrating what has become known as cracker night. They buy their fireworks from the Chinese shop, and the place where they celebrate is on land next to where Mr Wong's garden once was. This had been wasteland, later to become an iron factory. These changes are a result of connections to other people's cultural heritage: there is continuity through time and place and yet, while it is the same place in some respects, it is a different place in that it has been recreated as something else as a result of changed social relations. The text draws attention to the gaps but there is still a lot readers do not get to know about. It invites questions about what happened to the people within the place, such as what happened to the Wong family: did they move through choice to make way for the iron factory or were they forced off their land by the more powerful developers or industrialists? We also learn something about the inhabitants' connections to and interrelationships with other people who live in this local area, especially through the maps in which we can see how the land has been changed through being built on, enclosed, farmed, explored, enjoyed or polluted. Each map has imprints of what has gone before and intimations of what may come next.

Developing an interdisciplinary theoretical framework

Our research consisted of two phases: theory building and empirical work. From August to December 2009, we focused on the development of a new theoretical framework suitable for an interdisciplinary exploration of place-related identity (Charlton et al. 2011), which brought together the disciplinary perspectives of the members of the team: children's literature, English, geography and education. We were interested to learn more about how children conceptualise place and how their notions of place relate to their sense of identity by bringing to bear different theoretical perspectives from our respective disciplines. These disciplinary interests inclined us towards a study rooted in children's reading and creation of texts about place. We quickly became aware that interdisciplinarity, where thinking is advanced through interaction between disciplines (Moran 2002), is difficult to achieve;

multidisciplinarity, where disciplines are brought alongside one another but without interaction between them, is an easier although still valuable approach. The empirical phase is addressed later in the paper.

The development of an interdisciplinary approach firstly involved bringing together our different ideas on place. A preliminary exercise involved three of us reading the children's text *Gaffer Samson's Luck* by Jill Paton Walsh and comparing our respective responses (Cliff Hodges, Nikolajeva, and Taylor 2010). As a whole team, we also presented examples of our recent own work to one another in order to discuss similarities and differences within concepts and perspectives informing it, raise questions and try to clarify disciplinary distinctions. We then aimed to construct a theoretical framework whose component parts retained that distinctiveness but offered new ways of interpreting the data when used interactively. Two particular concepts that were brought together were the notions of space as space-time from cultural geography and the idea of reading as a transaction taken from reader-response theory. We will expand briefly on each of these and show, by way of illustration, how they might be applied to *My Place*, before discussing how the framework as a whole was used to inform our analysis of empirical data.

Space as a bundle of trajectories

In *for space* (2005), Doreen Massey proposes a way of re-conceptualising space, arguing in particular that we should always consider space in conjunction with time. Rather than representing space as static, as a surface to be covered or an area to be enclosed, she suggests that space should be conceived of as dynamic, formed by the encounter between different trajectories. Those trajectories may be created by living or non-living entities. If, says Massey, space is seen as 'a plurality of trajectories' (p. 12) temporarily coexisting rather than forming a chronological queue, there are critical implications for how people and their histories or geographies are perceived. People can no longer be homogenised, with some histories privileged over others or seen as being further ahead in a single queue. Massey's conception stresses that individuals contribute to the shape of the group (rather than merely being shaped by it) and different aspects of the local constitute the global (rather than the global being separate). So, if space is seen as a 'simultaneity of stories-so-far' (p. 9) a bundling together of individual trajectories each with their own histories, how might these ideas change the way we view children's perceptions and representations of their place-related identities?

Reading as a transaction

A second important idea within our interdisciplinary discussions was Louise Rosenblatt's notion of reading as a transaction, a perspective she first developed as long ago as the 1930s. Instead of thinking about reading as the printed page impressing its meaning on the reader's mind, Rosenblatt suggests readers actively construct meanings as they read over time in particular contexts or spaces: 'The relation between the reader and signs on the page proceeds in a to-and-fro spiral, in which each is continually being affected by what the other has contributed' (1938/1995, 26). Readers draw on their prior knowledge to construct meaning from texts; texts change readers' prior knowledge; new meanings are thus formed. The process is dynamic, not static. The reader's trajectory meets the text's trajectory to form a constantly shifting process of space-time which, following Massey, becomes a simultaneity of stories-so-far. If readers and texts are continually affected by one another in the transaction of reading, what evidence might we be able to find of children's place-related identities in their responses to reading and their own writing?

Reading the text

Reading My Place *from two theoretical perspectives*

My Place is a multi-layered, multi-modal book which brings place/space and time together and invites considerations of their relationship. However, the brief analysis which now follows focuses on just two double-page spreads, reading them from the two theoretical perspectives outlined above.

On the opening double-page spread of *My Place*, dated 1988, Laura is the narrator. She and her family have recently relocated to this town so that her father might find work. Hanging in the window of their home is the Aboriginal flag. Laura has a pet dog, Gully, and her family celebrates her birthday at the local McDonalds. They sit outside under a large, old tree. Laura writes about playing in the canal in a tin canoe. On the closing double-page spread of *My Place*, dated 1788, the narrator is Barangaroo. Barangaroo and her family stay in that location only during the summer and she swims in the creek and climbs in what turns out to be the 'same' tree as Laura sits under in 1988. Interestingly, these two pages – 1988 and 1788 – are the only pages in which reference is made to the Indigenous people of Australia; for the rest of the narratives Indigenous Australians are notably absent. As the pages open and close the book, this depiction appears symbolic of the way Indigenous Australians have been rendered invisible in representations of the country over the centuries since the arrival of European settlers, and indicates one of the many readings that may be constructed from the text.

Any individual reader's trajectory encounters Laura and her family with their history, particularly that which is signified by the flag, but also Laura's friends who, through their names (e.g. Fatima, Soriya, Tamara and Bianca), are signified as a multicultural community each with their own histories as well. Then there is the trajectory of McDonalds, a global corporation with its own controversial history, positioned in contrast to the writing on the T-shirt of one of Laura's family members, which reads 'FEED THE WORLD'. Interestingly, in the 2008 edition of *My Place*, McDonalds remains on the map, but has been deleted from the text. Rather than going to McDonalds for dinner and taking their food to eat under the tree, Laura states, 'For my birthday, Mum said we could have a picnic'. This alteration may point to the changed ideology and controversy surrounding McDonalds since the book was first published. The source of joy, expressed by exclamation marks after each mention of McDonalds in the earlier edition, has been shifted from the name of the coveted fast food franchise onto an ancient tree. A focus on Massey's conception of space as a bundle of trajectories prompts the question of what simultaneity of stories-so-far forms the spatial sphere in these pages.

In the 1788 double-page spread, an individual reader's trajectory encounters Barangaroo and her family with their history, the trajectories of the different Indigenous tribes invited to join for the feast, and that of a whale, washed up onto the beach. Meanwhile, the reader also travels across the pages from 1988 back to 1788, encountering not just a place and the people who live there but their histories through time as well. Features such as the ancient tree, a spatial point for each narrator and visible in every map in every double-page spread, afford apparent continuity across the time-span of the centuries, although of course the tree in 1988 cannot be the 'same' tree as the one in 1788 even though it appears to occupy the same 'place' as it did then. Analysis of two double-page spreads in *My Place* from spatial perspectives suggests that the text offers multiple vantage points from which young readers might scrutinise concepts of time and space in their own lives and hence encourage them to articulate representations of how they perceive their own place-related identities.

Analysing the same two double-page spreads from reader-response perspectives, especially the idea of reading as a transaction between text and reader, reinforces the notion that the text will prompt readers to draw and reflect on their own place-related identities in the process of reading itself. Amongst much else that they bring to bear, readers use their knowledge of language to engage in transactions with texts. For example, proper nouns, nouns and possessive pronouns are markers of identity within *My Place*. In 1988 Laura writes about 'my name', 'my place' and 'our house'. Her statement that 'This is a map of my place' is an assertion of rights of ownership. Similar assertions occur throughout the book. The exception to this is in 1788 where Barangaroo writes, 'I belong to this place... Everywhere we go is home ... This is a map of this place'. The shift in the narrators' respective stances towards ownership is significant, symbolising a completely different relationship between belonging and place. The title, *My Place*, reflects the first 19 narrators' ideological points of view. In spite of being an Indigenous Australian, Laura speaks of 'my place' and 'our house', and refers to her previous residence as 'home'. Only Barangaroo views herself as belonging to the place rather than the place being hers. Ownership is also demonstrated in the way the children talk about their relatives. Laura writes, 'he is my nephew', which is an assertion of family connectedness (although Laura does mention people who live in her house for whom the familial connection is not made, and it does appear to be more complex than a nuclear familial arrangement). As for proper nouns, the Indigenous Australian names Barangaroo and Bereewan in 1788 are preceded by a very broad cultural mix of names: Michaelis (1958), Heinrich (1878), Johanna (1848) and Sam (1798), whilst some of the shops and restaurants on the map in 1988 carry a variety of adjectives such as Lebanese, Vietnamese, Greek and Thai, signifying other spatial ways in which the place changes over time.

The different kinds of movement within and between places, reflected in these two double-page spreads, suggest both similarities and dissimilarities. Barangaroo says, 'Sometimes I wonder what it would be like to stop in the same place always, but my grandmother says no one does that'. Laura's family have relocated to the town from a place that Laura claims as home, somewhere where the earth is the colour of the Aboriginal flag. The distinction between house and home is also significant. 'Our house is the one with the flag on the window. Tony says it shows we're on Aboriginal land, but I think it means the colour of the earth, back home,' says Laura, adding later, 'We sat in the outside bit, under the tree, and it felt just like home'.

My Place proved to be a very stimulating but challenging text to use when provoking children's ideas about their place-related identities. The analysis above offers a glimpse of some of the opportunities we felt it would afford if it were used as a focal point in the research. We now move on to outline the methodology before presenting and analysing a selection of the data.

Methodology

As stated earlier, the project as a whole had two phases. The second phase – the empirical study of place-related identity through children's reading and writing, informed by our emerging theoretical framework – ran from January to July 2010. The research had three main questions:

- How can we draw upon a conceptualisation of place and space as a bundle of trajectories and theories of reading and writing, to generate analytical tools to develop understanding of children's representation of place-related identities?
- How do children perceive and represent their placed-related identities through reading and writing?
- In what ways do children's responses to and creation of texts shape their place-related identities?

The research involved an interpretive case study of two year 5 classes in two primary schools in Eastern England. While these schools were very different in their student population and landscape, they were only 15 miles apart. Willowmarsh Primary School[2] was a small rural school with a largely White British heritage student population and a small number of other European, Asian and African students. At Willowmarsh, we worked with a composite Year 5/6 class (30 students ages 9–11). Loftyrock Primary School was a big inner city school with a largely Pakistani heritage student population. At Loftyrock, we worked with a Year 5 class (28 students ages 9–10). A smaller sample of six children from each of the classes was selected for further in-depth study.

The data set includes field notes developed from classroom observations and audio recordings of the children at work; semi-structured interviews with the sample children; the texts the children engaged with and produced. The kinds of texts the children created include a timeline, a family tree, an autobiographical narrative, stories about 'a place I know', narratives from the perspective of a tree/animal/person in 'their place' in the past, a reading journal, a predictive chapter, and maps of 'their place'. In addition, when the headteachers and the class teachers came to the University of Cambridge for a day of reflection they decided to arrange for the children from their two schools to meet each other. These school exchanges were serendipitous events for the research, and evidence from them were incorporated into the data set. On the exchange visit to Willowmarsh, the rural school, the children did orienteering, went on a nature walk, planted lettuce seeds, built dens, and visited a farm where they patted and fed sheep and alpacas, and picked potatoes. At Loftyrock, the urban school, the children visited a mosque, learnt bollywood dancing, went shopping for fruit and cloth, had their hands painted with mehndi, ate fruit chaat, and were entertained by drumming and dancing. The schools hope to maintain this connection into the future.

In what follows, we present data selected from interviews, maps, stories about 'a place I know' and autobiographical narratives. These have been chosen because they provide particularly rich evidence of children's perceptions of their place-related identities. Together they offer a nuanced sense of the complexity of these perceptions and heighten our awareness of the multiple factors that comprise children's sense of place and identity.

The children's responses to My Place

In many ways, the children within our research found *My Place* challenging to talk about. A response typical of many children in the class is indicated by Ibrar, from Loftyrock, when he was talking with Emma, one of the research team:

Emma: So who tells the story?
Ibrar: Ah, Miss Bamford [*his class teacher*].
Emma: Sorry, who tells the story in the book? Who's telling this story? [*Emma points to 1988*].
Ibrar: Ah, Gully. No, Laura.
Emma: So on this page Laura's telling the story, who's telling the story on this page?
Ibrar: Mike.
Emma: So are they related these two people?
Ibrar: Yeah, I think. No.
Emma: No, not these two but the next two are related.
Ibrar: Yes.
Emma: So if there's different people telling the story on each page, what stays the same?
Ibrar: The animals, no no.
Emma: Well they're different animals aren't they. They always have animals.
Ibrar: The maps.
Emma: What's the same about the maps?
Ibrar: They be on each page.
Emma: There is a map on each page, yep.
Ibrar: And they have an animal to care about.
Emma: What about the house, is the house the same on every page, do they live in the same house?
Ibrar: No, but they quite look the same.
(Individual interview with Ibrar [Loftyrock])

Perhaps due to the non-conventional narrative structure of *My Place*, the children made fewer connections than we expected with the changing narrators, characters and maps. They appeared to enjoy looking very closely at the detailed artwork to identify similarities and differences across the decades of the book. However, the shifting timescales proved demanding for them to discuss. The aspects that resonated with the children more readily were to do with the animals. Ibrar noted not only that there are animals on each page, but that the relationship between each animal and each narrator is one of care and responsibility.

Santander, from Willowmarsh, presents another typical response which again makes a connection with animals in *My Place*. It was a connection, however, that took a while to identify.

Emma: How does it relate to life in [your village]?
Santander: It doesn't.
Emma: There's no similarities at all?
Santander: No, I don't think so
Emma: Do you have a favourite page inside?
Santander: Um, no.
Emma: Do you have a character that you remember?
Santander: I only looked at the pictures, and one has a pig.
Emma: So let's find the page with the pig.
Santander: I think we've gone past it, it's like halfway through.

Emma: *[Flipping through the pages]* So that's a cat, that's a budgy, he's got silkworms, the little girl's got a puppy, the little boy's got a chicken, this little girl looks after her little brother, the goat?

Santander: No it's a pig, a little pig.

Emma: Definitely a pig. There's a horse, not a horse? A cockatiel, a cat.

Santander: I just remember somebody with a pig.

Emma: Another cat, monkey.

Santander: I like the monkey too.

Emma: Another horse. There's the pig. So 1828. So what do you like about this page?

Santander: Because I like pigs, because when I used to live in Colombia I lived on a farm, it was made of wood and I liked it because we had cows and goat and pigs, and I most liked the pigs.

(Individual interview with Santander [Willowmarsh])

Seen from some perspectives, it might be tempting to conclude the children mainly read this book for information. However, if we focus on use of language and, crucially, bring to bear Rosenblatt's ideas about readers responding, not just generating information but activating feelings or the *aesthetic* response as she terms it (Rosenblatt 1938/1995), we see that stance clearly in these boys' responses as well. Yes, there are animals but they are always 'animals to care about'; yes there is a pig, but Santander likes the pigs in the book because he likes pigs in the real world, too. The pigs connect him with his former home in Colombia rather than home in England now. To this aesthetic response, we can also add a geographer's perspective which affords a view of place-related identity as not just locality-based, but relational to any living and non-living things with their own trajectories. Here, Santander's trajectory reaches back to his life in Colombia and jostles with other trajectories of pigs, real and fictional, portrayed in *My Place*.

Maps of 'My Place'

One of the activities the children did was make a map of what they considered to be 'their place'. It was intended to link with their reading of the maps on each double-page spread in *My Place*. The children at Willowmarsh made their maps as a homework task. The children at Loftyrock did it as a one of their classroom activities. These maps raise interesting questions about how the children perceived and represented place-related identities. The following maps belong to five of the children, two from Willowmarsh and three from Loftyrock.

Maria attended Willowmarsh. She and her family had lived in the village for just over a year following a move from Romania. Upon her arrival, Maria did not speak English, but was quite proficient by the time we did the research. Maria's map (Figure 1) is interesting for its relational accuracy. The streets are quite accurately portrayed, as is the detail in the housing, and the map is centrally arranged by roads and houses. Maria indicates a time/place relationship between the school and her home: it takes one and a half minutes for her to get to school. The street with the church on it is the main road in and out of the village. The streets to the right of the map are part of a cul-de-sac. The differential detail in these two areas reflects the boundaries of Maria's movement within the place she represents. In the interviews, Maria revealed that she is not allowed up on the main road without supervision. She is, however, allowed free movement in the cul-de-sac. Not all of the children's maps reflect the relational accuracy of Maria's map, although in different ways they all reveal the boundaries and limits of movement within 'their place'.

Nadia (Figure 2) attended Loftyrock. She was born in England, and her grandparents had emigrated to England from Pakistan. Her map includes four places of significance to her: home, school, mosque and shop. These are represented as the constellations of Nadia's world. The pathways between these places are a mixture of structured roads and direct (but inaccurate) lines. The yellow lines on the roads, and the 'partking tickets' indicate the way in which Nadia predominantly moves through this place, namely in a vehicle. She does, however, walk to school and ride her bike during the summer.

Darina also presents a map (Figure 3) in which the pathways between places are significant. Darina had come to England from the Czech Republic with her family in 2005. She had formerly lived closer to the school, but her family had since moved and now she was brought to school in a car by her uncle. Darina includes the school in her map. The features between the school and her house are not connected, although streets are included. This disconnection on the path to school may indicate Darina's awareness of the path. She has included shops such as Somerfield and Iceland, and a bank, but the connections between the roads are absent. This is not a path Darina walks. The path that she does walk is from her house to the park.

Ibrar was another student at Loftyrock. He was also a British-born student but his parents were born in Pakistan. He walked to school with family members, usually parents but sometimes older siblings. Ibrar's map (Figure 4) indicates movement within place, although interestingly it is one-directional movement to school, and

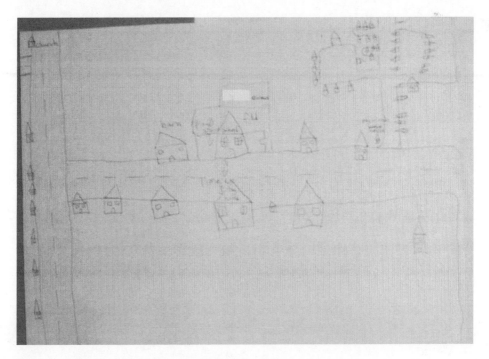

Figure 1.   Maria's map of her place (Willowmarsh).

Figure 2.   Nadia's map of her place (Loftyrock). Reproduced from Wyse et al. (2011, Figure 2) with kind permission of the British Educational Research Association.

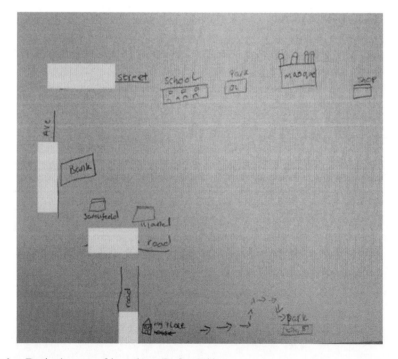

Figure 3.   Darina's map of her place (Loftyrock).

possibly to worship. (Ibrar mentioned that he attended a different mosque than those included on his map.)

While Ibrar's map showed movement within place, only children at Willowmarsh indicated movement beyond the local. It is possible that this may have been mentioned as something the teacher would like to see in the maps (along with how long it takes to get to school), but not all the children included this information; where they do, it demonstrates the children's awareness of places beyond their immediate village. Callum's map (Figure 5) is a good example. Callum was a British-born student from Willowmarsh. His map includes the path to school (235 metres) which he takes with his mother and his younger brother. He also indicates the directions to the neighbouring villages and the closest city. All of the roads are identified as leading somewhere else.

The five maps reveal much about the daily lives and routines of these children. The inclusion in these maps of church, mosque or shop also reflects the children wanting to represent spaces formed by the coming together of people and places. We cannot know what the children would have drawn if they had not read *My Place*, but there are connections between the representations in the text and the representations made by the children, visible, for example, in Maria's relational accuracy, Ibrar's labelling of the houses, Darina's labelling of important places, Callum's use of arrows, and Nadia's explanation of why some places are significant. Thus, their transactions with *My Place* seem to have informed the maps that were created. However, without Rosenblatt's theory we might have assumed they were imitating *My Place*; instead a combination of a transactional theory of reading with a notion of space as a bundle of trajectories enabled us to interpret their maps more subtly.

Children's perceptions of their place-related identities

One of the interview questions we asked the children was 'Where would you say you are from?'. They were asked this at the beginning and at the end of the research. A

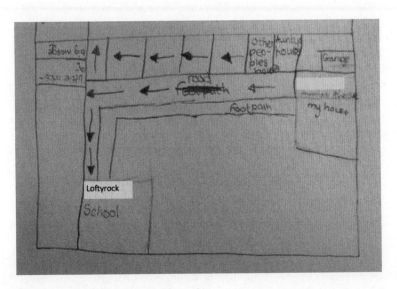

Figure 4.   Ibrar's map of his place (Loftyrock).

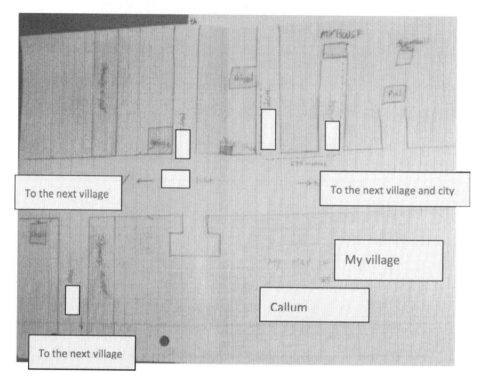

Figure 5.   Callum's map of his place (Willowmarsh).

sense of belonging for these children emerged not only through their responses to this question, but throughout the dataset in the texts they created and in their overheard conversations. In illustrating the complexity of how they perceived and represented their place-related identities, the following discussion focuses on two children from each of the schools. Callum and Simreet from Willowmarsh, and Dora and Ibrar from Loftyrock.

Callum, as mentioned in relation to his map mentioned earlier, was a British-born white boy who had resided in the village for 5 years, and whose maternal family could trace their heritage in the local area back to the early 1600s. Simreet was a British-born Indian girl whose parents were born in India and emigrated to England with their extended family. Both Callum and Simreet saw themselves as belonging to places where they were not born but which they had visited and with which one or both parents have a strong connection. For example, Simreet's immediate family had recently relocated to the village for work. When asked where she saw herself as being from Simreet stated:

> I am from India. ... That's where my mum and dad were born and the rest of my family. ... Because the rest of my family was born in India, because that's where we used to live until my granddad moved to England and then all my other, my dad, my aunties and everyone else moved to England, then I was born here. (Simreet, in small group interview with Callum [Willowmarsh])

Simreet was selected as a student to be interviewed because we predicted that she would exhibit more of a multiple sense of place due to her family's heritage and their movement between places. Callum, meanwhile, was selected because we predicted that he would show a stronger sense of local place since his mother's family had such a long local history. In neither instance, however, was this the case.

> Callum: I feel like I'm mostly part of Scotland.
> Emma: Oh okay, why do you say that?
> Callum: Because most of my family was born there and then some of my English family, which is Kate's [Callum's cousin, also in this class] part of the side, is just trying to get in, trying to settle into me, even though I was born in England I'm still used to Scotland.
> (Callum, in small group interview with Simreet [Willowmarsh])

Callum's father was born in Scotland and Callum identified more with his father's trajectory than his mother's. Callum's association with his father extended beyond seeing himself as Scottish. The activities Callum engaged in were strongly connected with his father and centred around farming. Each afternoon Callum would go out on the farm with his father, helping him with the lambing or going with him on the tractor. For Callum, his sense of place related to his father, and the tractor and land as much as the village, perhaps more so. Callum repeatedly referred to farming throughout the dataset: when Simreet told the sample group about cows in India, Callum mentioned 'I'd like to go there then'; when Simreet and the researcher were talking about rats on an excursion Callum commented, 'I've found a load of rats in my farm. You just look there and there's a rat right in front of you'; when Callum was selected to be a guard for his class's civil war re-enactment, but then told to create an appropriate alternative job for the character when the war wasn't on, he opted to be a farmer, 'Cause I already have a job, can I be that'; when Santander talked about shooting in Columbia Callum mentioned, 'On my farm we have guns and we go shooting'; and when asked about his favourite page in *My Place* Callum nominated the page with farming on it. Farming, therefore, was a strong aspect of his place-related identity.

Simreet's talk about place included regularly moving beyond the local for religious practices, which were not satisfied within the village. For example, on Sundays she and her family would travel to the closest city to attend the temple where there was also a strong emphasis on socialising with friends and family. For the time being, for Simreet, the trajectories of her Indian family jostling with her own trajectory shaped her identity strongly.

While at the beginning of the project both Simreet and Callum said they saw themselves as being from distant places more associated with their parents, at the end of the research process both offered different answers, perhaps indicating the effect of being asked regularly to reflect on a sense of place. When asked a second time, 'Where are you from?', Callum claimed to be from the village where he was born, which was close to where he now lived (and not in Scotland). And Simreet claimed: 'I am mostly from England 'cause I was born here but my mum and dad were born in India so basically I'm from India and England'.

The children at Loftyrock similarly reflected complex senses of identity. As mentioned earlier, Ibrar was a British-born boy. His parents had moved as children from Pakistan to England where they then met, married and had children themselves. Dora was born in Portugal. Her parents, both from East Timor, had then moved the family to England where they had now lived for 5 years. When first asked 'Where are you from?' Dora commented, 'East Timor's my dad's place because my mum and dad come from East Timor so we're kind of related to

Portugal and East Timor'. Dora's response the second time reflected the tension between place and heritage. Dora commented:

> I don't know 'cause Portugal is my place but my proper place is more Timor because my dad and my whole relations, my dad, my great granddad, they all fought in Timor and I was born in Portugal, don't know why. So I think it's more in Timor than in Portugal. (Individual interview with Dora [Loftyrock])

In fact, Dora would often talk about the political history of East Timor, and its landscape and location. She talked about East Timor in the group interview with the girls at Loftyrock, in classroom talk, and in her story 'about a place I know'. Reading her story to the group Dora stated: 'A long time ago Timor had to go, had to get their own food. They never had pizza or fanta, they only had water creatures and coconut. In 1999, East Timor was free from Indonesia they were having a big war and East Timor won. In Timor, it is very hot. It never rains or snow. It's just hot the whole time. Timor has the biggest beach'.

This place-related connection also emerged on excursions. As the students were leaving for the school exchange the researcher gave Dora a recorder. The transcript shows her talking to Mrs Murphy, the teaching assistant, about liking horses and ponies because her dad used to ride horses up the mountain in East Timor:

Dora: I'm going to talk about what I've seen on the way.
Mrs Murphy: That sounds like a good idea. What do you think you're gonna see on the way Jhangir [another student]?
Dora: Horses. Miss, you know my dad, my dad used to ride horses up the mountain.
Mrs Murphy: Oh wow. In Portugal?
Dora: Miss, he has photos.
Mrs Murphy: What part of Portugal did you live?
Dora: Not in Portugal, in East Timor.
Mrs Murphy: Where is East Timor?
Dora: Miss, here is Portugal and here is East Timor. In the middle of Australia and India. Miss, there's a map.
Mrs Murphy: When we come back tomorrow you can show me.
Dora: Miss, that's why I really like horse and ponies.
(Field notes [Loftyrock])

What was particularly interesting about how Dora claimed East Timor as her place was that she had never been there. Dora laid claim to place-related identity that involved a place she had not visited and yet it was a place with which she was familiar because of her father and the ways in which knowledge was conveyed in their family. Dora's family's trajectories continue to carry with them very apparent aspects from previous places. The tension between remembering a place was already emerging for Dora. She commented:

> I think I've kind of forgot about stuff in Portugal because it's been a long time, I've been here nearly more than Portugal, Portugal I only lived there for six years and here I'm already living for nearly five years. (Individual interview with Dora [Loftyrock])

Ibrar reveals a different sort of connection with his parents' sense of place. Ibrar talked and wrote positively of the city in which he lived.

Emma: Yeah? Would you be happy to stay here all your life?

Ibrar: Even if I was trapped in this world I would still be happy.

Emma: If you were trapped in the?

Ibrar: World, like a globe around England.

Emma: If you were trapped in England you'd still be happy because you like England?

Ibrar: Yes. But I would still miss the rain.

(Ibrar, in small group interview with Amjad and Idriss [Loftyrock])

Ibrar's story 'about a place I know' exhibited a strong sense of local place (Figure 6).

Ibrar was explicit about depicting his place as idyllic, justifying his images as 'beautiful' despite the cityscape of his environment. His autobiographical text similarly had a strong message to convey about his relationship with the local (see Figure 7).

The writing and then crossing out of 'Pakistan' is highly significant. The threat of return seems to be at the forefront of Ibrar's mind. 'I say to my family, I don't want to leave,' he writes. When later asked about this text, Ibrar denied feeling any connection with Pakistan, and talked about only speaking English. Ibrar was laying claim to his local place, and for him this entailed a rejection of what could have been a multiple sense of place.

Re-visiting the research questions

Having discussed a small number of extracts from the data, we now return to our original research questions to consider how our interdisciplinary framework affected our understanding of children's representation of place-related identities; how children perceived and represented their placed-related identities through reading and writing; and how children's responses to and creation of texts shaped their place-related identities.

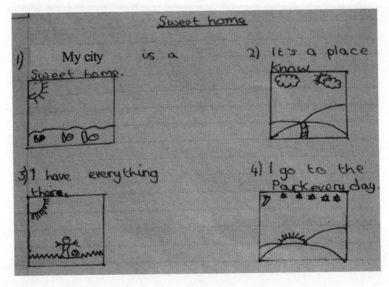

Figure 6.   Ibrar's first story 'about a place I know' (Loftyrock).

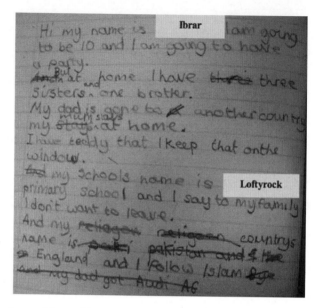

Figure 7.   Ibrar's autobiographical text (draft) (Loftyrock).

Our sense is that our interdisciplinary perspectives helped to move us away from thinking about place as fixed and static, or thinking about reading and writing as a mirroring of the world. Instead, taking the concepts of space as a constantly changing bundle of trajectories and of reading as a transactional process, and drawing on them as theoretical perspectives from which to analyse the children's talk, maps and stories, allowed a more complex representation of their place-related identities to emerge. A more commonplace, bounded notion of place might have led us to focus on how children's identity is influenced by their local place, how they experience their local area or place and what they like or dislike about it; but seeing space as formed by the coming together of different trajectories illuminated children's connections with other places beyond the immediate locality and with other spaces formed by social networks and cultural practices. Thus, if place and identity are seen as processes, place-related identity must be similarly dynamic and complex (see also Charlton et al. 2011).

My Place, in many respects, proved to be an interesting choice of text. Due to time constraints and unfamiliarity with its unique style, the children's readings of the text were sometimes limited. However, for many of the children the text was a rich stimulus for thinking about place and place-related identities. The text focused on individual trajectories and the importance of the narrators' families' identities as part of their own identities in the text. We can see echoes of this pattern in the children's own focus on their families' trajectories. The children's maps of their place are an indication of a transaction between them and *My Place*. An increased sense of place as multifaceted, as indicated by the changes between Dora's and Simreet's first and second responses to the question, 'Where are you from?' might also be evidence of a transaction with *My Place*, as well as being the result of heightened talk around place-related identities in interviews and other class activities.

The interdisciplinary framework developed during this project encouraged all those involved to pay due attention to the ways children bring their prior experiences into the classroom. Furthermore, it potentially encourages a move away from thinking about the local as fixed, something children should 'learn about', and more towards how children and their stories so far, along with the other living and non-living trajectories they encounter, contribute to the construction and re-creation of 'their place'.

Notes

1. There are no page numbers in *My Place*. Each double-page spread can therefore only be referred to by the date of the decade it represents.
2. All names have been changed.

References

Bavidge, J. 2006. Stories in space: The geographies of children's literature. *Children's Geographies* 4: 319–30.

Charlton, E., D. Wyse, G. Cliff Hodges, P. Pointon, M. Nikolajeva, and L. Taylor. 2011. Place-related identities through texts: From interdisciplinary theory to research agenda. *British Journal of Educational Studies* 59: 63–74.

Cliff Hodges, G., M. Nikolajeva, and L. Taylor. 2010. Three walks through fictional fens: multidisciplinary perspectives on Gaffer Samson's Luck. *Children's Literature in Education* 41: 189–206.

Comber, B., H. Nixon, L. Ashmore, S. Loo, and J. Cook. 2006. Urban renewal from the inside out: Spatial and critical literacies in a low socioeconomic school community. *Mind, Culture, and Activity* 13: 228–46.

Kostogriz, A., and G. Tsolidis. 2008. Transcultural literacy: Between the global and the local. *Pedagogy, Culture and Society* 16: 125–36.

Leander, K.M., and D.W. Rowe. 2006. Mapping literacy spaces in motion: A rhizomatic analysis of a classroom literacy performance. *Reading Research Quarterly* 41, 428–60.

Leander, K.M., and M. Sheehy, ed. 2004. *Spatialising literacy research and practice*. New York: Peter Lang.

Mackey, M. 2010. Reading from the feet up: The local work of literacy. *Children's Literature in Education* 41, 4: 323–39.

Massey, D. 2005. *For space*. London: Sage.

Moran, J. 2002. *Interdisciplinarity*. London: Routledge.

Rosenblatt, L.M. 1938/1995. *Literature as Exploration*. New York: Modern Language Association of America.

Soja, E.W. 2009. Taking space personally. In *The spatial turn: Interdisciplinary perspectives*, ed. B. Warf and S. Arias. London and New York: Routledge.

Wheatley, N., and D. Rawlins. 2008. *My Place*. Newtown, NSW, Australia: Walker Books.

Wyse, D., M. Nikolajeva, E. Charlton, G. Cliff Hodges, P. Pointon, and L. Taylor. 2011. Place-related identity, texts, and transcultural meanings. *British Educational Research Journal*, first published online 4 October 2011. http://dx.doi.org/10.1080/01411926.2011.608251.

Same old story: the problem of object-based thinking as a basis for teaching distant places

Fran Martin

Graduate School of Education, University of Exeter, St Luke's Campus, Exeter, UK

The English Geography National Curriculum encourages primary teachers to focus on similarities and differences when teaching distant places. The issues this raises are particularly acute when teaching geography in the context of the Global South. In this article I argue that comparisons based on object-based thinking can lead to views of the 'Other' that undermine attempts to challenge stereotypes and develop positive attitudes towards difference. Relational thinking is proposed as an alternative, where difference is seen as a relation rather than a distinction. Drawing on an Economic and Social Research Council research project, these alternative ways of thinking are explored through research participants' constructions of culture and identity during study visits to Southern India and The Gambia. The implications for primary teachers are considered.

Introduction

The English Geography National Curriculum (GNC) has, since its introduction (DES 1991), had a focus on knowledge and understanding of the concept of 'Place'. More specifically, when teaching about *distant* people and places, a comparative approach is suggested that encourages the identification of similarities and differences between the focus of study and pupils' own region. For example, in the current GNC (DfEE/QCA 1999, 111, 113) primary pupils are expected to be taught to 'recognise how places compare with other places' and to 'describe and explain how and why places are similar to and different from other places in the same country and elsewhere in the world'. This pattern continues in the proposals for the draft-revised English GNC where pupils are to be taught to 'understand geographical similarities and differences through studying the human and physical geography of a region or area of the United Kingdom' (DfE 2013, 163) and a contrasting region or area. Comparison is therefore embedded in the approach to understanding different places, with the UK being the benchmark against which similarities and differences are identified. This is quite natural since it is the curriculum for England; however it raises a number of issues which become particularly acute when the distant place is located in the Global South, and the focus is on human geography.

Between 2009 and 2013, an Economic and Social Research Council (ESRC) research project investigated what teachers and student teachers learn from their experiences during study visits to two contrasting areas of the world – The Gambia in West Africa and Southern India. The study gathered data from both visiting and host organisations and individuals. For the purposes of this article I focus on data gathered from two UK study-visit groups, the compositions of which were predominantly primary schoolteachers and student teachers. Over the course of the research it became evident that there were significant variations in how the UK individuals constructed knowledge about their own and others' culture and identity. These variations were partly influenced by their (changing) worldviews about the Global South and development, but at a more fundamental level we noticed differences which seem to connect to Nisbett's (2005) traditions of thought. In this article I explore these two traditions, object-based and relational, and show how they affect the ways in which cultural similarities and differences are understood, first in the context of my own identity, and then in the context of teaching about a distant place. These alternative ontological and epistemological positions are then used as lenses through which to analyse the UK data.

Based on the findings, I argue that, while subject knowledge is often cited as an issue for primary teachers, it is not only *what* teachers know that is an issue, but the epistemological basis for that knowledge that also needs to be considered. Drawing on the data, it is proposed that an object-based tradition focuses on assigning people and cultures to categories, identifying what is similar between people, and often unwittingly creating a standard from which difference is judged to be a deviation. I go on to argue that, in addition to object-based thinking, there is a need for relational thinking, in which difference is understood as a relation, rather than a distinction (Burbules 1997). I conclude by considering the implications of this for primary teachers and distant place studies in geography.

Literature review

As noted above, in primary geography education there is a tradition of teaching about distant places by making comparisons between the pupils' own locality and the contrasting place. Research has identified two key problems with such an approach (Picton 2008): the problem of essentialism and the problem of binary thinking. Picton's research was conducted with secondary pupils who were learning about Brazil. However, the findings are relevant to primary teachers because, as Catling (2004) and Martin (2008) have shown, many primary teachers ceased to study geography beyond the age of 14, with the result that their conceptions of the subject are similar to those of secondary pupils. With the amount of time given to prepare primary teachers to teach geography being between 0 and 16 hours on a Postgraduate Primary course (Catling et al. 2007) there are limited opportunities to change this situation, with the result that many teachers enter the profession with far greater pedagogical than subject knowledge, the latter of which is understood from the perspective of a non-specialist.

Adichie (2009)[1] identifies an essentialist Western view of Africa that she calls a 'Single Story', in which a group or nation is defined, by others, by a set of characteristics that create a stereotype. Adichie discusses how it is impossible to talk about a single story without talking about power; stories are defined by who tells them, how they are told, when they are told and how many stories are told. Adichie argues that stories about sub-Saharan Africa in the West are dominated by representations that focus on a mixture of the exotic, and 'people fighting senseless wars, dying of poverty and AIDS, unable to speak for themselves, and waiting to be saved by a kind, white foreigner' (Adichie 2009). The single story thus creates a category of Africa which is homogenising and presented as fixed and stable. Other stories about sub-Saharan Africa do exist in the West but, as Borowski (2011) observes, activities such as Red Nose Day (RND 2013) tend to perpetuate the deficit story, and incorporating such events into the curriculum in ways that counteract the stereotype requires a level of subject knowledge that many primary teachers do not have. This is further compounded by the binary, comparative approach to teaching distant places which is based on an object-based tradition as explained below.

Two traditions of thought

Richard Nisbett (2005) identifies two traditions of thought: an object-based tradition that has emerged from Greece and dominates Western-European thinking, and a relational tradition that has emerged from China and dominates Eastern-Asian thinking. He is careful to emphasise that the distinction is not intended to be used as a stereotype for how people think in the West and the East, but rather as a descriptor of the traditions' spatial and philosophical origins, and as a heuristic device for understanding alternative epistemologies.

An object-based tradition

Nisbett (2005) argues that object-based thinking is a highly linear way of understanding objects in isolation. Objects are viewed as things that possess certain properties, and properties are seen to remain static over time. If I apply this type of thinking to my identity – I am British – I am focusing on identity as an object and Britishness as a property of identity. This is a categorical way of thinking (Burbules 1997) in that I belong to a group of people who hold the same property, outside of which are those who are different, not-British. While categorisation is a useful means of making sense of the diverse nature of the living and non-living worlds, in the context of cultural difference and identity this becomes problematic. First, it creates a hierarchical binary of like–not like, us–them, which can create a sense of distance between cultures. Second, while the category itself creates a sense of belonging, this is a product of the focus on similarity and can smooth over the differences that exist *within* the category. Third, if culture is understood as an autonomous object that can be acquired, then decisions can be made about who can be included or (often unjustly) excluded from the group. Fourth, in a diverse world, 'boundary drawing becomes difficult, and must reify difference, ... and fix it as rooted in space and for all time' (Edensor 2002, 25). It is conceptualising culture, race and nationality as categories that are fixed and stable that Picton (2008) refers to as essentialising, and which Adichie (2009) and Borowski (2011) point out as problematic as bases for understanding alternative cultures and ways of life.

Similarity–difference as binary. As outlined above, an object-based tradition of thought creates a binary distinction of us–them. If applied to teaching about a distant place, pupils will naturally associate themselves with their place and culture and use this as the basis for identifying similarities and differences in the contrasting place to be studied. One can then see that similarity/like/us will be properties assigned to their own group, and difference/not like/them will be assigned to the contrasting group which, if linked to power, can lead to a sense of superiority in the group that is doing the assigning. It can also have the effect of increasing the distance between self and 'Other' (Said 1985).

In the 1980s, when I first started teaching, a solution to this perceived problem was to focus on a property we all share, thus identifying the inclusive category of 'human', to which everyone belongs. This is a problem because 'we are all the same because we are all human' is arguably another way of saying 'you are [or should be] like us'. So a focus on sameness as a way of levelling differences is as if there is no relevance to these differences – and it can have the effect of making differences invisible, of silencing them. Sharon Todd criticises the appeal for humanity in education on the grounds that it is an implicit appeal for universalism and intrinsic goodness such that differences that we feel *un*comfortable with are identified as *in*human, while being human is seen to be an automatic 'good'.

> ... the claim that education can ameliorate certain global conditions under this sign of humanity is a worrying proposition on two counts. First, it fails to recognise that the very injustices and antagonisms which are the targets of such educational endeavours in the first place are created and sustained precisely through our human ('all too human') talent for producing them; and secondly, as Simon Critchley has recently warned, humanity has often been used to justify the exclusion of those with whom 'we' are in conflict; enemies are turned into 'outlaws of humanity'. (2007, 142 cited in Todd 2008, 3)

Similarity–difference as diversity. In recognition of the problems with the all-inclusive category of 'human', during the 1990s there was a move in education towards a focus on difference, expressed as 'celebrating diversity'. Ostensibly, the focus is on valuing difference, but the differences continue to be externalised from the dominant group and are seen to be the property of the 'Other'. From this perspective, celebrating diversity is merely an accommodation of those aspects of difference that can be comprehended and classified in terms of dominant standards. The narrative continues to be 'we [the dominant group] are the same, you are different', with the dominant group identifying which aspects of difference to celebrate. This is sometimes evident in primary schools when, during the teaching of a distant place, there is a celebration of, for example, African culture through an African drumming event or Indian culture through the preparation and consumption of a 'typical' Indian meal. This approach can exoticise difference as something quaint, charming or curious, while differences that are more challenging to comprehend are ignored.

A relational tradition

In contrast to object-based thinking, relational thought, argues Nisbett (2005), has emerged from China as a way of thinking based on a sense of collective agency. In this tradition, a sense of self is developed through social relations, with individuals taking prescribed roles in working towards group goals. From this perspective, objects are understood as both part of, and inseparable from, their environment and because environments continually change, change and flux are seen to be natural properties of objects.

If I think about my identity from a relational perspective, I understand my 'Britishness' as a social relation (with people who are British, and those from other nationalities) and as a historic relation. Socially, in each moment of relation with another's difference, there is the possibility of understanding a further dimension of what being British means *to me*; thus aspects of my identity are constantly being made and remade (Brah 2007). Understanding the concept of identity as relational shows it as something that is fluid and open to change, complex and diverse – there is as much diversity within the category British as there is between British and other national identities.

This can be applied to other aspects of my identity. I am also a twin, a boogie boarder, a primary geographer, a teacher, a researcher, a sister, a dog owner and English with Scottish ancestry. There are multiple aspects to my identity, each of which has its own cultural traditions. If someone were to define me in terms of any one of these to the exclusion of the others, that would be a reductive sense of who I am and extremely limiting. These seem to me to be strong arguments for focusing on difference in ways that go beyond 'celebrating diversity' to acknowledging differences that are difficult to understand, including those that challenge ideas of what it means to be human. In order to do so, Burbules (1997) proposes that a deeper understanding of the concept of difference is required.

Difference as relational

Burbules (1997, 12) argues for a view of difference that is pre-categorical.

> Differences are enacted. They change over time. They take shape differently in varied contexts. They always surpass our attempts to classify or define them. They do not assume sameness; they are the conditions out of which we establish agreements about sameness. The word 'between' is itself a relational word: *difference here is seen as a relation, not a distinction* (my emphasis). Difference creates the sense of a 'between'. In this sense, then, difference represents a critique of binary thought and of the reification that categorical thinking falls prey to.

Conceptualising culture, race and nationality as relational implies understanding difference as a property of everyone, from which points of similarity can be identified but which create categories that are fluid, open to change (as individuals, societies and cultural traditions change over time) and the boundaries of which are permeable (Bashkow 2004; Posner 2004). In the same way that national boundaries are not fixed, as recent history of Eastern Europe testifies, neither are social and cultural boundaries 'barriers to outside influence or to historical change, but ... cultural distinctions that [are] irreducibly plural, perspectival, and permeable' (Bashkow 2004, 443).

It was on the basis of these traditions of thought as alternative (but not oppositional) epistemological stances from which to understand the spatial and cultural similarities and differences teachers encountered during study visits that we have interpreted data analysed from our study as is explained below.

Research methodology

Between October 2009 and January 2013, I led an ESRC project, as principal investigator (PI), for which the key research question was: What impact do two North–South study visits have on teachers' understanding of development issues and how does this inform their understanding of, and practice in, global partnerships? However, in the early stages of data gathering and analysis, it became clear that what respondents wanted to talk about was how they were making sense of, and learning from, the intercultural interactions that are at the heart of study visits. Our focus therefore began to shift to the questions below, which guide the focus for this article:

- What are the key factors that prompt changes in knowledge and beliefs about global and development issues?
- What influences how people learn from each other interculturally?

These questions were investigated through gathering data from participants in two study-visit courses: one for experiences of teachers from England to The Gambia, and one for student teachers from England to Tamil Nadu, India. Both study visits are facilitated by group leaders who are experienced educators. Each study visit has three components: a preparatory phase, the visit itself and a follow-up phase. The Gambia study visit is run by Tide~ global learning. A group of 8–10 teachers go to The Gambia for one week in February, with preparatory and follow-up phases taking place in the UK. Working with the National Environment Agency, they have some professional development with Gambian teachers, including fieldwork and a day conference to discuss pedagogical approaches to teaching about sustainability. The study visit to Tamil Nadu is run by staff at Canterbury Christ Church University. A group of between 14 and 18 students and lecturers go to India for 18 days. The preparatory and follow-up sessions take place in Kerala, with two weeks in-between staying and teaching at a children's home in Tamil Nadu where there is an on-site primary school.

Data analysed for this article were gathered from UK teachers who went to The Gambia in February 2010 ($n = 7$) and student teachers who went to India in July 2010 ($n = 14$). The gender split of the UK participants in 2010 was 6:1 females to males for the Gambia study visit and 15:1 for the India study visit. A multi-sited ethnographic approach was adopted by the research fellow (RF), who was a participant in both courses during 2010 and gathered data through participant observation, supplemented by semi-structured interviews, learning journals, end-of-study-visit written evaluations and biographical questionnaires. Participant observation entailed the RF keeping detailed notes in her own learning journal, including notes of reflective sessions run by study-visit leaders. For example, in the India study visit at the children's home a question wall was created where people could use post-its to stick up a question that had arisen for them. After a few days these were brought to a group session and discussed; this session was audio-recorded. The PI also participated in the study visits, gathering data through a research diary and in-depth interviews with study-visit leaders. To investigate whether changes in knowledge and practice were enduring, further data were gathered from participants in previous courses run between 2002 and 2009.Questionnaires were completed by 72 respondents (UK $n = 48$) with follow-up focus group and individual interviews being conducted a few weeks later (UK $n = 18$). The gender split across UK respondents was 35 females to13 males. In all cases, interviews were conducted as a form of professional conversation, with prompts for areas of discussion. In this way the researchers were led by the respondents' interests, rather than by sticking rigidly to questions of our own making. Since the researchers had also participated in the study visits, their perspectives as learners were seen as legitimate to include in the conversations.

As a former co-leader of the Gambia study-visit course and a colleague of the leader of the India study visit I came to the project as both researcher and participant. It was therefore clear that an objective 'bystander' stance to the research would neither be possible nor desirable. This had a profound effect on how the research was conducted. The ethical code developed by the BERA (2011) advises researchers to acknowledge how their experiences and values have affected their theoretical and methodological choices, in order to avoid the danger of those values being 'present in the form of unrecognised assumptions that shape what is done in an uncontrolled manner' (BERA 2011). Explicitly acknowledging my positionality 'is therefore part of good research practice' (BERA 2011). While this might be seen as being partisan in relation to the research, as researchers our ethical position was one of [self]-critical partisanship. We could not avoid being partisan, but we *could* constantly reflect on the nature and impact of that partisanship. We therefore negotiated the nature of our participation with both study-visit groups beforehand, gained informed consent from organisations, study-visit leaders and study-visit participants, assuring individuals of anonymity and the right to withdraw. As unanticipated ethical issues arose during the course of the study, we used these as a focal point for discussion with group leaders, and had recourse to the project's advisory group and our university's ethics committee when further advice was required.

Data analysis

Overall analysis of data sets from all three countries was conducted by the UK researchers using Nvivo. However, codings of samples of data from all three countries were shared and discussed with the PI at various points during the study, and this informed analyses made in the master copy of data sets. In addition, a code 'research processes' was created in Nvivo to enable us to keep records of differences in how data were coded by each researcher. In doing this we aimed to avoid imposing perspectives from the Western academy on the southern researchers (Shamim and Qureshi 2010; Andreotti 2011), and to attend to the ethical 'nature of what is legitimated as valid research and as appropriate research partnerships and research capacity building' (Barrett, Crossley, and Dachi 2011, 28).

A mixture of interpretive and reflexive approaches to data analysis was therefore taken (Welsh 2002). The first level of analysis, undertaken by researchers on their own data sets, was interpretive; the second level of analysis, when researchers came together and conducted additional collaborative analysis, was reflexive. At the first level, early data sets were coded *in vivo,* a process described by QSR (2011, 26) as using the selected word or phrase to name the node, which 'is useful if you want your nodes to reflect the language of the people you have interviewed'. As the number of nodes grows, they can then be grouped into overarching themes, which creates a hierarchical structure. For this article we have drawn on data under the key theme of Mutual Learning, and the codes of 'learning from similarity' and 'learning from difference'. Although there were two separate categories for similarity and difference, Nvivo allows for relationships between items coded under different headings to be noted.

Where direct quotes are taken from the data, the respondent is identified by gender and respondent number (F1/F2/M1), nationality (UK, Indian, Gambian), by study visit (Gambia – GSVC; India – ISSV), by the year they participated in a study visit (2002–2010) and, if part of the longitudinal sample, by the year in which they were interviewed (2011–2012). So a female participant in the India study visit in 2010 could be (F1/UK/ISSV 2010), a male participant in the Gambia study-visit course in 2005 could be (M5/UK/GSVC 2005, interviewed 2011) All the participants are primary schoolteachers and student teachers unless stated otherwise.

Findings

The findings are set out under the subheadings for similarity and difference identified in the review of literature. The first two sections thus give examples of object-based thinking from the data while the third section, with its two further subsections, give examples of relational thinking.

Similarity–difference as a binary

During the Gambia study visit in 2010, it became evident that some teachers were using the single story about Africa as a lens for making sense of their experiences. For example, a secondary schoolteacher focused on those aspects of life that fitted with the stereotype portrayed in teaching materials he used back home,

They [the streets] are absolutely piled with rubbish, which by pure coincidence is the first lesson back with Year 11, when we do about the Kibera slums and the flying toilets. I've got an extract from Bill Bryson's short book ... that he did for Tear Fund, and one of it is a walk through the Kibera slum in Nairobi. ... It starts off something like 'Kibera is a place that you might want to visit but you wouldn't want to visit alone and you certainly wouldn't want to visit after dark'. (M1/UK/GSVC 2010)

It seems as if this view of Kenya was acting as a filter to his experiences in The Gambia, which was perceived as another case study that could be used in his teaching. However, this was not common to other members of the study-visit group. Indeed, it was arguably the desire to avoid this kind of stereotyping that led other members of the group to focus on similarity as they attempted to comprehend the new culture.

When I went to see the Deputy Headmistresses' office and saw the bar charts of results and stats ... I thought yeah, this is exactly the same. (M2/UK/GSVC 2010)

We have more in common with people in other countries than we have differences. ... They've got the same issues. We've got common issues ... we do seem to be all singing to the same tune. (F1/UK/GSVC 2010)

The focus on similarity seems to be something that helped to make a connection with others, and to provide a good starting point for mutual learning.

Using commonality as a foundation for mutual learning is a powerful tool. Being able to compare cultures, family lives, workplaces and practices and realising similarities within them has developed ... relationships of which learning from each other can begin. (M2/UK/ GSVC 2010)

But some seemed to be avoiding difference, and suggesting that similarity is more comfortable to deal with.

I think it's nice for children to do as well, because I think it helps them understand different countries, they kind of realise what similarities [there are] rather than always focusing on the differences. I think sometimes you can say that people are different, and that's what you focus on rather than how you are. (F2/UK/ISSV 2010)

A focus on similarity as a means of connecting with others is understandable, particularly when one is spending time in a place and culture that contrast significantly from ones' own. The inclusive 'human' category is evident in the last quote, something that was much more prevalent in the ISSV data than the GSVC data, perhaps due to the younger age profile of the ISSV group. Disney (2009) conducted a study on the educational partnership between pupils in two primary schools in England and South India. The teachers in the UK school were keen to portray the whole diversity of urban, rural, rich and poor that make up modern India and so the UK children were shown that children in India have access to technology such as computer suites in school and televisions in their homes. However, as Disney noted, this was not without its drawbacks.

There is some indication from this research context that the children's estimation of the worth of their peers in the partner school is affected by the extent to which they possess modern consumer items. ... Teachers may also latch onto this, as it is a much more comfortable image with which to work. ... We cannot afford to dismantle some stereotypes and replace them with others. (2009, 145)

The implication is that a focus on differences would be negative, while a focus on similarities would be positive. This has the effect of devaluing differences and of avoiding the difficult task of trying to understand them. In the attempt to counteract what are perceived to be negative stereotypes, positive stereotypes are created and these are still underpinned by a whole set of assumptions that remain unexamined. The overall effect is a continuation of a single story, and one that is determined by those with the power to tell the story.

Similarity–difference as diversity

When asked about the impact of their study-visit experiences on their practice, many respondents talked about trying to avoid creating positive stereotypes through, for example, cultural weeks.

> … you're only going to reinforce stereotypes and children will come out of school thinking, oh, okay, all people in India [do this … or that]. (F3/UK/ISSV 2008)

It was evident that visiting a variety of places, and gaining a number of perspectives from different people they interacted with, contributed to this understanding.

> [you need to] reinforce to the children that that's just one perspective, and maybe compare it back to England to sort of get them to see differences in England to try and reinforce the idea about things being different in India as well. (F2/UK/ISSV 2010)

UK teachers were, therefore, increasingly avoiding generalisations and contextualising their knowledge as the diversity of experiences during their study visit expanded. Their single stories were being challenged and high levels of discomfort were evident as things they had felt certain about were questioned and deconstructed. As the study visit progressed, they began to talk about culture and lifestyles much more provisionally. The focus on specificity, rather than 'decontextualised, ungendered, disembodied, so-called "objective" knowledge' (Sharp 2009, 116), is an important step in appreciating that individuals and groups know and understand the world differently, according to their geographical, historical and cultural contexts; it assumes a view of knowledge that is socially constructed and thus relational.

Difference as relational, pre-categorical

In the earlier examples of how similarity and difference are understood from an object-based perspective, similarity was shown to be the starting point for understanding difference, with the latter being seen as a deviation from the standard of sameness. From a pre-categorical, relational perspective, difference becomes the starting point for a deeper understanding of self in relation to others. Many of the respondents in our research talked about how, in the face of differences encountered during study visits, those differences held up a mirror to their own culture and lifestyle.

> I think what you were saying earlier about sorting out our own relationship with otherness and diversity, and relational positioning, I think that happens most starkly when you're in a culture that's completely different. … I think what happens is, you get a mirror held up to you, because you see there are lots of different ways of doing things. There's no one right way of schooling, or traffic management, or whatever it is. I think that's when you start asking questions about things we might make assumptions about. (F4/UK/GSVC 2005; interviewed 2011)

Burbules (1997) warns that there is a danger the concept of difference might itself be treated as a unifying, homogenous category. He proposes three ways of understanding difference that is pre-categorical: difference beyond, difference within and difference against. The first two are discussed here as being particularly pertinent to intercultural understanding.

Difference beyond

Differences beyond categorisation are those that are beyond comprehension, for which there is no language to express the difference, no standards of sameness or analogy to work with: 'the difference of an Other always contains something beyond our capabilities of understanding' (Burbules 1997, 18). This is a difference that many in our research demonstrated in their interviews, when they found it hard to express the confusions they felt about some of what they were experiencing. In their end-of-study-visit evaluations, they were asked to write about something that had been troubling in some way, what insight it had given them and how they coped with the challenge.

> The most troubling insight for me whilst in India was the friendliness of people and how genuine their friendliness and acceptance of us was. I found this so troubling because looking back to England this is not the same, … in many cases people in England find it very difficult to tolerate and accept people from their own country and who are of the same nationality as themselves let alone people from another country. I therefore found it difficult to see and understand why it is so different in India to England. To try and cope with the challenge I found that the best thing to do was to try and work out why there is such a difference, however this was one of those questions that could not be answered as there are a number of reasons that could be speculated but no definite answers. I was able to speculate many reasons as to why the differences are present, the biggest being that in some of the places that we visited we were possibly the only foreign/white people that many of the Indian people had ever seen and they would therefore have been genuinely interested in us as they had never seen such people before and we were therefore a bit of a novelty … However, in England it is not the same as there are many different people from many different countries, races and nationalities and therefore it is not so interesting and different when you see someone who is so different to you walking down the street. … Although it was not possible to create a definite answer as to why the differences exist simply thinking about the possible answers and … about the concept helped to me to deal with the fact that it was troubling me and helped me to gain more of an insight into it. (F5/UK/ISSV 2008, interviewed 2012)

Here, the student demonstrates how difference can be a powerful teacher. She notes, first of all, that the difference between countries in acceptance of foreigners (as she perceives it) is beyond her understanding. She goes on to show curiosity and resilience in staying with the difference and trying to understand it. In doing so she comes to a deeper understanding of this aspect of her own culture. She draws on both object-based (people are tolerant of foreigners) and relational (the Indian and English contexts are different) thinking to help her make sense of the experience, and she shows awareness that the process of thinking about the difference, even though there was no resolution, helped her to a new understanding. Some educationalists argue that seeking resolution when differences are encountered can impede the educative processes of learning from and to live with difference; a 'pedagogy of dissensus' is proposed as an alternative (Souza 2008; Wånggren and Sellberg 2012).

Difference within

Difference within is described as within the concept, for example within the concept of woman is the concept of man – each contains and is essential to the understanding of the other. Therefore categories are never entirely stable: 'a thing is what it is but partly what it is not and these have a dialectic relationship' (Burbules 1997, 19). Here, a respondent who is of dual heritage reflects on how the Gambia study visit led to her and her partner doing Voluntary Service Overseas for two years in Nepal.

> My partner, who's English, who I'd had conversations with about how sometimes it's really hard because you feel so visible. He never understood [what it was like for me being a British Asian woman] … and suddenly he was the tall white guy in Nepal and everyone referred to him as the videshi, the foreigner. (F4/UK/GSVC 2005, interviewed 2011)

Through spending time in a racially and culturally contrasting culture her partner came to understand that the property of 'Other' existed within himself. Similarly, many of the students who went to India talked about trying on aspects of Indian culture such as wearing Saris and eating with their right hand. During a tape-recorded reflective session they discussed how this had affected their sense of self:

> F6   … it came from our touch section, which was how we were eating with our hands, and we were almost taking on a new identity by doing that and trying to fit in, … and trying to balance that with what you thought your identity was at home, and then [F7] added that it got her to kind of question what her identity was and how … sorry [F7], do you want to add something?
>
> F7   It just made me think about what makes me, me and not someone else. I just consider myself in relation to other people and, I don't know, it's a bit confusing really, I don't know … I don't really know who I am. (F6 & F7/UK/ISSV 2010)

The idea that one's identity is made up of elements of both self and other, and how these relate to each other, created confusion at the time but, with further opportunities to reflect with others and to articulate this confusion, deeper understanding of their multiple identities became evident. 'The experience was enjoyable and illuminating and on my return I find that I view things in a very different light that formerly I would not have questioned' (Hamilton 2012).

Implications and conclusions

In this article, the aim has been to look at the ways in which a comparative approach to teaching about distant people and places can unwittingly reinforce essentialist, single stories about the 'Other' that create binary spatial distinctions between the places being compared. A number of dangers associated with this approach have been identified (Picton 2008; Adichie 2009; Borowski 2011). Drawing on the work of Nisbett (2005) and Burbules (1997) I have shown how there seems to be a default position, as evident in the data from our study, that constructs knowledge from an object-based tradition, over-emphasising similarities and promoting an 'othering' disposition towards difference. Our study also showed that, over the course of the study visits and the periods following, as teachers continued to process their experiences, they began to focus more on relationships and the affordances offered by the differences encountered during intercultural interactions. The implications of this for primary teachers and approaches to teaching distant places are now considered.

As suggested by Burbules (1997), I propose that work needs to be done that deepens pupils' understanding of the concept of difference as applied to their own identities and the cultures of their families and communities (Wånggren and Sellberg

2012). Kent and Hannay (2012) conducted an investigation into the relationship between children's perception of difference and their self-image. Their findings on pupils' associations between skin colour and their identity have significant implications for teachers of primary geography. They showed how developing deeper, complex understandings of the relationship between individual and group differences provided a positive foundation for studying spatial and cultural differences of distant places. Normalising difference by constructing difference as natural, acceptable and ordinary has been shown to transform inclusion practices (Baglieri and Knopf 2004). However, normalising difference against a dominant standard can be just as effective in effacing people's experiences of cultural and racial difference as a focus on similarities, so it would be important to maintain a focus on individual's *experiences* of difference as they contribute to their sense of identity. As Kent and Hannay (2012, 13) point out,

> When we teach pupils about people, culture and places it is essential that we support them to form positive attitudes. One way is to avoid using stereotypical images of people and places. In geography we need to demonstrate the rich diversity in the world and help our pupils to see the unique contribution to society that each person makes. As pupils' knowledge about their own race and that of others evolves, we are in a unique position to influence and guide their thinking in a positive way.

I have argued elsewhere that stereotypes are part of making sense of the world (Martin 2005). It is *how* the stereotypes that are inherent in categorical thinking are perceived and acted on that primary teachers need to be aware of. If culture is understood as a category with permeable borders, that is not fixed in all time, that is constantly changing, this implies developing understandings based on multiple perspectives and multiple points of view. There are obvious implications for curriculum choices (focusing on a range of environments and lifestyles, rural and urban, wealthy and poor), the resources to support them and the range of perspectives evident in those resources. Teachers could take a critical stance asking themselves: who has created the resource, whose lives are portrayed and from whose perspectives, what is the primary purpose of the resource and who is the intended audience? Sedgebeer (2013), a teacher participant in the 2010 study visit to The Gambia, put this into practice with her year five and six (ages 9–11) pupils at the beginning of teaching a topic on India. She had been particularly influenced by Adichie's (2009) talk and began by doing some work on visual literacy using historical paintings. Her purpose was to raise their awareness of where their knowledge comes from (how do you know that?), and to introduce notions of bias, the partial nature of evidence and the fact that knowledge is socially constructed. She then showed about 10 photographs most of which were of India, but a couple of which were of England (a Sikh wedding in Birmingham and a temple in London). The pupils were asked to figure out which photos were of India and which of England, again justifying their choices.

> I ended with the question 'What picture had surprised them the most?' 'What had they discovered about India?', but also 'What had they discovered about themselves?' and that was really interesting and some of them actually answering using that terminology – 'I realised that my story is not the whole story, I can add to it all the other stories'. (Sedgebeer 2013, 2)

Sedgebeer's approach was to develop critical literacy skills (Andreotti 2011) by recognising that people, places and the resources representing them have a history, and by developing the pupils' awareness that resources are not inanimate objects in the sense that the pupils relate to them through their interpretations, which are in turn based on their own histories as shown in the comment that

> Sofia had decided that one of the pictures of three women who were wearing obviously traditional clothing of some sort, because they were all dressed exactly the same … [was] they were either Chinese or Japanese, and they all turned out to be Indian and she said 'I have never seen anyone in all the times I have been to India, I have never seen anyone wearing anything that looks like that'. (Sedgebeer 2013, 2)

In this way the pupils became aware that they each interpreted the resources according to their own stories, that there were potentially as many different interpretations as there were individual stories and that there were some stories (those of the people in the photograph) that they did not have access to, so what was possible to learn from them had to be conditional and subject to change in the light of other information and perspectives being made available.

There are implications of this for primary teachers' professional development. It was posited at the beginning of the article that primary teachers' subject knowledge is an issue. This is no doubt the case, but more fundamentally it is a question of how knowledge is perceived and knowledge construction understood. If I think about my own development since I first started taking groups of teachers to The Gambia, I recognise that it has been important for me to become aware of my own biases and single stories, and that this is an ongoing task. I have become aware, for example, that there are many models of development, the Western model of high mass consumption being just one; this has caused me to question economics as the sole basis for understanding development, and to seek other models such as the Happiness Index (Bhutan 2013). I have also become aware of how important it is to be a learner as well as a teacher, open to developing deeper understandings of myself and those I interact with through being attentive to, and learning from, our differences – even though this is very uncomfortable and challenging at times! As the examples from participants in our study show, sticking with uncomfortable differences can, when there is the chance to recollect and reflect in a more tranquil space, lead to long-lasting transformative changes in perspective.

Considering what the purposes of education (and therefore subjects such as geography) are, I would argue that geography has the potential to make a significant contribution to the sustainability of the planet. However, this does not mean providing ready-made solutions (turn off the lights, buy Fair Trade, Send My Friend to School) because this is object-focused and closes down possibilities. Rather than perpetuating single stories or single solutions, primary geography should be about opening up a world of possibilities for our learners and learning how to relate to difference. This is not a question of simply becoming aware of different perspectives, but of the worldviews and often deeply ingrained assumptions that underpin them, such as promoted by some of the initiatives linked to millennium Development Goals (Brundrett 2011). As teachers, awareness of the sociocultural and historical contexts that form our worldviews is an important first step in the process of being open to listening to others, of learning new ways of thinking and being in the world, and for the task of 'teaching for a world that is or is becoming out of joint' (Todd 2008, 5).

Note

1. It is well worth watching the full talk, which is about 15–20 minutes long and can be found at www.ted.com/talks/chimamanda_adichie_the_danger_of_a_single_story.html. It is also possible to download a transcript of the talk.

References

Adichie, C. N. 2009. "The Dangers of a Single Story." Talk given at TEDGlobal, July 2009. Accessed November 15, 2012. www.ted.com/talks/

Andreotti, V. 2011. *Actionable Postcolonial Theory in Education*. New York: Palgrave Macmillan.

Baglieri, S., and J. H. Knopf. 2004. "Normalising Difference in Inclusive Teaching." *Journal of Learning Disabilities* 37 (6): 525–529.

Barrett, A. M., M. Crossley, and H. A. Dachi. 2011. "International Collaboration and Research Capacity Building: Learning from the EdQual Experience." *Comparative Education* 47 (1): 25–43.

Bashkow, I. 2004. "A Neo-Boasian Conception of Cultural Boundaries." *American Anthropologist* 106 (3): 443–458.

BERA. 2011. *Ethical Guidelines for Educational Research*. London: BERA. http://www.bera.ac.uk/guidelines

Bhutan. 2013. "Gross National Happiness Index." Accessed May 10, 2013. http://www.grossnationalhappiness.com/articles/

Borowski, R. 2011. "The Hidden Cost of a Red Nose." *Primary Geography* 75 (Summer): 18–20.

Brah, A. 2007. "Non-Binarized Identities of Similarity and Difference." In *Identity, Ethnic Diversity and Community Cohesion*, edited by M. Wetherell, M. Laflèche, and R. Berkeley, 136–146. London: SAGE.

Brundrett, M. 2011. "The Global Challenge for Primary Schools: Education in a World of 7 Billion People." *Education 3–13: International Journal of Primary, Elementary and Early Years Education* 39 (5): 451–453.

Burbules, N. C. 1997. "A Grammar of Difference: Some Ways of Rethinking Difference and Diversity as Educational Topics." *Australian Educational Researcher* 24 (1): 97–116.

Catling, S. 2004. "Issues in Pre-Service Primary Teachers' Geographical Understanding." In *Symposium Proceedings: Expanding Horizons in a Shrinking World*, edited by A. Robinson, 71–76. Glasgow: IGU Commission on Geographical Education.

Catling, S., R. Bowles, J. Halocha, F. Martin, and S. Rawlinson. 2007. "The State of Geography in English Primary Schools." *Geography* 92 (2): 118–136.

DES (Department for Education and Science). 1991. *Geography in the National Curriculum*. London: HMSO.

DfE (Department for Education). 2013. *Reform of the National Curriculum in England*. London: DfE.

DfEE/QCA (Department for Education and Employment/Qualifications and Curriculum Authority). 1999. *The National Curriculum for England: Geography*. London: DfEE/QCA.

Disney, A. 2009. "The Contribution of International School Linking Partnerships to the Provision of Global Education." Unpublished PhD thesis, Nottingham Trent University.

Edensor, T. 2002. *National Identity, Popular Culture and Everyday Life*. Oxford: Berg.

Hamilton, M. 2012. "Images of India." *Primary Geography* 79 (Autumn): 8–9.

Kent, G., and L. Hannay. 2012. "Difference and Children's Self Image." *Primary Geography* 79 (Autumn): 12–13.

Martin, F. 2005. "North-South Linking as a Controversial Issue." *Prospero* 14 (4): 47–54.

Martin, F. 2008. "Ethnogeography: Towards Liberatory Geography Education." *Children's Geographies* 6 (4): 437–450.

Nisbett, R. 2005. *The Geography of Thought: How Asians and Westerners Think Differently and Why.* Boston, MA: Nicholas Brealey Publishing.

Picton, O. 2008. "Teaching and Learning about Distant Places: Conceptualising Diversity." *International Research in Geographical and Environmental Education* 17 (3): 227–249.

Posner, D. 2004. "The Political Salience of Cultural Difference: Why Chewas and Tumbukas Are Allies in Zambia and Adversaries in Malawi." *American Political Science Review* 98 (4): 529–545.

QSR. 2011. *Nvivo 9: Getting Started*. QSR International. Accessed March 11, 2013. www.qsrinternational.com

RND. 2013. "Red Nose Day." Accessed April 26, 2013. http://www.rednoseday.com

Said, E. 1985. *Orientalism*. Harmondsworth: Penguin.

Sedgebeer, M. 2013. A Relational Approach to Teaching India. Accessed May 6, 2013. http://education.exeter.ac.uk/projects.php?id=468

Shamim, F., and R. Qureshi, eds. 2010. *Perils, Pitfalls and Reflexivity in Qualitative Research in Education*. Oxford: Oxford University Press.

Sharp, J. 2009. *Geographies of Postcolonialism*. London: Sage.

Souza, L. M. T. 2008. "A Pedagogy of Dissensus." Keynote address at the Shifting margins, shifting centres: Negotiating difference in education in the 21st century conference, Institute of Education, University of London, September 17. Audio version. Accessed August 6, 2010. http://www.throughothereyes.org.uk/audio/index.html

Todd, S. 2008. "Facing Humanity: The Difficult Task of Cosmopolitan Education." Paper presented at the annual conference of the Philosophy of Education Society of Great Britain, New College, Oxford, 28–30 March 2008.

Wånggren, L., and K. Sellberg. 2012. "Intersectionality and Dissensus: A Negotiation of the Feminist Classroom." *Equality, Diversity and Inclusion: An International Journal* 31 (5/6): 542–555.

Welsh, E. 2002. "Dealing with Data: Using NVivo in the Qualitative Data Analysis Process." *Forum Qualitative Sozialforschung/Forum: Qualitative Social Research* 3 (2): 1–7. Accessed March 10, 2012. http://nbn-resolving.de/urn:nbn:de:0114-fqs0202260

'They are like us' – teaching about Europe through the eyes of children[†]

Daniela Schmeinck

Institute of Primary Science and Social Sciences, University of Cologne, Köln, Germany

For some time the theme of the 'European dimension' in education has had a prominent place in school curricula across Europe. In practice the implementation of a European dimension in primary-school education still shows significant shortcomings. In some school systems Europe is not taken into consideration at all, while other school systems focus rather on formal aspects concerning Europe such as facts, names and figures. Compared to this, the ideas, preconceptions and experiences of children concerning Europe or other European countries are rarely taken into account. This paper, therefore, aims to provide an up-to-date contribution to European education taking into account the voices of children. Based on research results about children's perceptions of the world and of European countries, the paper offers perspectives on and suggestions about the implementation of a 'European dimension' in education, with special attention given to peer-learning. Methods of intercultural group learning and peer assessment are thereby used to underpin the co-operative learning environment for children.

Introduction

What is our knowledge worth if we know nothing about the world that sustains us, nothing about natural systems and climate, nothing about other countries and cultures? (Jonathan Porrit in DfEE/QCA 1999, 108)

For more than half a century geographical education has been engaged with tackling questions about individual perceptions of space. Particularly since the 1990s this interest has increased significantly within geographical education, and importantly in geography in primary education. The studies undertaken in this area can be divided into five different subgroups (Schmeinck 2007, 2010):

- Studies which focus on *the cartographic knowledge of pupils*, e.g. Brucker (1980), Oeser (1987), Wastl (2000), Livni and Bar (2001) and Umek (2003). These

---

[†]The paper presents results of a study published by the Julius Klinkhardt publishing house under the title 'Wie Kinder die Welt sehen. Eine empirische Ländervergleichststudie zur räumlichen Vorstellung von Grundschulkindern', as well as of the COMENIUS 2.1 Project: 'The Implementation of a European Dimension by Peer Learning in Primary School (E-PLIPS)'. Grant Agreement number: 128766-CP-1-2006-1-DE-Comenius-C21.

publications focus in particular on the differences in cartographical knowledge of children and questions about how cartographic competence can be promoted through teacher, media and teaching methodology.

- Studies investigating *awareness and understanding of topographic terms*, e.g. Kelly (1997, 2004), Baldwin and Opie (1998) and Ward (1998). Results from these studies show that even though children are using particular geographical words they do not automatically possess the same understanding of or attribute the same meaning to these terms as adult geographers do.

- Studies of *spatial concepts and knowledge of pupils concerning Europe and the world*, e.g. Achilles (1979), Kullen (1986), Kasper (1986), Kasper and Kullen (1991), Rösler, Steinen, and Thümmel (1996), Hüttermann and Schade (1997), Halocha (1998), Schade and Hüttermann (1999), Lambrinos (2001), Büker (2001) and Schniotalle (2003). The various studies in this group range from studies on representations of Europe and spatial distances in sketch maps of pupils to research on the influence of travel experiences and media on the perceptions and knowledge of pupils.

- Studies about *perceptions concerning proximity and foreign countries*, e.g. Stückrath (1958, 1963), Apfelstedt (1960), Wagner (1974), Aboud (1988), Graham and Lynn (1989), Harrington (1998) and Barrett (2007). The perceptions of children concerning other nations take centre stage in these studies. The studies show that even primary-school children have developed concepts about foreign countries. Nevertheless they show also that these concepts are often clearly clichés and stereotypical and are mainly affected by media such as television.

- Studies on *the impact of school and out-of-school knowledge and experiences on the perceptions of learners*, e.g. Saarinen (1988), Saarinen and MacCabe (1990), Walmsley, Saarinen, and MacCabe (1990), Dale, Saarinen, and MacCabe (1995), Wiegand (1995, 1998), Harwood and Rawlings (2001) and Schmeinck (2007, 2010) for knowledge and experiences gained in school; and Kosmella (1979), Achilles (1979), Geiger (1982), Øverjordet (1984), Kullen (1986), Holl-Giese (2004), Hüttermann and Schade (2004), Schmeinck (2006, 2007, 2010) and Schmeinck and Thurston (2007) for knowledge and experiences acquired out of school. The main issue arising from these studies is the question of representation of the world and/or Europe by children and understanding the factors of influence that directly contributed to these perceptions.

Many of these studies focus on secondary-school children. In fact in recent decades in many primary-school systems in Europe, geographical aspects have only played a marginal role. This may account for the lack of research on primary-school-age children's perception of space. In primary education at present solid empirical data and analyses that allow for well-founded conclusions about children's perceptions concerning Europe and the world remain rather scarce. Worse still is the situation in early-years education.

Primary-school children live in places, in different spaces, together with different people and in relation to their environment. They experience and engage with and within different situations, with spatial and everyday life connections locally and with distant places (Martin 2006a; Catling and Willy 2009). Increasing Europeanisation and globalisation, growing mobility of the population, and the rising flood of daily information through a variety of different media such as television, mobile phones, and the Internet are having an impact on the fields of learning and experience of primary-school children. Dealing with foreign countries and cultures is, therefore, part of everyday life of many and increasingly more of today's children. According to Negt (1998) the understanding of issues and changes, nearby or at a distance, as well as the recognition of those aspects affecting children personally is not an unnecessary luxury but rather a fundamental prerequisite for primary education.

Milestones for the implementation of Europe in German primary schools

As one example of the development of a European Dimension, Germany has taken steps since the 1970s to encourage schools to include studies of Europe in its states' curricula for all schools. The outline below indicates the directions of this development at European, national, and state levels. It is illustrative of decisions that have been taken in many European nations over the same period.

1978	Resolution of the Standing Conference of the Ministers of Education and Cultural Affairs of the Länder in the Federal Republic of Germany (KMK) for a realisation of 'Europe in School'. Initially the resolution only applied to secondary schools (Sekretariat der Ständigen Konferenz der Kultusminister der Länder in der Bundesrepublik Deutschland 1978)
1988	The Council of Europe and its Ministers for Education underline their willingness to focus on the promotion of the European Dimension in education (Amtsblatt der Europäischen Gemeinschaft 1988, 5)
1990	Extended Resolution of the Standing Conference of the Ministers of Education and Cultural Affairs of the Länder in the Federal Republic of Germany (KMK) for a realisation of 'Europe in School'. This version of the resolution also applied to primary schools (Sekretariat der Ständigen Konferenz der Kultusminister der Länder in der Bundesrepublik Deutschland 1990)
1992	German Ministers of Education sign a ministerial letter of intent to integrate the European Dimension into the new curricula (Büker 2001, 38)
2002	The Perspective Framework for General Studies in Primary Education provides as examples of contents and processes in the spatial perspective: the state, Germany, Europe, and the world in overview (Gesellschaft für Didaktik des Sachunterrichts 2002)
2008	Recommendation of the Standing Conference of the Ministers of Education and Cultural Affairs of the Länder in the Federal Republic of Germany (KMK) for a realisation of Europe in all schools (Sekretariat der Ständigen Konferenz der Kultusminister der Länder in der Bundesrepublik Deutschland 2008)

(see Schmeinck, 2008, 2010)

The state of the art concerning a European dimension in primary schools

What does 'distance' mean to today's and future primary-school children? What role does Europe play for them? What ideas about foreign countries, cultures, and the world do they have? Which qualifications and skills do learners need in the future? How should knowledge be organised so that primary-age children can orientate themselves in a continuously changing environment. Especially, what can and should primary schools do in this context?

Assessing the current teaching praxis concerning spatial learning in the primary-school years in many European countries, there still appears to be a clear orientation towards the principle 'from nearby to distance'. For instance, despite all the effort, demands, and resolutions noted above, as well as the different didactic discourses in many German federal states, spatial learning in German primary schools is still taking place mainly in the home region (Schmeinck 2008). Even the reorientation in education which has taken place since the 1980s – and considering the changes in children's knowledge and perceptions as a consequence of the integration of knowledge into already existing structures (Carey 1985; Vosniadou 1994) – has not yet led to sufficient changes in school education to support the effective development of a European Dimension.

The situation in other European countries is quite similar. For instance, the Greek curriculum mentions Europe as a topic in primary-school education. Yet analysing almost six thousand paragraphs of text in Greek elementary-school textbooks, Flouris and Ivrideli (2002) found out that Europe is mentioned rather more in history books (4%) than in geography textbooks (0.4%). Furthermore, at primary-school level, Europe is mainly included in the fifth grade. The available teaching materials about Europe consist of maps of the European Union, including its new and possible future members. In summary, the 'European dimension' is given little importance in Greek primary education (Schmeinck et al. 2010).

In English primary schools, there is currently no legal requirement to include the European Dimension as a distinctive focus within primary education, though this will change from 2014 (DfE 2013). Even though geography, as a statutory subject in the National Curriculum, states that pupils should 'study a range of places and environments in different parts of the world, including the United Kingdom and the European Union' (DfEE, 1999, 20), this formulation leaves much to the decision-making and interpretative freedom of primary teachers. In practice some primary schools make no reference to the European Dimension in their whole school planning, while others have highly developed schemes of work that integrate the European Dimension across the curriculum (Schmeinck et al. 2010). It is very variable.

The requirement that teaching and learning should build upon prior experiences and the individual learning conditions of learners is neither new nor unknown for primary teachers. The implementation of a European dimension into primary-school education therefore should be obvious. However, as long as educational programmes and curricula remain directed by education ministries and thus by adults, based on their perspectives, interest, beliefs and aims, the realisation of this requirement seems to be possible only to a very limited extent. Against the background of growing Europeanisation and globalisation this close and local focus appears as too narrowly conceptualised and too restricted. At a time that is characterised by discussions about the coming together of Europe, the reality of the 'Euro-crisis', reports of wars, famines and natural disasters, the broadcasting of international sporting events and, furthermore, where the prior knowledge of learners about events and places in Europe and the wider world is recognised – that understanding is not simply limited to their local region (Schmeinck 2007) – this range of children's interests needs to be taken seriously. Thus, the development of children's spatial concepts and understanding, of the nearby as well as distant, should be taken up and addressed in primary school and in the early years of education, particularly through geographical education.

Following Bale (1987), the importance of 'the world inside their heads' should be taken into account to a much greater extent. Catling (2003), Catling and Willy (2009) and Martin (2006b) demand a stronger focus on the geographies of children, 'their uses of places and the environment, their awareness of the world about them, and their concerns' (Catling 2003, 169).

> Children's local experiences, and their (personal and through a myriad of other sources) experience of the wider world, [ought] to be a basis for their exploration, investigation, knowledge, understanding and judgement about the world – its people, places and environments – locally and at a distance'. (Catling 2003, 169)

Reasons for the implementation of a European dimension in primary schools

Examining the various areas of life and experience of today's primary-school children concerning Europe and a European dimension five different areas for development can be identified. These concern inter-cultural living, mobility, the impact of the media, access to European and global products, and greater European integration (Schmeinck 2009).

(1) *Experiences based on the living together of and with people from different countries and cultures.* The increasing percentage of foreign citizens and visitors all over Europe lead more than ever to a multicultural society in which people from different countries with different lifestyles (e.g. habits, attitudes, religions, values, etc.) live together. The multicultural society not only becomes visible in everyday life, but it also shows itself in the school context. Thus, even primary-school children are already part of this multiculturally composed society and experience this in their everyday life. In their so-called sub-communities, such as the school, the class, the kindergarten, the nursery, the sports club and in their neighbourhood, they gain their first insights in and experiences with other cultures.

(2) *Increasing mobility and growing travel activities of the society.* Increasing mobility of people across society as well as the growing travel activities and experiences of families have changed and influenced the lives of many children. However, it remains unclear whether the travel experiences of children also have an impact on their concepts and/or their knowledge concerning Europe through their individual estimation of their (European) holiday destinations.

(3) *Influence through (the mass) media.* These days the mass media are rated as important carriers of information concerning foreign countries and cultures. Wherever direct access is not possible, such media still allow insights into history and future, the 'here' and 'elsewhere', as well as into the considerable variety of human life and behaviour.

(4) *Accessing a growing European and international range of products.* Bausinger (1988) noted that for today's youngsters 'Lacoste' and 'Benetton' are familiar terms. But not only in fashion areas are people confronted with the culture of Europe or other countries. Swedish furniture stores, Italian furniture design and ice cream, French cuisine, Czech or Polish automobile brands, Dutch tomatoes, Greek or Spanish olives, and many more products have found their way into our lives and hence also into the lives of our children.

(5) *Official programmes supporting the integration and coming together of Europe.* Particularly in recent years, the number of special programmes supporting the implementation of a European dimension in (primary) education has increased immensely. Of particular significance in this context are support actions of the European Commission such as the SOCRATES programme,[1] which enables teachers (and children) to visit and exchange with teachers in schools in other European countries as a key means to enhancing their awareness of others and their knowledge of Europe.

Aims for the implementation of a European dimension in primary school

To enable the effective implementation of a European dimension in primary-school education four different areas of interacting educational competence can be identified as highly relevant. These are: knowledge, attitudes, understanding, and skills. Their interlocking nature is indicated in Figure 1. These are explained briefly below (Schmeinck 2009).

- *Knowledge.* Learners should possess fundamental but flexible knowledge about Europe. This knowledge should be interdisciplinarily orientated and, therefore, take into account cultural, geographical, historical, and political aspects, for instance the development of the EU, EU member states, climate and nature, languages, and history.
- *Understanding.* On the one hand, learners need to develop an understanding of inter-dependencies, connections, and correlations within Europe and in relation to the world. On the other hand, they should become aware of and be able to understand the effects of their personal actions and engagement concerning the future development of the European Union, their own life and, respectively, the lives of European people in general, for instance the Schengen agreement, European law, flows of goods and transport in Europe, and the single currency.
- *Attitudes.* Effective participation as a European citizen can only be constructed upon clear, positive, and constructive – but also critical – attitudes towards European ideas, as well as relationships with other peoples and their cultures. Education, aiming to improve attitudes towards European ideas, therefore, needs to offer opportunities to investigate and validate different perspectives and ideas, attitudes, perceptions, and views as well as to revise and question prejudices and stereotypes, such as aware-ness of the environmental problems and issues within Europe.
- *Skills.* Effective participation is based upon practical life-long learning skills, like language, communication, social and geographic skills, for example the ability to acquire, arrange, and use geographic information for decision-making processes in everyday life (Schmeinck et al. 2010, 26).

In the context of formal (primary-school) education, it is essential to promote effectively all four elements simultaneously.

Teaching about Europe through the eyes of children

How should we teach about Europe in primary schools? How should we implement a Euro-pean Dimension in primary-school learning and teaching? In conjunction with the E-PLIPS

Figure 1.   Key elements for implementing a European dimension in learning and teaching in primary schools (Schmeinck et al. 2010, 26).

project (*The Implementation of a European Dimension by Peer-Learning in Primary School*) (Schmeinck et al. 2010), the project partners from five different European countries worked together to develop teaching materials to enable children from different European countries to communicate with one another. As has been noted above, the everyday life experiences of children can work as a good link for implementing a European Dimension into primary-school education, particularly through geographical education. The learning conditions and interests of the children involved in the project, as well as their individual levels of learning, were taken as the starting point and an orientation framework for the teaching activities within the E-PLIPS project. Thus, among the project phase materials and modules were topics based on such aspects of children's lives as a day at school, a day at home, our town events and attractions, the weather in my country, special annual events and attractions (for instance Christmas, Easter), and languages. All the materials and modules were developed, prepared, and exchanged by the pupils themselves.

'The weather in my country' – an example

The first thing that comes to my mind is that in Germany it snows often and I've never felt snow. (Girl, 9 years old, Malta)

In general children possess a huge range of everyday experiences due to meteorological phenomena (such as temperature, rainfall, humidity, and surface wind). These phenomena can change everyday as well as during a day. They also vary very much between different places. Therefore it can be assumed that children living in Northern Europe have a different experience of how the weather is during summer than, for example, those living in the South of Europe. These differences can be sensed and identified by the children and thus their everyday experience becomes important in showing key similarities and differences between places (Schmeinck et al. 2010, 158). Based on their own experiences children prepare a presentation about the weather in their own town and/or country (Figures 2–5) and exchange these presentations with children from other places in Europe.

Figure 2.   Summer in Malta (Schmeinck et al. 2010).

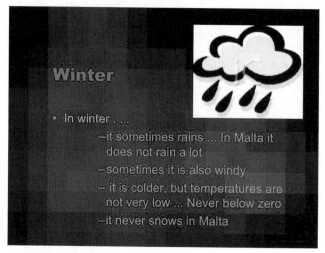

Figure 3.   Winter in Malta (Schmeinck et al. 2010).

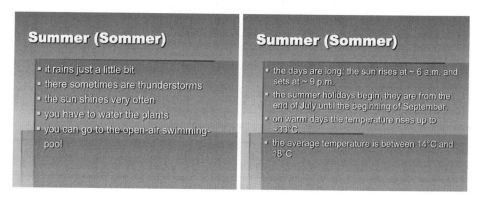

Figure 4.   Summer in Germany (Schmeinck et al. 2010).

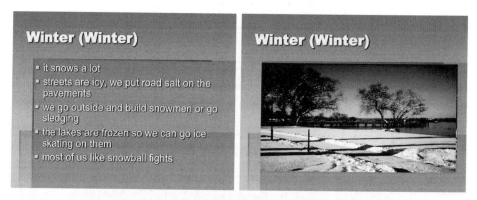

Figure 5.   Winter in Germany (Schmeinck et al. 2010).

By having several examples from different places in Europe, children can analyse similarities and differences between places. It is important that first they have a good look at their own situation and at their perceptions about other places before they compare them with the information given by children from these countries.

The following geographical questions can build the basis of discussions between the children:

- What is this place like?
- Why is this place as it is?
- How is this place connected to other places?
- How is this place changing?
- What would it feel like to be in this place?
- Where is this place?
- How is it similar to/different from another place?

These geographical questions, postulated by Storm (1989) and supplemented by Foley and Janikoun (1992), allow children to develop a context-related, individual, as well as emotional relationship towards the topic and the countries they investigate and with the children they interact with. The prepared presentations enable children to establish a further level of meaning and relationship towards other countries.

Results

To demonstrate the effectiveness of the developed materials all project-based outcomes and activities were longitudinally and simultaneously tested in a Pretest/Post-test Design research study. The results of the study indicate that by using the proposed materials and modules children gain knowledge and understanding about similarities and differences concerning themselves, their own, and other European countries. They changed their attitudes into clear, positive, and constructive – but also critical – attitudes towards European countries, ideas, and relationships with other peoples and their cultures. This was grounded in their evolving knowledge and understanding about European countries and peoples, based in the development of their topics and modules during the project. Last but not least, they improved their practical life-long learning skills such as communication and social skills. Although the implementation of a European dimension has to be seen as a long-term process, which exceeds the duration of the project, the results of the project can be perceived as a starting point for developing efficient educational policy in Europe (Schmeinck et al. 2010).

Conclusion

In the era of globalisation and of Europe's coming together, it should be a matter of course that the development of geographical and cultural knowledge and understanding in primary schooling is not limited to the local region or home region. Life-long learning in the area of European education needs to begin in primary education or even earlier. For a long time the official decisions and recommendations have built a basis for the implementation of a European Dimension in primary schools. Yet these elements are not enough on their own. Implementing a European dimension in primary education requires more than policy guidelines and recommendations. In light of the fact that Europe is still insufficiently consolidated into many school systems, the aim should be to implement a binding European Dimension into school curricula. In addition, educational approaches for teaching about Europe and its countries need to be further developed. Europe should not be handled as a detached Project or just added on as an additional or afterthought topic for teaching. It is rather a new perspective, in which the European Dimension is included in all areas of the curriculum, and thus it becomes a comprehensive educational principle.

Note

1. The SOCRATES programme, named after the Greek philosopher Socrates, was an educational initiative (in the meantime replaced by the Life-long Learning Programme 2007–2013) aiming to strengthen the European dimension of education at all levels and to encourage transnational cooperation between schools.

References

Aboud, F. E. 1988. *Children and Prejudice*. Oxford: Basil Blackwell.

Achilles, F. W. 1979. "Das Europabild unserer Schüler – Topographisches Wissen heute und Methoden der Vermittlung." *Geographie im Unterricht* 4 (4): 289–306.

Amtsblatt der Europäischen Gemeinschaft. 1988. Entschließung des Rates und der im Rat vereinigten Minister für das Bildungswesen zur europäischen Dimension im Bildungswesen vom 24. Mai 1988. In *Amtsblatt C 177 vom 06/07/1988*, 5–7. Accessed May 30, 2010. http://eur-lex.europa.eu/Notice.do?val=140191:cs&lang=de&list=140192:cs,140191:cs,140190:cs,&pos=2&page=1&nbl=3&pgs=10&hwords=&checktexte=checkbox&visu=#texte

Apfelstedt, H. 1960. "Erdkundliche Vorkenntnisse zehn- und elfjähriger Volksschüler." *Pädagogische Welt* 14: 123–132.

Baldwin, H., and M. Opie. 1998. "Child's Eye View of Cities." In *Primary Sources. Research Findings in Primary Geography*, edited by S. Scoffham, 40–41. Sheffield: Geographical Association.

Bale, J. 1987. *Geography in the Primary School*. London: Routledge & Kegan Paul Ltd.

Barrett, M. 2007. *Children's Knowledge, Beliefs and Feelings about Nations and National Groups*. Hove: Psychology Press.

Bausinger, H. 1988. "Das Bild der Fremde in der Alltagskultur." *Universitas* 43 (2/9): 946–955.

Brucker, A. 1980. "Topographiekenntnisse früher und heute." *Praxis Geographie* 10 (8): 329–332.

Büker, P. 2001. "Europa – (k)ein Thema für die Grundschule?." *Grundschule* 33 (4): 34–40.

Carey, S. 1985. *Conceptual Change in Childhood*. Cambridge: Bradfort Books/MIT Press.

Catling, S. 2003. "Curriculum Contested: Primary Geography and Social Justice." *Geography* 92 (3): 164–210.

Catling, S., and T. Willy. 2009. *Teaching Primary Geography*. Exeter: Learning Matters Ltd.

Dale, B. E., T. F. Saarinen, and C. L. MacCabe. 1995. *World Images, Geographical Knowledge, and Gender Differences: A Case Study of Norway*. Trondheim 1995 (Papers from The Department of Geography University of Trondheim, 8).

DfE (Department for Education). 2013. *The National Curriculum in England: Framework Document for Consultation*. London: HMSO.

DfEE/QCA (Department for Education and Employment and Qualifications and Curriculum Authority) 1999. *The National Curriculum for England. Geography: Key Stages 1–3*. Accessed May 30, 2010. http://curriculum.qcda.gov.uk/key-stages-1-and-2/index.aspx

Foley, M., and J. Janikoun. 1992. *The Really Practical Guide to Primary Geography*. Cheltenham: Nelson Thornes Ltd.

Flouris, G., and M. Ivrideli. 2002. "The Image of Europe in the Curriculum of Greek Primary Education: Comparative Perspective of the Last Three Decades of 20th Century (1976–77, 1982, 2000)." In *Contemporary Issues of the History of Education*, edited by S. Bouzakis, 473–510. Athens: Gutenberg.

Geiger, M. 1982. "Vorwissen durch Fernsehen?" *Praxis Geographie* 12 (1): 10–14.

Gesellschaft für Didaktik des Sachunterrichts (GDSU) (ed.) 2002. *Perspektivrahmen Sachunterricht*. Bad Heilbrunn: Klinkhardt.

Graham, L., and S. Lynn. 1989. "Mud Huts and Flints: Children's Images of the Third World." *Education 3–13* 17 (2): 29–32.

Halocha, J. 1998. "The European Dimension." In *Primary Sources. Research Findings in Primary Geography*, edited by S. Scoffham, 42–45. Sheffield: Geographical Association.

Harrington, V. 1998. "Teaching About Distant Places." In *Primary Sources. Research Findings in Primary Geography*, edited by S. Scoffham, 46–47. Sheffield: Geographical Association.

Harwood, D., and K. Rawlings. 2001. "Assessing Young Children's Freehand Sketch Maps of the World." *International Research in Geographical and Environmental Education* 10 (1): 20–45.

Holl-Giese, W. 2004. "Geographisches Weltbild aus Grundschulsicht." In *Untersuchungen zum Aufbau eines geographischen Weltbildes bei Schülerinnen und Schülern. Ergebnisse des "Weltbild"-Projektes an der Pädagogischen Hochschule Ludwigsburg*, edited by A. Hüttermann, 18–34. Ludwigsburg: Pädagogische Hochschule.

Hüttermann, A., and U. Schade. 1997. "Untersuchungen zum Aufbau eines Weltbildes bei Schülern." *Geographie und Schule* 20 (112): 22–33.

Hüttermann, A., and U. Schade. 2004. "Das Weltbild-Projekt des Fachs Geographie an der Pädagogischen Hochschule Ludwigsburg." In *Untersuchungen zum Aufbau eines geographischen Weltbildes bei Schülerinnen und Schülern. Ergebnisse des "Weltbild"-Projektes an der Pädagogischen Hochschule Ludwigsburg*, edited by A. Hüttermann, 3–9. Ludwigsburg: Pädagogische Hochschule.

Kasper, H. 1986. Projekt Europa. In: *Politik und Unterricht* (= Baustein B) 2: 7–29.

Kasper, H., and S. Kullen. 1991. *Europa-Kartei*. Heinsberg: Agentur Dieck.

Kelly, A. 1997. *An Exploration of the Meanings which Primary Age Children Ascribe to the Spatial Dimensions of 'Country' and 'Continent'* (unpublished). University of Liverpool.

Kelly, A. 2004. "'It's Geography Jim, but not as we know it': Exploring Children's Geographies at Key Stage Two." In *Register of Research in Primary Geography. Occasional paper: No. 4: Place and Space*, ed. R. Bowles, 104–109. London: Register of Research in Primary Geography.

Kosmella, C. 1979. *Die Entwicklung des „länderkundlichen Verständnisses"*. München (Schriften für die Schulpraxis, Band 87).

Kullen, S. 1986. "Wie stellen sich Kinder Europa vor? Untersuchungen kindlicher Europakarten." *Sachunterricht und Mathematik in der Primarstufe* 14 (4): 131–138.

Lambrinos, N. 2001. "World Maps: A Pupils' Approach." Proceedings of the third international conference on 'Science Education Research in Knowledge Based Society' Vol. II, 505–507. Thessaloniki.

Livni, S., and V. Bar. 2001. "A Controlled Experiment in Teaching Physical Map Skills to Grade 4 Pupils in Elementary Schools." *International Research in Geographical and Environmental Education* 10 (2): 149–167.

Martin, F. 2006a. "Everyday Geography." *Primary Geographer* 61 (3): 4–7.

Martin, F. 2006b. *Teaching Geography in Primary Education, Learning to Live in the World*. Cambridge: Chris Kington Publishing.

Negt, O. 1998. "Lernen in einer Welt gesellschaftlicher Umbrüche." In *Lernkonzepte im Wandel. Die Zukunft der Bildung*, edited by H. Dieckmann and B. Schlachtsieck, 21–45. Stuttgart: Klett Cotta Verlag.

Oeser, R. 1987. Untersuchungen zum Lernbereich „Topographie". Ein Beitrag zur Quantitativen Methodik in der Fachdidaktik Geographie. Lüneburg (Geographiedidaktische Forschungen, Band 16).

Øverjordet, A. H. 1984. "Children's View of the World During an International Media Covered Conflict." In *Perception of People and Places Through Media. Vol. 1: Perception of People and Places – a Goal for International Understanding and a Topic for Geographical Education*, edited by H. Haubrich, 208–219. Freiburg: Pädagogische Hochschule.

Rösler, W., S. v. d. Steinen, and I. Thümmel. 1996. "Was wissen Grundschulkinder über Europa? Eine Pilotstudie zur Repräsentanz der Euro-Thematik?" *Grundschule* 28 (4): 47–48.

Saarinen, T. F. 1988. "Centering of Mental Maps of the World." *National Geographic Research* 4 (1): 112–127.

Saarinen, T. F., and C. L. MacCabe. 1990. "The World Image of Germany." *Erdkunde* 44 (4): 260–268.

Schade, U., and A. Hüttermann. 1999. "Empirische Untersuchungen zur Entstehung eines geographischen Weltbildes bei Schülerinnen und Schülern." In *Geographieunterricht und*

Gesellschaft. Vorträge des gleichnamigen Symposiums vom 12.-15. Okt. 1998 in Landau, edited by H. Köck, 194–206. Nürnberg (Geographiedidaktische Forschungen, 32).

Schmeinck, D. 2006. "Images of the World or Do Travel Experiences and the Presence of Media Influence Children's Perception of the World?" In *Research on Learning and Teaching in Primary* Geography, edited by D. Schmeinck, 37–59. Norderstedt: Books on Demand.

Schmeinck, D. 2007. *Wie Kinder die Welt sehen – Eine empirische Ländervergleichsstudie über die räumliche Vorstellung von Grundschulkindern.* Bad Heilbrunn: Klinkhardt.

Schmeinck, D. 2008. "Europa im Sachunterricht – historische Entwicklungen und aktueller Stand in den Bildungs-, Rahmen- und Lehrplänen in Deutschland." *Geographie und ihre Didaktik* 35 (4): 161–177.

Schmeinck, D. 2009. "Europa in der Grundschule – Voraussetzungen, didaktische Konkretisierung und Umsetzungsmöglichkeiten am Beispiel des COMENIUS 2.1 Projekts E-PLIPS – The Implementation of a European Dimension by Peer Learning in Primary School." *Karlsruher Pädagogische Beiträge* 70: 87–117.

Schmeinck, D. 2010. *Die Entwicklung der geographischen Raumvorstellung im Grundschulalter* (unpublished). Karlsruhe.

Schmeinck, D., P. Knecht, W. Kosack, N. Lambrinos, M. Musumeci, and S. Gatt. 2010. *Europe through the Eyes of Children. The Implementation of a European Dimension by Peer Learning in Primary School.* Berlin: Mensch & Buch.

Schmeinck, D., and A. Thurston. 2007. "The Influence of Travel Experiences and Exposure to Cartographic Media on the Ability of Ten-year-old Children to Draw Cognitive Maps of the World." *Scottish Geographical Journal* 123 (1): 1–15.

Schniotalle, M. 2003. *Räumliche Schülervorstellungen von Europa. Ein Unterrichtsexperiment zur Bedeutung kartographischer Medien für den Aufbau räumlicher Orientierung im Sachunterricht der Grundschule.* Berlin: Tenea.

Sekretariat der ständigen Konferenz der Kultusminister der Länder in der Bundesrepublik Deutschland (KMK) (ed.): *Europa im Unterricht. Beschluss der Kultusministerkonferenz vom 08.06.1978.* Bonn.

Sekretariat der ständigen Konferenz der Kultusminister der Länder in der Bundesrepublik Deutschland (KMK) (ed.): *Europa im Unterricht. Beschluss der Kultusministerkonferenz vom 08.06.1978 in der Fassung vom 07.12.1990.* Bonn.

Sekretariat der ständigen Konferenz der Kultusminister der Länder in der Bundesrepublik Deutschland (KMK) (ed.): *Europabildung in der Schule. Beschluss der Kultusministerkonferenz vom 08.06.1978 in der Fassung vom 05.05.2008.* Bonn.

Storm, M. 1989. "The Five Basic Questions for Primary Geography." *Primary Geographer* 2 (3): 4–5.

Stückrath, F. 1958. "Das geographische Weltbild des Kindes." *Westermanns Pädagogische Beiträge* 10 (4): 135–145.

Stückrath, F. 1963. *Kind und Raum. Psychologische Voraussetzungen der Raumlehre in der Volksschule.* München: Kösel-Verlag.

Umek, M. 2003. "A Comparison of the Effectiveness of Drawing Maps and Reading Maps in Beginning Map Teaching." *International Research in Geographical and Environmental Education* 12 (1): 18–31.

Vosniadou, S. 1994. "Capturing and Modeling the Process of Conceptual Change." *Learning and Instruction* 4 (1): 45–69.

Wagner, E. 1974. "Umwelterfahrungen von Grundschülern. Untersuchungen über außerschulische Bedingungen für das geographische Verständnis in der Primarstufe." *Geographische Rundschau, Beiheft* 13 (1): 4–9.

Walmsley, D. J., T. F. Saarinen, and C. L. MacCabe. 1990. "Down Under or Centre Stage? The World Images of Australian Students." *Australian Geographer* 21 (2): 164–173.

Ward, H. 1998. "Geographical Vocabulary." In *Primary Sources. Research Findings in Primary Geography*, edited by S. Scoffham, 20–21. Sheffield: Geographical Association.

Wastl, R. 2000. *Orientierung und Raumvorstellung. Evaluierung unterschiedlicher kartographischer Darstellungsarten.* Klagenfurt (Klagenfurter Geographische Schriften, 20).

Wiegand, P. 1995. "Young Children's Freehand Sketch Maps of the World." *International Research in Geographical and Environmental Education* 4 (1): 19–28.

Wiegand, P. 1998. "Understanding the World Map." In *Primary Sources. Research Findings in Primary Geography*, edited by S. Scoffham, 50–51. Sheffield: Geographical Association.

Giving younger children voice in primary geography: empowering pedagogy – a personal perspective

Simon Catling

School of Education, Oxford Brookes University, Oxford, United Kingdom

It is argued that children's voice can and should be enhanced in primary schooling, and particularly in geographical learning. Using examples from different aspects of geographical experience and content, four approaches to engaging children's voice are presented: children leading and developing geographical topics; children bringing their ethno-geographical expertise into the classroom; children being listened to beyond the classroom and children learning from and heeding other children's voices from around the world. Interwoven with discussion of these approaches are matters concerning the purpose of locational knowledge, identity, geographical knowledge as powerful knowledge and the value of hazards education. The case is that this strengthens the teachers' role through its focus in empowering children's and teachers' learning, not only in geography but more widely for the primary curriculum. This argument draws on critical pedagogy, which supports strongly children's agency in schooling. It concludes by specifying principles to enable children's voice in their learning and which empower pedagogy.

Introduction

Embracing the child-centred, child-enabling and child-empowering values underlying participation is one thing. Putting these values into practice is another (Woodhead, 2010, xxi).

Education is a political activity. Which subjects or areas of learning should be included in the school curriculum, and what these subjects might be about, has always been a matter of convincing whoever has authority and control, whether in schools, governments or other interest parties. There is rarely agreement. Inevitably, education is controversial. Schooling is claimed to be about empowering children, teachers and society (Woodhead, 2010), but there may be different intentions at work among these dimensions. Education is not and cannot be outside the interests of those who wield power and the purse strings, whether tax-payers approve of or desire to challenge the purposes laid out for education and the school curriculum by politicians. Schooling is never a neutral activity. Notions of behaviour are value-laden, just as is the specification of content in curriculum subjects and how it is inter-preted. Perspectives on children and children's roles in their education are also varied and influence the values of schools and teaching in them. Education is a social event loosely or closely determined by those in political power, as they prefer, desire or consider. Politicians may occasionally be benign but, more often than not, they wish to influence overarching social outcomes, be they about a more equal society or focused on children as future

This article is based on Professor Simon Catling's illustrated celebratory lecture 'Giving Children Voice: Empowering Pedagogy', given on 21 June 2012, at the School of Education, Oxford Brookes University, to mark his retirement.

economic units and outputs, fitted for various levels of work. Education can be forward looking or regressive. It can be a shared learning journey or a matter in which children must succeed, or not, subserviently, in what is required of them. All education is based in and inducts children, one way or the other, into value systems. This is my setting. I now add a context, about perspectives on children and childhood.

A simple truism is that every adult was a child and young person earlier in life, a time perhaps treasured in the memory or put aside as a necessary part of growing up! There are differing perspectives on childhood. One characterisation is that we, as children, were not very pleasant, veritable ignoramuses in need of knowledge-based schooling, wilful and incorrigible, quite often out of place and out of control, being where we should not have been, doing things we should not have done, and generally being little demons who needed to be taught what we should be and must be, what is right, and what not to question. Research into adult attitudes towards children, as well as reports and opinion in our tabloid (and at times broadsheet) press, indicate this is a commonly held view of children (Corsaro, 2011; Jenks, 2005; Valentine, 2004; Wyness, 2012). It supports the argument that children should be acquiescent and to keep their voices to themselves. In this perspective, children are not really proper people; they have to 'grow up'. This view has a long history, from Greek and Roman times, through the eighteenth, nineteenth and twentieth centuries into the present. But none of *us*, dear readers, fit this stereotype! None of *us* hold these views about our own childhood and children. We would not recognise our children in the critical reviews of children out and about, or of children in schools. We see children more as little 'angels'. We know they should be listened to, share their ideas and viewpoints, can speak for themselves, are able to take responsibility and act with thought and care, appreciate the concerns that confront our world and develop ideas about how we can and ought to tackle these. In this understanding, children of all ages are people with views to respect as much as any adult is to be respected (Flutter & Rudduck, 2004). Children are benevolent, thoughtful and positive.

I have posed polarising views of childhood, and it is, we know, much more complex than this. In a 2012 local community *Newsletter*, a resident challenged the village council's efforts to provide a youth shelter as a place for children and young people to meet in the village recreational ground, a place surrounded by housing. The case put was that to site the shelter there was not far enough away for some people's liking (Grant, 2012)! The children using it would be noisy, rowdy and untidy, even uncouth: the wrong children. We tend to be contradictory in our viewpoints. While we are inclusive of those we know well and find 'fit in' with us, we tend to *other* those children we do not know, who resultantly we mistrust, fear or want nothing to do with. From a post-colonial and subaltern perspective (Apple, 2006; Gregory, 2004), we can recognise in society and schooling a dominant yet implicit approach which *subordinates* children, that takes them to be naïve, ill-informed, untutored in the ways they should be, and thoughtless and unappreciative in their everyday lives. Schooling is to be their salvation – done *to* them, perhaps *for* them – where they are expected to be compliant, complicit and comforted by it. We wish to manage children through our pedagogy: through the curriculum and what we allow children to know and from which we exclude them; through the ways we choose to teach and manage them and through the sorts of learning we expect children to achieve, sustained through assessment and approval or disapproval. My challenge to this perspective is that we stop *othering* and *subordinating* children. I contend that in doing this we empower our pedagogy rather than inhibit it, by bringing children 'back in', to adapt Michael Young's phrase (Catling & Martin, 2011; Young, 2008) as co-learner participants, working with, not working to, their teachers.

This argument is problematic in the current climate, not least because when government ministers tell us that they are only concerned about the content of the curriculum, what children should know and understand (e.g. in England: DfE, 2010), we know full well that they dissemble. They hold clear and barely camouflaged views about how teaching should properly occur, what should be learnt, the ways children's understanding should be assessed and judged, how children should be distinguished and discriminated between, and how they must behave in classes, schools and the street. In their eyes, children are objects to whom education is 'done', not younger and less experienced people who must be inside the educational process, shaping their learning, not independently but with their teachers and others, as participants. I do not see this as abrogating the teachers' role; rather it enhances it, not simply in terms of power or as a facilitator but because it demands greater responsibility when teachers and children learn together, mutually engaged and supportive, with shared respect for each other as people, regardless of age, as a core tenet of the educational enterprise.

This article considers bringing children more centrally into our pedagogy. By *pedagogy* I follow the European perspective (Alexander, 2000, 2010) and include within its meaning the curriculum, how we teach and manage and children's and adults' learning. This is what education is about, the full experience of schooling, formal and informal, explicit and hidden. Geographical education is my medium for exploring several aspects of pedagogy and of children's participation, but my focus has wider implications. I draw on the English context but also more widely. I offer some pointers about how we might engage children more directly and empower our pedagogy more effectively. I am not proposing anything particularly new or radical. I am reflecting on how we view children through pedagogy. In doing so, I shall make some points about school knowledge in relation to children. Initially, I shall focus on aspects of children's voice in primary geography. I shall connect this to empowering pedagogy, though I shall not be offering guidance on specific approaches to teaching geography. This article concludes by setting out several principles which might enable further developments in classroom practices in primary geography.

Listening to children's voice

I shall consider children's voice in terms of their role in their learning, developing their school knowledge, expressing their learning and perspectives and sharing learning by listening to other children. In doing this I set contexts, some from experience, which reflect on some of the wider concerns in geographical learning, such as about locational awareness, identity, personal geographies, geographical knowledge and children's experience in our hazardous world. I offer four examples for learning, these notions interplaying across them. In doing this, I use these geographical interests: knowing place locations in the world, children's geographical experience, and responses to local and global situations and learning from children's lives in hazardous environments.

Learning locations: children and teachers together

I start with a story. In Ann Lawrence's (1976) engagingly geographical children's novel, *The Travel of Oggy*, a young hedgehog sets out to find a family who moved from their home in north London but left him bereft in the back garden. He determines to find them, knowing nothing of the world, near or far. On his journey from the city into the countryside, he learns about the wider world of the local area and Britain from the various creatures he encounters. He begins to build a mental map of his neighbourhood, the countryside and of Britain, though he does not readily appreciate that Britain is an island. Later, after various adventures, he meets a kestrel who has been blown inland from Ireland by a storm but who hails from New Zealand. Oggy discovers the idea of 'a country', that there are countries all over the world and that we live on a largely ocean-covered globe, not a flat Earth. His concluding comment on learning all this is cogent,

It must be very beautiful – the Whole World, I mean.

Through his travels and encounters Oggy began to learn something of the planet on which we live, of its geography. He was awed by it and curious. Developing awareness of the world is inspiring. Simply summarised, geography is about describing, understanding and explaining the world. Geography studies Earth's natural, modified and social environments, with particular interests in the interplay within and between human and physical environments, what they are like, what happens and why and about the impact. Geographers are fascinated by the spatial interrelationships we see, summarised by 'where?', 'why there?' and 'with what effect?' (Bonnett, 2008). They are interested in how we perceive all this and how this affects the ways we use our planet. They are stimulated by what can be done to resolve concerns and issues that arise and what the possible and probable futures of its people and the planet might be (Brunet, 2011; Holt-Jensen, 2009; Reinfried & Hertig, 2011). Geography is not, and cannot be, value-free, as the range of views on exploitation of and care for the world amply indicate, whether for self-interest or altruism. Within all of this is the idea that we ought to know where the world's features, places, environments and events are and occur. How do you know the world if we do not know where things happen? This is one aspect of basic geographical information, the 'vocabulary' of core geographical knowledge, as the Geographical Association puts it (GA, 2011).

Consider the photograph in Figure 1. When asked the question 'Where is it?', initially we are likely to say what it is: "the Grand Canyon". We may well add: 'in North America'

Source: Author

Figure 1. Where in the world would you see this view?
Source: Author.

or 'in the USA', even 'in Arizona'. We could, to be precise, state that it is in 'northern Arizona, USA, North America, at latitude 36° 15' north, longitude 112° 30' west'. Such an enquiry about a location is a typical quiz 'geography' question. It is the way geography is often characterised in the popular mind. It is how people 'know' geography – 'know' as in: can say what they believe the subject is about: that is, geography is about knowing locations and information about the world. This is the public face of geography (Taggart, 2011). Anecdotally, many people may be reticent about admitting not really 'knowing' geographical information. Too many of us appear not to know where in the world even some well-known places are (though we feel perhaps that we ought to know). This is a current concern about England's school geography: children leave school not sure where many places they study are on the map and in the world; they do not seem to have a mental national or global framework within which to set their knowledge about Britain or the world (Ofsted, 2011). Geographers discuss whether and in what sense such *locational knowledge* matters (Gersmehl, 2008; Martin, 2005; Matthews & Herbert, 2008). As the residual sense of geography that many adults retain from their schooling, it does matter; lay perspectives about subjects have meaning and influence, not least for and on politicians.

Since *locational knowledge* is embedded in the idea of geographical knowledge, it raises questions. Why should we know where the Grand Canyon is? Does it matter? Indeed, does the location of anywhere in particular matter? In the world of email and twitter has location any relevance? Though spatial location might not seem to some to be particularly relevant any longer (O'Brien, 1992), there are those who think that knowing where places are remains important. I am one (Catling, 2002, 2013a). Geographers, historians, linguists, business people and even travel agents agree – and so do politicians! Indeed, alongside government ministers, expert geography education panels think *locational knowledge* important (DES/WO, 1990; Dunn, 2011; GA, 2012).

Locational knowledge has always been a core element in geography education, from the subject's earliest years into the twenty-first century (DES, 1991; DfE, 1995; DfE, 2013; DfEE/QCA, 1999). Its focus has been on national, continental and global place knowledge. In England it has been included in all the versions of national curriculum primary and secondary geography. Why? There are many arguments put, but here are three basic reasons (Catling, 2002):

- to have a rudimentary notion of the layout of our locality, and of our country and of our planet, the Earth, its key major physical features such as land masses and oceans, and key human features such as countries and cities, which may be mentioned in the news, conversations, our reading, and so forth (alongside having some idea about these features and environments);
- to help us find the location of places we hear about or want to visit using atlases, Internet map sites, even GPS, and to appreciate that our knowledge is always limited, partial and even transient;
- to whet our curiosity, broaden our limited knowledge and challenge our ignorance, partiality, bias and preferences about the world.

This is rational and reasonable, but then there is a deeper question: Which places *should* be known and why these places? In my own primary education, more than 50 years ago, learning to recall the sites of places on maps and by drawing detailed maps from memory – places such as the cities, coalfields, wool towns, rivers of the British Isles (in fact, mainly on Britain, with the emphasis on England) – meant I encountered the pinky–red 'British' areas on the world map, the chief human and physical features of the continents, and certain 'important' countries, such as the USSR and the USA and some of the European nations. My early geography education, in the mid-1950s, occurred at the time of transition, of the British Empire mutating into the British Commonwealth. I learnt about Nyasaland and Tanganyika and then re-learnt their names as Malawi and Tanzania. I enjoyed this and could recall and locate all 'our' nations as I went round the continents. But why? Why these places? Why not Vietnam or Peru, Iran or Albania? This was decided for me; I had *no say* in 'where' to learn.

Given the geographical relevance of locational knowledge, there are various contexts in which children find they learn about place locations in Britain and the rest of the world: those set, those encountered and those sought.

- *'Powerfully' determined places to remember and recall*: Locations for children and teachers to learn are selected by those who know about these things, by expert geographers, historians and others, as has been done in England's Geography National Curriculum since the start of the 1990s (DES, 1991; DfE, 2013). This is the knowledge of 'the powerful' in the context of the subject. They are places, sites and locations 'the powerful' want known by the populous. Here teachers are simply teaching what they are told. They have no pedagogic authority. Children learn what is ordered, to order their knowledge.
- *Encouraging encounters for remembrance, formally and informally*: Children use atlases, Google Earth and so forth to identify places they come across during their geographical studies, through topics and from current events. Key locational knowledge is specified and encouraged. Teachers have some control but to an extent are working to others' decisions, such as about what is in the news or the places named in resources used in place and other studies, alongside their own selections. Still, though, children may have little say, but can have some, particularly out of school.
- *Enquiring about locations to know*: Children are involved in identifying where it is they should know about. This could well produce arbitrary knowledge unless a process is adopted which involves them in investigations and problem-solving activities, where teachers facilitate and challenge children in their proposals, their reasons and their arguments. They will use a variety of sources and resources and learn through engagement, debate, critique and decision-making. A pertinent question always for the children will be: Why is it important and/or useful for you and me to know about this place and where it is? And another: How does your list compare with others' views? Why are they similar, yet divergent? Of course, this knowledge of places will change for children over time, so children should do this more than once across their geographical studies during schooling. It fosters interest in being aware of and informed about the world in which we all live (Catling, 2013a).

This third option provides a real opportunity for *children's voice*: children leading their learning. This is my first instance of giving children voice in pedagogy. I suggest that children can be inquirers and make sound judgements. They need advice, guidance and challenge, for instance in not taking a single line of enquiry, and through their teachers always questioning why some places seem to be more privileged than others in our atlases, news and so on. Children must be required to justify their selection criteria and choices, more than once. The teacher remains very much involved in teaching. In this approach, children have agency and take ownership of their learning, appreciating why the location of the places they name is worth knowing. Indeed, while there may be some common places named by a class's children, there will be differences between individual children. This is inevitable, appropriate and to be valued. Children's senses of geography — and equally of place knowledge — will be what makes best sense to them, relevant to their experiences and interests (Rickinson, Lundholm, & Hopwood, 2009). They contribute to and have a stake in the core knowledge — the vocabulary — they learn. We should take the opportunity to be more honest and open about this, for common sense and social justice reasons.

Considering identity: subject knowledge and children's voice

Developing locational knowledge engages us with another question, about locational understanding: Where am *I* in all of this? In learning the whereabouts of Commonwealth countries, I did not have a choice about which places I was required to learn to locate! Why was I given these places to learn? What is learning *locational knowledge* really about? Why learn the locations of Kenya and Jamaica, or of Britain's glove and pottery industries? What had they to do with me, as a primary school child? What is this public, traditional sense of geography about and for?

I was taught what I learnt later were already outdated stereotypes of Commonwealth countries, and it was only after my schooling that I realised how much more important globally nations like the USA and USSR were in the 1950s, compared to our 'world workshop' of the fabled British iron ore and coal fields, Australian sheep and Ghanaian groundnuts! Yet learning locational information about Britain and Commonwealth countries had a purpose. Implicitly the idea of location encompassed notions of *identity*. Learning about the pinky-red areas on the world map was part of a quite recent 'tradition' to create and enhance my sense of being 'British'. It linked to the feel-good effects of imperialism, of global importance, and of engendering a sense of service and a range of other 'correct' beliefs and feelings, increasingly less grounded in reality but still to be instilled. On reflection, it demonstrated how schooling lags behind reality, while serving political desires to preserve the 'dying' images of yesterday. Learning about the Commonwealth was about the transmission of heritage, of a global place in the world, and of British 'right' (birthright and access to/ownership of elsewheres), though the 'might' was slipping speedily away, despite pretences otherwise. It was cultural and nationalistic, even though not laid down by law. My geography (and history) school learning was about embedding deeply my British identity and, in effect, about *othering* the rest of the world, even as very many members of the British Empire/Commonwealth were recruited to work in the UK, British citizens through and through, people who had and held an identity as British as my own (Ahier, 1988; Phillips & Phillips, 1998) — and, of course, it had other despicable, though perhaps unintended, outcomes.

What was happening through my geographical learning represented a type and use of *powerful knowledge*. This was about what was right and proper to be studied, to be learnt, cognitively and affectively, through geography the subject; it was a nationalistic literacy. It was what those who influenced education and subject experts thought was the 'right' focus for school geography from the late nineteenth to the mid-twentieth century. Senses of identity were underpinned by key geographical concepts, particularly the regional concept and aerial study (Hartshorne, 1939; Herbertson, 1905; Martin, 2005) and on imperialist paternalism. This is the stuff of the '*I-used-to-know-that-Geography*' style of book that has appeared nostalgically in recent years (Taggart, 2011). Some of these books evidently reflect *my* school geography curriculum, which focused on a multitude of locations

and information. This shaping of my values of 'Britishness' was inculcated through studies of the more fully (white) 'British' parts of the world, such as Australia and New
Zealand. School geography, inadvertently or not, differentiated and was benevolently
nationalistic, even implicitly racist. This use of internalised value systems, I contend, is
in the nature of school subjects, which some have misunderstood (Standish, 2009). School
subjects provide not simply understanding and skills alongside information but instil values, which discerning writers about geographical education have long recognised (Bailey,
1974; Graves, 1975; Morgan, 2012; Scoffham, 2010; Walford, 2001).

Powerful knowledge incorporates values, but it is rather more than information. The
argument for the conceptual and capability notions (Lambert & Morgan, 2010) of a subject is that this really provides a subject's 'powerful knowledge', that it has objectivity,
and that it is constructed over time and has authority as high-status knowledge which
takes young people beyond their immediate and constrained everyday lives and learning
(Young, 2008). Indeed it seems to do so, but it is based in values which it transmits. This
apparent 'objectivity' provides rationality, since it has been through the hands of many
experts and emerged in an organised form, with structure and coherence, systematic in its
use of concepts to underpin the nature of the subject and its studies. Yet it is a pretence
that school subjects are neutral. That they are value-based and espouse values gives them
interests that focus their 'objectivity' and makes them interesting, stimulating and motivating. And, they are not static in their values, structure, core ideas and information. The
'powerful' disciplinary version of my school geography came under severe challenge
from the late 1950s. During the 1960s and 1970s geography, the discipline, shifted its theoretical underpinnings in major ways (Agnew & Livingstone, 2011; Johnston &
Williams, 2003; Livingstone, 1992; Peet, 1998) – which gradually affected school geography (the educational lag) – emerging from these revolutions and diffusions as more
eclectic and diverse as well as stronger in its theoretical underpinnings, more surely
rooted in the foundational concepts of space, place and environment (Bonnett, 2008;
Clifford, Holloway, Rice, & Valentine, 2009; Holt-Jensen, 2009; Matthews & Herbert,
2004). Through these shifts, geography remained systematic and coherent. It retained
authority and vitality, and now we understand and appreciate it to be far more complex,
insightful, valued and contested than it was imagined to be in earlier embodiments.
Indeed, geography thrives with the challenge as the complexity of the world is ever more
apparent. This is what gives the subject power, makes it powerful: that it is alive,
dynamic, evolves and has important things to say about the nature and state of the world
in the past, the present and the future; and that it provides a secure base from which to
challenge received wisdom and hegemony.

Disciplinary power and authority have parallels in children and their geographical
learning, their knowledge and how they gain and use this. Notions of children as demons
or angels, in need of control and development, assumes they are naïve, ill-informed and
unsystematic in their lives and learning in contrast to, and *othered* in relation to, school
subjects. Yet there is good evidence through studies of children's geographies, for example, that their understandings of their worlds are more sophisticated, structured, diverse
and useful than we grant them credit for (Barrett, 2007; Catling, 2006, 2011; Freeman &
Tranter, 2011; Matthews, 1992). This is not to say their knowledge, understanding and
ideas are fully developed, but no discipline is in this state. That this is so does not diminish children, their understandings and contributions.

Fran Martin and I have contended that children construct their own ethno-knowledge
of places, spaces and environments from life experience – their *folk* context (Catling,
2003; Catling & Martin, 2011; Martin, 2008). They develop environmental knowledge

and life skills and construct values and attitudes concerning their experience of the world from first and second hand engagement (Alexander, 2010). The evidence suggests clearly that it encompasses their familiar places, environmental perspectives and attitudes, spatial understanding and use, and awareness of the wider world (Freeman & Tranter, 2011; Matthews, 1992; Spencer & Blades, 2006). What we argue is that children's understanding and knowledge is *powerful* and to be valued, that it has rationality, is systematic and structured, has coherence, and is conceptually grounded. We note equally that it evolves and grows with experience and maturity. Hopefully, school geography − primary and secondary − contributes to this. Certainly children's sense and appreciation of the local and wider world is *different* from the school subject geography, though the core structural concepts of space, place and environment underpin both real life geography and disciplinary geography. But *difference* does not mean 'inferior', the implicit notion in claims about subject 'objectivity' and 'authority' (Young, 2008) over children, and indeed more widely as a basis for *othering* (Martin, 2012). Our argument is that children's knowledge and ways of learning are matters to take into our pedagogy, to value and to engage with in a *joint venture* in pedagogy, teachers and children together (Cox, 2011).

This identifies my second perspective on giving children voice, that pedagogy can and should be empowered and empowering through working with children as *knowing* individuals and groups. What children bring to school is not simply some experience to elicit as a starting point because their teacher 'knows best', but rather that they engage with their teacher as a co-learners, exploring through geographical investigations, concerns and issues, challenges and problems. It infers that children can be 'co-teachers', working with and for each other, using their personal and everyday geographies as constructs to aid their own and their teacher's learning in the context, for instance, of curriculum making (Catling, 2013b; Mercer, 1995). This does not diminish the subject knowledge and understanding of their teachers, but given that many primary teachers lack confidence in and appreciation and understanding of geography (Ofsted, 2008, 2011), giving children pedagogical voice may well be a way to enhance geographical learning, understanding and values for all in any primary classroom.

Responding to challenges: sharing learning for others

I turn now to examples from a different area of geography and geographical education, environmental hazards and issues, connecting formal and informal geographies. These are further contexts through which children have taken or been given voice. They, too, enable and empower pedagogy. They concern the ideas and impact of disasters and climate change, for some children events seen in the media and taught about, while for others very real occurrences and experiences in their own lives. They are part of children's personal geographies just as much as those aspects already mentioned.

School geography can have powerful impacts on children's lives, not simply in exciting their curiosity and interest but also in enabling them to understand and use their evolving and new knowledge. The 2004 Boxing Day Indian Ocean tsunami was a horrifying disaster, killing almost a quarter of a million people (Karan & Subbiah, 2011). Having investigated with primary-age children the structure, forces and energy of the Earth, I know they can be stimulated and enthralled by such events, not morbidly, but fascinated to understand what happened, where, how and with what impact, just as they have been more recently by the earthquakes affecting Japan in 2011 and Italy in 2012 (Kington, 2012; Pisa & Gavaghan, 2012). While such topics can be highly engaging and foster informative enquiries, they can, on the spot and in a single instance, have an impact on

---

Girl, 10, uses geography lesson to save lives

A 10-year-old girl saved her family and 100 other tourists from the Asian tsunami because she had learnt about the giant waves in a geography lesson, it has emerged.

Tilly Smith, from Oxshott, Surrey, was holidaying with her parents and seven-year-old sister on Maikhao beach in Phuket, Thailand, when the tide rushed out.

As the other tourists watched in amazement, the water began to bubble and the boats on the horizon started to violently bob up and down.

Tilly, who had studied tsunamis in a geography class two weeks earlier, quickly realised they were in danger.

She told her mother they had to get off the beach immediately and warned that it could be a tsunami.

She explained she had just completed a school project on the huge waves and said they were seeing the warning signs that a tsunami was minutes away.

Her parents alerted the other holidaymakers and staff at their hotel, which was quickly evacuated. The wave crashed a few minutes later, but no one on the beach was killed or seriously injured.

In an interview with the Sun, Tilly gave the credit to her geography teacher, Andrew Kearney, at Oxshott's Danes Hill Prep School.

She said "Last term Mr Kearney taught us about earthquakes and how they can cause tsunamis.

"I was on the beach and the water started to go funny. There were bubbles and the tide went out all of a sudden.

"I recognised what was happening and had a feeling there was going to be a tsunami. I told mummy."

Source: *The Telegraph*, January 1st, 2005.
www.telegraph.co.uk/news/1480192/Girl-10-used-geography-lesson-to-save-lives.html
(Accessed: 16/4/2012)

Figure 2.   10-year-old uses geographical understanding during 2004 tsunami.

lives. One primary child's geographical learning at school not only saved her life, but her quick thinking saved her family and the lives of many others, as the newspaper report in Figure 2 about the local and immediate effect of the 2004 tsunami describes. A 10-year-old child who voiced her geographical learning was heard, her learning in school appreciated by her family and acted instantly upon; trust in their child was the basis for this family's survival. This is dramatic, but there are many examples in local environmental work, for instance, where children have had impacts through implementing suggestions to develop aspects of their school's grounds, to be actively eco-friendly and to contribute to local improvements (Baraldi, 2003; Bellamy, 2003; Freeman, Henderson, & Kettle, 1999; Hart, 1997). Such school learning gives children a real voice in their communities. It shows that geographical learning matters and can be invaluable.

Another example, reported in Figure 3, alerts us to a child's voice arising from his primary teacher's evident flexibility and sense of trust in the children. On 11 March 2011, a devastating tsunami hit north-eastern Japan (BBC, 2011; Fackler, 2011). That evening Raja went home, clearly moved by what he had heard about and learnt during the day. He probably watched the evening news and may have sought more information and photographs via Google, resources which were readily available in considerable numbers already that evening in England. Perhaps he should have been asleep, but this 10-year-old

> ## Heathfield primary school: Year 6 blog, March 11th 2011
>
> "Recently, the news has been lit up about Japan. It has been absolutely devastating for them. The earthquake has spread 80 miles from where it started. Japan must have been terrified when it started. The disastrous strike had set fire to buildings, that have killed people. Houses have been demolished and have trapped loads of people and made them die. This trecherous earthquake has caused two more disasters in Japan. It has caused a tsunami which has rised about 10 metres high. It has smashed against Japan, and has cleared everything in it's path. 100's of people have died by this, and we hope there is no more. The tsunami has drived boats under the water, drowning people and killing them. Many boats have collided and pushed by the waves. Helicopters have flew over Japan and have recorded what has happened, when the tsnuanami rised to its highest today. We hope that this is the highest, because we don't want it to rise even more. Some people have survived in their building, however the water is nearly up to their roof. People are waving for help, and we are trying our best to help them. After that, I heard on the news that on a radar people have spotted a whirlpool next to Japan I really hope that this whirlpool does not touch Japan or any of their people, because they Are suffering enough already, and they have lost so much. It is very sad news that this has happened to them, because I think they don't deserve it! I believe that all these disasters will go away, and lets just hope they do. Please watch the videos."
>
> *Raja, 9.58pm.*

Source: Heathfield Primary School Blog Site, March 12th, 2011.
http://y62011.heathfieldcps.net/2011/03/11/earthquake-strikes-at-japan/
(Accessed: 12/3/2011) [Spellings and syntax in the text have not been corrected.]

Figure 3. A 10-year-old's blog about the 2011 Japanese tsunami impact.

posted his contribution to his primary school's blog just before 10.00 pm. He added his voice to those trying to understand and appreciate this horrifying event. His voice, too, went beyond his school as he shared his thoughts, understanding and explanation. Of course, he had more to find out and understand – there are misunderstandings evident in his writing – but here is a primary school child who felt confident enough to post his understanding and views, in this social networking age, whose voice was supported in a school that was confident enough in its children to let them have out-of-school access to its blog site to post their perspectives from home. Geography, for children, is not only about information and ideas; it is about personal responses and actions.

A third, but differently focused and seemingly innocuous, example illustrates this directly. It is provided by nine-year-old Martha Payne through her NeverSeconds blog (Payne, 2012). She wrote about her school dinners during the late spring of 2012, receiving surprising feedback (Walker, 2012). Her blogging began following a school-inspired writing project which she was so enamoured with that she maintained it, writing daily for her family and friends about the nature and quality of her school lunches (Payne, 2013; Press Association, 2011). She posted photographs and rated the meals. It aroused her geographical curiosity, for instance, about where the food came from and how it was processed into what appeared on her plate. Six weeks into her blog, the local authority, Argyle & Bute Council in Scotland, became aware of her writing and photographs. The Council moved quickly to ban her from photographing her school meals, but this ban unintentionally and unexpectedly caused her blog to go viral. It raised a very real concern and much ire about such politically motivated censorship, with the result that the council hastily backed down. Martha then began to use her blog to raise funds for a kitchen and school feeding project in Malawi, run by international charity Mary's Meals (www.justgiving.com/marys-meals). In the ensuing months she raised many tens of thousands of pounds for the project (Payne, 2013). One result has been that she visited the project in Malawi and learnt much through this visit and through the interest her focus on school dinners had raised, about farming, access to food, poverty and the global power of the Internet. Her informal geographical learning was deepened locally and globally.

Using geographical knowledge in a disaster, trying to understand what happens when a disaster unfolds, and developing geographical awareness informally and inadvertently through the unintended consequences of blogging about an everyday event – all aspects of a child's ethno-geography (Martin, 2008) – are contexts in which learning has developed and been applied: subject and children's powerful knowledges mutually embracing, enabling and emboldening each other. Crucially, these examples illustrate pedagogy – formal and informal – empowering children as learners, sharers and communicators. My third focus, then, for giving children voice, is to enable their voices to be heard, listened to and appreciated not only in but also beyond the classroom.

Engaging with risk: ways to act in a hazardous world

My fourth focus for children's voice uses a related context. We need to understand the contested issue of climate change (Boyce & Lewis, 2009; Hulme, 2009). There are those, in the UK and elsewhere, who argue that teaching about climate change, sustainability and global citizenship are simply brainwashing activities which irrevocably damage younger children (Carbura, 2012; Fyall, 2012; Standish, 2009, 2012), because they lack the knowledge and simply have opinions. It ought to be that the climate change debate has been put to rest, but this is not the case for everyone; it is politically charged. While we are well aware that climate change has always occurred, what is keeping the debate lively is the concern about our human impact on our atmosphere and the environment, the result of human industrial and personal activities, such as our energy production and use, over the past 200 or so years. It is argued that our recent period of steady increases in Earth's temperatures, which are projected to continue to rise over the next century, cannot be accounted for other than by human 'interference' and impact (Giddens, 2009; Goudie, 2013; Lovelock, 2009). The overwhelming view of earth climate scientists is that this is so. Recent re-analysis of the global temperature data, funded by sceptics and convinced scientists (Muller, 2011; Sample, 2011) has confirmed the findings of earlier studies, recording the rise in Earth's temperatures by 1 °C during the last 50 years of the twentieth century. Some still do not accept this and continue to challenge the case that human-generated additions to the atmosphere are driving a speedier rise in temperatures than ever before (Plimer, 2009). For geographers, climate change is not a topic that can be ducked, even for primary age children, for which age group, Oxfam for instance, has produced learning activities and resources (Oxfam, 2008).

Do children have ideas and views about climate change? Does it concern them? Studies of younger and older children's views about environmental care and sustainability indicate that they do (Alexander & Hargreaves, 2007; Gayford, 2009; Hicks, 2002; O'Brien, 2003), though there is limited research into younger children's understanding of and perspectives on climate change (Gautam & Oswald, 2008; Kempster & Witt, 2009; Lovell & O'Brien, 2009). There is a greater range of research into the impact of climate change on children (Back & Cameron, 2007; Baker, 2009; Bartlett, 2008a, 2008b; Ebi &

Paulson, 2007; UNICEF, 2007, 2008) and what might be undertaken by schools and communities to help children's preparation for, and participation in, disaster risk management (ActionAid, 2009; Plan/World Vision, 2010; Seballos, Tanner, Tarazona, & Gallegos, 2011; UNICEF, 2009; UNICEF/Plan, 2010). This is socially important (Bator, 2012; Button, 2010; Stoltman, Lidstone, & DeChano, 2004) for both the present and the future. From the array of research we can note several important findings and directions for children's engagement.

- Across the world, many younger children have some rudimentary knowledge and understanding of what climate change is about, though, just as they talk about the ideas inherent in sustainability, they may reiterate views heard via adults and in the news (rather than through school learning) which go unchallenged and are uncritically accepted. They seem aware of such events as ice cap melting, some effects of air pollution, a sense of the Earth warming, and changes in the weather and its effects. More and more children have experience of such events. They have misunderstandings and misconceptions, for instance related to the causes of global warming, which may be ill-informed, anthropomorphic and naturalistic or from simplistic, even inaccurate, adult explanations. This provides a good reason for initiating and developing teaching about weather, climate and climate change with younger children. To fail to do so leaves children's opinions uninformed.
- Children are concerned about the climatic and weather challenges facing the Earth and its inhabitants, and some are fearful. Knowledge, concern and emotion are all involved. Teaching positively about climate change can be both informative and reassuring. This is important in developing understanding and for being thoughtful about the future.
- In some parts of the world, including the UK, children and young people realise some of the more direct impacts on their lives, through increasing water shortages or flooding resulting from shifts in weather patterns, and in relation to the greater effects of pollution and environmental degradation, which can affect their health and well-being. They seem aware that energy needs are not simple to resolve, when balancing energy provision with environmental care, and debates about finite and renewable resources. What concern them are the consequences of current and future human activities negatively affecting the planet and people's lives.
- National and global reviews report children's real desire is to have a voice in this issue. It is a constant refrain in policy directions raised by researchers and strategists, particularly in areas of the world more likely to be hit by devastating weather and its impacts, now intruding into more places.
- Children want to be involved in practical activities which help to improve life locally and which help them consider their attitudes and values about the environment, how to enhance sustainability and the future. These activities include tree planting, eco-activities concerned with the reduction in energy and water use in schools and at home, gardening and growing food, food sourcing, waste reduction, evaluating classroom resource use, local conservation projects, arguing for eco-friendly new developments, and recycling and re-use.
- Children wish and need to understand what climate change is, how and why it might affect their lives, and to be engaged in monitoring their localities for hazards, in the stewardship of their communities, in participating in discussions and decisions that affect their futures in such circumstances, and in having equal and full access to understandable information.

- Children should be and want to be properly prepared to know what to do when emergencies arise. This is underway in various parts of the world, where, for instance, tsunamis may batter coasts, earthquakes occur, tornadoes strike, and drought, wildfires and severe floods happen. Indeed, it is happening already in southern and Southeast Asia, Australia and the USA.
- Climate change affects us in ways we would not anticipate, making inland urban children everywhere similarly open to its detrimental effects as are children in rural and more exposed coastal areas. More than half the world's population now live in cities. Changes in weather patterns can lead to such events as food shortages and urban floods, creating major disruption to urban life. No child is immune from the effects of climate change, whether directly or indirectly.
- Children need to be more aware of the health risks associated with flooding, clean water loss and sanitary pollution so that they know about precautions to take to adapt to short and long term changes. They must appreciate the challenges in organising shelter and access to food, in helping to bring some order and routine back to their own, their family's and neighbour's lives through co-operative activities, and by knowing where to turn for help.
- Children can and should study the science and geography underpinning global warming, investigate the apparent and varied causes, debate different standpoints about action and inaction, and consider present and future impacts and outcomes resulting from climate change and their role in abetting, moderating and adapting to these.

These findings indicate that children's personal geographies are engaged with the world they encounter, just as there are geographies, physical and human, events and decisions, which affect them (Catling, 2003). But surely, these are matters that concern only children who live in the world's hazard zones? Such activities are not relevant to them in places like the UK and some other parts of the world – except that increasingly they are, for, while climate changes may yet have limited effects in less obviously affected places, local changes to rainfall patterns and dealing with more frequent floods, for instance, requires understanding and responses. In the context of giving children voice my case is that when we investigate fascinating geographical (and wider curriculum) topics like climate change and natural hazard events such as earthquakes and volcanic eruptions, we must ensure that learning covers not only the processes involved and their impacts where they happen and elsewhere, but also the ways in which children's lives are affected, what children can be involved in doing, and how children view this. It is not only because such geographical education is important for them, but because they also see it as vital for their futures (Smawfield, 2013).

Thus my fourth focus for giving children voice is that we need to hear directly from children in those parts of the world that are and stand greater chances of being affected by natural hazards. They are closer than we admit. This is because we need to understand more fully and appreciatively children's (and their wider community's) contexts and perspectives. We need to learn *from* them about how we might be more thoughtful and better prepared ourselves. Such might be the culmination of curriculum projects focused on local and global hazards and effects and about climate change (Hickman, 2009; Save the Children, 2008a, 2008b; Practical Action, n.d.), with children in the UK and elsewhere considering what they need to understand, who they need information and advice from, what they might do, and how they might have some say in decisions and actions. For instance they might have a say in the way that their school can be prepared and respond to a natural or human event and its impact. They might draw up the 'hazard response' blueprint for the school's governing body. In this way children's voices contribute from across the globe for the benefit of all, and we make active and effective use of our learning as well as use a proactive and challenging pedagogy. Perhaps a hazard action plan for a school will never be needed, but much will be gained if we take children seriously as participants in such pedagogy (European Panel on Sustainable Development, 2010) and we learn from the voices of other children.

Empowering pedagogy

I have presented four ways through which to encourage, engender and engage children's voice in primary and geographical pedagogy.

- Children lead the development of a topic. They take forward their investigations, certainly facilitated by the teacher, but not constrained by experts and politicians!
- Children are appreciated as authoritative co-learners, acting as co-teachers in subjects like geography, particularly in topics where they can contribute everyday expertise. To this they bring ways they understand the world around them which are conceptually consistent with the subject's core concepts; they bring their 'powerful knowledge' – a capability to be recognised and engaged with, and which brings mutual benefits.
- Children's learning can and should be heard beyond the classroom whether, through their life experiences, by being the expert for their family and others or in communicating, sharing and contributing with and to others beyond their school and community, trusted and able to show their understanding and effectiveness.
- Children elsewhere nationally and globally have knowledge which may be daunting and challenging, such as through their experience of and preparation for disasters, or exciting and energising, for instance in their contributions to environmental improvement and community development. Other children's voices, providing perspectives on their experiences and contributions, need to be heard by all and can help us learn and develop.

These are approaches which any high-quality primary teacher of geography and planner of an entitling curriculum uses (CACE, 1967; MacGilchrist & Buttress, 2005; Rogers, 1970; Swann, Peacock, Hart, & Drummond, 2012). Children's voices already matter to such teachers in empowering children's learning, her teaching and the curriculum. Children's voices, when given a key place in pedagogy, provide vitality, essence, focus and centrality for pedagogy. Some contest this approach. It is too *critical* a pedagogy. Indeed it is: critical in that it is about impact and effects in our own and our children's lives; critical in its concern to ask challenging questions; critical through engaging with controversy; critical through seeking, critiquing and not simply accepting the decisions of others and critical in not accepting given perceptions and persuasions either about children, subjects or the curriculum. It is *critical pedagogy*. It is challenged and challenging (Burney, 2012; Giroux, 2011; Kincheloe, 2008). Critical pedagogy, put succinctly, is emancipatory, based, among other aspects, in seeking equality and justice, in question making and problem orientation, in critical thinking, in its challenge to dominant power and hegemony, in working democratically, in freedom to debate and argue and in providing voice for the learner. Gatto has put this in more direct terms, arguing that we must challenge the effects of much teaching which obfuscates meaning, is disconnected with learners' own lives and realities and creates teacher dependency among children (Gatto,

1992, 2009). Three aspects of critical pedagogy seem pertinent in giving children voice in primary geography and across the curriculum.

In education policy the case for listening to children was made and appreciated some time ago (DfES, 2004). Yet does 'listening to children' go beyond hearing children's voices to involving those children, to engaging them in real participation in and out of school (Cox, Dyer, Robinson-Plant, & Schweisfurth, 2010; Gibson & Haynes, 2009; Percy-Smith & Thomas, 2010; Reid, Bruun Jensen, Nikel, & Simovska, 2008)? A primary school Eco-Council which has elected representatives and is managed by a teacher may note children's viewpoints and ideas, but does it provide children with a central role, or are the children managed rather than having *agency*? Agency involves judgement and decision making. Giving children a real voice in their learning of geography and other subjects often remains elusive. Johnson argues that giving children voice must focus on enabling them to take leadership and real responsibility (Johnson, 2004). To illustrate this she describes one primary school which involved all children in cross-age-phase meetings, led by children, contributing to decision making about pedagogy. Debate and responsibility are real, fully engaged with and enjoyed by children, providing benefit to the school and its community and having a strong impact on their learning. This is active involvement. But we need to discriminate between children's engagement through active learning (Monk & Silman, 2011), important and valuable as that is, though often constructed to keep children 'on track', and deep involvement in *liberatory learning*, with children transformed through a creative, challenging and demanding pedagogy, in which they have agency (Freire, 1970). Decisions on which topics, geographical and other, to study and how this is done will engage with argument and judgements. Not everyone will be content with the directions taken, but teachers and children engage with democratic principles and processes and learning becomes empowering.

Pedagogy is usually teacher, school and even externally directed. In an era of heavy political control in education, from the classroom to school systems and accessibility, this seems inevitable and for many it is beyond challenge. Yet, we can draw on a different pedagogy, critical, contested and never still. An aspect of this is the nature and role of subject knowledge, the foundation of the curriculum. The disciplines school subjects connect with evolve, are internally critical, seeking new interpretations, understandings and foci for study, in many cases looking beyond their discipline, as geography does. This provides opportunities to draw on children's knowledge and involve them in exploring current understandings of subjects such as geography. It provides openings for critical pedagogy. Within their overall responsibility, teachers can open the direction and development of what is taught and learnt to involve the children, as learners together, in this quest, through identifying the questions and problems, concerns or issues to investigate and with the children constructing enquiries which explore these (Roberts, 2003). This can occur within a subject framework, with where this leads and its outcomes kept open, while foregrounding children's everyday subject-connected constructs alongside the key ideas, constructs and topics of school subjects. For Freire knowledge is interpreted through dialectical practice and review involving all learners, so by children and teachers together (Darder, 2002). This provides an emancipatory basis for understanding and appreciating curriculum subject knowledge within pedagogy. Teachers and children need to be engaged in evaluating and directing where learning leads, through a consistently critical awareness of their studies, the value of this learning and its subject and wider social contexts. This empowers pedagogy.

The teacher's responsibility is not diminished; rather it is enhanced. The role of the teacher is, in Freire's terms, to be knowledgeable and informed, to be, he argues, an intellectual (Freire & Horton, 1990; Leach & Moon, 2008). He asks: If teachers do not know their subject(s), what are they there for? This is a question as pertinent for primary as for secondary teachers. Critical pedagogy extols the role of the teacher but demands that it is a dialectical role and, in Alexander's term, dialogic (Alexander, 2008), taking into account the everyday realities of learners, connecting with them through their current experiences and understandings, drawing on, accepting and valuing these, and engaging the learners' authority with subject authority in order to enhance their learning (Catling & Martin, 2011). The teacher is required to know and understand the curriculum subjects and topics they teach, to understand and relate to their learners (including themselves) and to teach responsively, engagingly and to empower the learner through learning. In this context teachers and children together and children with children, all as learners, are engaged in what Mercer has termed 'the guided construction of knowledge' (Mercer, 1995). This is a natural expectation of teachers (DfE, 2012). Such an approach requires teachers to understand the possibilities of school pedagogies and to appreciate and value alongside them what Bruner has termed 'folk pedagogies' (Bruner, 1996). This involves being self-critical about our 'insider' understandings of school pedagogy, such as the recommended approaches to teaching geography. It demands that we keep extending our subject and topic understanding. It means that we take into account in our pedagogies children's ways of learning in the out-of-school world, where learning through experience, dealing with problems and rising to challenges, as well as learning by direction from the experienced and wise are key elements in the armoury of folk pedagogies. This connects directly with teachers' acceptance, alongside their expertise, that their children also have 'expertise', and to give it credence and to value and use it.

Conclusion

We have encountered a variety of arguments in this discussion, from the nature and purpose of school knowledge and its links with forging identity to the hazardous nature of the world and its effect on your lives. We have encountered four approaches to engaging with children's voices, not only with our own children's but with those of others. We are aware that children's ethno-geographies are there whether we wish it or not. That subjects are of educational value is not disputed, but we recognise that disciplines are adventurous, about learning and evolve. Drawing on these debates, not uncontested certainly, leads, it seems to me, to a number of principles concerned with 'giving children voice' and 'empowering pedagogy'. These are pertinent for younger children's geographical education, in and beyond school, and they owe more than a little to Alexander's arguments about dialogic teaching and Kincheloe's perspectives on critical pedagogy (Alexander, 2008; Kincheloe, 2008).

- *Hearing children*: Children have the right to be heard and to be appreciated as persons and citizens, able to make positive contributions and commitments in their community, in school and in subjects such as geography.
- *Aware children*: Children bring awareness into school, however limited or embryonic in development. They become increasingly aware of the world around and beyond them and wish to and can, variously, articulate their perspectives about that world. Their teacher's role is to provide the opportunities and to enable them to do so, for which they need to be knowledgeable, in geography as in other subjects and aspects for learning.

- *Enabling participation*: Children need participatory and open contexts in which to develop their contributions and to learn from each other. This implies pedagogical flexibility in the curriculum, in teachers' attitudes and approaches, and in terms of what is valued in learning by learners and teachers.
- *Critically thoughtful citizens*: All societies, particularly democracies (even imperfect ones) need citizens able to argue, question, challenge, reason and develop interpretations and meanings, distinguish reason from polemic, recognise diverse viewpoints, critique, present arguments, evaluate cases put to them, and offer alternatives, even if not agreeable. Learners need to be self-evaluative. Children must be engaged fully in and by pedagogies that provide for and enhance these developments throughout their education.
- *Social justice*: Children are to be encouraged to value and work for equity and just approaches in their lives, their class and school, and more widely. This means tackling problems and issues, and at the least trying to understand them even though they cannot resolve them. It infers quizzing those who have responsible and powerful roles and arguing points with them.
- *Being fully engaged*: Children should be motivated, stimulated and focus their attention, being provided with opportunities and time to be absorbed in what they do – as teachers should be.
- *Exploring personal and disciplinary knowledge*: Knowledge needs to be recognised as conceptual, based in deep constructs, connected with information, about reality and relevance, mutable and changing and evolving, never static. It is not held by 'one' person or by some 'objective' external force, but is within us and shared between us, which can give it credibility and value. Teachers must recognise and balance the knowledge children bring and develop with the knowledge disciplines hold, revise and reconstruct.
- *Social learning*: Children learn most effectively through social engagement and interaction, which should be the nature of their classroom and school environment. In 'folk' and school pedagogies, children learn where they have real involvement and responsibilities, which are genuine and engaging, not tokenistic (Hart, 1997). Their voice matters and is valued.
- *Integrity in learning*: Children should have their confidence and self-esteem fostered through experiences which enable all these principles, in an environment with integrity, where they matter as co-participants, co-learners and co-teachers.

What I have argued is a case for thinking and working beyond national curriculum requirements and the schooling straightjacket. I have argued for the centrality of children's engagement as participants in learning through a range of ways we can involve their voices as co-participants. If we want the children we say we do – empowered and social individuals, critical and independent learners, informed and seekers after knowledge and participants in and contributors to our society and lives – then, whatever the school's pedagogy currently provides, be critical, be open, be creative, be challenging, be inclusive – and continually recreate it as a place of and for learning together. Children's voices empower pedagogy.

References

ActionAid. (2009). A right to participate: Securing children's role in climate change adaption. Retrieved from http://www.childreninachangingclimate.org

Agnew, J., & Livingstone, D. (Eds.). (2011). *The Sage handbook of geographical knowledge.* London: Sage.

Ahier, J. (1988). *Industry, children and the nation.* Lewes: Falmer Press.

Alexander, R. (2000). *Culture and pedagogy: International comparisons in primary education.* Oxford: Blackwells.

Alexander, R. (2008). *Towards dialogic teaching: Rethinking classroom talk.* York: Dialogos.

Alexander, R. (2010). *Children, their world, their education: Final report and recommendations of the Cambridge primary review.* London: Routledge.

Alexander, R., & Hargreaves, L. (2007). *The primary review interim reports: Community soundings.* Cambridge: University of Cambridge Faculty of Education.

Apple, M. (2006). *The subaltern speak: Curriculum, power and educational struggles* (2nd ed.). London: Routledge.

Back, E., & Cameron, C. (2007). *Our climate, our children, our responsibility: The implications of climate change for the world's children.* Paris: UNICEF.

Bailey, P. (1974). *Teaching geography.* Newton Abbot: David & Charles.

Baker, L. (2009). *Feeling the heat: Child survival in a changing climate.* London: Save the Children.

Baraldi, C. (2003). Planning childhood: Children's social participation in the town of adults. In P. Christensen & M. O'Brien (Eds.), *Children in the city: Home neighbourhood and community* (pp. 184–205). London: RoutledgeFalmer.

Barrett, M. (2007). *Children's knowledge, beliefs and feelings about nations and national groups.* Hove: Psychology Press.

Bartlett, S. (2008a). *Climate change and urban children.* Retrieved from pubs.iied.org/pdfs/10556IIED.pdf.

Bartlett, S. (2008b). The implications of climate change for children in lower-income countries. *Children, Youth and Environment, 18*(1), 71–98.

Bator, J. (2012). The cultural meaning of disaster: Remarks on Gregory button's work. *International Journal of Japanese Sociology, 21,* 92–97.

BBC (British Broadcasting Authority). (2011). Japanese earthquake: Tsunami hits north-east. Retrieved from http://www.bbc.co.uk/news/world-asia-pacific-12709598

Bellamy, C. (2003). *The state of the world's children 2003: Child participation.* New York, NY: UNICEF.

Bonnett, A. (2008). *What is geography?* London: Sage.

Boyce, T., & Lewis, J. (Eds.). (2009). *Climate change and the media.* New York, NY: Peter Lang.

Bruner, J. (1996). *The culture of education.* Cambridge, MA: Harvard University Press.

Brunet, R. (2011). *Sustainable geography.* London: ISTE/Wiley.

Burney, S. (2012). *Pedagogy of the other.* London: Peter Lang.

Button, G. (2010). *Disaster culture: Knowledge and uncertainty in the wake of human and environmental catastrophe.* Walnut Creek: Left Coast Press.

CACE [Central Advisory Council for Education (England)]. (1967). *Children and their primary schools: A report of the central advisory council for education (England)* (The Plowden Report). London: HMSO.

Carbura, A. (2012). *The environmental terrorising of children.* Retrieved from http://www.climatechangedispatch.com/home/10088-the-environmental-terrorizing-of-children.

Catling, S. (2002). *Placing places.* Sheffield: Geographical Association.

Catling, S. (2003). Curriculum contested: Primary geography and social justice. *Geography, 88*(3), 164–210.

Catling, S. (2006). Younger children's geographical worlds and primary geography. In D. Schmeinck (Ed.), *Research on learning and teaching primary geography* (pp. 9–35). Karlsruhe: Karlsruhe Pädagogische Studien.

Catling, S. (2011). Children's geographies in the primary school. In G. Butt (Ed.), *Geography, education and the future* (pp. 15–29). London: Continuum.

Catling, S. (2013a). Learning about places around the world. In S. Scoffham (Ed.), *Teaching geography creatively* (pp. 59–73). London: Routledge.

Catling, S. (2013b). Teachers perspectives on curriculum making in primary geography in England. *Curriculum Journal, 24*(3), 425–442.

Catling, S., & Martin, F. (2011). Contesting powerful knowledge: the primary geography curriculum as an articulation between academic and children's ethno-) geographies. *The Curriculum Journal, 22*(3), 317–335.

Clifford, N., Holloway, S., Rice, S., & Valentine, G. (Eds.). (2009). *Key concepts in geography* (2nd ed.). London: Sage.

Corsaro, W. (2011). *The sociology of childhood* (3rd ed.). London: Sage.

Cox, S. (2011). *New perspectives in primary education*. Maidenhead: Open University Press.

Cox, S., Dyer, C., Robinson-Plant, A., & Schweisfurth, M. (Eds.). (2010). *Children as decision makers in education*. London: Continuum.

Darder, A. (2002). *Reinventing Paulo Freire: A pedagogy of love*. Cambridge, MA: Westview Press.

DES (Department of Education and Science). (1991). *Geography in the national curriculum (England)*. London: HMSO.

DES/WO (Department of Education and Science/Welsh Office). (1990). *Geography for ages 5 to 16*. London: DES/WO.

DfE (Department for Education). (1995). *Geography in the national curriculum: England*. London: HMSO.

DfE. (2010). *The importance of teaching: The schools white paper 2010*. London: TSO.

DfE. (2012). *Teachers' standards*. Retrieved from http://www.education.gov.uk.

DfE. (2013). *The national curriculum in England: Framework document*. Retrieved from http://www.education.gov.uk/nationalcurriculum

DfEE/QCA (Department for Education and Employment/Qualifications and Curriculum Authority). (1999). *The national curriculum for England: Geography*. London: DfEE/QCA.

DfES (Department for Education and Skills). (2004). *Every child matters: Change for children*. Nottingham: DfES.

Dunn, J. (2011). Locational knowledge: Assessment, spatial thinking and the new geography standards. *Journal of Geography, 110*, 81–89.

Ebi, K., & Paulson, J. (2007). Climate change and children. *Pediatric Clinics of North America, 54*, 213–226.

European Panel on Sustainable Development. (2010). *Taking children seriously – How the EU can invest in early childhood education for a sustainable future*. Centre for Environment and Sustainability. Retrieved from http://www.ecesustainability.org.

Fackler, M. (2011, March 11). Powerful quake and tsunami devastate Northern Japan. *New York Times*. Retrieved from http://www.nytimes.com/2011/03/12/world/asia/12japan.html?pagewanted=all

Flutter, J., & Rudduck, J. (2004). *Consulting pupils: What's in it for schools?* London: RoutledgeFalmer.

Freeman, C., Henderson, P., & Kettle, J. (1999). *Planning with children for better communities*. Bristol: Policy Press.

Freeman, C., & Tranter, P. (2011). *Children and their urban environment: Changing worlds*. London: Earthscan.

Freire, P. (1970). *Pedagogy of the oppressed*. London: Penguin Books (1993 revised ed)

Freire, P., & Horton, M. (1990). *We made the road by walking: Conversations on education and social change*. Philadelphia, PA: Temple University Press.

Fyall, J. (2012, February 16). Climate change sceptics plan to 'brainwash' US children. *The Scotsman*. Retrieved from http://www.scotsman.com/the-scotsman/environment/climate-change

GA (Geographical Association). 2011. *The national curriculum: GA Proposals and Rationale*. Retrieved from http://www.geography.org.uk/geographycurriculumconsultation.

GA. 2012. Curriculum consultation feedback report. Retrieved from http://www.geography.org.uk/download/GA_GINNCConsultationFeedbackReport.pdf

Gatto, J. (1992). *Dumbing us down: The hidden curriculum of compulsory schooling*. Philadelphia, PA: New Society Publishers.

Gatto, J. (2009). *Weapons of mass instruction*. Philadelphia, PA: New Society Publishers.

Gautam, D., & Oswald, K. (2008). *Child voices: Children of Nepal speak out on climate change adaptation*. Bristol: ActionAid.

Gayford, C. (2009). *Learning for sustainability: From the pupils' perspective*. Godalming: WWF (World Wildlife Fund).

Gersmehl, P. (2008). *Teaching geography* (2nd ed.). London: Guildford Press.

Gibson, S., & Haynes, J. (Eds.). (2009). *Perspectives on participation and inclusion: Engaging education*. London: Continuum.

Giddens, A. (2009). *The politics of climate change*. Cambridge: Polity Press.

Giroux, H. (2011). *On critical pedagogy*. London: Continuum.

Goudie, A. (2013). *The human impact on the natural environment* (7th ed.). Oxford: Blackwell.

Grant, J. (2012). Letter to the editor: Reply to Ellie Stacey, *Wheatley Newsletter,* June-July (p. 15). Wheatley: Wheatley Parish Council.

Graves, N. (1975). *Geography in education*. London: Heinemann.

Gregory, D. (2004). *The colonial present*. Oxford: Blackwell.

Hart, R. (1997). *Children's participation: The theory and practice of involving young citizens in community development and environmental care*. London: Earthscan.

Hartshorne, R. (1939). *The nature of geography*. Lancaster, PA: The Association of American Geographers.

Herbertson, A. (1905). The major natural regions: An essay in systematic geography. *Geographical Journal, 25,* 300–312.

Hickman, L. (2009, May 2). Why don't we stop hurting the planet? *The Guardian*. Retrieved from http://www.guardian.co.uk/environment/2009/may/22/climate-change-children-education-books.

Hicks, D. (2002). *Lessons for the future*. London: Routledge.

Holt-Jensen, A. (2009). *Geography – history and concepts: A student guide* (4th ed.). London: Sage.

Hulme, M. (2009). *Why we disagree about climate change*. Cambridge: Cambridge University Press.

Jenks, C. (2005). *Childhood* (2nd ed.). London: Routledge.

Johnson, K. (2004). *Children's voices: Pupil leadership in primary schools*. Nottingham: National College for School Leadership.

Johnston, R., & Williams, M. (Eds.). (2003). *A century of British geography*. Oxford: Oxford University Press.

Karan, P., & Subbiah, S. (Eds.). (2011). *The Indian Ocean tsunami*. Lexington: The University Press of Kentucky.

Kempster, E., & Witt, S. (2009). Children's ideas on climate change. *Primary Geographer, 70,* 16–18.

Kincheloe, J. (2008). *Critical pedagogy* (2nd ed.). New York, NY: Peter Lang.

Kington, T. (2012, May 29). Italian earthquakes: 800 aftershocks in Emelia-Romagna and 'more to come'. *The Guardian*. Retrieved from http://www.guardian.co.uk/world/2012/may/29/italy-earthquakes-800-aftershocks-emelia.

Lambert, D., & Morgan, J. (2010). *Teaching geography 11–18*. Maidenhead: Open University Press.

Lawrence, A. (1976). *The Travels of Oggy*. London: Pan Books (1973; originally Gollancz).

Leach, J., & Moon, B. (2008). *The power of pedagogy*. London: Sage.

Livingstone, D. (1992). *The geographical tradition*. Oxford: Blackwell.

Lovell, R., & O'Brien, L. (2009). *Wood you believe it? Children and young people's perceptions of climate change and the role of trees, woods and forests*. Farnham: Forest Research. Retrieved from http://www.forestry.gov.uk/pdf/SERG_Wood_you_believe_it.pdf.

Lovelock, J. (2009). *The Vanishing face of Gaia: A final warning*. London: Allen Lane.

MacGilchrist, B., & Buttress, M. (2005). *Transforming learning and teaching*. London: Paul Chapman.

Martin, F. (2008). Ethnogeography: Towards a liberatory geography education. *Children's Geographies, 6*(4), 437–450.

Martin, F. (2012). The geographies of difference. *Geography, 97*(2), 116–122.

Martin, G. (2005). *All possible worlds: A history of geographical ideas* (4th ed.). Oxford: Oxford University Press.

Matthews, H. (1992). *Making sense of place: Children's understanding of large-scale places*. Hemel Hempstead: Harvester-Wheatsheaf.

Matthews, J., & Herbert, D. (Eds.). (2004). *Unifying geography: Common heritage, shared future*. London: Routledge.

Matthews, J., & Herbert, D. (2008). *Geography: A very short introduction*. Oxford: Oxford University Press.

Mercer, N. (1995). *The guided construction of knowledge*. Clevedon: Multilingual Matters.

Monk, J., & Silman, C. (2011). *Active learning in primary classrooms: A case study approach*. Harlow: Longman.

Morgan, J. (2012). *Teaching secondary geography as if the planet matters*. London: David Fulton.

Muller, E. (2011). *Cooling the warming debate*. Retrieved from http://www.BerkeleyEarth.org

O'Brien, M. (2003). Regenerating children's neighbourhoods: What do children want? In P. Christensen & M. O'Brien (Eds.), *Children in the city: Home neighbourhood and community* (pp. 142–161). London: RoutledgeFalmer.

O'Brien, R. (1992). *Global financial integration: The end of geography*. London: Pinter Publishers/ Royal Institute of International Affairs.

Ofsted (Office for Standards in Education). (2008). *Geography in schools: Changing practice*. Retrieved from http://www.ofsted.gov.uk/publications.

Ofsted. (2011). *Learning to make a world of difference*. Retrieved from http://www.ofsted.gov.uk/ publications.

Oxfam. (2008). Climate change [Resources for key stage 2]. Retrieved from http://www.oxfam.org. uk/education/resources/climate-change

Payne, M. (2012). Matha's meals [blog]. Retrieved from http://neverseconds.blogspot.co.uk./

Payne, M. (2013). The primary geography interview: Martha Payne. *Primary Geography, 81*, 8–9.

Peet, R. (1998). *Modern geographical thought*. Oxford: Blackwell.

Percy-Smith, B., & Thomas, N. (Eds.). (2010). *A handbook of children and young people's participation*. London: Routledge.

Phillips, M., & Phillips, T. (1998). *Windrush: The irresistible rise of multi-racial Britain*. London: HarperCollins.

Pisa, N., & Gavaghan, J. (2012, May 30). Priest dies in church collapse while trying to rescue statue as second major earthquake to hit Italy in days kills at least 15 others. *Mail Online*. Retrieved from http://www.dailymail.co.uk/news/article-2151469/Italy-earthquake-2012-15-dead-5-8-quake-hits-region-7-died-week.html

Plan/World Vision. (2010). *Children on the frontline: Children and young people in disaster risk reduction*. London: Plan.

Plimer, I. (2009). *Heaven and earth: Global warming: The missing science*. London: Quartet.

Practical Action (n.d.) *Climate choices – Children's voices*. Retrieved from http://www. climatechoices.org.uk.

Press Association. (2011, June 19). The Malawi school kitchen that Martha's blog built. *The Guardian*, p. 13.

Reid, A., Bruun Jensen, B., Nikel, J., & Simovska, V. (Eds.). (2008). *Participation and learning: Perspectives on education and environment, health and sustainability*. New York: Springer.

Reinfried, S., & Hertig, P. (2011). Geographical education: How human-environment-society processes work. In UNESCO-EOLSS Joint Committee (Eds.), *Geography, in EOLSS, encyclopedia of life support systems*. Oxford: Eolss Publishers. Retrieved from http://www.eolss.net

Rickinson, M., Lundholm, C., & Hopwood, N. (2009). *Environmental learning*. London: Springer.

Roberts, M. (2003). *Learning through enquiry*. Sheffield: Geographical Association.

Rogers, V. (1970). *Teaching in the British primary school*. New York, NY: Macmillan.

Sample, I. (2011, October 21). Global warming study finds no grounds for the climate sceptics' concerns. *The Guardian*. Retrieved from http://www.theguardian.com/environment/2011/oct/20/ global–warming–study-climate–sceptics

Save the Children. (2008a). *The alert rabbit*. Bangkok: Save the Children.

Save the Children. (2008b). *Child-led disaster risk reduction: A practical guide*. London: Save the Children.

Scoffham, S. (Ed.). (2010). *Primary geography handbook*. Sheffield: Geographical Association.

Seballos, F., Tanner, T., Tarazona, M., & Gallegos, J. (2011). *Children and disasters: Understanding impact and enabling agency*. Brighton: Institute of Development Studies.

Smawfield, D. (2013). *Education and natural disasters*. London: Bloomsbury.

Spencer, C., & Blades, M. (Eds.). (2006). *Children and their environment*. Cambridge: Cambridge University Press.

Standish, A. (2009). *Global perspectives in the geography curriculum: Reviewing the moral case for geography*. London: Routledge.

Standish, A. (2012). *The false promise of global learning*. London: Continuum.

Stoltman, J., Lidstone, J., & DeChano, L. (Eds.). (2004). *International perspectives on natural disasters: Occurrence, mitigation and consequences*. London: Kluwer Academic Publishers.

Swann, M., Peacock, A., Hart, S., & Drummond, M. (2012). *Creating learning without limits*. Maidenhead: Open University Press.

Taggart, C. (2011). *I used to know that*. London: Michael O'Mara Books.

UNICEF (United Nations International Children's Emergency Fund). (2007). *Climate change and children: Unite for children*. New York: UNICEF.

UNICEF. (2008). *Climate change and children: A human security challenge*. Florence: UNICEF Innocenti Research Centre.

UNICEF. (2009). *Children and disaster risk reduction: Taking stock and moving forward*. Brighton: Institute of Development Studies.

UNICEF/Plan. (2010). *The benefits of a child-centred approach to climate change adaptation*. London: UNICEF.

Valentine, G. (2004). *Public space and the culture of childhood*. Aldershot: Ashgate.

Walford, R. (2001). *Geography in British schools 1850–2000*. London: Woburn Press.

Walker, P. (2012, June 16). *Victory on a plate: Council backs down as Martha's school dinner blog goes global*. The Guardian, p. 3.

Woodhead, M. (2010). Foreward. In B. Percy-Smith & N. Thomas (Eds.), *A handbook of children and young people's participation* (pp. xix–xxii). London: Routledge.

Wyness, M. (2012). *Childhood and society* (2nd ed.). Basingstoke: Palgrave Macmillan.

Young, M. (2008). *Bringing knowledge back in*. London: Routledge.

Index

Note: Page numbers in *italics* represent tables
    Page numbers in **bold** represent figures
    Page numbers followed by 'n' refer to notes

academic geography: and ethno-geography 25
academic knowledge 59
academic perceptions: of knowledge 61
access to resources 10
accessibility to all 30–1
Action Plan for Geography (APG) 74, 88, 89, 138
active curriculum agents 145
active engagement 64
active learning approaches 135
Adichie, C.N. 201; *The Dangers of a Single Story* 191
adversity: inspiration in 106
age groups: geographical learning 11
Alexander, R. 57–8, 90, 94, 113, 151
Alkis, S. 42, 46, 47, 48
All out Futures (1999) 107
American Study (Clayton) 137
Amman (Jordan) 64
Areas of Learning: Northern Ireland Curriculum (NIC) 117–20, 122, 124, 125
areas of the world 9
artists 106
attachment 64
attitude to change 127–8
Australia 78, 174, 176–7
authority: disciplinary power 224
autonomy: teacher 126

Bale, J. 208
Barlow, C.: and Brook, A. 118
Barnes, J. 32, 110; and Scoffham, S. 106
Barrett Hacking, E. 40; and Barrett, R. 18, 160–72
becoming: notion of (Giroux) 66
Biddulph, M. 51, 140
Boaler, J. 77, 85
Bobbitt, J. 134–5, 138, 152
Bradbeer, J.: Healey, M. and Kneale, P. 41, 42, 48

Brazil 9
Britishness 224
broaden and build theory (Fredrickson) 105
Brook, A.: and Barlow, C. 118
Brooks, C. 34, 48, 140
Bruner, J. 79, 83, 223
Burbules, N.C. 191, 192, 194, 199, 200

Calderhead, J. 40; and Shorrock, S. 76
Cambridge Primary Review 40
Catling, S. 1–19, 74, 75–6, 82, 87–8, 109, 119, 133–59, 217–39; earthist perspective **42**, 46, 47; interactionist and placeist perspective **41**, **42**, 44, 47, 49; and Martin, F. 17, 40, 54–72, 191; and Morley, E. 16, 21, 21–38; and Pickering, S. 111; postgraduate trainees' conceptions of geography 41, **42**; and Taylor, L. 81
change: attitude to 127–8
characterisation 218
Charlton, E.: et al. 173–89
child-centered approach 74, 135, 217
children: secondary-school 29, 206
Children's Bill (2003) 162
Children's Commissioner 162
citizenship 74
classroom: working outside 5, *see also* outdoor learning
classroom-based teacher development project 18
Claxton, G.: and Lucas, B. 104
Clayton, C. 136, 151; American Study 137
Cliff Hodges, G.: et al. 173–89
climate change 23, 228, 229
comfort zone 18
conceptions of geography: student teachers 75–6, 77, 79
concepts: key 97
connected learning approach 125, 126
content knowledge: pedagogical 23

contextual factors 150
continuum view (Martin) 97
Cook, I.: Montamedi, M. and Williams, A. 82
core knowledge 87–102, 103; notion of 28;
  politicians 32
Craft, A. 104–5; possibility thinking notion 110
creative play 111
creativity 17, 104–5, 113; curriculum-making
  99–100; learning 103–16; personal growth
  105–6
cross-curricular teaching 124
cross-curricularity (CC) (NIC) 117–30;
  arguments against 121; arguments in favour
  120–1; pre-and post-curriculum revision
  surveys 124, **124**
Csikszentmihalyi, M. 105, 108
culture 57, 61; difference 194
curriculum: active agents 145; factors 150;
  integration 118; -knowledge relationship
  65–6; Knowledge and Understanding of the
  World (3-7 year olds) 1; spiral 83–4, **83**;
  (2014) 3
curriculum (2000-14): change in 4–5; Key
  Stage 1 & 2 framework 4, 5; place locations
  4; revisions 4
Curriculum Consultation Report (GA, 2011b)
  30
curriculum-makers: teachers 98–9
curriculum-making 129, 134–41, **138**, 153, 155;
  attitudes and underpinning 153; creativity
  99–100; decision-making organisational
  aspects 154; five factors 136–7; GA's
  interpretation 138–41; key ingredients 139;
  learning about 149–53; living geography 140

Damasio, A.: and Immordino-Yang, M. 103–4
D'Ambrosio, U. 60, 77
Darling, J. 120–1
data analysis 196; child engagement 166–8
De Bono 104
De Koning, K.: and Martin, M. 163
Department for Education and Employment
  (DfEE): National Curriculum (NC) 39
Deputy Headteachers 167
development: children 15, 94, **95**; teacher 18
dialectic 57
dialogic interactions 58
difference 198; culture 194; principal
  investigator (PI) 194; relational 194;
  self-image 201; within 199–200
disciplinary power: authority 224
diversity: similarity-difference 193, 198–9
Dobson, K. 106
Draper, E.. 135, 151

earth climate scientists 228
earthist perspective (Catling) **42**, 46, 47
Eaude, C. 23, 28, 34, 35

Economic and Social Research Council (ESRC)
  70, 191, 194
educational fashion: pendulum 119
educational value 30
Edwards, R. 150; Miller, K. and Priestley, M.
  136, 137
effective learning 128
effectiveness pedagogy 23
empowering pedagogy 231–3; principles
  233–4; teacher responsibility 232
empowerment: teacher autonomy 126
engagement: active 64; in data analysis 166–8
England 3–15
English primary schools 208
enough understanding 23
Enquiring Minds project 66
enquiry: and skills *12–13*, 114–15
enquiry-based fieldwork: personal sense of
  space **81**
Entwistle, H. 121
environment: physical geography 48;
  sustainability 112–13; urban 160–72
environmental change: sustainability 10
environmentalists perspective 42, **42**, 47, 49
essential knowledge 29
ethical approach: children's research findings
  168–9
ethical debates 164
ethno-geography 50, 57, 77, 79–80, 81–4; and
  academic geography 25; concept of 17;
  disconnection to 55; Initial Teacher Training
  (ITT) 56; learner 76; liberatory education
  73–86; National Curriculum 80–1; primary
  education 79, 79–80; primary phase 56–60;
  spiral curriculum **83**; teacher education 78–9
ethno-mathematics 57, 67–9, 73, 76–8, 84, 85n
Europe: German primary schools 207; teaching
  about 205–16
European dimension 205–16; aims for
  implementation 209–10; German primary
  schools 207–13; home continent 8; reasons
  for implementation 209; teaching 210–11
Every Child Matters (DfES, 2004) 106
everyday knowledge 59, 60–2; inferiority 62
Excellence and enjoyment (DfES, 2003) 106
expectations: geographical learning and
  thinking 10–11, *12–13*; progression statement
  for geographical learning (GA) 11
expert teachers 15, 34
explorations and uses of knowledge: children's
  thinking 2

facilitators *45*, 47, 165, 209
fact finder: global *45*, 46, 47
fieldwork: enquiry-based 80, **81**
Firth, R. 32, 96
Flouris, G.: and Ivrideli, M. 208
folk pedagogies 223

For Space (Massey) 109, 173, 175–6
foreign countries: perceptions 206
Foundation Stage 122; Knowledge and
  Understanding of the World 1
Frankenstein, M.: and Powell, A.B. 76, 77, 83
Fredrickson, B.: broaden and build theory 105
Freire, P. 56, 60, 61, 65, 76–7, 83–4, 232–3;
  liberatory education 58; politicization and
  consciousness raising 73, 84; post-colonial
  theory 60–1

Gaffer Samson's Luck (Walsh) 175
Gambia study visit 9, 18, 190, 191, 194–7, 200,
  201, 202
General Certificate in Secondary Education
  (GCSE) 49–50
Geographical Association (GA) 11, 25–6, 88,
  133; Curriculum Consultation Report (2011b)
  30; curriculum-making 138–41; Global
  Learning Programme (GLP) 11; high quality
  teaching 13–14; living geography model 134;
  progression expectations 10–13, *12–13*;
  progression statement 10, *see also Young
  Geographers – A Living Geography Project
  for Primary Schools* (GA)
geographical development: children 94, **95**
geographical knowledge 22–5, 34, **59**, 63;
  children 148; as powerful knowledge 17;
  pre-service teachers 17; teachers 17, 21–38;
  teaching 34; and understanding 17
geographical learning 10–13; content 11;
  different age groups 11; expectations of
  progress statement (GA) 11; and thinking
  expectations 11, *12–13*
geographical skills 98
geographical thinking 3, 78, 97; children 2;
  expectations of progress statement (GA) 11;
  geographical learning 11, *12–13*;
  geographical understanding 3; intrinsic
  elements 5; physical geography 49
geographical understanding 3, 225–6, **226**
*Geography: Learning to Make a World of
  Difference* (Ofsted, 2011) 107
geography: definitions 40, **41**, 94, **95**; Turkey 42
Geography National Curriculum (GNC) 190
Geography Quality Mark (GQM) 26
Gerdes, P. 77, 78–9, 85n; four dimensions 78
German primary schools 207–8
Giddens, A. 78, 228
Gilmer, G. 57, 85n
Giroux, H.A.: notion of becoming 66
Global Citizenship and Sustainable
  Development 82
global fact finder *45*, 46, 47
Global Learning Programme (GLP) (GA) 11
global processor *45*, 47
global warming 113
globalist perspective **42**, 46, 48

grammar 32
Greek curriculum 208
Greenwood, R. 17, 117–32

Hannay, L.: and Kent, G. 201
Happiness Index 202
Hart, T. 66
Hayes, D. 121
hazardous world: risk 228
Healey, M.: Kneale, P. and Bradbeer, J. 41, 42,
  48
Held, B. 106
Hicks, D. 87, 112
high quality geography 87
high quality teaching: children's development
  15; Geographical Association (GA) 14; HMI
  13; practices of expert teachers 15; primary
  geography 13–15; review processes 14;
  subject leadership 13, 15, 16–17, 23–5
HMIs (Her Majesty's Inspector of Schools) 13
holistic geographies 27–8, 32–3
holistic subject 33, 125
home continent: European dimensions 8
Hopwood, N. 48, 79
House of Commons Education Committee 23
human nature: moment 61

identity: place-related 127–89; relational
  perspective 193
image of geography: trainee teachers 44–8
Immordino-Yang, M.: and Damasio, A. 103
Importance of Teaching White Paper (DfE,
  2010) 94, 103
India study visit 18, 191, 194–6, 197–202
individual factors 137
inferiority: everyday knowledge 62
information: knowledge as 32, 33, 56–7
Initial Teacher Training (ITT) 22, 25, 35;
  ethno-geography 56; Post Graduate Primary
  Education (PGCE) 75, 76
innovative practices: impact 152
interactionist perspective **41**, **42**, 44, 47, 49
interdisciplinary theoretical framework 174–6
interest in geography: teachers 31
interpretivist approach: Young Geographers'
  Project 141–2
Ivrideli, M.: and Flouris, G. 208

Jackson, P. 81–2; thinking geographically 27;
  underpinning concepts 2
Jamaica 223
James, M.: and Pollard, A. 23
Japan: tsunami **226**, 227, **227**

Kent, G.: and Hannay, L. 201
Kenya 8, 95, 197, 223
key concepts 97
key principles: of living geography 140

Key Stage (KS) 1 & 2 framework: NC aspects comparison (2000 and 2014) 4, *5*; NC summary comparison (2000 and 2014) 5–10, *6–8*

Key Stage (KS) 3 programme of study (POS) 81

Al-Khalaileh, E. 64

Kirby, P. 165, 167, 168–9

Kneale, P.: Bradbeer, J. and Healey, M. 41, 42, 48

Knight, P. 120

knowledge: about the world 28–9; academic 59; academic perceptions 61; co-construction 66; core 28, 32, 87–102, 103; of geography 32–4; as information 32, 33, 56–7; locational 221; mathematical activity 77; out-of-school 206; pedagogical content 23; powerful 17, 54–72, 223, 224, 225; primary experience 55; procedural 32–3; subject 21, 22, 33, 137, 152, 223–5; subject concept 32; thinking geographical 32; traditional 28, *see also* geographical knowledge

Knowledge and Understanding of the World (3-7 year olds) 1

knowledge-curriculum relationship 65–6

Lambert, D. 29, 30, 33, 94, 140; and Morgan, J. 51, 140; and Owens, P. 98; and Young, M. 17

land: settlements 8

Lawrence, A.: *The Travels of Oggy* 219–20

leadership, subject 15, 16–17, 23–5, 26, 31, 88, 90; and high quality teaching 13; and PGQM 88, 90–100, **91**, **93**

learner: ethno-geography 76

learning: active 135; connected 125, 126; creativity 103–16; effective 128; geographical 10–14; liberatory 232; locations 219–20; outdoor 5, 14, 47, 109, 111–12, 146; place making 111; shared 225–31; social space 83; spatial 207–8; start activities 110; stories 110; trails 110–11

liberatory education 56, 62, 83; and ethnogeography 73–86; Freirean 58

listening: to children's voice 219

Listening to Children: environmental perspectives and the school curriculum (L2C) 160–2, 166

literature review 191–4

living geography 29, 84; accessibility 30–1; curriculum-making 140; dynamism 29; GA model 134; key principles 140, *see also* *Young Geographers – A Living Geography Project for Primary Schools* (GA)

living subject 29–30

local care projects 10

locational knowledge 221

Loftyrock Primary School 178–88

London children 64

Louv, R. 111

Lucas, B.: and Claxton, G. 104

map skills 28

Martin, F. 17, 18, 25, 40, 41, 73–86, 190–204, 224; and Catling, S. 17, 40, 54–72, 191; continuum 97; ethnogeography 50; primary teachers 24; teacher lack of understanding 25

Martin, M.: and De Koning, K. 163

Massey, D. 109, 173, 175–6

mathematics 21, 22, 39, 67–8, 76–8, 84, 85n, 107, 110; activity and knowledge 77

micro-political factors 137, 150

Miller, K.: Priestley, M. and Edwards, R. 136, 137

moment: human nature 61

Montamedi, M.: Williams, A. and Cook, I. 82

Moore, R.: and Muller, J. 58, 60

Moran, D.: and John-Steiner, V. 104

Morgan, A. 87, 95

Morgan, J. 2; and Lambert, D. 51, 140; and Slater, F. 69; and Williamson, B. 60, 66

Morley, E. 16, 39–53; and Catling, S. 16, 21–38

motivation improvements: and skills development 125–6

Muller, J.: and Moore, R. 58, 60

My Place (Wheatley) 173–89; Australian names 177; children's response 179–80; maps of 180–3, **181**, **182**, **183**; and Rosenblatt 180

National Curriculum (NC) 73, 74–5, 79; Department for Education and Employment (DfEE) 39; ethno-geography 80–1, **80**; programmes of study (POS) 4, 5, *5*, *6–8*, 80, **80**, 81, 119, 150, *see also* Key Stage (KS) 1 & 2; Key Stage (KS) 3

National Moderation Team: for PGQM 92

Nikolajeva, M.: et al. 173–89

Nisbett, R. 191, 192, 193, 200

nominal group technique 44, **46**

North America 9

Northern Ireland: Council for Curriculum, Examination and Assessment (CCEA) 117

Northern Ireland Curriculum (NIC): Areas of Learning 117; Areas of Learning – The World Around Us (WAU) 117, 122–4, 126–30; cross-curricular and subject-based approach approaches 117–30

novice teachers 21, 22, 25, 34, 56, 68, 76, 137

object-based thinking 190–204

object-based tradition 192

O'Brien, M. 63, 64

Ofsted (Office for Standards in Education) 21, 23–4, 31, 68, 87, 89, 120; *Geography: Learning to Make a World of Difference* (2011) 107

organisational factors 137, 150

Other 199, 200
Othering 62, 66
out-of-school knowledge 206
outdoor learning 5, 14, 47, 109, 111–12, 146
outside 5
Owens, P. 17, 87–102, 129; and Lambert, D. 98
ownership 126

Payne, M. 227–8; and Wattchow, B. 111
Payne, Martha 227–8
pedagogical content knowledge 23
pedagogical repertoire 120
pedagogy 2; effectiveness 23; empowering 217–39, 231–3, 233–4; folk 223; social constructivist 60
people-environment perspective 40
personal exploration 64
personal growth: and creativity 105–6
personal sense of space: enquiry-based fieldwork 80, **81**
perspectives: teachers 135–59
physical geography 4, *5*, *6–8*, 8, 9, 33, *43*, 48–9, 96, 190
physical-human linkage 42
Pickering, S.: and Catling, S. 111
Pike, S. 63, 64
place making: learning 111
place-related identities 127–89; children's perceptions 183–7
placeist perspective **41**, **42**, 44, 47, 49
planning 15, 18, 24, 33–4, 92, 94, 97, 104, 111; cross-curricular 99, 117–20, 121–2, 126, 128–30, 168; progression 10–11, *see also* curriculum-making
play: creative 111, 112
Pointon, P.: et al. 173–89
politicians: core knowledge 32
politicization and consciousness raising 84
Pollard, A.: and James, M. 23
possibility thinking notion (Craft) 110
Post Graduate Certificate in Education (PGCE) 75, 76
post-colonial theory 60–1
Powell, A.B.: and Frankenstein, M. 76, 77, 83
power: disciplinary 224; schools and classrooms 62
powerful knowledge 17, 54–72, 223, 224, 225
Priestley, M.: Edwards, R. and Miller, K. 136, 137
primary geography 3–13; high quality teaching 13–16; sense of purpose 5–10
Primary Geography Quality Mark (PGQM) framework 89, 94, 95; content knowledge 94; core knowledge 94–6; evidencing criteria 92; feedback from schools 90–1; levels 90, **91**; National Moderation Team 92; procedural knowledge 94; revised 92, **93**; and subject

leadership 88, 90–100, **91**, **93**; underpinning criteria 91–2
Primary Review (2007) 24
principal investigator (PI): difference 194
principles: key 140
procedural knowledge 32–3
processor: global *45*, 47
programmes of study (POS) 4, 5, *5*, *6–8*, 80, **80**, 81, 119, 150; KS3 81
progression in learning: expectations (GA) 11–13, *12–13*; five dimensions 11
progressive child-centred approach 135
pupils 140; concepts and knowledge 206

Qualified Teacher Status (QTS) 39
quality *see* high quality teaching

Rawding, C. 27
reading 175; transaction 175–6, *see also My Place* (Wheatley)
relational perspective: identity 193
relational tradition 192, 193–4
research methods 122–3
Research Team: Data Analysis Conference 166
resources 15, 201–2, 222, 226, 228, 229; access 10; personal 105–6
risk: hazardous world 228
Rosenblatt, L. 175, 180

Schmeinck, D. 205–16
school localities 10
school setting 163
Scoffham, S. 17, 30, 87, 103–16; and Barnes, J. 106
seasons 8; weather 8
secondary postgraduate teacher trainees 40
secondary teachers 23, 151
secondary-school children 29, 206
Sedgebeer, M. 201–2
self-image: difference 201
sense of geography: teacher's 25–34
settlements 8
shared learning 225–31
Shorrock, S.: and Calderhead, J. 76
Shulman, L. 23
similarity-difference: binary 192–3, 196–7; diversity 193, 198–9; Kenya 197
Single Story (Adichie) 191–2
skills 3–5, *5*, *6–8*, 28, 31–2, 63, 65, 87–8, 98, 209, 210; development and motivation improvements 125–6; and enquiry *12–13*, 73, 114–15; lifelong-learning 213; map 28; trainee teachers 39, 43, **46**, 49–50, *51*
Slater, F.: and Morgan, J. 69
social constructivist pedagogy 60
social interaction 64
space: personal sense of 80, **81**; social 83
spatial context 82, 87, 91, 95, 100, 108, 206

spatial learning 207–8
spatialists 40, **41**
spiral curriculum: and ethno-geography 83–4, **83**
Spring, E.: et al. 17, 173–89
Standish, A. 97
starter activities 110
stereotypes 201
stories 110, 219–20
student teachers: conceptions of geography 75–6, 77, 79, *see also* trainee teachers
subject breadth 27–9
subject dynamics: Young Geographers Project 146–9
subject knowledge 21, 137; children's voice 223–5; teachers 22, 152
subject leader: Primary Geography Quality Mark (PGQM) framework 95–6
subject resource 138
subject specialist schools 39
subject-based approach: Northern Ireland Curriculum (NIC) 117–30
sustainability: environment 112–13; environmental change 10
synthesisers **41**, 44, *45*

Tanner, J.: and Whittle, J. 110
Taylor, L.: and Catling, S. 81; et al. 17, 173–89
Taylor, P. 35
teacher development project: classroom-based 18
teacher education 79; course 39; ethno-geography 78–9
teachers 76; autonomy empowerment 126; concept of geography 22; curriculum-makers 98–9; curriculum-making perspectives 133–59; empowering pedagogy responsibility 232; enjoyment 126; expert 15, 34; flexibility and adaptability 99; geographical knowledge and understanding 16, 21–38; interest in geography 31; lack of understanding 25; liberation 149–50; novice 21, 22, 25, 34, 56, 68, 76, 137; pre-service 16; responsibility and empowering pedagogy 232; secondary 23, 151; sense of geography 25–34; subject knowledge 22, 152; UK 198; weaker 24, *see also* trainee teachers
teaching: cross-curricular 124; European dimension 210–11; geographical vocabulary 24, *see also* high quality teaching
Teaching and Learning Research Programme (UK) 23
thinking 3; children's 2; object-based 190–204
thinking geographically 27, 32, 49; intrinsic elements 5
topographic terms 206
traditional knowledge: notion of 28
traditions of thought (Nisbett) 191, 192

trails: learning 110–11
trainee teachers 49; conceptions of geography 44, *45*; image of geography 44–8; perception of themes covered 43, *43*; secondary postgraduate 40; skills 39, 43, **46**, 49–50, *51*; subjects by rank 43, *43*
Training and Development Agency for Schools (TDA) 39, 134
Travels of Oggy, The (Lawrence) 219–20
truism 218
truth 57
tsunami: Japan 227, **227**
Turkey: geography 42
typology 33

underpinnings of geography 2, 87, 153, 224, 230; PGQM 91–2
understanding 3, 153–5, 190, 193–4, 198–202, 206–10, 213, 225–6, **226**; enough 23; locational 223; tsunami **226**
United Kingdom (UK) 112; teachers 198; Teaching and Learning Research Programme (UK) 23
United Nations (UN): Convention on the Rights of the Child (CRC) 162
United States of America (USA) 9, 221
universal activity 78
urban environment: children's research 160–72

value: of creativity 106, 110; of geography 2, 30, 33, 34, 51, 139–40, 148
values 88, 97–8, 151, 195, 217, 229; powerful knowledge 224–5
visibility 31–2
vocabulary *6–8*, 15, 24, 32, 68, 82, 96, 97
voices: children's 219, 222, 223–5
Voluntary Service Overseas (VSO) 200

Walford, R. 40, 41, 44, 47; definition of geography 40, **41**
Walshe, N. 41–2
Wattchow, B: and Payne, M. 111
weather 8, 211–13, **212**, 229–30
Western model: high mass consumption 202
White Paper: *Importance of Teaching* (DfE, 2010) 94, 103
Whittle, J.: and Tanner, J. 110
Whyte, T. 110
Williams, A.: Cook, I. and Montamedi, M. 82
Williamson, B.: and Morgan, J. 60, 66
Willowmarsh Primary School 178–88
Witt, S. 111, 112
world: areas 9; geography as knowledge about 28–9
World Around Us (WAU) Area of Learning (NI) 17–18, 117, 122–4, 126–30
writing *see My Place* (Wheatley)
Wyse, D.: et al. 18, 173–89

INDEX

*Young Geographers – A Living Geography
Project for Primary Schools* (GA) 89,
99–100, 133, 134, 137, 140, 146–50, 155;
active curriculum agents 145; attitudes 143;
contextual dynamics 144–6; five aspects of

practice 141; interpretivist approach 141–2;
local solutions 141; subject dynamics 146,
146–9; teacher's involvement 143
Young, M. 17; and Lambert, D. 17; powerful
knowledge notion 55–66